Regional Development Agencies in Europe

Regional Policy and Developmental Series

Series Editor: Ron Martin, Department of Geography, University of Cambridge

Throughout the industrialised world, widespread economic restructuring, rapid technological change, the reconfiguration of state intervention, and increasing globalisation are giving greater prominence to the nature and performance of individual regional and local economies within nations. The old patterns and processes of regional development that characterised the post-war period are being fundamentally redrawn, creating new problems of uneven development and new theoretical and policy challenges. Whatever interpretation of this contemporary transformation is adopted, regions and localities are back on the academic and political agenda. *Regional Policy and Development* is an international series which aims to provide authoritative analyses of this new regional political economy. It seeks to combine fresh theoretical insights with detailed empirical enquiry and constructive policy debate to produce a comprehensive set of conceptual, practical and topical studies in this field. The series is not intended as a collection of synthetic reviews, but rather as original contributions to understanding the processes, problems and policies of regional and local economic development in today's changing world.

Regional Development Agencies in Europe

Edited by Henrik Halkier, Mike Danson
& Charlotte Damborg

Regional Policy and Development Series 21

Jessica Kingsley Publishers
London and Philadelphia

Regional Studies Association
London

First published in the United Kingdom in 1998 by
Jessica Kingsley Publishers Ltd
116 Pentonville Road, London N1 9JB, England
and
325 Chestnut Street, Philadelphia, PA19106, USA.

with the Regional Studies Association
Registered Charity 252269

Copyright © 1998 Jessica Kingsley Publishers

Library of Congress Cataloging in Publication Data

A CIP catalogue record for this book is available from the Library of Congress

British Library Cataloguing in Publication Data

Regional development agencies in Europe. -
(Regional policy and development series; 21)
1. Regional planning - Europe 2. Regional economics
I. Title II. Danson, Mike III. Damborg, Charlotte
352.2'88'094

ISBN 1 85302 602 6

Printed and Bound in Great Britain by
Athenaeum Press, Gateshead, Tyne and Wear

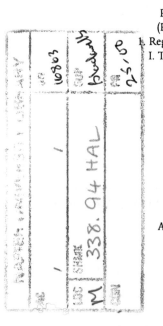

Contents

Tables

Figures

Preface

This volume brings together papers presented to two conferences on 'Regional Development Agencies in Europe' held in Gothenburg, Sweden in May 1995 and in Aalborg, Denmark in August 1996. These meetings and the associated research network of policy makers, practitioners and academics from across the continent focus on applied studies of the work of regional development agencies in Europe. The activities of the network are ongoing and will continue to address the evolving research agenda described in the conclusion to this volume. Further seminars have been organised and publications are forthcoming. The network is inclusive and all are welcome to contact the editors for further information.

PART I

Introduction

CHAPTER I

Regional Development Agencies in Europe
An Introduction and Framework for Analysis
Mike Danson, Henrik Halkier & Charlotte Damborg

Introduction

Europe is facing a period of profound economic change at the turn of the century. On the one hand we witness a large-scale opening up of new trading possibilities following the completion of the single European market, the transition to market-oriented economies in the former COMECON area, and the moves towards greater liberalisation of international trade in general. On the other hand the trend towards economic globalisation would seem to be accompanied by the increased importance of local systems of production. It is clear that some regions are more likely to benefit from these developments than others, and as national governments and international institutions attempt to address increasing disparities and regions strive to improve their position, regional policies are set to become a prominent feature. This situation has generated widespread interest in the strengths and weaknesses of the options available to policy makers in terms of institutional arrangements and development strategies (Bachtler and Turok 1997; Alden and Boland 1996; Wannop 1995), and hence an examination of the experiences of individual approaches to regional policy is a highly relevant undertaking. Further, the last two decades have witnessed a considerable

13

degree of change and experimentation in the field of regional policy in Europe. Traditional spatial policies, primarily aimed at redistributing economic activity within the national economy from prosperous to disadvantaged areas, have been supplemented by supra-national EU programmes and, partly related to this, an explosive growth in local initiatives promoting economic development 'from below'. Despite these institutional innovations regional inequalities, however, have remained conspicuous, and in the wake of the single market and the transformations in Eastern Europe, regional policies can rightly be said to be 'at the crossroads' (Albrechts and Swyngedouw 1989), searching for more efficient strategies in a climate of economic uncertainty and political change.

Regional development agencies (RDAs) have long been part of the institutional set-up in a number of European countries (Yuill 1982), and this type of semi-autonomous organisation operating on the regional level would appear to offer significant advantages for policy makers in the 1990s. RDAs can easily be construed as the 'manageable' bottom-up alternative, avoiding the bewildering maze of local initiatives but allowing for flexibility and receptiveness to the specific problems of indigenous industry within the region. At the same time, a position outside the mainstream government apparatus appears to make it possible to pursue public policies without evoking the ghosts of interventionism or state dirigisme, and so to make it easier to adopt a long-term perspective, while the distance from government frequently generates an operating environment more closely attuned to the needs of enterprise.

In Western Europe, development agencies have been a part of regional policy in a number of countries since the 1950s/60s, and lately this approach has provoked considerable interest in Central and Eastern Europe as a possible way of coping with the difficulties of industrial restructuring. However, with the exception of Yuill (1982), the existing European experience has not been addressed on a comparative basis, and this would seem to be a highly unsatisfactory state of affairs in a situation where regionally based policy initiatives are likely to play an important part in shaping the new Europe (Alden 1996).

Based on an analytical framework developed by Halkier and Danson (1995) for exploring RDAs in Europe, this volume has contributions from all parts of Europe, north and south, east and west, and on the key issues of institutions, governance and accountability, public-private partnerships, policies and evaluation.

The aim of this book on regional development agencies in Europe is to explore the long-term potentials and limitations of this approach to the promotion of economic development at the regional level. The focus, therefore, is on the extent to which existing bodies have lived up to expectations by developing tailor-made, integrated and proactive strategies, and whether unforeseen side effects have occurred, such as a failure to address certain types of regional problems or an inability to employ particular methods of implementation. From this, institutional and other preconditions for successful regional policies have been identified. On this basis, a much clearer picture of the significance of development agencies emerges, including their relevance in the context of Eastern Europe.

The book, in other words, not only provides a much-needed update of previous surveys of development agencies dating from the early 1980s, but also represents a considerable broadening of analytical and geographical coverage. However, although the separate chapters advance examples of techniques which have been used to review the programmes and policies of RDAs and criteria against which alternative approaches to regional economic regeneration can be assessed, it is clear that there is still no accepted methodology for evaluating such institutions as institutions. In particular, the discussion in this introduction and conclusion demonstrate that standard economic and political analyses have not been applied with much success to the assessment of these institutional forms. Nevertheless, work based on theories of organisations, corporate governance and fiscal federalism has opened up the debate once more on how to address the evaluation of development agencies directly (see Brown and Danson 1997, and Armstrong 1997 for some discussion on these developments).

It is noteworthy that the current debate surrounding the proposed development agencies for the English regions is particular to its time and place. Given their long histories and range of initiatives, the experiences in Scotland, Wales and Northern Ireland would have been expected to inform the discussions over the form and functions of the institutions planned for England. However, the deliberations of the commission which considered the potential strategies for regional economic development in England (Regional Policy Commission of the Labour Party 1996) and the recent White Paper (Department of the Environment, Transport, and the Regions 1997) which sets out the proposals for the establishment of RDAs in England both neglect any lessons from the Celtic countries, apart from references to the original Acts which established the Scottish and Welsh Development Agencies. The current accompanying academic debate over the potential advantages of introducing this particular form of intervention are similarly specific to the concerns of the 1990s: globalisation and European integration, regulation theory, regional competitiveness under new regimes of flexible specialisation. While the current shift in the theoretical underpinnings of the rationale and critique of RDAs reflect these issues of the

1990s, it is clear that these were not apposite to the concerns of those who planned the RDAs which were established under Fordism, for instance, in earlier decades. It would be incorrect to evaluate these older institutions according to a new set of criteria, as much as it is inappropriate to establish RDAs in England using outdated philosophies. This underlines the importance of *both* being precise about what is meant by the RDA concept *and* being aware of the changing economic and political context in which these organisations operate. Only then can the performance of RDAs in Europe be assessed in a way that can be useful also for future development initiatives.

Almost as a prolegomena to this evolving agenda, this volume covers a number of areas of interest to researchers, policy makers and practitioners. Addressing the need for an update to the form and nature of these organisations, there is a review and analysis of the types and general characteristics of regional development agencies in Europe, their activities and key features. This second chapter includes a consideration of their strategies for development, methods of policy implementation, evaluation and performance indicators, relationship with financial and political sponsors and the wider policy environment.

Reflecting the need to understand the uniqueness of each institution, most chapters present case studies of selected organisations where the specific experience of individual regions is analysed in greater depth in order to understand the diversity of the European experience. Because of the very different economic and political conditions in the former COMECON countries, there is a discussion of the institutional arrangements for local and regional development in Central and Eastern Europe countries in several contributions. Drawing together the lessons for all parts of the continent of this form of intervention, the conclusion incorporates an assessment of the future prospects for the role of regional development agencies in Europe, both within the European Union and in the former COMECON countries.

The individual chapters are written by a team of European specialists who in the main have tended to focus their own contributions on a particular development agency but with particular emphasis on a sub-theme, for instance regional governance and accountability. Because our own contributions on the analytical framework and the survey of European RDAs were adopted by many of the contributors to this volume, there is a strong commitment to a comparative European perspective across the chapters. This initial approach to addressing the role and form of RDAs in the 1990s has led, we believe, to a satisfactory degree of coherence in the range of definitions and forms of research applied; and so to a move beyond descriptive and *ad hoc* analyses which typically characterise individual case studies of development bodies.

The remainder of this introduction discusses a definition of RDAs and key issues relating to this particular approach to regional policy, evolving from the initial work of Yuill and Allen (1982) which underpinned the procedures used to set the agendas of the ongoing seminars and research network and this book. This is followed by an outline of the structure of the book and the different sections.

RDAs – defining a profile

In connection with a European survey, Yuill and Allen (1982, p.1) defined an RDA as 'any publicly-financed institution outside the mainstream of central and local government administration' designed to promote economic development 'in regions that are generally designated as problem or priority areas'. This broad definition of a non-departmental body involved in regional policy does introduce an element of ambiguity, however, because it includes organisations operating on the national level, some of which are even involved in the administration of traditional top-down regional policy programmes such as grant assistance. DATAR in France and the IDA (Industrial Development Agency) in Ireland are prominent examples of this pattern: essentially national bodies hived off as non-departmental organisations by central government.

In order to be able to develop an understanding of the specific features of 'regional' development agencies, this volume employs a more restrictive definition, namely:

> a regionally based, publicly financed institution outside the mainstream of central and local government administration designed to promote economic development.

This definition deliberately leaves open the question of what exactly is required to situate an institution 'outside' the mainstream apparatus of public administration. First, discrepancies between the legal position and actual degree of autonomy are likely to occur, and hence adopting a restrictive practice as to which institutions to include and exclude may be grossly misleading. And second, the use of 'development agency' as a 'trade mark' has proliferated in the last few decades and thus examining the nature of self-proclaimed RDAs will be useful. In practice this means that the chapters in this volume have targeted:

> regionally based organisations that *appear* to *claim* to play an independent role in the promotion of economic development on the regional level.

As was apparent in the conducting of the survey of institutions described in Chapter 2, some of the self-proclaimed agencies across the EU turned out, on closer inspection, to function as integrated parts of, for example, regional government and hence not to comply with the definition of an RDA. It was believed that, by adopting a fairly liberal approach to the initial selection of the organisations studied and to the papers admitted to the conferences, the analysis and debate would prove to be more fruitful as it would enable the research to identify the nature of the mechanisms by which some organisations achieve a high degree of operational freedom – and others effectively become or remain part of the mainstream administrative apparatus.

Despite their history, as suggested above the relationship between RDAs and traditional regional policies has received little systematic treatment. However, on the basis of an analysis of the key institutional features of the two approaches to regional development and of scattered comments in the literature, a distinct pattern nonetheless emerges.

While national-level policies are the domain of central government departments, RDAs are established as semi-autonomous bodies at the regional level. The latter organisational set-up is perceived as having four advantages. First, a regional institution is better placed to develop strategies tailored to the specific problems of the individual region, especially if production systems are becoming increasingly localised and differentiated; this is indeed a crucial point. Second, this bottom-up approach to regional policy requires staff capable of dealing with individual firms in a business-like manner, and a position outside the mainstream bureaucracy would make it easier to attract specialist expertise. Third, a semi-autonomous position limits direct political interference and, hence, allows the adoption of a long-term perspective capable of tackling structural weaknesses of the regional economy that could not have been effectively addressed within the short-term horizon of party political manoeuvring. Within this arrangement, often described as an arm's-length degree of operational freedom, the sponsoring authority only interferes with the activities of the policy-making organisation on a very general level, such as allocation of resources and broad policy guidelines, whereas the strategic initiative and important discretionary powers are left with the front-line bureaucracy. And finally, compared with the more discrete impact of national-level policies, a separate regional institution not only may enhance the regional clout of the political sponsors in relation to other public bodies, but also may function as a visible symbol of party political commitment to the development of the region.

The accompanying table presents a *précis* of the discussions of a number of authors of these differences between national-level regional policies and

Table 1.1 National-level regional policies and RDAs compared

Characteristics	Traditional top-down	New-model bottom-up
Organisation	National	Regional
	Government department	Semi-autonomous body
	Bureaucracy	Business-like
	Generalist qualifications	Specific expertise
Operational freedom	Limited	Arm's length
Economic objectives	Interregional equality	Interregional competitiveness
	Growth of national economy	Growth of regional economy
	Redistributed growth	Indigenous/imported growth
Mode of operation	Non-selective	Selective
	Automatic/discretionary	Discretionary
	Reactive	Proactive
Policy instruments	Bureaucratic regulation	Financial inducements
	Financial inducements	Advisory services
	Advisory services	Public provision
	Public provision	

Source: based on Young and Lowe (1974), Stephen (1975), Grant (1982), Wannop (1984), Firn (1985), McCrone and Randall (1985), Hood (1991), Martin and Townroe (1992), Danson, Lloyd and Newlands (1992), Halkier (1992).

those initiated through and by regional development agencies. To explore these various dimensions both analytically and descriptively, to a greater or lesser extent the chapters in this volume contrast and compare national government top-down and RDA bottom-up approaches. Present across the debates, but increasingly to the fore, are questions over the inter-relationships between these different levels of institution and of the significance of issues of the efficiency and effectiveness of the alternative forms of regional policy delivery mechanisms. In the conferences, therefore, areas of governance, partnership and networking were introduced on to the agenda, reflecting this perceived relevance of institutional thickness and regulation theories to the analysis.

Thus, in the burgeoning literature on regional governance, it is argued that differences in organisational form and conduct clearly affect the ways policy objectives are determined and the methods by which they are implemented (see Armstrong 1997; Roberts 1997 *inter alia* in Danson, Lloyd and Hill 1997 for an introduction). Whereas central governments have targeted national problems such as inter-regional disparities in unemployment or congestion, it is believed that RDAs are able to establish specific priorities and to promote their regions *vis-à-vis* others, both as regards the competitiveness of indigenous firms and in the attraction of economic activity from outside the area. In contrast to the generally indiscriminate redistributive programmes of central government, the inherent emphasis on regional targeting in RDA policies prompts a much more selective approach. Together with differences in staff, this also should explain the importance of discretionary decision making and of the critical capability to play a proactive role in fostering new development initiatives. As regards policy instruments, however, non-departmental bodies like RDAs would seem to lack the legitimacy and power to force individual firms or industries to act against their private interests by means of bureaucratic regulation.

The regional governance discussion referenced above has demonstrated that the combination of operational freedom and a capacity for proactive and selective initiatives would appear to enable RDAs to play an important role as a supplement, or alternative, to central government policies and local development activities. In other words, a picture of a 'model agency' has emerged, not as a blueprint for particular policies, but in the sense that a number of key features can be identified that distinguish RDAs from traditional regional policies, and thus potentially denote a set of analytical criteria against which the activities of individual organisations can be described. The next chapter applies these features in the investigation of the form and nature of RDAs across the European Union, assessing their autonomy and range of functions as a means of determining how appropriate these classifications and criteria can be in analysing alternative policy approaches.

The realisation of these advantages does appear, however, to be somewhat precarious. An RDA's scope for action still ultimately depends on its support from the political sponsors, and innovative exploits in policy development may test the boundaries of party political tolerance and/or give rise to conflicts with central government departments and other public sector bodies. In essence, testing a would-be 'model RDA' requires a dual approach, *both policy oriented and institutional*, because the capacity to develop adequate responses to the specific problems of the region hinges on the delicate position of the organisation as a semi-autonomous body (Halkier and Danson 1997).

An RDA therefore may be attempting to move towards a more innovative portfolio of activities, but be constrained in this by the need to be perceived as delivering at least the minimal range of traditional development practices expected by its sponsors. Thus, perhaps by necessity, most RDAs are involved in a number of very different activities like construction and administration of industrial property, attraction of inward investment, financial support of individual firms or particular activities, provision of various types of infrastructure, and delivery of advisory services on a variety of subjects from general management to specific technologies and market intelligence.

For reasons of space and focus, most of the chapters have concentrated on an in-depth analysis of the most important activities of their RDAs. This, however, makes it easier to clarify the way individual policies operate, i.e. the nature of the interaction between the RDA and the private sector, and thereby this:

- facilitates comparisons between regions and nations with regard to forms of governance and policy regimes

- provides at least part of the explanation for the success or otherwise of RDAs in meeting the objectives of particular programmes by identifying relationships of power and interests in the policy-implementation process.

To analyse such dimensions of the role and nature of regional development agencies at the close of the century cannot be undertaken as a simple desk exercise based on annual reports nor on an evaluation of studies of limited comparability. An extensive period of interaction and feedback between a network of academics, practitioners and policy makers was required to promote the context for such research, hence the creation of the series of meetings and seminars in the 1990s which have given rise to this book amongst other outputs.

Outline of contents and structure of the book

In compiling this book, we have selected those chapters which address the evolving issues in the analysis of RDAs most critically. Similarly, where new approaches to the study of the RDA model have been suggested, borrowing from alternative paradigms and disciplines, then such contributions to the seminars have been included.

The volume is in seven parts. The next chapter in this first part presents the results of a survey of regional development agencies in Western Europe. This survey provides a review of the activities and key features of RDAs; an introductory analysis of the general characteristics of European development agencies, including strategies for development, methods of policy implementation, and relationships with financial and political sponsors and the wider policy environment. It therefore offers a much-needed update of previous surveys of development agencies dating from the early 1980s, but also represents a considerable broadening of analytical breadth and geographical coverage.

The second part is on regional development agencies in Western Europe, expanding on this survey. Three national case studies of Austria, the Netherlands and Denmark are covered, with their differing planning, economic and institutional regimes. Part III describes the position in Central and Eastern Europe, tracing the introduction, application and development of this model of regional economic regeneration and restructuring in Poland, the Czech Republic and Hungary.

Whilst not all countries of Europe are represented separately in the chapters of this book, we are confident that the approaches and models which each nation of Europe has adopted are analysed here. From the continent-wide surveys and the other detailed descriptions, it is apparent that broad similarities can be identified in the overall environments, institutions and regimes across countries. Although individual chapters may focus on the differences, the comparability of institutional forms, of regulation regimes and of the dominating system-wide characteristics imposed by the European Union and the European Commission on any RDA are such as to convince us of the universality of many apparently specific conclusions.

Thus the first two parts of the book should be considered as demonstrating the applicability of the research findings more broadly as well as setting the scene for the remaining, cross-cutting themes of the remainder of the volume.

The following three parts of the book address the issues concerning regional development agencies in their regional economic environment. While there have been descriptive studies of many RDAs across Europe, as we suggest above, there has been but seldom attempts at their systematic analysis. As this project was assembled and developed, so the original research agenda to address this neglect evolved according to the new concerns and modes of operation of the 1990s. The contents of this book reflect this changing emphasis within the initial framework of the project. Part IV focuses on RDAs, regional governance and accountability, and discusses the evolving role and debate over the position of development agencies within their regional political setting. Introducing theoretical approaches to such issues from a number of disciplines, these chapters open up new lines of enquiry into the philosophy and accountability of regional economic planning, broadly defined, and economic agencies. Increasingly, even where 'model' agencies have been established, they are being regulated and organised within wider and more imposing environments than hitherto: at regional, national and EU levels. The varying forms of regulation within differing constitutional frameworks is examined in this section. Clearly, however, RDAs are having to work with and alongside other institutions, often within formal planning regimes; the significance of planning and regulation theories in analysing RDAs are enhanced as a result.

With the move to a partnership model of regional economic development across the European Union, in particular the following part considers RDAs and public–private partnerships. A common theme running through the three chapters in Part V is the recognition that agencies are becoming progressively but one partner in strategic regional policy interventions, rather than unique multi-functional organisations able to deliver all elements of economic development in the locality. As the evolution of RDAs into networking institutions complements the adoption by the EC of the partnership model for the delivery of structural fund assistance through Community Support Frameworks (Danson *et al.* 1997), there has been a significant growth in the need to examine this changing environment.

Part VI returns to the traditional themes of policies and evaluation, but again in the changed circumstances of the last decade with the emphasis on new firm formation and indigenous potential. These three chapters analyse the strategies and effectiveness of the endogenous development perspective. As in the two preceding parts, they utilise techniques and theoretical frameworks which have tended not to be in evidence in previous analyses of RDAs.

The final section on perspectives pulls together the current and future issues we have identified through the chapters and the research network regarding the continuing evolution of regional development agencies.

Conclusion

As can be seen from the selected bibliography below, there is a very limited literature in this field with regard to international or cross-national studies. The best-known publication, *Regional Development Agencies in Europe* (Yuill 1982), is now markedly dated. While in the recent past the EU have commissioned EURADA (the European Association of Development Agencies) to publish reports on development agencies across the Union, these have not become well known nor have they entered the literature reviews of many of those interested in regional economic development and governance more generally.

In organising the seminars and research network and in editing this book, we have been impressed by the breadth of research on the agency approach to addressing regional economic development. We believe, therefore, that this book should appeal to practitioners, academics and policy makers alike. As the contributions are drawn from more than 15 countries across the continent, have a cohesive objective and structure, and cover the critical themes in the areas of regional economic development, the volume should be of value both as a whole, but also in terms of its individual chapters and sections. To realise the benefits of this thematic structure, each section has a brief introduction by the editors which focuses on the specific arguments, regional distinctiveness, and conclusions of that theme.

The following discussions and debates in the network, planning and reflective meetings have generated a new research agenda which is explored in the final section. This suggests that RDAs are now not only almost universally well embedded into the institutional framework of economic development, but also are being reinvented to meet the new challenges of the evolving Europe.

References

Albrechts, L. and Swyngedouw, E. (1989) 'The challenges for regional policy under a flexible regime of accumulation.' In L. Albrechts, F. Moulaert, P. Roberts and E. Swyngedouw (eds) *Regional Policy at the Crossroads – European Perspectives.* London: Jessica Kingsley Publishers.

Alden, J. (1996) 'Regional development strategies in the European Union: Europe 2000+.' In J. Alden and P. Boland (eds) *Regional Development Strategies: A European Perspective.* London: Jessica Kingsley Publishers.

Alden, J. and Boland, P. (eds) (1996) *Regional Development Strategies: A European Perspective.* London: Jessica Kingsley Publishers.

Armstrong, H. (1997) 'Regional-level jurisdictions and economic regeneration initiatives.' In M. Danson, G. Lloyd, and S. Hill (eds) *Regional Governance and Economic Development.* London: Pion.

Bachtler, J. and Turok, I. (1997) *The Coherence of EU Policy: Contrasting Perspectives on the Structural Funds.* London: Jessica Kingsley Publishers.

Brown, G. and Danson, M. (1997) 'The European Partnership Model and the Changing Role of Regional Development Agencies. A Regional Development and Organisation Perspective.' Paper presented to the European Urban and Regional Research Network Conference, Frankfurt an der Oder, Germany, 20–23 September.

Danson, M., Fairley, J., Lloyd, G. and Turok, I. (1997) *The Governance of European Structural Funds: The Experience of the Scottish Regional Partnerships.* Brussels: Scotland Europa Paper No. 10.

Danson, M., Lloyd G. and Newlands, D. (1992) 'Regional development agencies in the UK.' In P. Townroe, and R. Martin (eds) *Regional Development in the 1990s: The British Isles in Transition.* London: Jessica Kingsley Publishers.

Danson, M., Lloyd, G. and Hill, S. (eds) (1997) *Regional Governance and Economic Development.* London: Pion.

Department of the Environment, Transport and the Regions (1997): *Building Partnerships for Prosperity: Sustainable Growth, Competitiveness and Employment in the English Regions.* CM3814, London: HMSO.

Firn, J. (1985) 'Industry.' In U. Wannop and R. Smith (eds) *Strategic Planning in Action. The Impact of the Clyde Valley Regional Plan 1946–1982.* Aldershot: Gower.

Grant, W. (1982) *The Political Economy of Industrial Policy.* London: Butterworths.

Halkier, H. (1992) 'Development agencies and regional policy: the case of the Scottish Development Agency.' *Regional Politics and Policy 2,* 3, 1–26.

Halkier, H. and Danson, M. (1995) *Regional Development Agencies in Western Europe: A Survey of Key Characteristics and Trends.* University of Paisley: European Studies Working Papers 7.

Halkier, H. and Danson, M. (1997) 'Regional development agencies in Western Europe: a survey of key characteristics and trends.' *European Urban and Regional Studies 4,* 3, 241–254.

Hood, N. (1991) 'The Scottish Development Agency in retrospect.' *The Royal Bank of Scotland Review,* 3–21.

Martin, R. and Townroe, P. (1992) 'Changing trends and pressures in regional development.' In P. Townroe and R. Martin (eds) *Regional Development in the 1990s: The British Isles in Transition.* London: Jessica Kingsley Publishers.

McCrone, G. and Randall, J. (1985) 'The Scottish Development Agency.' In R. Saville (ed) *The Economic Development of Modern Scotland 1950–1980.* Edinburgh: Donald.

Regional Policy Commission of the Labour Party (1996): *Renewing the Regions – Strategies for Regional Economic Development.* Sheffield: Sheffield Hallam University.

Roberts, P. (1997) 'Sustainability and spatial competence: an examination of the evolution, ephemeral nature, and possible future development of regional planning in Britain.' In M. Danson, G. Lloyd, and S. Hill (eds) *Regional Governance and Economic Development.* London: Pion.

Stephen, F. (1975) 'The Scottish Development Agency.' In G. Brown (ed) *The Red Paper on Scotland.* Edinburgh: EUSPB.

Wannop, U. (1984) 'The evolution and roles of the Scottish Development Agency.' *Town Planning Review 55,* 313–321.

Wannop, U. (1995) *The Regional Imperative: Regional Planning in Britain, Europe and the United States.* London: Jessica Kingsley Publishers.

Young, S. and Lowe, A. (1974) *Intervention in the Mixed Economy: The Evolution of British Industrial Policy 1964–72.* London: Croom Helm.

Yuill, D. (ed) (1982) *Regional Development Agencies in Europe.* Aldershot: Gower.

Yuill, D. and Allen, K. (1982) 'European regional development agencies – an overview.' In D. Yuill (ed) *Regional Development Agencies in Europe.* Aldershot: Gower.

CHAPTER 2

Regional Development Agencies in Western Europe

A Survey of Key Characteristics and Trends

Henrik Halkier & Mike Danson

Introduction

One of the most conspicuous developments in the field of regional policy over the last two decades has been the rise of bottom-up initiatives conducted from within the regions, and an important part in this process has been played by semi-autonomous public bodies, the so-called regional development agencies. Such institutions have existed in a number of European countries since the 1950s, but in the academic literature their increasing importance has mainly been reflected in case studies of individual organisations. The last major comparative study of RDAs on a European scale was undertaken under the direction of Douglas Yuill in the early 1980s (Yuill 1982), and following a decade of rapid expansion of bottom-up activities, an updated overview would seem to be highly relevant. It would, for instance, be good to know to what extent the increased activity on the regional level also implies a new strategic perspective: do RDAs attempt to strengthen the competitiveness of indigenous firms, or do they instead concentrate their efforts on attracting investment from outside the region and thereby become a regionally based complement to the traditional regional subsidies of central government?

The aim of the present chapter is to identify systematic differences between various types of regionally based development bodies and illuminate possible origins of this pattern. The discussion is based on a survey of selected institutions in eight Western European countries with regard to organisation, policy profile and modes of implementation. By comparing existing bodies with the general qualities expected to be found in a model RDA, a multi-dimensional picture of bottom-up regional policy in Western Europe in the 1990s can be produced as a point of departure for further analysis.

The chapter proceeds in four steps. First, the survey is introduced and basic information on the selected development bodies presented. Second, key characteristics of the institutions are discussed in relation to the general expectations of model RDAs with regard to organisation, policy profiles and modes of implementation. Third, a typology of regionally based development organisations is proposed, and finally possible origins of these patterns are considered.

The survey takes as its point of departure the definition of an RDA proposed in Chapter 1, and thus a model RDA in this chapter therefore denotes a development body that complies with the following three criteria:

1. *Organisationally* it is in a semi-autonomous position *vis-à-vis* its sponsoring political authority.

2. *Strategically* it supports mainly indigenous firms by means of 'soft' policy instruments.

3. *Implementation* is integrated, i.e. it draws upon a broad range of policy instruments.

The operational version of these criteria will be given as part of the empirical analysis, but it is important to stress that the notion of a model RDA should be seen as a Weberian ideal type and in no way be construed as prescriptive. By using the model, three key dimensions of bottom-up regional policy will be captured – its relationship to politics, its policy profile and its mode of implementation – that taken together will provide a multi-dimensional picture of regionally based development activities.

The Survey

The task of identifying regionally based development bodies in Western Europe is complicated by the ambiguity of the term 'region' and the position of many development bodies outside mainstream administrative structures, and it was therefore decided to base the survey on members of the European Association of Development Agencies, set up in 1991 and supported by DG XVI of the European Commission (EURADA 1992). Although the Association comprises development bodies across the EU, its membership still appears to be biased:

- it is biased geographically; in particular some southern countries are clearly under-represented

- given that information about the possibilities for attracting EU support to regional development activities is a central service to members, one could expect an over-representation of organisations working in areas designated by EU regional policies, and/or organisations with relatively few resources incapable of maintaining a permanent presence in Brussels.

Even when these factors are taken into account in selecting the sample, the survey cannot claim to be representative of all regionally based development bodies in Western Europe, but this should, however, not prevent us from developing a typology of regionally based development organisations. The value of a survey of this nature should in other words be to identify possible patterns and refine concepts and methodologies that at a later stage can be employed in a larger research project.

Table 2.1 Organisations included in the survey

Region (country)	Organisation
Flemish Brabantine (B)	Gewestelijke Ontwikkelingsmaatschappijen voor Vlaams Brabant
West Flanders (B)	Gewwesteijke Ontwikkelingsmaatschappijen voor West-Vlaanderen
Liege Province (B)	Société Provinciale d'Industrialisation (SPI)
Viborg County (DK)	Erhvervs- og arbejdsmarkedsafdelingen Viborg Amt
Storstrøm County (DK)	Storstrøms Business Development Center
West Zealand County (DK)	West Zealand Business Development Center
Val d'Oise (F)	Comité d'Expansion Économique du Val d'Oise
Alpes-Maritimes (F)	Côte d'Azur Développement
Creuse (F)	Creuse Expansion
Nord-Pas-de-Calais (F)	Agence Régionale de Développement Nord-Pas-de-Calais
Greater Aachen (D)	Aachener Gesellschaft für Innovation und Technologietransfer (AGIT)
North Rhine-Westphalia (D)	Gesellschaft für Wirtschaftsförderung Nordrhein-Westfalen
Hessen (D)	HLT – Wirtschaftsförderung Hessen Investitionsbank & Gesellschaft für Forschung Planung Entwicklung
Greater Hanover (D)	Kommunalverband Grossraum Hannover
Berlin (D)	Wirtschaftsförderung Berlin
Schleswig-Holstein (D)	Wirtschaftsförderungsgesellschaft Schleswig-Holstein
Mid-West (IRL)	Shannon Development
Gaeltacht (IRL)	Udarás na Gaeltachta
Setubal (P)	Sociedada de Desenvolvimento Regional de Península de Setúbal (SoSet)

Alto Tamega (P)	Associação de Desenvolvimento da Região do Alto Tâmega (ADRAT)
Catalonia (E)	Centre d'Informació i Desenvolupament Empresarial (CIDEM)
Aragon (E)	Instituto Aragenoés de Fomento
Andalusia (E)	Instituto de Fomento de Andalucía
Murcia (E)	Instituto de Fomento de la Región de Murcia
Isle of Wight (UK)	Isle of Wight Development Board
Northern Ireland (UK)	Local Enterprise Development Unit (LEDU)
North Nottinghamshire (UK)	North Nottinghamshire Training & Enterprise Council
Scottish Lowland (UK)	Scottish Enterprise
Wearside (UK)	Wearside Training & Enterprise Council
Non-rural Wales (UK)	Welsh Development Agency

Fifty-seven organisations from ten countries responded positively to an initial postal inquiry, and in excess of 400 more or less glossy publications were obtained, ranging from annual reports to PR leaflets. On the basis of this a manageable sample of 30 organisations with a reasonable geographical spread was selected for closer scrutiny, and, as can be seen from Table 2.1, the sample represents eight member states from Spain in the south to Denmark in the north, with four small and four large countries included. Due to the timing of the postal inquiry, most of the annual reports and so on reported activities in the years 1991 and 1992, and thus the results presented below reflect the situation in the early 1990s.

The diverse character of the sample is also underlined by the basic characteristics of the organisations included. With regard to age, three 'generations' of development bodies are clearly in evidence, the first two stemming from around 1960 and 1970 respectively, and the largest group dating from the 1980s or early 1990s, in line with the general view of the last decade as one in which bottom-up organisations mushroomed.[1]

The resources at the disposal of the organisations also vary considerably, as illustrated by Table 2.2.[2] Although externally funded activities – e.g. central government or European grant schemes – may have been omitted from the accounts in some cases, small and large organisations would still appear not to be playing in the same league. The smallest organisations on

1 Of the 26 organisations for which information was available, 15% had been founded in the period 1959–62, 15% in the period 1969–72, and 50% from 1982 onwards (source: RDA survey).

2 All figures have been converted to pound sterling, using the exchange rates given by Yuill et al. (1992, p.vii).

average report 12 staff and a budget of £1.4m, whereas the equivalent figures for their large counterparts are 229 persons and £133m respectively.

Table 2.2 Organisations by size

Size band	Staff	Survey results	Funding (£m)	Survey results
Small	–20	9	–2.5	10
Medium	21–100	7	2.5–25	5
Large	101–500	6	25–500	6

Source: RDA survey.

All in all, the sample would appear to be sufficiently diverse to enable a preliminary mapping of different types of regionally based development bodies in Western Europe, and we therefore proceed to analysing the organisations by comparing their key characteristics to those of a model RDA.

Bureaucratic autonomy

To qualify as a model RDA, a development organisation is by definition required to be situated outside the mainstream government apparatus in a semi-autonomous position *vis-à-vis* its political sponsors. Although 'semi-autonomy' may seem a contradiction in terms, it is possible to define a sequence of possible relationships between the political authority legitimising a development operation and the bureaucratic executive in the frontline of policy implementation, and by means of this conceptual framework determine the degree of bureaucratic autonomy enjoyed by the latter (Halkier 1992).

As illustrated by Table 2.3, a basic distinction can be drawn between development organisations positioned either inside or outside the core administrative apparatus of politically elected government. While a development body incorporated into, for example, a regional council is likely to be subjected to a high degree of direct political control, the bureaucratic autonomy of an independent institution is potentially higher both with regard to long-term strategic decisions and day-to-day business. In an arm's-length situation the sponsoring authority only interferes with the activities of the policy-making organisation on a very general level such as allocation of resources and broad policy guidelines while both the strategic initiative and important discretionary powers are left with the frontline bureaucracy. In both departmental and arm's-length situations the relationship between the political sponsors and the frontline bureaucracy can be influenced by the involvement of other public or private organisations, broadening the legitimacy of the development body and at the same time making it less dependent on a single main sponsor and, potentially, increasing its freedom of manoeuvre. In the following an organisation will, however, be counted as a model RDA *only* if it is found to be in an arm's-length position *and* regardless of the number of sponsors involved.

Table 2.3 Organisations by bureaucratic autonomy –
definitions and results

Legal position	Position vis-à-vis political sponsor	Survey results
Part of govern-ment	DEPARTMENTAL direct political control	0
	SEMI-DEPARTMENTAL direct political control mediated by advisory council	4
Independent body	ARM'S-LENGTH/SINGLE political supervision, board appointed by govern-ment	13
	ARM'S-LENGTH/DOMINANT political supervision, board appointed mainly by government but influenced by other public/private organisations	7
	ARM'S-LENGTH/PLURAL political supervision, board appointed by govern-ment(s) and other public/private organisations	5

Source: RDA survey.

The information available has made it possible to establish the position of each development organisation *vis-à-vis* its political sponsor(s).[3] As can be seen from Table 2.3, four were incorporated in the apparatus of mainstream government, none was in an outright departmental position, while more than 80 per cent of the organisations surveyed were found to be in an arm's-length position, mostly sponsored solely or predominantly by one particular

3   One organisation, SoSet in Portugal, is a private company with no formal links to elected political authorities.

political authority. It can thus be concluded that the vast majority of organisations in the sample live up to the requirements of a model RDA, at least at the level of their legal and institutional position. Furthermore, this pattern of political sponsorship is clearly reinforced by the sources of funding: more than 80 per cent of organisations for which information has been available rely exclusively or primarily on a single source of finance, and this source is of course the sponsoring political authority.[4]

All in all it can be concluded that from an organisational perspective the development bodies surveyed comply remarkably well with the expectations of a model RDA, with more than 80 per cent positioned at arm's-length distance from the sponsoring political authority. At the same time the precarious nature of this semi-autonomous position was, however, also underlined by the fact that the vast majority of organisations rely exclusively or predominantly on one single economic and political sponsor, and hence the potential for extensive political interference in the activities of the legally independent RDAs is obvious.

Policy instruments and development strategies

To qualify as a model RDA, a strengthening of the indigenous sector by means of 'soft' policy instruments should be an important part of the policy profile of a development body. In order to operationalise this requirement, the activities in which the organisations engage have been classified according to the basic resources involved – supply of advice, finance or infrastructure – and the specific type of support provided[5], and the resulting policy areas have then been distributed into three groups according to their strategic orientation, as illustrated by Table 2.4. First we have the 'traditional' measures complementing or replacing the redistributive policies of central government by facilitating the import of growth from outside the region. Then follow the 'new' measures, not found in the traditional armoury of central government and primarily aimed at stimulating the growth and competitiveness of indigenous firms. And finally there is a small number of policy areas for which the strategic nature is so variable that classification is not possible.[6]

---

4   Of the 30 bodies surveyed, 11 depended on a single sponsor, for 11 one sponsor played a
    dominant role, and 5 organisations had a pluralistic funding structure.
5   The subdivisions reflect a number of rather different considerations rather than one particular
    principle, but it is still, we would argue, the most suitable for a survey primarily based on
    published information, and also not dissimilar to the one applied by Yuill (1982).
6   Grant schemes, both regionally based and those administered for national or European
    authorities, and land renewal can target both indigenous and incoming firms.

Table 2.4 Growth strategies and policy areas

Strategic orientation	Resource	Policy area	Occurence in survey
Traditional	Advice	Investment attraction	19
		Access to grants	12
	Infrastructure	General factories	11
New	Advice	General management	23
		Markets	23
		Production/technology	17
	Finance	Equity, loans etc.	16
	Infrastructure	Science parks etc.	9
		Training	6
Other	Finance	Own grants	8
		Grant administration	5
	Infrastructure	Land renewal	5

Source: RDA survey.

As can be seen from the aggregate figures included in Table 2.4, the three most common activities are all advisory services. Two of them clearly focus on indigenous firms through general management support, especially for small and medium-sized enterprises (SMEs), and information about market opportunities, for example the promotion of subcontracting or trade fairs. Contrary to this the third most common advisory service, attraction of inward investment, entails a rather different perspective on regional development and its prominence underlines the diversity of the activities undertaken by the organisations investigated. Furthermore, amongst the development bodies the internal balance between traditional and new policy areas vary greatly: some organisations engage both in traditional and new activities while others concentrate heavily on policy programmes involving a particular type of resource or strategic orientation, such as either promotion of inward investment[7] or advice to regionally based firms.[8]

7   Examples in the survey include the development bodies in German Schleswig-Holstein and Spanish Aragon.
8   Examples in the survey include the three Danish development organisations and two French ones, from Creuse and Nord-Pas-de-Calais.

Table 2.5 Organisations by policy profile

Degree of specialisation	Primary activity	
	Traditional	*New*
Specialised	8	13
Mixed	4	5

Source: RDA survey.

In order to take both the relative weight and the overall distribution of different types of development activities into account, the character of the policy profile of each organisation in the sample was determined by combining two criteria, namely: 1) the traditional/new nature of the most important policy area; 2) the degree to which the organisation specialises in activities with a strategic perspective similar to that of its most important policy programme. This divides the sample into four groups according to priority activity and degree of specialisation[9], and, as can be seen from Table 2.5, nearly half of the organisations surveyed specialise in new policy areas, while the remainder are evenly divided between those specialising in traditional measures and development bodies with a mixed policy profile. Again the overall picture is, in other words, a very heterogenous one.

As model RDAs are supposed to give an important, but not necessarily exclusive, role to policies focusing on the needs of indigenous firms, organisations that specialise in traditional policy areas cannot be said to comply with this requirement. From the perspective of policy profiles and strategic orientation, only those with either specialised-new or mixed policy profiles fulfil the model-RDA criteria[10], and thus 75 per cent of the organisations pass the second of the three tests.

9   In order to allow for the greater number of policy areas with an indigenous strategic focus (cf. Table 2.4), an organisation with predominantly new activities will be regarded as specialised if it engages in no more than one traditional activity, and an organisation with predominantly traditional activities will be regarded as specialised if it engages in no more than two new policy areas.
10 The additional requirement to rely mainly on soft policy instruments is fulfilled by all non-specialised-traditional organisations in that advisory services account for more than half of their new policy areas.

Modes of implementation

A model RDA was not only expected to be involved in new types of policy areas but also to go about its task in a way that differed from that of the traditional regional incentive schemes of central government. Whereas the latter consisted primarily of segregated programmes, RDAs were expected to operate in an integrated manner, being able to draw upon a range of policy instruments in order to tackle structural problems within the regional economy or specific difficulties faced by individual firms in an effective manner.

The capacity for integrated implementation depends on two features: the number of policy areas in which an organisation is engaged, and the diversity of the policy instruments at its disposal. The exact number of policy areas that will allow integrated implementation of course cannot be established once and for all, but for the purpose of this text only organisations involved in four or more different policy areas will qualify as model RDAs. In terms of diversity, only organisations having both 'soft' (advice) and 'hard' (finance, infrastructure) resources at their disposal are accepted as being able to tailor a specific incentive structure that can induce private and other actors to adopt new patterns of behaviour and thereby address a particular weakness in the regional economy.

Table 2.6 Organisations by capacity for integrated implementation

Diversity of policy instruments	No. of policy areas	
	1–3	4+
Either hard/soft	3	1
Both hard/soft	4	22

Source: RDA survey.

As can be seen from Table 2.6, nearly 75 per cent of the organisations surveyed fulfil both criteria, while involvement in too few policy areas appears to be a more common cause of non-compliance than is exclusive reliance on either hard or soft resources. What these findings do not reveal, of course, is the extent to which the potential for integration has actually been fulfilled. It is perfectly possible to imagine a development body with a large number of diverse policy instruments at its disposal than nonetheless operates in a compartmentalised, and hence ultimately segregated, manner due to internal divisions of labour within the organisation or external constraints imposed by political sponsors.

Again, however, the picture emerging is a heterogenous one, with a sizeable majority of organisations complying with the third requirement for being a model RDA, and a significant minority of the sample failing to do so.

A typology of regional development organisations

As will be remembered, the thinking behind the RDA approach to regional development requires a 'model agency' to fulfil three different criteria, focusing on sponsorship, policy profile and implementation respectively. We have already established that for each of these characteristics a significant majority of the organisations surveyed comply with these requirements, and in order to get a fuller, multi-dimensional picture of bottom-up regional policy in Western Europe, attention is now turned on the extent to which a particular organisation fulfils all of these criteria. Although the research methodology employed limits both the comprehensiveness and degree of detail attainable – cf. the comments above on the nature of the sample and the empirical indicators – this will enable us not only to identify a group of model RDAs within the sample, but also to develop a preliminary typology of regionally based development bodies on the basis of shared key characteristics.

Table 2.7 RDAs and other development bodies

Classification	Survey results
Model RDAs	16
Potential RDAs	8
Non-RDAs	6

Source: RDA survey.

By combining the three criteria, the 30 development bodies surveyed can be divided into three groups: 'model RDAs' fulfilling all three criteria; 'potential RDAs' fulfilling two out of three; 'non-RDAs' complying with only one or none of them. As can be seen from Table 2.7, more than half of the organisations can be classified as 'model agencies', while the rest is evenly divided between those failing by only one criterion and those clearly not complying with the expectations of an RDA. This of course does not imply that the current state of development policy in half of the regions surveyed is inherently superior to that in the other half, but merely that the existing patterns are in varying degree of accordance with the RDA approach to regional policy with its integrated implementation of new-model policies by an arm's-length institution. But before moving on to consider possible origins of the differences recorded between regionally based development bodies, it is worth taking a closer look at the organisational characteristics of the three groups.

Amongst the model RDAs, three distinct subgroupings can be identified on the basis of particular combinations of policy profile and resources. Organisations with a mixed-traditional policy profile are generally large, probably reflecting the relatively costly nature of many traditional policies with their reliance on grants and factory building[11], while most of those with mixed-new[12] or specialised-new[13] profiles generally operate on a much smaller scale. Within the sample the basic requirements of a model RDA in other words are fulfilled by three distinct types of development bodies, namely:

- relatively large organisations with mixed-traditional policy profiles

- medium to small organisations with mixed-new profiles and

- relatively small organisations specialising in new policy areas. Although RDAs are by definition characterised by relatively broad policy profiles, this clearly does not necessarily require a large organisation in terms of financial resources.

A closer look at the group of organisations dubbed 'potential RDAs' justifies the adoption of this apparently prejudicial label,[14] as the more diverse of the organisations specialising in traditional activities lack only one additional new policy area each to achieve a mixed profile and qualify as RDAs.[15] A fairly large group of relatively small organisations in other words would appear to be capable of making the transformation into fully-fledged RDAs if they, and/or their political sponsors, should decide to go down this road – although the seemingly high degree of concentration on one particular

11 Model RDAs with mixed-traditional policy profiles are Shannon Development, the Welsh Development Agency and the development bodies in Murcia and Greater Hannover.
12 Model RDAs with mixed-new policy profiles are Portuguese ADRAT, and the development bodies in Flemish Brabantine, West Flanders and Hessen. Scottish Enterprise, by far the largest organisation in the sample, is an exception to this rule.
13 Model RDAs with specialised-new policy profiles are the two English TECs, LEDU, Udaras na Gaeltachta and the development bodies in Greater Aachen, Andalusia and Catalonia.
14 Potential RDAs were found in the following regions: Alpes-Maritimes, Berlin, the Liege Province, Val d'Oise, Nord-Pas-de-Calais, Isle of Wight, Viborg County and Storstrøm County.
15 This is the case in Alpes-Maritimes, Val d'Oise, Berlin and SPI in the province of Liege.

activity in many cases may make it difficult to develop an integrated approach in practice.

The non-RDA group is dominated by development bodies under relatively strict political supervision and organisations narrowly specialised in traditional regional policy activities[16], and as all of them comply with only one of the three criteria, major changes would have to be undertaken should it be decided to move these organisations in the direction of the model RDAs.

Origins of diversity amongst regional development bodies

Given the importance attached to adapting to the specific circumstances of the individual region entailed in the thinking informing bottom-up regional policy, it is not unexpected that the 30 organisations included in the survey have turned out to be a heterogenous group. It, however, would be surprising if this diversity was purely a reflection of the different economic problems faced by the regions – such a hyper-rational explanation in fact would set regional policy apart from most other areas of public policy[17] – and it is therefore necessary to explore what factors might influence the character of individual organisations. The survey methodology underlying this chapter is by no means ideal for this particular purpose, but as will become evident some preliminary points can be made that could inform future research in the area. In the following the results of the survey will be reconsidered with a view to examining the possible importance of three factors that could all potentially have had a bearing upon regionally based development policies, namely the economic characteristics of the region, the broader institutional environment, and the changing paradigms of regional policy.

In order to get a first, and admittedly rough, indication of the economic position of the 30 regions, their designation for European regional support has been used. This allows us to distinguish between structurally backward regions (Objective 1), areas affected by industrial decline (Objective 2), rural areas (Objective 5b) and non-designated areas where the latter must generally be assumed to be relatively better off. As can be seen from Table 2.8, even in this limited sample practically all possible combinations of RDA status and EU designation can be found, and the only feature worth commenting on is the relatively high frequency of model RDAs in Objective 1 regions, perhaps indicating that extensive problem have been translated into a comprehensive approach to development policy.

---

16 Non-RDAs were found in the following regions: West Zealand County, Creuse, Aragon, North Rhine-Westphalia, Schleswig-Holstein and Setubal (SoSet).

17 See e.g. Ham and Hill (1984), Hogwood and Gunn (1986) and Mayntz (1993).

Table 2.8 Development bodies
and EU regional support

	Non RDAs	Potential RDAs	Model RDAs			Total
			spec.-new	mixed-new	mixed-trad.	
Objective 1	1	1	3	1	2	8
Objective 2	2	4	4	1	1	12
Objective 5b	3	1	1	2	1	8
Undesignated	1	3	0	1	1	6
Total	6	8	7	5	4	30

Source: RDA survey.

The most important conclusion, however, still would seem to be that neither model RDAs nor other types of development bodies are firmly linked to particular structural problems of the regional economy, and thus there are good reasons for proceeding to consider other possible sources of influence upon bottom-up policy in the regions.

Regional development agencies are public bodies, and despite in some cases being situated at arm's-length from mainstream government, political sponsorship could well influence their organisation and policies. Amongst the Western European democracies, the political systems differ both on the central and sub-central level (Bennett 1989), and this could give rise to distinct national policy patterns (Richardson 1982) also in the field of regional development. Table 2.9 breaks down the sample according to nation and the level of political sponsorship in order to see whether certain types of development bodies are found in particular political environments. If this is generally the case, the political and institutional environment would appear to have a major influence on bottom-up regional policy.

As can be seen from Table 2.9, the pattern varies considerably across Western Europe. First, in three countries the development bodies surveyed would seem to be fairly homogenous: while the two Irish organisations are both model RDAs, none of the Danish and French organisations qualify. Second, in three countries variation is limited and may well reflect differences in political sponsorship: in the UK all the 'model agencies' are sponsored by central government while the potential RDA has a regional sponsor, and in Belgium the two 'model agencies' are sponsored by Flemish provinces while the potential RDA is co-sponsored by a Wallonian province. In Spain the predominance of regionally sponsored model RDAs is also pronounced, but

Table 2.9 Developmental bodies
and political sponsorship

Country	Political sponsorship	Non RDAs	Potential RDAs	Model RDAs			Total
				spec.-new	mixed-new	mixed-trad.	
Portugal	local	1	0	0	1	0	2
Ireland	central	0	0	1	0	1	2
France	regional	1	2	0	0	0	3
	reg./local	0	1	0	0	0	1
Denmark	regional	1	1	0	0	0	2
	reg./local	0	1	0	0	0	1
UK	central	0	0	3	1	1	5
	regional	0	1	0	0	0	1
Spain	regional	1	0	2	0	1	4
Belgium	regional	0	0	0	2	0	2
	reg./local	0	1	0	0	0	1
Germany	regional	2	1	0	1	0	4
	local	0	0	1	0	1	2
Total		6	8	7	5	4	30

Source: RDA survey.

as the non-RDA in Aragon is also sponsored by its Autonomous Community, this cannot be accounted for solely by reference to the political system. Third, two countries, Portugal and Germany, display great internal variation, defying any particular kind of pattern.

It is interesting to note that the three homogenous countries are all unitary states, the three near-homogenous countries all had quasi-federal constitutional features despite being essentially unitary[18], and the greatest degree of diversity is found in the Federal Republic of Germany[19]. Perhaps this suggests that the degree of internal diversity is greater in countries with a more decentralised political system. A closer look at the policy profiles of model RDAs found in the various countries, however, does not suggest a

18 The survey was undertaken before the federalisation of Belgium was completed.
19 Portugal, a highly centralised country with a new and weak tradition of regional government, is the only exception to this rule.

relationship between their policies and the position of the sponsoring political authority, and thus while the survey certainly does suggest that the national and regional political setting can influence the shape of development bodies, it also underlines the need to take other factors into account.

The development paradigms informing regional policy have changed over the years, and the characteristics of individual organisations may therefore be influenced by their history. Although the transition from traditional top-down policies towards new-model bottom-up policies was an uneven process rather than something that happened throughout Western Europe at one particular moment in time, it is generally thought that the traditional approach prevailed until the mid-1970s after which the new approach gradually became more widespread (Stöhr 1989). As reported earlier, the 26 development bodies for which information on their year of creation was available make up three generations, comprising organisations founded before the early 1960s, between the late 1960s and late 1970s, and from the 1980s onwards. In other words, we would expect that the oldest generation is more in line with traditional forms of regional policy, the youngest one primarily involved in new-model activities, and the middle one perhaps presenting a more mixed picture.

In Table 2.10 the sample of organisations is broken down according to year of creation and RDA status. From this it is immediately evident that the relative distribution of model, potential and non-RDAs is almost the same within each of the three generations of development bodies. A sizeable part of the 'model agencies' thus predates the rise of new-model regional policy, and this may indicate that extensive processes of organisational learning and change have taken place in some of the older development bodies. Furthermore, it is also noticeable that the policy profiles of the three generations of model RDAs differ: while organisations with a specialised-new profile are very prominent among the youngest generation, there appears to be an over-representation of organisations with a mixed-traditional policy profile in the oldest generation of development bodies, and thus the three forms of 'model agencies' identified above would appear to have thrived in different phases of the development of regional policy in Western Europe.

Table 2.10 Development bodies and their historical origins

Year of creation	Non RDAs	Potential RDAs	Model RDAs			Total
			spec.-new	mixed-new	mixed-trad.	
Before 1963	1	1	1	1	2	6
1968–78	1	2	1	2	1	7
1982 onwards	1	4	5	2	1	13

Source: RDA survey.

All in all the results of the survey clearly suggest that attempts to explain the origins of the current patterns of bottom-up initiatives must be as multi-dimensional as the analysis of the organisations themselves. The political-institutional setting and the historical links with particular paradigms in regional policy certainly cannot be ignored, while the possible influence of the economic environment requires further examination.

Conclusions and future perspectives

The above analysis of regional development organisations in Western Europe has led us to three conclusions.

First, the organisations surveyed turned out to be a very heterogeneous group with regard to most key characteristics, but by employing the ideal-type of a model RDA it was found that around half of the organisations complied with all three key requirements of a model agency: operating at arm's-length from their political sponsors, primarily stimulating the growth of indigenous enterprise and having the capacity to adopt an integrated approach to regional development. Furthermore, it was possible to distinguish between three different types of model RDAs within this group on the basis of their policy profiles and organisational resources. The other half of the sample, however, diverges from the prescriptions of the RDA approach, mainly because they concentrate on a limited number of often rather traditional policy programmes and hence do not have the capacity for developing an integrated approach with an indigenous strategic thrust.

Second, although a small group of organisations is near-exclusively geared to promoting the region as a location for incoming investment, the overwhelming majority to a greater or lesser extent are involved in activities aimed at strengthening the competitiveness of local firms. New types of policy activities are by no means the exclusive domain of model RDAs, and thus regional-level promotion of economic development is clearly much more than just a lower-tier mirror of traditional central government policies. The bottom-up sector would seem to hold important potentials as a source of innovation in regional policy.

Third, the preliminary probing of possible origins of the diversity recorded amongst regionally based development organisations suggested the importance of factors such as the political environment, nationally and regionally, and the historical heritage from the policy paradigm predominating at the creation of the organisation. The influence of other factors, including the structural characteristics of the regional economy, may well have escaped the current survey, but future analyses of bottom-up regional policy clearly would have to take qualitative and institutional factors, more often than not downplayed in studies of regional policy, into account.

In addition to these conclusions, the discussion of the survey has also pointed to a number of areas in which further work remains to be undertaken. In the current research design, the analysis of development organisations is partly based on measures of the capacity to fulfil the model-RDA criteria, and it would be interesting to know more about the extent to which this potential has actually been fulfilled. Moreover, if the focus of research were broadened from individual organisations to the region as a spatial unit, it would be possible to understand the division of labour between development bodies co-existing in a particular regions and the ways in which they interact amongst themselves and with national and international actors. And lastly, an inquiry into the origins of the differences observed in the survey could cast additional light upon the interplay between organisational and strategic aspects of regional policy, and the relationship between development organisations and their economic and political environment. In terms of methodology the findings of the present survey confirmed the importance of approaching bottom-up regional policy from a multi-dimensional perspective, but also clearly demonstrated the limits of the survey approach itself. A better understanding of this area would therefore require *not only* a vastly extended international survey of regionally based development organisations in order to establish the broader picture, *but also* in-depth studies of the development of individual RDAs, aiming especially to identify patterns of interaction with other actors involved in regional development. As regional policy in Europe is gradually being transformed into a complex multi-level operation, research along these lines could further our understanding of the potentials and limits of bottom-up initiatives and the position of the RDA approach within the overall picture of regional policy in Western Europe.

Acknowledgements

Thanks are due to Mr Christian Saublens, Director of EURADA, for making available the addresses of his membership, to British Council and Aalborg University for financial support, and to Helle Weiergang and Runa Olesen for help in carrying out the survey. We gratefully acknowledge constructive comments on earlier versions of the text from two anonymous referees from *European Urban and Regional Studies*, and from Charlotte Damborg and other members of the European Research Unit, Aalborg University, although full responsibility for the text in its present form remains with the authors.

An earlier version of the text appeared in *European Urban and Regional Studies 4, 3*, 1997. Thanks are due to Sage Publications for permission to reproduce material previously published elsewhere.

References

Bennett, R. (1989) 'European economy, society, politics and administration: symmetry and disjuncture.' In R. Bennett (ed) *Territory and Administration in Europe*. London: Pinter.

EURADA (1992) *European Association of Development Agencies*. Brussels: EURADA.

Halkier, H. (1992) 'Development agencies and regional policy: the case of the Scottish Development Agency.' *Regional Politics and Policy 2*, 3, 1–26.

Ham, C. and Hill, M. (1984) *The Policy Process in the Modern Capitalist State*. Brighton: Wheatsheaf.

Hogwood, B. and Gunn, L.A. (1986) *Policy Analysis for the Real World*. Oxford: OUP.

Mayntz, R. (1993) 'Governing failures and the problem of governability: some comments on a theoretical paradigm.' In J. Kooiman (ed) *Modern Governance: New Government-Society Interactions*. London: Sage.

Richardson, J. (ed) (1982) *Policy Styles in Western Europe*. London: Allen and Unwin.

Stöhr, W. (1989) 'Regional policy at the crossroads: an overview.' In L. Albrechts *et al.* (eds) *Regional Policy at the Crossroads: European Perspectives*. London: Jessica Kingsley Publishers.

Yuill, D. (ed) (1982) *Regional Development Agencies in Europe*. Aldershot: Gower.

Yuill, D., Allen, K., Bachtler, J., Clement, K. and Wishlade, F. (1992) *European Regional Incentives 1992–93*. London: Bowker-Saur.

PART II

RDAs in Western Europe – National Surveys

The general picture with regard to the role of RDAs in regional policy in Western Europe is reasonably clear. Since the 1970s national incentive schemes have in many cases been reduced, and as the number of regionally based development organisations such as RDAs has continued to grow, the overall importance of bottom-up initiatives would appear to have increased.

RDAs and their activities are supposed to reflect the needs of individual regions, and the growing prominence of new-model regional policy would therefore seem to make it more difficult to get a comprehensive overview of spatial economic policy on the national level. Although diversity is to be expected, there are, however, also factors that are likely to prompt a certain degree of homogeneity in the heterogeneous bottom-up scene. Despite local variations, the economic problems faced by Western European regions are essentially variations on a limited number of themes: industrial decline, sectoral change, urban congestion and rural depopulation to name but the most obvious. Similarly, the strategies of development organisations rely on combinations of a limited set of policy instruments like finance, advice and infrastructure. And finally the political environment is likely to have a bearing on the role of RDAs, both with regard to the institutional set-up, the position *vis-à-vis* other organisations involved in regional and local economic policy, and the types of initiatives in which they primarily engage. At the end of the day the seemingly arbitrary permutations of bottom-up regional policy may well constitute an intricate pattern.

One approach to the study of RDAs is to analyse the experience in a particular national setting. International surveys have pointed to the existence of differences along national lines, and investigations of bottom-up regional policy on a national scale can help illuminate some of the features that distinguish development bodies from those in other countries, and possibly also point towards the origins of national peculiarities by linking them to institutional characteristics, economic structures, political traditions and historical trends. Furthermore, national surveys have the advantage of comprising a large number of agencies and should therefore also be able to highlight inter-regional differences and perhaps also suggest some reasons for the pattern of variation uncovered.

Part II contains three national surveys, covering Austria, the Netherlands and Denmark respectively. The unifying aspect is, in other words, the method – they all report findings of comprehensive nation-wide studies that insert individual agencies in a broader national context – and it must be underlined that the three countries are not seen as being representative of different types of RDA regimes or indeed the general situation in Western Europe. Although contributions elsewhere in this volume, notably the chapters on Belgium and Spain, are not dissimilar to the surveys presented in the following, bottom-up regional policy in major nations such as Germany, France and Britain clearly seem to have avoided systematic treatment on a national basis. The reasons for this are open to speculation, but the logistics involved in studying regionally based organisations are likely to have been at least a contributing factor: national surveys are certainly easier to conduct in small and relatively homogenous countries. The concluding chapter in this volume will, however, in a small way attempt to redress this balance by attempting to identify national characteristics of RDAs across Europe at large.

Although the three Western European countries surveyed are similar in that they are small, open and relatively prosperous economies with consensual political traditions, the subsequent chapters reveal that the role and development of RDAs in Austria, the Netherlands and Denmark have by no means been identical. In Chapter 3 Michael Steiner and Thomas Jud analyse the Austrian case by setting the development of regionally based bodies in the changing context of regional policy within the federal state, and offer an in-depth case study of policy towards new technology-based firms in the region of Styria. In Chapter 4 Wilfred Sleegers discusses the evolving role of regional development bodies in the Netherlands, especially with regard to provision of long-term share investments, and relates the changing fortunes of Dutch RDAs to the changing general approach to economic policy taken by central government. Finally in Chapter 5 Charlotte Damborg and Henrik Halkier chart the recent rise in Denmark of regional initiatives in economic development, focusing especially on issues of organisation and policy profiles in an attempt to identify a 'Danish approach' to bottom up regional policy.

As should be apparent, the three national surveys have a number of themes in common that are of a more general relevance. First, the change from traditional policies based on 'hard' resources towards a new approach involving more specialised resources such as information and organisational capacities is very much in evidence, and, despite national differences with regard to institutional position and policy profile, RDAs have been part and parcel of this process. Second, the nature of the relationship between different tiers of government emerges as a major issue, involving both constitutional differences between federal and unitary states, and the different ways in which these rules are employed in the process of institution building and policy implementation with regard to RDAs. The significance of inter-tier relations has been increased, of course, by the growing role of the European Structural Funds as a source of finance and policy programmes for regional development. Third, the question of coordination at the regional level between different organisations is clearly also of great importance because of the existence of a plethora of public or semi-public bodies with economic development as part of their remit. While some degree of duplication may not necessarily be a major problem – a certain 'institutional thickness' might be necessary to ensure a reasonable rate of response from the firms targeted – the potential for overall inefficiency as a result of organisational parochialism is a very real one indeed. All in all the national surveys would thus seem to suggest that the environment in which the RDAs operate and the ways in which the organisations attempt to negotiate it must be borne in mind when studying individual development bodies.

CHAPTER 3

Regional Development Institutions in Austria
Trends in Organisation, Policies and Implementation
Michael Steiner & Thomas Jud

Introduction

Until the 1980s the Austrian regional policy system was characterised by a traditional view of regional economic problems with respect to the interpretation of regional inequality, the instrumental set-up and the instruments used. Rough regional indicators such as the growth rates of the economy, the income level and the unemployment rate were used to measure regional disparities which were to be equalised or at least decreased with the help of policy intervention. Reasons for the disparities between the well-developed regions and the problem regions were traced back mainly to the lack of capital, market imperfections and the existence of mobility barriers concerning production resources. Correspondingly the instruments of economic policy were designed to cope with these problems. It was necessary to reduce production costs of firms in the problem regions in order to stimulate transfer of capital from relatively richer regions, and this was to be achieved by the induced settlement of new firms and by subsidising investments. This approach of regional economic policy was supported by promotional activities aiming at the strengthening of national economic competitiveness in general by subsidising investments in key industries.

The entire system of economic promotion was highly centralised and led by aggregated economic indicators. As a result, two problems arose which could not be solved by the traditional instruments of economic policy:

- The continuous technological change caused structural alterations of the economy, which could not be taken into account by the undifferentiated instruments used.

- The macro-orientated economic policy did not recognise the importance of immobile factors of regional development (e.g. infrastructure, knowledge base, etc.) which were not covered by the purely financial promotional activities. Especially the problems of old industrial areas in the late 1970s and early 1980s represented a regional problem which showed the need for a new kind of regional policy.

The increasing ineffectiveness of traditional regional policy, the progress in regional economic research and the availability of foreign examples of new solutions for existing problems finally brought about a shift from the old model to a new philosophy of regional development in Austria.

In the following, the change of the Austrian regional policy is reported and a description of the current situation in the Austrian provinces is given and illustrated by examples.[1] It is shown that a new philosophy of regional policy is increasingly taking place characterised by the emergence of new institutions with a wider range of tasks using sophisticated methods to develop the indigenous potential of regions. Finally, the paper is concluded and an overview is provided of major new tasks and challenges which will arise for Austrian regional policy institutions in the near future.[2]

Austrian regional policy between traditional instruments and new solutions

Changes in the Austrian regional policy system have taken place very gradually. Today the available instruments of economic policy are thus characterised both by traditional elements and new approaches. However there is strong evidence to show that extensive changes are taking place. We have attempted to document these changes by carrying out a passive screening of printed information about all major Austrian regional policy institutions together with selective informal telephone contacts. We identified major changes at three different levels.

The organisational level first of all describes the position of the particular economic policy institution within the broader organisational framework; it can best be understood in terms of the legal position of the institution (private or public). Second, it provides information about the scope for action

---

1   The survey in this paper is based upon information from spring 1995, so the facts presented may not correspond entirely with the situation in 1998.
2   At the conference *Regional Development Agencies in Europe – Past Experiences and Future Perspectives* (Aalborg, Denmark, 29 August – 1 September 1996) a long version of this paper was presented describing our empirical findings about the features of individual development institutions in more detail.

and the objectives of the particular institution, and its ability to concentrate on the demands of the region involved by using discretionary measures.

The functional or instrumental level describes the range of the provided services of regional policy institutions: from providing financial support, soft factors of regional development (e.g. information and advisory services) to the takeover of regional coordination and catalyst functions (e.g. initiating and balancing regional infrastructure projects).

The implementation level describes changes in the target groups and economic activities focused by promotional activities.

The organisational level

Austria is a federal republic with a powerful central government. Beside the federal government and the federal parliament it consists of nine provinces with their own provincial governments and parliaments which autonomously use a considerable share of the public budget. Therefore regional economic policy represents a cross-section of policies carried out by various institutions.

At the federal level, the federal parliament, the federal government and its ministries are responsible for regulatory and discretionary regional policy tasks. The strategic guidelines designed by these bodies are implemented mainly by two legally separated promotional institutions which are responsible for allocating available funds along a variety of different financial support schemes. Additionally, a specific forum has been established to discuss regional policy subjects in Austria and coordinate activities and initiatives at the federal and provincial levels.

The only significant institutional change which took place at the federal level during recent years was the foundation of the *Gesellschaft des Bundes für industriepolitische Maßnahmen* (GBI); an institution designed to play a more active role in regional development beyond the pure granting of financial aid.

At the provincial level, the regional governments and regional parliaments are responsible for developing regional policy guidelines. These used to be implemented by institutions within the mainstream administrative apparatus, but about a decade ago the organisational structure and targets of regional policy began to change. In many provinces the tasks of implementing policy guidelines have been handed over to semi-autonomous institutions.[3] Most of them are legally separated from the mainstream administrative apparatus and

---

3   It should be emphasised that both traditional and newly founded regional policy institutions are responsible for administrative regions and not functional regions with specific economic characteristics.

set up as private companies but are publicly financed and owned. Their activities are limited by legally defined guidelines of the respective province and are orientated towards certain tasks. An essential difference between the traditional view and the new philosophy lies in the different objectives of the old and new institutions. Until now it was believed that regional differences were caused by differences in the capital stock of the regions. Recently, however, a quite different view has been discovered: differences between regions also arise from differences in the immobile factors of a region, e.g. its (physical) infrastructure, the abilities and skills of the workforce, the local economic structure, the local technical and organisational know-how and the social and institutional structures. Therefore, the starting points of regional policy activities of new institutions have shifted. It is essential to promote the strengths of the indigenous regional potential, to balance existing deficiencies and to link the regions to the international context.

The functional or instrumental level

Only minor changes have taken place at the federal level in recent years. With the establishment of the GBI an institution has been created which provides a wider range of services than more traditional institutions supplying only financial support programmes. It not only offers different kinds of infrastructure (e.g. technology and industrial parks, telecommunication infrastructure, etc.) but also carries out, initiates and finances regional restructuring projects and regional economic research projects.

At the regional level the range of services provided by regional policy institutions in the last few years has changed dramatically. A wide range of new instruments has been introduced and particularly is being used by newly founded institutions. Besides financial support services, infrastructure institutions such as technology parks, industrial parks and incubator centres are provided, information and advisory services are offered, trade fairs and meetings for certain target groups are arranged as well as many other activities. A characteristic feature of the new approach is the increasing number of border-crossing activities by regional policy institutions. Financial incentives to conduct international projects, particularly R&D collaboration, together with the establishment of cross-border industrial and technology parks will help form international links.

New institutions are becoming the centre of efforts of regional development. Instead of being passive institutions of the 'mainstream administrative apparatus', they build up regional networks, generate incentives for firms and entrepreneurs to increase their innovation activities and coordinate the use of regional resources to accelerate the indigenous development of the regions.

In the course of this development the provinces follow two different strategies. Either the entire range of regional policy services is combined in one institution or several different specialised institutions are founded. In this second strategy, one might have, for example, individual suppliers of infrastructure, individual suppliers of risk and equity capital, individual institutions for providing financial support, and so on.

The implementation level

Besides the expansion of the range of instruments of regional policy the last few years have brought about a markedly new way of implementing traditional financial support services. At federal and provincial levels a shift has occurred with respect to both the target groups and the activities which are supported by public funds. Formerly, funds were provided as subsidies for investments in problem regions, key industries and small and medium-sized firms. Nowadays financial support schemes focus on supporting comprehensive innovation, infrastructure, modernisation, internationalisation or application-orientated R&D projects; they have become project-orientated. Thereby a strong emphasis is laid on promoting young, small and newly founded firms. Therefore regional economic promotion activities no longer aim at the transfer of capital between regions, but try to increase the competitiveness of regional economies by developing the regional innovation potential.

Summary

Austrian regional economic policy is carried out both by the federal government and the individual provinces.

At the organisational level the changes can be seen in a tendency to establish new regionally based policy institutions outside the mainstream administrative apparatus which are characterised by an arm's-length autonomy with respect to their activities and a changing nature of the targets to be followed.

In contrast to the federal level, a distinct change in the range of tasks provided by regional policy institutions took place at the regional level. It can be seen in the expansion of services for border-crossing activities and soft factors of regional development (e.g. information and advisory services) and the takeover of coordination and catalytic tasks by regionally based institutions.

Both at federal and regional levels, public funds used to support economic activities are now granted in a more diversified way. Financial support activities essentially aim at: applied R&D, innovation, internationalisation, infrastructure and modernisation projects, innovative SMEs and newly established firms.

Surveying the Austrian situation at the provincial level

As can be seen from the above explanations, the changes of instruments and modes of implementation of regional policy in Austria were complementary to the emergence of new institutions at the regional level with a strong RDA-like character. Following the definition of a regional development agency given by Halkier and Danson (1995) as

> a regionally based organisation that appears to claim to play an independent role in the promotion of economic development, which is publicly financed and outside the mainstream of central and local government administration (p.3)

three major criteria were identified:

1. regionally based
2. outside the mainstream of central and local government administration
3. having an independent role in the promotion of economic development.[4]

Using these criteria, Austrian institutions were classified into institutions with strong, medium, weak and no RDA character. Institutions were awarded one point for each criterion they satisfied. Institutions with one point have a weak RDA character, those with two points have a medium, those with three points are strong and those with no points have no RDA character.

Figure 3.1 presents the outcome of the classification procedure. The vertical axis represents the number of existing development institutions and on the horizontal axis are the nine Austrian provinces. The shaded areas indicate the RDA-like character of the different regional policy institutions. The pictures do not include regional policy institutions at the national level, because they are not regionally based.[5]

---

4 In the context of this paper an institution plays an independent role in the promotion of regional economic development if it is able to design and implement initiatives and support schemes autonomously, i.e. institutions are not directly influenced by short-term political decisions.
5 For more detailed information see Steiner and Jud (1996).

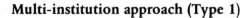

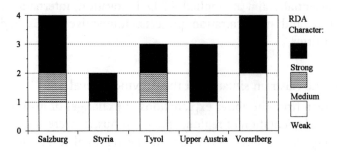

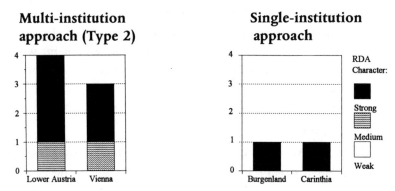

Figure 3.1 Regional policy institutions in Austrian provinces

We see that there are two general strategies of change for regional policy institutions in Austria at the regional level: the *multi-institution approach* and the *single-institution approach.*

The multi-institution approach

For different activities like providing financial support, infrastructure, or the typical soft factors of economic development, there are separate institutions with different institutional modes (outside or inside the mainstream apparatus, independent or dependent role in economic development) – the Austrian provinces Lower Austria, Upper Austria, Salzburg, Styria[6], Tyrol, Vorarlberg and Vienna adopt this philosophy. As most political changes can only occur gradually, it is difficult to reconstruct whether this approach is

6   Styria has since adopted the single-institution approach.

part of a consistent strategy or whether it represents a by-product on the way towards RDA-like institutions for the individual provinces.

Within this multi-institution approach two different trends can be recognised. Type 1 is represented by the provinces Upper Austria, Salzburg, Styria, Tyrol and Vorarlberg, which implement a twofold 'strategy' of policy change combining traditional elements with the new philosophy. They have pushed ahead the spreading of regional policy tasks by establishing new institutions and have left at least part of the field of financial economic promotion to the mainstream administrative apparatus with weak RDA character. The newly established institutions (medium or strong RDA character) either take over the tasks of a qualified infrastructure supplier, provide information, coordination and advisory services, or offer funding services with a strong focus on applied R&D and innovative activities.

In the Type 2 provinces, Lower Austria and Vienna, all existing institutions have medium or strong RDA characters because they are all separated from the mainstream administrative apparatus. Therefore not only the new tasks of regional policy, but also traditional financial support activities are carried out by RDA-like institutions. Their regional development activities are project orientated and their focus lies on promoting technology and innovation-orientated activities of firms and other institutions.

The single-institution approach

Carinthia and Burgenland adopt the single-institution approach. In these two provinces all different regional policy tasks have been tied together and handed over to just one institution. Thus *Kärntner Wirtschaftsförderungsfond* and *Wirtschaftsservice Burgenland AG* provide all the different services for financial economic promotion, infrastructure facilities and the soft factors of regional development on a central basis. In both provinces these institutions have a strong RDA-like character matching all of the three criteria.

The case of Styria as an example
A twofold 'strategy' of policy change

Styria has been chosen as a good example of both the twofold 'strategy' of policy change followed by most provinces (multi-institution approach – Type 1) and for illustrating the working of one of the newly established RDA-like institutions in Austria.[7]

Styria has two regional policy institutions covering the whole area and all sectors of the province with their promotional services: the *Steirische Wirtschaftsförderungsgesellschaft* (SFG) and *Amt der Steiermärkischen Landesregierung (Fachabteilung für Wirtschaftsförderung)*.

The division of regional economic policy between two distinct institutions is very difficult to reconstruct. The reasons for this strategy cannot easily be attributed to efficiency considerations, but are mainly an outcome of the political process. The following explanations will merely focus on the characteristics of the two institutions without considering the rationale behind the twofold 'strategy'.

Amt der Steiermärkischen Landesregierung (Fachabteilung für Wirtschaftsförderung)

Amt der Steiermärkischen Landesregierung is a typical institution of the mainstream administrative apparatus. Its activities concentrate exclusively on financial economic promotion activities which follow strictly defined guidelines. It has only a limited scope of action and no extended range of tasks. The financial support services are not particularly differentiated and rather meet the concept of traditional economic support. But also in this field there is an increasing focus on economic support for technology- and innovation-orientated projects.

Regarding the characteristics of regional development agencies the *Amt der Steiermärkischen Landesregierung* can be classified as an institution with weak RDA character. Though it is regionally based, it is inside the mainstream administrative apparatus and its activities are influenced by short-term political decisions.

The Steirische Wirtschaftsförderungsgesellschaft (SFG)

To allow a better comparison between the explanations in section two of this chapter and the following descriptions, we shall use a similar structure.

---

7   The situation in Styria has since changed. *Amt der Steiermärkischen Landesregierung* is about to be integrated into the SFG. Consequently, the SFG will develop into the main regional development institution in Styria. Nevertheless, the description of the former twofold strategy in Styria is still a valid illustration of the policy followed by the other representatives of the multi-institution approach (Type 1).

The organisational level

The SFG is an independent institution operating under private law outside the mainstream administrative apparatus. It is owned by and financed out of the budget of the province, and its activities are limited by legal regulations which are written down in the Styrian economic promotion law. These regulations include precise guidelines for granting financial support. They define to whom support can be given, which circumstances have to be fulfilled, what procedure must be followed and they limit the promotional activities of the SFG to the regional area of the province. To safeguard the interests of Styria, an evaluating committee was established which supervises the activities of the institution.

With respect to the soft factors of economic development the SFG can select its specific measures of support independently. Due to its legal status and its greater autonomy with respect to soft activities, the SFG does not just provide financial support in correspondence with its guidelines, but actively collaborates with Styrian companies, assisting them in conducting profitable innovation projects. Additionally, it promotes important infrastructure projects of municipalities and other institutions. This puts it in the role of an important coordinating authority. It is an essential contact partner for the Styrian economy and can also stimulate economic development across regional and national borders.

The objectives of the SFG are not precisely defined and furthermore not operational. But with a long-term orientation in mind, the objectives should merely function as guidelines for development activities and thus should not be defined too narrowly. The objectives include improving preconditions for economic development in Styria, increasing economic growth in disadvantaged regions, and strengthening indigenous regional potentials.

THE FUNCTIONAL OR INSTRUMENTAL LEVEL

The SFG carries out a wide spectrum of tasks divided into different activity areas. The main focus is on granting differentiated financial support, providing information and advisory services, supporting the creation of new firms, establishing and managing technology parks, initiating border-crossing initiatives and organising trade fairs, seminars and workshops to improve technology transfer. These activity areas are divided into seven subdivisions:

- *Regions*: marketing for locations, funds for infrastructure projects, information services.

- *Founders of firms*: encouraging business start-ups, providing information and advisory services, financial support and infrastructure such as business parks, technology parks etc.

- *Growing firms*: information and advisory services, financial support, equity capital.

- *Technology transfer*: mediation of cooperation, internationalisation, innovation transfer, organisational management, organisation of fairs.

- *Settlement of firms*: acquisition of investors, informing and taking care of investors, mediating information, providing infrastructure, mediating promotions.

- *Technology parks, innovation and incubation centres*: establishing and managing, providing infrastructure, mediating contacts, information for firms, acquisition of firms.

- *Training*: improvement of quality, globalisation, information for firms, personnel development.

THE IMPLEMENTATION LEVEL

Financial support and the provision of soft factors of economic development usually occur in the framework of comprehensive projects which are worked out together with the supported firms and organisations. Thus the different instruments or activities mentioned above are combined to a coordinated whole which is orientated towards an explicit goal. Using such a mode of action, a significant improvement of the effects of the instruments can be expected with respect to the development goals defined above.

The basis of financial support activities in the framework of particular projects is the legally defined guidelines prescribing preconditions which have to be fulfilled by projects. Basically, only innovation projects which either eliminate regional disparities, strengthen the economy of Styria, or contribute to the realisation of new technologies and the strengthening of the regional innovative potential can be supported. As a part of its strong project orientation, the SFG subsidises all costs arising out of a project: fees for external advisory services and training costs as well as costs that are directly connected to the projects. Thereby a strong emphasis lies on the promotion of innovative SMEs in the phase of growth and newly established firms.

NEW TECHNOLOGY-BASED FIRMS IN SYRIA - THE SFG AT WORK

A main focus of the SFG's work lies on supporting new technology-based firms (NTBFs). NTBFs are newly founded, profit-orientated firms aiming at selling products or services based on new technological ideas or research results. They represent a major factor in supporting the economic development of Styria because they perform four essential tasks:

- accelerating the transfer of knowledge from universities and research institutions to the economy
- facilitating economic structural change by developing new products for new markets
- supporting the formation of competitive economic networks of firms
- creating qualified employment.

Compared with the rest of Austria, Styrian new technology-orientated entrepreneurs play a dominant role (along with Vienna's NTBFs), as indicated by the portion of public funds allocated to their activities: about 35 per cent of all NTBFs supported under the Austrian seed financing programme[8] in 1993 were located in Styria and received a total of 50 per cent of the allocated funds compared to the share of Styrian employment in total national employment of about 12 per cent. This regional concentration of technology-intensive firm formation activities in Styria can be traced back to the availability of a highly developed technology infrastructure (universities, research institutions, technology parks) which is closely reconciled with the main economic foci of the different Styrian industries (e.g. engineering, new materials, electronics, etc.)

In spite of these facts indicating a considerable entrepreneurial activity in the high-tech sector, Styrian NTBFs are facing severe problems which are responsible for lowering actual foundation rates, preventing new ventures from reaching the market and impeding the expansion of successful firms. As various studies (see e.g. Steiner et al. 1996; Kulicke 1993) have reported, the main NTBF-specific problems can be classified in the following way: informational (e.g. lack of information about adequate partners), qualification-related (e.g. lack of management skills), financial (e.g. lack of equity capital and external funds), demand-related (e.g. high after sales risk of customers) and competition-related (e.g. different kinds of entry barriers).

---

8 The seed financing programme is the only Austrian-wide initiative designed to support NTBFs.

Though highly diversified, these obstacles are not independent from each other but on the contrary are closely interconnected. Any successful initiative designed to support NTBFs has to take these inter-relations into account and consequently should deal at best with all the problems simultaneously.

In many European countries and especially in the USA during the last decades, an industry has evolved specialised in funding and developing high-risk ventures, particularly NTBFs. In search of high returns for their investment, venture capitalists and 'Business Angels' offer equity capital for seed, start-up and expansion projects together with adequate management support. They use sophisticated networks of different actors directly or indirectly involved in the development process of NTBFs to generate and dissipate high-value information about competitors, potential customers, adequate partners for collaboration etc., thereby offering the set of complementary services needed to overcome existing problems and to propel the development of technology-orientated entrepreneurship. Success stories like Silicon Valley or Route 128 are good examples of the working of these markets (see e.g. Robertson and Langlois 1995).

In Styria and the whole of Austria the venture capital market is barely developed, thus available capital is very scarce and not high-risk orientated. It is primarily allocated to mergers and acquisitions in the form of management buy-out and management buy-in transactions and not to seed, start-up and expansion projects of NTBFs.

Naturally it is impossible for a public-funded RDA – like the SFG – bound by precise guidelines to compensate for all the services supplied on specialised private financial markets. But its autonomous position, especially with respect to the soft factors of regional development, offers a considerable potential for initiatives to be taken in some respects beyond the services a profit-driven market can offer.

To support technology-orientated entrepreneurship in Styria the SFG elaborated a twofold approach. First, it tries to establish adequate preconditions for the successful development of entrepreneurial activities, and second, it offers a phased or project-orientated structuring of its financial and soft promotional services aimed at NTBFs.

Preconditions for successful development

The SFG provides a rather diversified set of services relating to preconditions for a successful development of NTBFs:

- It establishes and runs technology parks and incubator centres to offer necessary infrastructure for newly established firms and to generate synergies between them.

- It organises meetings and workshops to put young entrepreneurs in touch with experienced managers, potential customers, collaborators and investors.

- It manages the presentation of new products and services of NTBFs at international trade fairs and exhibitions.

- It runs demonstration centres to put potential customers in touch with innovative products and services of NTBFs etc.

It is evident that the SFG is strongly engaged in building up networks of different actors (customers, partners for collaboration, potential investors, etc.) to generate and dissipate information important for the development of NTBFs. One major breakthrough in this direction is a recently established network called *Technologiepartner Steiermark* (TP). The TP network emerged from a long process of discussion and collaboration of now 15 different partners actively engaged or indirectly involved in local or regional economic development activities (e.g. research institutions, external institutes of regional universities, chambers of commerce, technology transfer centres, science parks, training institutions, labour market policy agencies, etc.)

The members of the TP network agreed to develop and establish a common information system designed as an Internet-based 'One-Stop-Shop'. Styrian NTBFs and regional businesses in general can send requests in terms of technology, training, funding and other support to the internet home page of the TP-network. All requests are categorised according to the services offered by the different members of the TP-network and immediately distributed to the individual members with appropriate expertise. Coordination of requests and management of the Internet server lies within the responsibility of the SFG.

The advantages of this system are threefold. First, any request of a regional business is dealt with by the multiplied intelligence of an interdisciplinary group of public or semi-public business service providers. Second, solutions can be delivered quickly and with high quality. Thus the system can be seen as a major advance in supporting innovative firms in general and NTBFs in particular. Third, this system also gives regional agencies the opportunity to 'listen to the market', constantly to review their services and coordinate measures and policies.

Project-orientated promotional services

In contrast to traditional modes of supporting regional economic activities, the SFG has released the purely financial focus, has broadened its supply of services and offers comprehensive packages of different programmes closely reconciled with the different needs of their target groups. With regard to NTBFs, two packages are offered in accordance with the two major stages during their evolution: promotion of the seed and start-up phase and promotion of the expansion phase.

Besides the granting of non-refundable subsidies and refundable seed capital (in the form of loans with interest rates below the market level), the start-up package contains financial grants for external advisory services and direct management support in elaborating business plans, financial projections and so on. In contrast to the start-up programmes, the package for expanding firms does not contain seed capital but real equity capital provision instead.

If contacted by entrepreneurs, the SFG designs an individual promotion scheme most appropriate to the venture at stake and puts them in touch with other public or semi-public providers of related services. In this respect the newly established TP network will play a major role in the near future. The interconnection of different providers of soft factors of regional development will guarantee a fast dissipation of information and a transparent and comprehensive system of promotional services with fast access to effective support for entrepreneurs.

Summary

- *Amt der Steiermärkischen Landesregierung* is a typical institution of the mainstream administrative apparatus: it is regionally based but within the mainstream administrative apparatus; its activities are influenced by short term political decisions.

- In contrast, the SFG is separated from the mainstream administrative apparatus, highly autonomous in designing and implementing its supply of soft factors of regional development and in adjusting its financial support schemes to the needs of its target groups.

- NTBFs – a major factor for the economic development of Styria – are facing severe problems which are preventing new ventures from reaching the market and impeding the expansion of successful firms.

- To support technology-orientated entrepreneurship in Styria, the SFG elaborated a twofold approach. It tries to establish adequate preconditions for the successful development of entrepreneurial activities (e.g. networks like *Technologiepartner Steiermark*) and offers project-orientated structuring of its services aimed at NTBFs.

Conclusions

So far we have described the process of change and the current situation of the Austrian regional policy system regarding the nature of traditionally and newly founded regional policy institutions, their range of tasks and the increasing differentiation of regional policy instruments together with Styrian examples. In contrast to the traditional strategy of regional development, the new philosophy concentrates more strongly on promoting the indigenous potential of regions and their internationalisation. The thus expanded range of policy tasks is transferred to newly founded institutions. In some provinces, however, there are still institutions within the mainstream administrative apparatus which provide mainly financial support services. In spite of this there is a strong tendency to transfer regional policy tasks to regionally based institutions outside the mainstream of central and local government administrations, with an independent role in the promotion of economic development. Thereby institutions are created which have a strong RDA-like character.

In addition to changes which have already taken place, the intensifying of direct international contacts of regions will become an increasingly important task for the future, especially for a small open economy like Austria. This situation has intensified even more since Austria recently joined the EU. Until now there have been basically two different but strongly connected strategies for implementing the internationalisation of regions.

The first is characterised by the use of financial instruments to support direct foreign investment and the penetration of foreign markets. Corresponding to the new philosophy of regional policy, financial instruments are implemented selectively (strong focus on technology and innovation orientated projects) and mostly complemented by elements of the second strategy.

The second strategy is aimed at intensifying and implementing contacts for collaboration between Austrian and foreign firms in different fields (e.g. with respect to R&D and innovation activities, marketing and distribution activities, etc.). Usually different soft factors of regional development are used, such as information services, the organisation of trade fairs or mediation of collaborations. Another instrument used for promoting international collaborations is the setting up of border crossing technology and industrial parks especially along Austria's eastern border. Such projects are intended to generate impetus for growth for this formerly 'dead' border region by developing collaborative and competitive relations to the advantage of both sides. Examples of this approach are the 'Access Industrial Park' on the north-eastern border to the Czech Republic and the technology park between Graz and Maribor on Austria's south-eastern border which is at the realisation stage.

To become a valuable partner within the EU, these two strategies must be supplemented by additional efforts. It will be necessary to improve the implementation of integrated programme planning of the European Structural Funds and increasingly to take advantage of available community programmes and European inter-regional networks. For Austrian regional development institutions this will bring about alterations at two levels.

First, the internal mode of operation of the institutions must be changed. So far different institutions have been able to use fixed budgets to run their support programmes within certain legal guidelines. Now target-orientated programmes need to be defined and then evaluated with respect to main and side effects before they can be carried out. However, in the promotion guidelines of many institutions an increased programme-orientation of regional policy initiatives can already be found. Therefore Austrian institutions will surely meet this challenge.

Second, existing regional policy institutions must strengthen their collaborative relations with one other and with foreign institutions to be able to participate in international networks. On a long-term basis this could bring about new forms of the division of labour between regional policy institutions. Thereby a further development of regional policy institutions is possible, particularly for those with an RDA-like character. Institutions of the future will probably focus more strongly on functional regions with specific economic characteristics and not merely on administrative regional entities.

References

Halkier, H. and Danson, M. (1995) 'Regional Development Agencies in Europe: A Preliminary Framework for Analysis.' Paper presented at the conference *Regional Futures: Past and Present, East and West*, Gothenburg, Sweden, 6–9 May.

Kulicke, M. (1993) *Chancen und Risiken junger Technologieunternehmer – Ergebnisse des Modellversuchs 'Förderung technologieorientierter Unternehmensgründungen'*. Karlsruhe: report Fraunhofer-ISI.

Robertson, P.L. and Langlois, R.N. (1995) 'Innovation, networks, and vertical integration.' *Research Policy 24*, 4, 543–562.

Steiner, M., Jud, T., Poeschl, A. and Sturn, D. (1996) *Technologiepolitisches Konzept Steiermark*. Graz: Leykam.

Steiner, M. and Jud, T. (1996) 'Regional Development Institutions – A Descriptive Analysis for Austria' (updated version). Paper presented at the conference *Regional Development Agencies in Europe – Past Experiences and Future Perspective*. Aalborg, Denmark, 29 August – 1 September.

Further reading

Buggrave, W. and Timmons, J. (1992) *Venture Capital at the Crossboards.* Boston: Harvard Business School Press.

Halkier, H. and Danson, M. (1996) 'Regional Development Agencies in Western Europe: A Survey of Key Characteristics and Trends.' Paper presented at the conference *Regional Development Agencies in Europe – Past Experiences and Future Perspectives.* Aalborg, Denmark, 29 August – 1 September.

Kögerler, R. (1995) 'Technologietransfer in Österreich.' In M. Steiner (ed) *Regionale Innovation – Durch Technologiepolitik zu neuen Strukturen.* Graz: Leykam.

OECD (1996) *Financial Market Trends.* Paris: OECD.

Steiner, M. (1995) 'Regionale Entwicklung zwischen neuem Innovationsverständnis und technologispolitischer Herausforderung.' In M. Steiner (ed) *Regionale Innovation – Durch Technologiepolitik zu neuen Strukturen.* Graz: Leykam.

Steiner, M., Sturn, D. and Wendner, R. (1991) *Eine neue Philosophie: Orientierungs- und Maßnahmenvorschläge für die steirische Wirtschaftsförderungs Ges.m.b.H.* Graz: Joanneum Research.

Steiner, M. and Sturn, D. (1992) 'Mehr Wirtschaftsmacht nach unten – Ökonomische Leitlinien für neue regionale Verantwortungen.' In M. Steiner, H. Isak and J. Marko (eds) *Alle Macht nach unten? Regionen und Gemeinden gestalten die neuen Demokratien Europas.* Graz: Leykam.

Sturn, D. (1995) 'Welchen Raum brauchen Kooperationen, Netzwerke und Cluster? Ein Werkstattbericht.' In M. Steiner (ed) *Regionale Innovation – Durch Technologiepolitik zu neuen Strukturen.* Graz: Leykam.

CHAPTER 4

Regional Development Agencies In the Netherlands

Twenty Years of Shareholding

Wilfred Sleegers

Introduction

In 1974 five regional development agencies were founded in the Netherlands to support the national policy aiming to develop the lagging regions. From the constitution of the Dutch RDAs one can deduce that the general intention which led to their foundation can be described as 'to contribute to the improvement of the socioeconomic structure and employment of its region of action'. To achieve this general objective the RDAs have three essential tasks (Ministry of Economic Affairs 1976):

- to stimulate initiatives that lead to new firm formation
- the acquisition of branches of industrial enterprises (both national and foreign)
- to develop initiatives that contribute to the preservation (and reinforcement) of favourable economic activities.

There are significant differences among the five Dutch RDAs which are partly related to the different economic structures of the region in which the individual RDA functions and also due to the fact that they were founded at different moments in time. Moreover, the economic situation and the related national policies have also changed over time. The objective of this paper therefore is neither to try to evaluate the usefulness of RDAs as a policy instrument, nor to compare the effectiveness of the RDAs with each other, but to present an overview of the way in which the different RDAs have reacted to the changes in their external environment. Hence specific attention is given to the provision of venture capital as this is one of the most direct ways to support firms in their financial needs.

The structure of this contribution is as follows. First, by way of general background, the five RDAs and their regions are introduced, and then several developments are described which over time have influenced the RDAs, with particular attention paid to the role and provision of venture capital. This is followed by a more detailed study of the development over time of this specific activity of the Dutch RDAs, undertaken on the basis of an analysis of their available financial annual reports.

RDAS in Dutch regional policy

Regional background and moment of foundation

The five RDAs were established by the Dutch national government at different moments in time. (The specific spatial location of the various regions of the RDAs is given in Figure 4.1.) The Northern Development Agency NOM (*Noordelijke Ontwikkelingsmaatschappij*) was the first to be founded, in 1974, and was set up to deal with the problems in the northern part of the country. At that time this area was designated by the national government as the northern stimulation area '*Noorden des lands*'. It is formed by the provinces Groningen, Friesland, Drenthe and part of the province Overijssel, and its general character was (and still is) dominated by agricultural activities.

In 1975 two additional agencies were founded. In the south of the country was the Limburg Institute for Development and Finance (LIOF – *Limburgs Instituut voor Ontwikkeling en Financiering*). The regional problem in this area can be traced back to the fact that the Dutch coal mining industry was located here. The relatively high labour costs and unfavourable geological structures meant that the production of coal gradually had to be stopped, and the national government was faced with the necessity of restructuring the industrial base.

Also in 1975 the Overijsselse Development Agency (OOM) was founded, covering the province Overijssel in the eastern part of the country. This region is characterised by the concentration of the Dutch textile industry and hence also engine building in the eastern part of the province (the region Twenthe). The decline in these old industries meant that this region too was confronted with a relatively high and increasing level of unemployment.

In 1978 the Gelderse Development Agency (GOM) was founded, and finally in 1983 the Brabantse Development Agency (BOM) was founded to support the development in this southern province. In the northwestern and central part of this region traditional industries (such as the footwear industry, the cigar industry and the textile industry) were over-represented, and although the industrial base was much stronger than in other regions, it also had its weaker parts that needed to be modernised.

General economic development and change in Dutch regional economic policy

The debut of RDAs in the Netherlands in the middle of the 1970s came at an unfortunate moment in time. This period followed the first energy crisis in 1973; the ensuing economic stagnation was characterised by high and rapidly increasing unemployment figures in the lagging regions, and government policy was generally more focused on the preservation of existing regional employment than on renewal of the industrial base (Bartels and van Duijn 1981). Especially in the early period of the RDAs, their function of providing financial support to regional industry was very important. The provision of (state-guaranteed) loans and venture capital was aimed, however, much more at the possible 'rescue' of regional employment than at the development of 'new' initiatives.

In addition to the general consequences of the economic stagnation, the Dutch economy as a whole was also influenced by the global developments of modernisation and internationalisation of industrial production. These tendencies led to the overall weakening of the Dutch manufacturing industries and meant a general decline in employment, and it will become clear that especially in regions with a weak economy the disappearance of economic activities has not been compensated for by the starting up of new activities. There are, however, two contrasting viewpoints with regard to the relative position of lagging regions in a period of general economic stagnation. Frost and Spence (1983) for instance show that in Britain in the 1970s and the 1980s regions characterised by high unemployment figures were more sensitive to the national economic situation. Recently van Oort (1995) has shown that in the case of the Netherlands in the 1980s the peripheral regions show an anti-cyclical pattern: in this period of overall stagnation the development in the lagging regions was also negative but the relative decrease in employment was much smaller. He explains his finding by the assumption that core regions generally suffer more from economic stagnation as in absolute terms the decrease in employment has more severe effects. In absolute numbers it is also more difficult for core areas to retain similar positive growth percentages than in peripheral regions.

In the context of the general economic situation in the Netherlands in the 1970s and the 1980s it is not surprising that attraction of foreign firms by RDAs was relatively low. The majority of foreign companies which came to the Netherlands in this period are located in the western part of the country, mainly due to the fact that the activities of these companies generally are in the field of producer services or transportation, economic sectors which are also generally located in the central western part of the country. It might be concluded that the RDAs were rather unsuccessful in attracting foreign companies to their region, although from the 1980s it has also been learned that 'branch plant economies' have disadvantageous characteristics for regional development in the long run and therefore, taking this into account, the failure to attract foreign companies (and with that the growth of externally controlled employment) perhaps should not be judged as a negative development for the lagging Dutch regions.

Associated with these changes in the international setting and the globalisation and the modernisation of industrial production, there also has been a significant change in national policy with regard to the lagging regions. As mentioned above, in the early years of the RDAs the general policy was characterised by financial support of individual firms and was oriented towards the preservation of employment, and in this sense the RDAs functioned as the 'local desk' of the national policy makers. In the late 1970s the policy to support individual firms which faced temporary difficulties was, however, largely abandoned. The reason for this change was mainly that due to the recession the financial cost of this policy increased enormously. At the same time the awareness also grew that it was rather inefficient to support firms that in the long run had no economic future. These developments stimulated initiatives to restructure the industrial base, and in 1974 (note that this was in the same year as the first RDA) a national institute called NEHEM (*Nederlandse Herstructurerings Maatschappij*) was founded. Although there was, as we have seen, a clear regional pattern in the industries to be restructured, the creation of a separate national institution in effect meant that restructuring was not carried out at the regional, but at the sectoral level. For the Dutch RDAs this implied that restructuring issues were not their primary task but that of the NEHEM.

In the mid-1980s it was realised that next to the preservation and restructuring of industries it was also worthwhile focusing upon 'new' activities. It must be noted that in this context there are three main areas of concern, each of which involves specific issues associated with renewal and economic development. The first area of concern regards the techno-institutional issues that are related to the development of new products and new production processes (Malecki 1991). These R&D activities are generally expected to be carried out in the 'core' of the country (Dicken 1992), and Louter (1993) has shown that apart from these general patterns clear regional clusters exist in the Netherlands associated with specific types of industrial activities.

The second area of concern regards the aspects that are associated with the spread of knowledge and new opportunities from a country's 'centres of knowledge' towards the individual entrepreneur. Although the Dutch national government has acknowledged the fact that the five RDAs can be seen as their 'regional' agents, the government also founded 18 regional innovation centres in the two-year period 1988–89. These institutions are entirely publicly financed, and their main task is to provide local small and medium-sized firms with general information regarding new technologies and opportunities. Apart from this main task – which in the opinion of the author is similar to the development task of the RDAs – a second intention of these centres is to stimulate the development of network relations between local and regional entrepreneurs. As can be seen from Figure 4.1, these regional innovation centres are spread all over the country; note that 10 out of the 18 centres are located within the working area of an RDA, and it is evident that in the lagging regions innovation centres must be seen as direct competitors of the RDAs.

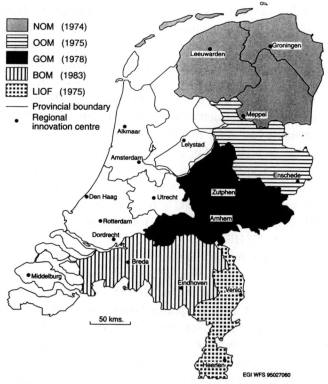

Figure 4.1 Regional innovation centres and the five RDAs in the Netherlands

The third area of concern regarding 'new' activities is related to the issues of stimulation of 'setting up in business' activities and support of newly founded enterprises. When these three fields are compared with the original intention and main tasks of the RDAs then it is obvious that at the regional level the RDAs could in theory function well in all three fields of renewal.

In relation to the developments discussed above one can claim that the national policy in support of lagging regions has changed over time. From the middle of the 1960s the general and traditional view was based upon the 'social-justice' principle. From this viewpoint it is undesirable that regional differences exist, especially with regard to unemployment or disposable income. In the period from 1960 to the mid-1980s Dutch regional policy thus attempted to reduce the gap between the well-developed western part of the country and the lagging regions (Ministry of Economic Affairs 1976; Bartels and van Duijn 1981). After the economic stagnation and the rise of new activities in the 1980s, Dutch regional policy is today more based upon an 'efficiency' approach, in which regional policy focuses on the spatial allocation of activities across the regions with a view to allocating them in such a way that they contribute most to national production. Regional specialisation (and as a consequence of this, regional difference) is no longer seen as undesirable, but support for lagging regions is justified in this 'efficiency approach' when the potentials of these regions are not (yet) fully exploited.

In summary one can conclude that the socioeconomic policy aimed at the reduction of regional differences in the 1970s over time is gradually replaced by a regional policy in which the economic performance of regions and the efficiency of spatial allocation of activities across the regions have become more important. One may argue that this new approach still is in line with the development task of the RDAs, but with the introduction of new institutions like NEHEM and especially the regional innovation centres the development task (i.e. the task of renewing the structure of the industrial base) has become less important for the RDAs.

The development in the role and provision of venture capital

In 1974, when the first RDA was founded, the provision of venture capital in the Netherlands was very limited and exclusively in the hands of officially registered banks. Through the provision of (state-guaranteed) loans and the possibility of participation in the firm by becoming a shareholder, the RDAs had an almost monopolistic position in supporting firms in their financial needs. As discussed above, in the mid-1970s and the years of stagnation thereafter the financial support provided by RDAs was dominated by the preservation of employment and thus was not so much oriented towards the stimulation of new activities. Over time this situation has changed considerably.

As described in the previous section, the stimulation of new activities is in general related to three areas of concern, and in two of these fields – the development of new technologies and the 'setting up in business' activities – the provision of venture capital plays an important role. In both these fields projects generally involve a relatively high level of risk and, with a relatively high probability of project failure, the commercial price for high risk capital is also relatively high. On the other hand, when a project is a success it will not only generate profits in financial terms – the indirect revenues are supposed to be even more important. With respect to these indirect benefits one should think of the multiplier effects that are generated by the realisation of the project and thus through the gearing of activities have a positive effect upon other (regional) activities. The justification for financing new regional activities with public funds is generally based upon the supposed importance of these indirect effects and, as a result, the level of risk aversion is meant to be lower in public institutions such as an RDA than that it is in commercial financial institutions.

It will be evident that 'setting up in business' activities and other related local initiatives in general will yield only small indirect benefits as the size of the projects are comparatively small. In contrast the stimulation of new activities in the sense of the development of new technologies will relate to much larger projects and, given their nature and size, the spin-off effects of such projects go well beyond the regional scale. One therefore may question whether the stimulation of such projects, even when they are realised in lagging regions, can be considered as regional support. On top of this, in the context of the product lifecycle theory, one may furthermore question whether the production environment of lagging regions in reality is suited to such activities (Dicken and Lloyd, 1990).

Furthermore, the monopolistic position that the RDAs enjoyed with regard to the provision of venture capital has completely disappeared over time. In 1980 the law regulating the activities of credit establishments (*Wet Toezicht Kredietwezen*) was changed significantly, giving private banks more freedom to provide individual firms with risk capital, and in 1981 new rules were introduced at the national level allowing private venture capital firms to provide risk capital to firms. Although in theory these developments could have undermined the position of the RDAs as a provider of risk capital, in practice this has not been the case. The next section shows that although the general pattern of development is the same for all RDAs, there nevertheless are significant differences between them, relating both to the absolute level and to the distribution of funding over the various economic sectors.

The RDAs as shareholders

In the introduction it was mentioned that the RDAs were founded at different moments in time, but they also differ from each other in other characteristics. A characteristic such as size can be measured on the basis of several indicators, for example in terms of number of employees, in terms of balance sheet total, or in terms of total operating costs. From Figures 4.2 and 4.3, in which the development of the RDAs with respect to size is depicted, it can be seen that the latecomers GOM and BOM stay behind. However when the size of the operating costs is scaled with the number of employees it can be seen that over time the relative positions have changed. When one looks at the level of average operating costs (see Figure 4.4), it is evident that at the end of the research period only small differences exist between the RDAs. Nonetheless the small RDAs, the OOM and the GOM, have somewhat lower values, and this suggests that the large RDAs in terms of organisation have no, or only very small-scale, advantages. With regard to development over time it is notable that until the mid-1980s the indicator for the NOM, the LIOF and the OOM increases, while thereafter the levels stabilise. There is also a striking similarity in the pattern over time between the NOM and the OOM, while the magnitude of the difference between these two, in absolute terms, remains more or less the same. The increase in the average level of operating costs is the highest for the LIOF. This development deserves special attention as in the same period the number of employees at this RDA also grew. The growth in the number of employees at the NOM and the LIOF took place in the period 1975–82, after which the number of employees remained more or less the same; after 1981 the increase in total operating costs for the LIOF is thus not related to an increase in labour costs. The development of the OOM shows a clearly different pattern. The OOM started as a small RDA with only 8 employees in 1977, but after continuous growth had around 35 employees in 1993 and was by that time about the same size as the early starters NOM and LIOF. The increase in operating costs for the OOM thus was completely in line with the development in the number of employees. The late starters GOM and BOM only gradually increased in number of employees; their level is now at around 17. Over time the difference in average level of operating costs between these small RDAs have stayed more or less the same.

The indicators as described above relate to all the activities of the RDAs. In the remainder of this contribution we will focus on the provision of venture capital. In Figure 4.5 the average value of the shareholdings is given

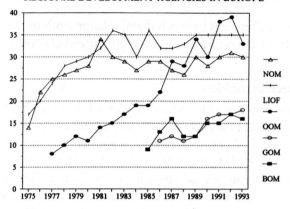

Figure 4.2 Number of employees

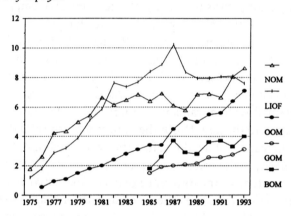

Figure 4.3 Operating costs (mio. NLG)

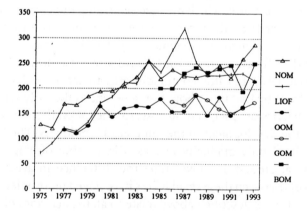

Figure 4.4 Average operating costs per employee (✕ 1000 NLG)

for the research period. For each RDA the average values are calculated by dividing the balance sheet total of the entry 'participations' by the total number of individual shareholdings in a given year. The amounts are given in current prices, not corrected for inflation. The large RDAs (NOM and LIOF) have remarkably higher values than the other RDAs. Since the mid-1980s their values decreased in such a way that at the end of the period only the value of the NOM still stood out. The other RDAs had similar values of around 50,000 guilders, while the value for the NOM was approximately six times as large.

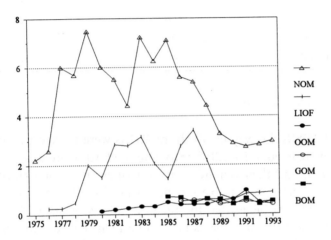

Figure 4.5 Average size of shareholdings (× 10,000 NLG)

This conspicuous development over time can for the most part be explained by changes in the policy of the national government with regard to the financing of the RDAs. Until the mid-1980s the RDAs could finance their venture capital activities by means of loans which were provided by the commercial capital market, but where the interest costs and commitments of repayments were carried by the Dutch government. Financial ceilings were set for each RDA within which the organisation had freedom of action. In addition to these payments the national government also contributed to the operating costs of the organisations. The extent to which this happened is different for the various RDAs, and Table 4.1 gives an overview of the percentages which the national government contributed in financing costs and operating costs. The figures in this table are in line with the relative sizes of the RDAs. Note that the small RDAs (OOM, GOM and BOM) had to provide 50 per cent of the operating costs and 40 per cent of their financing costs from their own means. For these regions actually the Chambers of Commerce and the provincial governments shared these costs.

Table 4.1 Proportional contribution of central government to operating costs and financing costs (percentage)

	Financing costs	Operating costs
NOM	100	100
LIOF	100	75
OOM	60	50
BOM	60	50
GOM	60	50

Source: Annual reports of Dutch RDAs.

In the mid-1980s the way in which the RDAs were funded by the Dutch government changed. A so-called 'revolving fund' structure was introduced, aimed at hiving off their venture capital activities. In the new situation the RDAs became more responsible for the financial results of these activities with the basic idea being that the financial means of an RDA over time circulate so that new participants have to be financed from the fund. The 'revolving fund' was created by converting debt capital into equity capital: the debts of RDAs to the national government, incurred through the borrowing of money for the provision of equity capital to private firms, were now converted so that the national government became a shareholder of the RDA. This change in financial structure was introduced at different times for the various RDAs: to the NOM in the year 1986, to the LIOF in 1989, to the BOM and the GOM in 1990, and to the OOM in 1991. As a result of this renewal of their financial basis it became more important for the RDAs to look at the risks and financial revenues of their shareholdings, and the new funding regime also generally prompted them to screen their portfolios. The downward trend that we noted in the average size of shareholdings for the NOM and the LIOF is associated with this behaviour. Especially at the NOM a number of rather old and large participations in the metal industry were written off.

As a side effect of the hiving off of the financial activities of the RDAs, the distribution of shareholdings over industrial sectors has also changed significantly. In Table 4.2 the columns to the left give the distribution between industrial sectors for all RDAs for the years 1985 and 1992. The year 1985 was chosen as this was the last year before the new system was introduced, and the year 1992 was the first year in which all RDAs had converted to the new system. The table shows that the proportion of shareholdings in modern manufacturing significantly decreased while there was an increase in the proportion of shareholdings in traditional manufacturing. In spite of the decrease from 75.7 to 69.4 per cent the dominance of manufacturing remained. Table 4.2 also breaks down the figures according to the size of the RDAs, small and large. Note that for all RDAs together the total number of 196 participations in 1992 is about twice the number of 1985 (i.e. 107). This doubling in the number of participations is more or less the case for both the small RDAs (from 57 to 106) and the large RDAs (from 50 to 90).

Table 4.2 Distribution of shareholdings according to industrial sectors (percentage of portfolio)

Industrial Sector	Total		Small		Large		NOM		LIOF	
	1985	1992	1985	1992	1985	1992	1985	1992	1985	1992
Traditional manufacturing	13.1	17.9	19.3	19.8	6.0	15.6	5.3	18.2	6.4	11.4
Modern manufacturing	62.6	51.5	66.7	55.7	58.0	46.7	89.4	50.9	38.7	40.0
Transport and wholesale	3.7	9.2	1.8	8.5	6.0	10.0	-	9.1	9.7	11.4
Producer services	14.1	16.3	10.5	13.2	18.0	20.0	5.3	14.5	25.8	28.6
Consumer services	6.5	5.1	1.8	2.8	12.0	7.8	-	7.3	19.4	8.6
Number of shareholdings	107	196	57	106	50	90	19	55	31	35

Source: Annual report of Dutch RDAs.

For the three small RDAs the dominance of shareholdings in manufacturing was even stronger than was the case for the overall pattern. Also here the percentage decreased over time (from 86.0 to 75.5), but for these RDAs this development was entirely due to the reduction of shareholdings in modern manufacturing as the share of participation in traditional industries stayed more or less the same. Although significant differences exist between the two large RDAs (NOM and LIOF), in contrast to the small RDAs they both show an increase in the relative importance of shareholdings in traditional manufacturing. Table 4.2 also gives the distribution between the industrial sectors separately for the two large RDAs, NOM and LIOF. Note that the dominance of manufacturing is only found in the NOM, and that the decrease in the proportion of shareholdings in these types of industries is very significant. The percentages for the LIOF are much smaller but more or less also stayed the same over time, and in contrast to all other RDAs the portfolio of this organisation was and still is more oriented towards the service sectors.

Conclusion

In the last five years significant changes have occurred in the financial operation of the RDAs. First, the types of industries that have been funded by venture capital have changed; second, a continuous reduction in the average size of shareholdings can be noticed. As a result of these developments one can conclude that the financial support to individual firms through the provision of venture capital nowadays is much more oriented towards new firm formation and the financial support of young firms. The emphasis towards the financial support of large projects that in the longer run will generate large (regional) multiplier effects has in other words decreased. When the five RDAs are compared only the NOM has a clearly different position with on average a much larger financial involvement in individual firms than the other RDAs.

In line with the general changes in regional policy discussed above, the Dutch government has decided that the state funding of those four RDAs will be ended. The reason for this decision is that in practice the operation of these RDAs is not very different from the generic policy aimed at supporting SMEs, and that a specific regional approach is not thought to be necessary. These four RDAs will not cease to exist, but as of 1997 they are in financial terms completely dependent upon their own revolving fund' and further regional financial support. In the last regional policy report of the Dutch government (Ministry of Economic Affairs 1995) it was, however, acknowledged that the development of the northern part of the country still is not in phase with the overall expansion and recovery of the Dutch economy. In the future only the NOM will therefore continue to function as a regional development agency in the proper meaning of the word, i.e. as a state-financed institution that is oriented to the development of a specific region of the Netherlands.

References

Bartels, C.P.A. and van Duijn, J.J. (1981) *Regionaal-Economisch Beleid in Nederland.* Assen: van Gorcum.

BOM (1985–1993): *Annual Financial Reports.* S-Hertogenbosch: BOM RDA.

Dicken, P. (1992) *Global Shift: The Internationalisation of Economic Activity, 2nd Edition.* London: Paul Chapman Publishing.

Dicken, P. and Lloyd, P.E. (1990) *Location in Space, 3rd Edition.* New York: HarperCollins.

Frost, M.E. and Spence, N.A. (1983) 'Unemployment change.' In J. Goddard (ed) *The Urban and Regional Transformation of Britain.* London: Methuen.

GOM (1985–1993): *Annual Financial Reports.* Arnhem: GOM RDA.

LIOF (1975–1993): *Annual Financial Reports.* Maastricht: LIOF RDA.

Louter, P.J. (1993) 'Kijk op Kennis: regionale verschillen in kennisintensiteit van bedrijvigheid.' *Onderzoekspublicaties 13*, Economisch Geografisch Instituut, Erasmus Universiteit Rotterdam.

Malecki, E.J. (1991) *Technology and Economic Development.* Harlow: Longman.

Ministry of Economic Affairs (1976) *Nota Selectieve Groei: Economische Structuurnota.* The Hague: Staatsuitgeverij.

Ministry of Economic Affairs (1995) *Ruimte voor Regio's.* The Hague: Staatsuitgeverij.

NOM (1974/5–1993): *Annual Financial Reports.* Groningen: NOM RDA.

OOM (1975–1993): *Annual Financial Reports.* Hengelo: OOM RDA.

Van Oort (1995) 'Regionale variaties in welvaart in Nederland.' *Onderzoekspublicaties 31*, Economisch Geografisch Instituut, Erasmus Universiteit Rotterdam.

CHAPTER 5

Regional Development Agencies in Denmark

Towards a Danish Approach to Bottom-up Regional Policy

Charlotte Damborg & Henrik Halkier

Introduction

The last decade has witnessed a considerable degree of change in regional policy in Denmark. Towards the end of the 1980s large development programmes supported by the European Structural Funds were introduced in eligible regions. At the same time the Danish government came to see policies of preferential treatment for peripheral regions as outdated, and in 1991 all central government regional incentive schemes were terminated. Generally, regional authorities became increasingly committed to regional development, and this led to a mushrooming of regional bottom-up development initiatives from the end of the 1980s onwards.

Today, regional development policy in Denmark is therefore to a large extent in the hands of regional actors. All regional authorities have set aside funds for economic development activities and most authorities have established a separate department of regional development. In addition to these departments of regional government – and mostly somehow related to them – there is a large number of public and semi-public development organisations also operating at a regional level.

The purpose of the present paper is to illuminate the characteristics of Danish bottom-up regional development initiatives and consider how these are positioned in the broader context of different approaches to regional policy in Europe.

The theoretical point of departure of the paper is the approach presented in Chapters 1 and 2, according to which a model regional development agency has to comply with the following three requirements:

- it has to be positioned at arm's length from its political sponsor because, presumably, this will allow it to focus on long-term solutions to the problems of the regional economy

- it has to take initiatives that stimulate indigenous enterprise rather than rely primarily on the attraction of firms from outside the region

- it has to have an integrated approach to regional development, i.e. be able to draw upon a wide range of policy instruments.

Clearly not each and every body involved in development activities on the regional level will fulfil these criteria, but by positioning individual organisations against the model RDA, their degree of (non-)compliance in the three fields will produce a multi-dimensional picture of the current state of affairs. This should provide us with an indication of whether such a thing as a 'Danish approach' exists and, in turn, place Denmark on the map of bottom-up regional policy in Europe.

The paper proceeds in the following steps. The next section introduces the methodology of the survey and presents basic information on the selected organisations. The main section of the paper then analyses the key characteristics of these organisations with regard to organisation and policy programmes, and the findings are discussed in relation to the general expectations of regional development organisations. On the basis of this a model of the 'Danish approach' to bottom-up regional policy is put forward and its position in relation to other actors on the regional policy scene is considered.

Methods

Research design

Although Denmark is a relatively small country by European standards, the task of conducting a survey of regional bottom-up development initiatives is complicated by several factors.

First, there is, as ever, the ambiguity of the term 'region'. Denmark has a two-tier system of local government with 14 counties and 275 municipalities, but development organisations do not necessarily follow these administrative boundaries. To avoid the bewildering complexity of having to deal with all kinds of sub-national levels, it was decided for the purposes of this survey to define a region as no smaller than the county. This means that cooperation between municipalities is *not* included in the survey unless it covers an entire county, whereas a few organisations covering an area larger than one county are included.[1] Moreover, the development organisations had to be 'true' bottom-up organisations established on the initiative of regional actors in order to focus on the regional capacity for action. This distinction is important because it means that deconcentrated central government bodies such as the technological institutes and the technology information centres – both operating at a regional level – have not been examined.

Bottom-up regional development is in the making as a research area in Denmark and there was no previous survey or listing of regionally based development organisations upon which the present survey could be based or which could provide a preliminary impression of the organisation of bottom-up initiatives in Denmark.[2] Questionnaires were forwarded to both county council departments and other regional development organisations in order to obtain information on organisation, resources, objectives and policies. Of the 42 questionnaires sent out, 32 were returned. The information from two of the county departments was judged insufficient to provide a basis for comparative analysis between the counties and one development organisation turned out to be an entirely private initiative. Accordingly, the survey includes the 11 county departments and 20 regional development organisations listed in Table 5.1, and as the organisations represent a very broad and varied section of the development bodies active in the Danish regions, it should be able to identify both typical and particularly interesting patterns.

In addition to the postal survey, six counties were selected for closer scrutiny and a total of 14 interviews were carried out in April/June 1996.[3] Interviews were carried out in both county council departments and selected regional development organisations, as well as in the Association of County Councils and the Danish Agency for the Development of Trade and Industry, the central government body responsible for regional development policy on the national level.

---

1   This set-up occurs in tourist development organisations and development organisations in the Copenhagen metropolitan area where counties and municipalities have made a joint effort.
2   A basic survey of the organisation of regional development in the Danish counties was conducted by the Association of County Councils in Denmark in 1993 (Amtsrådsforeningen i Danmark 1993). However, this primarily described the development policies of the departments of regional government and could not be relied on to provide information about other regionally based development organisations. Moreover, the survey of the Association represents a snapshot in time (as, indeed, does the present survey) and much has happened during the last three years as regards bottom-up initiatives.
3   Interviews were carried out by Charlotte Damborg in the counties of Nordjylland, Viborg, Århus, Sønderjylland, Vestsjælland and Storstrøm (a list of interviewees is included at the end of the paper).

Although the present paper is based on a substantial amount of data, the exploratory nature of the survey must still be stressed, and an important subsidiary aim of this paper – besides providing an insight into Danish bottom-up regional policy – is therefore to improve the general understanding of bottom-up initiatives and their institutional setting in order to help develop an analytical approach that can be used in comparisons between regions on an international scale.

Table 5.1 Organisations included in the survey
(by county)

County	County council department responsible for regional development	Other regional development organisations
Bornholm		Bornholms Erhvervsfond Bornholms Erhvervsråd
Frederiksborg	Erhvervsudviklingsafdelingen	
Fyn	Kontor for regional udvikling	Fyns Erhvervsråd
København	Erhvervskontoret	Copenhagen Capacity Wonderful Copenhagen
Nordjylland	Erhvervssekretariatet	Nordjyllands Erhvervsservice Nordjyllands Udviklingsfond
Ribe		Turistgruppen Vestjylland
Ringkøbing	Budget- og erhvervasfdelingen	EURA A/S
Roskilde	Kontoret for erhvervsfremme og internationale anliggender	
Storstrøm	Erhvervssektionen	Storstrøms Erhvervscenter Storstrøms Turistråd
Sønderjylland	Udviklingsafdelingen	Sønderjyllands Erhvervsråd Sønderjyllands Investeringsfond Sønderjyllands Udviklingsselskab A/S
Vejle		Servicekontoret for Turisterhvervet
Vestsjælland	Vestsjællands Erhvervscenter	Zealand Care A/S
Viborg	Erhvervs- og arbejdsmarkedsafdelingen	
Århus	Erhvervsafdelingen	Center for Virksomhedsudvikling Chef-Leasing A/S Danish Business Service Procon

Organisation

This section examines the organisational characteristics of regionally based development bodies in Denmark and establishes a typology of their interaction on the regional level. When no specific source is indicated, the exposition is based on analysis of a database constructed on the basis of the information supplied by the questionnaires as well as the personal interviews.

Origins and objectives

During the 1980s and the 1990s the Danish counties have gradually increased their commitment to the promotion of regional development. This field of activity has been added to their statutory activities which include significant parts of welfare services such as health, education, regional planning, environment and major roads, and today promotion of economic development is a field of activity in which all counties are involved, mostly through a separate department of regional development.

As regional development is not a statutory activity, the counties have themselves put regional development on the agenda and set aside funds for development activities. However, with the demise of the centrally operated regional incentive policies in 1991 and the relaxation of restrictions on local and regional authorities' participation in regional development activities in 1992, greater emphasis is being placed on regional and local initiatives, and in this sense the *political* responsibility for regional development is increasingly being placed with the local and regional authorities (Erhvervsministeriet 1995).

In many counties it is difficult to determine exactly when their involvement in regional development began as their commitment developed gradually. Generally, however, the first counties to become involved in it were those suffering the highest rates of unemployment. Parts of these counties had traditionally been covered by central government incentive schemes and towards the mid-1980s assistance from the European Structural Funds was made available.[4] In the counties of Nordjylland, Viborg, Sønderjylland, Størstrom and Bornholm large EU-funded development programmes were initiated, and the administration of these programmes – and the fact that the unemployment rates were higher in these areas – inspired the counties to increase their commitment to regional development and draw up their own

---

4   Until 1984 assistance from the European Structural Funds was primarily directed at areas in Greenland. When Greenland left the EC in 1984, the government decided that the Danish assisted areas under the Regional Development Act were to be eligible under the Structural Funds as from 1985.

regional development programmes. An exception to this general rule is Århus County which from an early point has pursued a very proactive role in regional development despite its status as one of the more prosperous counties in Denmark.

At the beginning of the 1990s, regional development was also put on the agenda in counties that had not previously had specific activities in this field. The topicality of regional bottom-up initiatives can be traced back to several sources: the Danish government had relaxed restrictions on local government activities in the area; some counties in Denmark had already embraced the sphere of regional development and thereby inspired – or prompted – other counties to do the same; and, finally, there was a general European orientation towards bottom-up initiatives.

As regards the development organisations operating outside the mainstream administrative apparatus of the counties, the vast majority of those included in the survey have been established during the last decade. Only four organisations date back before 1980, namely two regional development committees and two regional investment funds which were set up between 1947 and 1973.

The regional development organisations included in this survey are very diverse, but one of the features most of them have in common is that they have been established either on the sole initiative of the county or on the initiative of the county in cooperation with other regional actors (especially municipalities, development organisations and/or the business community).[5]

Resources

The questionnaires supplied the following information on the resources of the development bodies. As regards the financial resources set aside for regional development activities by the counties, yearly expenditure varies from DKK 10m to DKK 26m in the 11 counties included in the survey. The majority of the counties spend between DKK 10m and DKK 15m on regional development activities, and only two counties spend over DKK 20m. The number of staff in the central regional development departments of the counties varies from 2 to 18, with an average of 8.

Both financially and in terms of personnel the resources committed to regional development by the counties are therefore modest – especially when

---

5   In fact, the only organisations that have been established unassisted by the county are the two regional development committees and the two investment funds mentioned before and a more recent development company, Sønderjyllands Udviklingsselskab A/S, initiated by the regional development committee in Sønderjylland.

seen in an international perspective. A survey by Halkier and Danson of selected regional development agencies in Europe showed that most agencies had budgets of over £2.5m (c. DKK 25m) and that the largest agencies had average staffs and budgets of 229 persons and £133m (c. DKK 1330m) respectively (Halkier and Danson 1998). It should of course be kept in mind that regional development is a voluntary sphere of activity for the counties in Denmark, not one of their statutory activities, and that the Danish regions are small compared to the regions in many other countries in Europe and consequently do not justify the same size of expenditure. Besides, regional development projects have other sources of funding than the county, so the budgets of the counties do not reveal the total expenditure on regional development in the regions. For example, Nordjylland County has a yearly regional development budget of DKK 24m, but EU funding in the region amounts to a yearly DKK 200m and releases an additional DKK 70m from central government in matching funding, and so especially in counties where large European programmes operate the total level of expenditure will be significantly higher than in counties where the presence of the Structural Funds is less conspicuous.

With regard to the resources of the Danish regional development organisations, budgets range from a yearly DKK 3m to DKK 59m with an average of DKK 10m, and the number of staff ranges from 1 to 50 with an average of 10. As can be seen from Table 5.2, most organisations are relatively small and the resources at their disposal limited.

All in all it can thus be concluded that in terms of resources, bottom-up regional policy in Denmark is dominated by relatively small organisations, both inside and outside the system of regional government, and that availability of external funding, especially from the EU Structural Funds, is therefore likely to make a major difference between the regions in terms of their capacity to influence economic developments within their area.

Table 5.2 Regional development organisations by size

Staff	Survey results	Budget (DKKm)	Survey results
1 –10	14	<10	14
11–20	5	10–25	5
20+	1	25+	1

Source: Survey.

Bureaucratic autonomy

The question of bureaucratic autonomy has been examined in order to establish the degree of operational freedom that the various organisations enjoy *vis-à-vis* their elected political sponsors and thereby to determine the extent to which they comply with the general organisational qualities expected to be found in a model RDA.

The formal position of the policy-making organisation *vis-à-vis* its political sponsor(s) was established according to the definitions presented by Halkier and Danson in Table 2.3 (Chapter 2 of this volume) and produced the results in Table 5.3.

**Table 5.3 Departments and organisations
by degree of bureaucratic autonomy**

Category	Survey results	
	County departments	*Development organisations*
Departmental	4	1
Semi-departmental	7	1
Arm's-length/single	0	0
Arm's-length/dominant	0	0
Arm's-length/plural	0	18

Source: Survey.

Four of the regional development departments in the survey are in a departmental position and refer exclusively to the finance committee of their respective counties. The seven departments in the category 'semi-departmental' also refer to the finance committee, but in addition to this have a separate advisory council consisting of representatives from, for example, the county council, municipalities, local and regional development committees, trade organisations and the business community. The fact that most counties have put together an advisory council does of course indicate an intention to hear the views of a broad spectrum of regional actors with an interest in development decisions – a point of view which was also emphasised in the personal interviews. However, the significance of the advisory councils in terms of actual influence may vary and cannot be fully evaluated on the basis of the data in this survey, although indications were given in some of the counties where interviews were carried out pointing to a substantial influence of the advisory councils and a more formal role of the finance committee. This may, for example, be the case when the county mayor chairs the advisory council and/or members of the finance committee are also members of the advisory council.[6]

The vast majority of the regional development organisations in the survey are in an arm's-length position *vis-à-vis* the county and are organised under a variety of organisational forms: funds, self-governing institutions and limited companies. The only two organisations that are in a departmental or semi-departmental position are Procon and Center for Virksom-hedsudvikling, both decentralised service institutions set up by Århus County.

The regional development organisations rely on a wide range of sources of finance. Most development organisations receive yearly grants from the counties, while other external sources of finance include EU funding, and municipal and central government grants. Moreover, internally generated income (fees) is an important source of income in many organisations. The extent of the county's contribution to the yearly budget of the regional development organisations will appear from Table 5.4.[7]

Table 5.4 The contribution of counties to the budgets of regional development organisations

Sponsorship	Survey results
County sole sponsor (100%)	1
County dominant sponsor (50–99%)	5
County minor sponsor (–49%)	9

Source: Survey.

In short, even though many of the organisations have been initiated and sponsored, at least partly, by the county and even though the county may continue to allocate a substantial yearly grant to the organisation, most regional development organisations – with the two in Århus county as a notable exception – are in an arm's-length position *vis-à-vis* the county, at least in terms of their legal and political position. They exist as separate

6   In Nordjylland County, where a separate organisation financed by the county has been set up to initiate regional development activities, the decisions of the board have to be approved by the finance committee of the county – but this is only a formal approval as the county mayor chairs the board. In Viborg the finance committee has been integrated in a council which also brings in other social actors and decisions taken here need no further approval.

7   As regards the remaining five organisations not mentioned in Table 5.4, in two cases the county does not contribute to the yearly budgets, and for three organisations the information was insufficient.

entities and, presumably, have a certain degree of operational freedom to go about their tasks as they see fit – although this may of course be influenced by other factors, such as the range of policy instruments at the disposal of the organisation.

Implementation and inter-organisational relations

The analysis of the general characteristics of the relationship between the counties and external regional development organisations can be extended by looking at the degree to which regional government as the main sponsor of bottom-up initiatives attempts to influence the implementation of individual policy programmes. This can be examined along two key dimensions: first, the extent to which a county has its own detailed plan of action or, alternatively, relies on external actors to fill in broad regional policy guidelines in terms of actual projects; second, the extent to which the county implements regional development programmes itself or buys external partners to implement the programmes.

**Table 5.5 Counties categorised by implementation
form and degree of planning**

Degree of planning	Implementation	
	County	External
High	2	6
Low	0	3

Source: Survey.

On the basis of these distinctions, three different approaches to regional development can be identified in the Danish counties, as can be seen from Table 5.5. First, there are counties combining a low degree of planning with implementation by external bodies. These counties draw up some general priorities within the field of regional development and set aside a regional development pool from which other regional actors can apply for resources for their projects, i.e. the county does not carry out its own projects, but relies on other regional actors to formulate and carry through regional development projects. Resources from the pool are therefore only triggered in so far as external actors come up with suitable projects. The counties of Sønderjylland and Storstrøm favour this approach. Roskilde County is an extreme version in that no priorities have been formulated, although block grants are still allocated to various organisations.

Second, some counties develop their own plans of action with very specific priorities where money is earmarked for particular purposes, but leave the actual implementation of the programmes to external partners. The freedom of initiative of the external partner is therefore likely to be restricted. Such an approach has been found in the counties of Nordjylland, Viborg, Ringkøbing, Fyn, Vestsjælland and København.

Third, there are the counties which draw up detailed policy programmes and plans of action, but – unlike the second type – undertake the actual implementation of regional development programmes themselves, either through their core administrative apparatus or via decentralised centres with little or no operational freedom. This is the case in the counties of Århus and Frederiksborg.

In addition to the above criteria, it should be noted that most counties spend part of their regional development budget as grants to regional development institutions to support their activities. Traditionally, these grants were allocated as block grants to the institutions with no conditions attached, but increasingly the counties have shown a determination to ensure value for money and to make sure that their resources are spent in accordance with their own regional development objectives. In this way the regional development organisations may be required to provide certain types of services or undertake certain types of projects. The counties most eager to ensure value for money are, hardly surprisingly, the counties which have their own detailed policy programmes and plans of actions whereas counties whose strategy is to encourage external initiatives and support these are less inclined to let their grants to regional development organisations depend on the provision of certain types of services.

Despite the above differences between the counties some general trends of development can be detected. Increasingly, the counties demonstrate a determination to pursue a more active role in regional development and there seems to be a move towards a higher degree of planning and control both as regards formulation of policies and control with implementing bodies. At the same time most counties favour the role of a policy unit which formulates strategies, programmes and development policies, but leave the actual implementation to external bodies often initiated and established by the counties themselves. Danish bottom-up regional policy, in other words, would seem to be moving towards an institutional set-up characterised at the same time by external implementation and a relatively detailed control of policies by regional government.

Policies

This section examines the policies of the Danish regional development organisations in order to establish the extent to which they give priority to stimulating growth of indigenous enterprise and have the capacity to adopt an integrated approach to regional development. The exposition is still based on the database created from the information supplied by the questionnaires as well as the personal interviews.

Policy profiles of the counties

Danish counties are not allowed to grant direct subsidies to individual firms, and it is therefore hardly surprising that the survey demonstrated that their regional development policies first and foremost support the provision of advice and infrastructure in the regions.

As regards the policies implemented directly by the regional development departments themselves, they vary along a wide spectrum. Most counties are engaged in international activities and some counties have their own representation in Brussels or have established offices in, for example, Poland to support exporting enterprises. The counties may also develop regional development programmes or projects internally in the county or in cooperation with other regional actors, either aimed directly at the regional enterprises by providing advice, training etc.,[8] or designed to improve the general conditions of business more indirectly by drawing on the counties' statutory activities within, for example, the health sector, or aiming to improve their administrative procedures vis-à-vis the private sector.[9] Activities within the field of public-private cooperation have been a particular focus of interest since the new acts in 1992 gave the counties and municipalities some limited rights to form partnerships with private companies.[10] Moreover, and in connection with this, some counties are also examining how they can plan their purchase policies to benefit the regional trades and industries.[11] All in all, the regional development departments would thus mainly seem to concentrate on one-off projects and improvement of the business environment via third parties and do not provide programmes directly that would involve contact with individual firms on a routinised ongoing basis.

In terms of total expenditure, the 11 counties included in the survey have an aggregate regional development budget of around DKK 170m, but over

8 E.g. Viborg County.
9 A particular focus of interest in København County.
10 E.g. Fyn County has made several development contracts with enterprises in the region based on the county's knowledge within the hospital sector.
11 E.g. Århus County and København County.

half of this amount is spent as grants to external regional development organisations. In the following the policies of these development organisations will be examined, therefore, both with a view to gaining an overall impression of the regional development priorities in the Danish counties, but also – as explained above – to establish the extent to which individual organisations qualify as model RDAs.

Policy profiles of the regional development organisations

The activities in which the regional development organisations engage have been classified according to the three basic policy instruments applied *vis-à-vis* individual firms – supply of advice, finance or infrastructure – and subdivided into 14 policy areas on the basis of the specific type of support provided. Furthermore, these policy areas have been distributed into 'traditional measures', associated with 'import' of growth from outside the region, and 'new measures', primarily aimed at stimulating the growth and competitiveness of indigenous firms (cf. Halkier and Danson 1998).

Table 5.6 Types of regional support

Strategic orientation	Resource	Policy area	Occurrence in survey
Traditional	Advice	Investment attraction	5
		Access to grants	0
	Infrastructure	General factories	0
New	Advice	General management	8
		Markets	8
		Production/technology	3
		Tourism	6
	Finance	Equity, loans etc.	4
	Infrastructure	Science parks etc.	0
		Training	1
Other	Advice	EU advice	5
	Finance	Own grants	0
		Grant administration	0
	Infrastructure	Land renewal	0

Source: Survey.

The presence or absence of each type of regional support within the policies of each of the 20 regional development organisations was recorded and the findings are summarised in Table 5.6.

As can be seen, provision of advice is by far the most prominent type of service offered by the regional development organisations. The financial instruments, direct investment in the form of equity or loans, are offered by only four organisations, and moreover, the absence of traditional policy instruments such as grants and factory building is notable. Overall, the predominance of new activities is thus very much in evidence. Using the criteria for analysis of policy profiles proposed by Halkier and Danson, most of the organisations therefore turn out to specialise in new policy areas, while only one organisation, Copenhagen Capacity, specialises in a traditional activity, namely the attraction of foreign investment.

Even though Table 5.6 clearly demonstrates the new policy profile of most organisations and the predominance of advisory services, it does not reveal how the different kinds of activities are distributed in the various organisations; whether several different activities co-exist within the same organisation or whether the organisations specialise in a few activities. In order to measure the degree of specialisation of the various organisations and thereby their capacity for an integrated approach to regional development, the number of different activities undertaken by the organisations was calculated, producing the results in Table 5.7.

The main impression is one of rather specialised units. A striking number of nine organisations engage in one activity only and a closer look at the individual organisations reveals that the organisations specialised in only one activity are primarily tourism development organisations or investment funds. The remaining development organisations which undertake two or more activities are involved in a range of advisory services with one organisation also involved in the training of entrepreneurs.

Table 5.7 Degrees of specialisation

No. of policy areas in organisation	Survey results
1	9
2	4
3	4
4	3
5+	0

Source: Survey.

Compared with the results of the survey of RDAs in Europe by Halkier and Danson (1998), where much diversity was established both with regard to the mix of old and traditional activities as well as the range of activities undertaken by individual organisations, Danish RDAs are thus characterised by the predominance of new policy profiles and rather specialised RDAs.

With these characteristics of Danish bottom-up initiatives in mind we will turn to the question of how they are positioned *vis-à-vis* the concept of model RDAs.

From model RDAs towards a Danish model

As will be remembered, a model RDA is positioned at arm's length from its political sponsor, because – presumably – this will allow it to focus on the long-term competitiveness of the economy of the region by means of initiatives that stimulate indigenous enterprise in an integrated manner. In order to qualify as a model RDA in the following the regional development organisation therefore has to fulfil *all* of these criteria.

As regards the first criteria, most Danish regional development organisations were found to be in an arm's-length position in terms of their formal legal and political position. The only exceptions were the two development centres in Århus, Procon and Center for Virksom-hedsudvikling, which were found to be in a departmental and semi-departmental position. However, it should also be remembered that most organisations receive a substantial yearly grant from the counties and that the allocation and size of this grant – on which many organisations depend – may be used to ensure that the activities undertaken by the development organisations are in line with the political priorities of the counties. Moreover, the comparatively small budgets of most organisations and the fact that they have a somewhat specialised policy profile of course also limits their room for manoeuvre in practice.

The second criteria, according to which the development organisations have to stimulate the growth of indigenous enterprises to qualify as model RDAs, also proves relatively easy to fulfil. Only organisations which have specialised in a traditional policy area cannot be said to comply with this criteria, and only one of the Danish organisations was found to be in this category, namely Copenhagen Capacity.

The third criteria concerning the organisations' capacity for an integrated approach to regional development turns out to be most difficult criteria for the development organisations to fulfil. In order to have an integrated approach to regional development the organisation has to be able to draw upon a wide range of policy instruments, and the fact that most Danish development organisations are involved in a narrow range of policy areas of course limits their capacity for operating in such a manner.[12] The Danish development organisations are simply too specialised in the particular areas of advice, finance or tourism to have the capacity for developing an integrated approach and none of them complied with this requirement.

All in all, none of the development organisations satisfied all three criteria and the conclusion therefore must be that there are no model RDAs in Denmark. Instead, there is a range of rather small, specialised development organisations which in most cases are in an arm's-length position *vis-à-vis* their political sponsors.

Two features in particular would seem to stand out and mark what could be called the Danish model of bottom-up regional policy. First, an organisational set-up with regional government (the counties) being the political and economic centre around which many specialised regional development units are positioned. Second, a general policy profile where new policy instruments are in focus and different types of advisory services the most prominent feature.

The most important difference between the Danish model and the notion of model RDAs is in other words the existence at the regional level of a number of separate, specialised implementing organisations and a potential problem would therefore be to ensure that policies delivered by separate organisations are adequately coordinated and thus provide policy integration on a network level rather than within the individual development body.

Current and future issues

The demise in 1991 of the regional incentive schemes operated by central government decreased the responsibility of central government for regional development and signalled a reorientation as regards the objectives and policy instruments in regional policy in general. The objective of equal development in the Danish regions was now seen as outdated and instead the regions were encouraged to focus on the growth opportunities specific to their region. Moreover, direct subsidies to individual firms had traditionally been the main policy instrument in regional development, but 'framework measures'[13] were now considered to be preferable to financial subsidies (Erhvervsministeriet 1995).

---

12 To qualify as model RDA in terms of policy integration an organisation must be involved in at least four different policy areas with at least one based on hard resources, i.e. finance or property (cf. Halkier and Danson 1998).

13 Framework measures are forms of support that are not directed exclusively towards one particular firm, i.e. advisory services, technological support facilities, training, etc.

While central government has decreased its direct involvement in regional development policies significantly, local and regional authorities have increased their commitment in the field. Traditionally, the possibilities for counties and municipalities to pursue economic development policies and engage in private sector activities have been strictly regulated, but during recent years the local authorities have been allowed more scope for manoeuvre (Erhvervsministeriet 1995). Collective arrangements in support of local/regional business development were made possible by national legislation in 1992 and the political responsibility for regional development policies is now very much placed with the local and regional authorities, as explained earlier.

However, despite a considerable degree of latitude in the field of regional development policy which undoubtedly facilitated the mushrooming of initiatives during the last decade, bottom-up policies still operate within the parameters set by national and supra-national institutions. First, the uneven access to resources from the EU Structural Funds counteracts the advantages of the more well-off areas in inter-regional competition and thus recreates the uneven playing field associated with the traditional regional policies of central government. Second, the activities of local and regional actors are still restricted by central government in that sub-national bodies are not allowed to grant direct subsidies to individual firms.

Moreover, a recent initiative by central government promoting the creation of so-called 'Business Nodes' has highlighted many of the contradictions between the actors involved in bottom-up regional policy. These Nodes are to provide a forum for discussion between development organisations active in a particular geographical area, but do not infringe the control of participating organisations over their own activities or necessarily involve the creation of a separate organisation (Erhvervsministeriet 1995). From a *functional* perspective the Nodes are intended to counteract risks of duplication on the regional level by providing a forum where policy coordination between the various actors can be ensured, but from an *institutional* perspective what was originally designed as a vehicle to increase coordination on the regional level may end up increasing competition between the tiers; the Nodes are typically groups of local authorities which do not cover an entire region and some counties have therefore seen the initiative as an attempt to promote the role of the local authorities at the expense of the counties.

Apart from potentially aggravating the problem of coordination it was originally intended to address, it is also interesting to note that the concept of Business Nodes does not attempt to address the perhaps even more complex problem of how to ensure policy integration. When regional development organisations exist as independent and highly specialised bodies, the problems of individual private firms are likely to be treated in a piecemeal manner, unless the different implementing organisations are networking in an efficient manner. This specific problem, however, seems to be less prominent in the Danish debates on policy coordination than that of the risks of duplication, and this might indicate that a public sector perspective (avoid waste of resources) continues to dominate the thinking of key actors.

All in all the picture of the current situation with regard to bottom-up regional policy in Denmark would very much seem to take the shape of a mosaic. The basic pattern – regional government taking the general political responsibility while policy implementation is left to an array of external bodies – is sufficiently clear to warrant talk about a Danish model, although a complex series of variations on this pattern is also in evidence. It is also obvious that although the regional level has gained significantly in importance over the last decade, its new position in regional policy is still being challenged by local initiatives, partly depending on economic resources from Europe, and being regulated by central government especially with regard to policy instruments. The Danish regions are in other words still 'sandwiched in' between the inter/national levels of government above and local spatial interests below.

While this chapter has provided a first overview of bottom-up regional policy and identified the key characteristics and inherent problems in the 'Danish model', in terms of research the next step forward will be to focus on interaction – horizontally within regions as well as vertically between local-regional-national-EU actors – in order to get an insight into how policy coordination and policy integration are assured between the separate, specialised development organisations and the different levels of government – something that will require fieldwork of a qualitative nature on a much more extensive scale than the present survey.

Acknowledgements

Thanks are due to the Association of County Councils, the Danish Agency for the Development of Trade and Industry, and the counties and the regional development organisations participating in the survey for supplying the information upon which the present paper is based. However, full responsibility for the text in its present form of course remains with the authors. We also gratefully acknowledge the financial and other support for our research from the Department of Languages and International Culture Studies and the Faculty of the Humanities, University of Aalborg.

Interviewees

Henning Christensen, Head of the Industrial Policy Division, Nordjylland County.

Ejner Frederiksen, Manager of Procon, Århus.

Ebbe Jensen, Head of the Development Division, Sønderjylland County.

Anne Hyldegaard, Economic development officer, Århus County Industrial Policy Division.

Tyge Korsgaard, Manager of Sønderjylland Regional Development Committee, and Managing Director of Sønderjylland Development Company Ltd., Aabenraa.

Tonni Kragh, Head of the Industrial Policy Division, Storstrøm County.

Henrik Lodberg, Senior civil servant, the Danish Agency for the Development of Trade and Industry, Silkeborg.

Bent Mikkelsen, Head of the Industrial Policy and Labour Division, Viborg County.

Anette Møller, Managing Director of Nordjylland Turism Development Group Ltd., Åbybro.

Kristian Primdal, Manager of Storstrøm Business Development Centre, Vordingborg.

Michael Schwedler, Deputy Chief of Vestsjælland County Business Development Centre.

Thorsten Tyndeskov, Controller, Vestsjælland County Business Centre, and temporary Managing Director of Zealand Care Ltd., Sorø.

Lone Vingtoft, Head Clerk, Office for Economy and Industrial Policy, the Association of County Councils, Copenhagen.

Susanne Willumsen, Advisory officer, Nordjylland Business Service, Aalborg.

References

Amtsrådsforeningen i Danmark (1993) *Erhvervsfremme. Amternes organisering, funktioner og udgifter på området.* Kobenhavn: Amtsrådsforeningen i Danmark.

Erhvervsministeriet (1995) *Regionalpolitisk Redegørelse 1995.* København: Erhvervsministeriet.

Halkier, H. and Danson, M. (1998) 'Regional development agencies in Western Europe: A survey of key characteristics and trends.' Chapter 2 in this volume.

Further reading

Amtsrådsforeningen i Danmark (1995) *Amternes erhvervsfremme – status og udviklingsmuligheder.* København: Amtsrådsforeningen i Danmark.

Bogason, P. and Jensen, L. (1991) 'Statens ansvar for regional udvikling i Danmark.' *NordREFO 3*, 51–81.

Cornett, A.P. (1989) 'Regionalpolitik i Danmark efter 1992? – muligheder og perspektiver.' *Politica 21*, 4, 431–440.

Gaardmand, A. (1988) 'Jobbet til manden eller manden til jobbet? Om dansk regionalpolitik fra 1945–1985.' In NordREFO (ed) *Regionalpolitikken som politikområde.* Helsinki: NordREFO.

Halkier, H. (1996) 'Denmark.' In D. Yuill *et al.*, *European Regional Incentives, 16th edition.* East Grinstead: Bowker-Saur.

Industri- og samordningsministeriet (1994) *Koordinering af regional erhvervsfremme.* Betænkning afgivet af et udvalg nedsat af industriministeren, Betænkning nr. 1262. København: Industri- og Samordningsministeriet.

Jensen, L. (1994) 'Ændringen i dansk opfattelse af statens ansvar i 80erne og 90erne.' *NordREFO 3,* 89–111.

Yuill, D., Allen, K., Bachtler, J., Clement, K. and Wishlade, F. (1994) *European Regional Incentives 1994–95, 14th Edition.* London: Bowker-Saur.

PART III

Regional Development Agencies in Central and Eastern Europe

Whereas the general picture with regard to the role of RDAs in Western Europe was reasonably clear as stated in the last section, the situation of RDAs in Central and Eastern Europe (CEE) is much less so. The CEE economies have undergone a period of profound and rapid political, economic and social transition, and the process of change is still ongoing.

Before 1989 the CEE countries were characterised by strongly centralised planned economies, the general approach being top-down rather than bottom-up. The introduction in the wake of 1989 of a more market-oriented approach therefore represented a dramatic change and posed significant new challenges for the post-command economies. One side effect of the transition and the less interventionist approach of the state was the re-emergence of territorial differences which had earlier been disguised by the strong equalisation policies of the socialist system of central planning. However, the question of how – or even whether – to counteract these emerging regional imbalances in the transition countries is not a straightforward one. Nor is it necessarily an issue which ranges high on the agendas of the central governments.

In this light examining the introduction and track record of bottom-up initiatives and Western-inspired RDAs in the CEE countries becomes a highly relevant and interesting undertaking, but also a pioneering one. The following three chapters discuss the role of RDAs in Poland, the Czech Republic and Hungary.

In Chapter 6 Grzegorz Gorzelak, Marek Kozak and Wojciech Roszkowski present the results of a survey of 42 RDAs in Poland, focusing on their origins, organisational patterns, financial resources and policy profiles. In Chapter 7 Jan Vozáb describes the development of RDAs in the Czech Republic and their changing roles and position in society including a description of the two RDAs currently operating in the Czech Republic.

Finally, in Chapter 8 Anne Lorentzen analyses the institutional changes related to regional development in Hungary, focusing on selected RDAs and presenting BAZ county as a case study.

As will appear from these chapters, the three countries have faced a similar set of general problems during the transition period with regard to the establishment of RDAs. A typical problem in the initial period, which can be traced in all countries, has been the question of defining the role of the RDA. The transition from top-down policies to a bottom-up approach does not happen overnight; attitudes rooted in culture and history change only slowly. In addition, there is the question of competition from other authorities/institutions. Not only RDAs are attempting to define a role for themselves. Local authorities have come into power and are trying to position themselves, making an integrated approach more difficult and, moreover, in some countries (e.g. Hungary) RDAs have to coexist with old institutions favouring a more traditional centralised approach.

At the same time the new, more liberal winds blowing over Central and Eastern Europe have presented another problem. New dogmas of state non-interference with economic life as well as the reduced influence or even absence of a regional level of government have left the RDAs in a vacuum that complicates an integrated approach to regional development and also aggravates a general obstacle to the operations of the RDAs, namely the problem of finance. The shortage and unstable stream of financial resources obviously influence the profile of the agencies, both as regards the type of regional development activities the RDA is able to undertake/offer, but also, as is the case in Poland, forcing some agencies to create their own sources of revenue by undertaking commercial activities – a feature familiar to many Western European RDAs, although the types of commercial activity undertaken by Polish RDAs are arguably different.

However, the achievement of the RDAs should also be emphasised. In many ways the situation is gradually improving. The RDAs have managed to fill in the gaps in economic and public administration and have assumed a mediating and coordinating role as well as pointing the way to overcoming barriers between the public and the private. In this sense the RDAs also contribute to changing the attitudes and motivation in the regions and to the creation of new networks.

Despite these general similarities in the situation of RDAs in Eastern Europe, important differences between the CEE countries are also in evidence, notably as regards the scale of the problems presented above as well as that of regional differences in general. The extent of reform (e.g. as regards economic reform and decentralisation), the pace of it as well as the approach chosen varies in different CEE countries, and all this sets out different basic premises for the operations of the RDAs. So does, for example, the role of the PHARE programme and the amount of resources made available under it (PHARE is the EU's support programme directed towards the CEE countries). Hungary especially would seem to stand out in the following chapters as having a more well-defined state regional policy and a better record of institution-building than, for instance, Poland and the Czech Republic. In terms of the number of RDAs established, Poland clearly takes the lead, possibly as a result of its strong local government, whereas the Czech Republic has only two RDAs, possibly reflecting its rather low rates of unemployment (1995).

As will appear from the following three chapters, the challenges facing RDAs in Eastern Europe are therefore of a different nature than those facing RDAs in Western Europe as described in the previous section. They are newly established and are operating in an environment where regional policy is in its infancy and where there is scepticism about strong state intervention, making the question of trust and strategy a crucial one. The deficiencies in the institutional environment have meant a lack of central coordination of policies and also that many agencies have to be financially self-reliant. Access to external funds, state or EU, again influences the ability of RDAs to meet expectations and affects attitudes towards and acceptance of the agencies. Finally, the requirement to adapt to rapidly changing economic and social conditions in an unstable environment and constantly to develop and redefine their role would very much seem to be a basic premise for the operations of RDAs in the CEE countries, and hence a state of flux would seem to characterise the present mid-1990s situation.

CHAPTER 6

Regional Development Agencies in Poland

Grzegorz Gorzelak, Marek Kozak
& Wojciech Roszkowski

Agencies in Central and Eastern Europe

There is no post-communist country without at least one regional development agency, although as a rule not more than two or three agencies have been established. Poland, with its 66 RDAs (including local ones), is an absolute exception: by comparison, one agency operates, in Ukraine, in Zaporoze; two agencies operate, in the Czech Republic, in Ostrava and in Most; and one agency operates in Slovakia, in Zilina. Two agencies, with changing luck, operate in Bulgaria (in August 1995 their financing was suspended it is hoped temporarily; one agency operates in the Russian-speaking Narva (Estonia). Sometimes one encounters an opinion that a well-developed network of agencies has been set up in Hungary, but it should be noted that they are not so much regional development agencies as centres for supporting SMEs, operating on a sub-regional scale.

Particular transition countries have had different experiences. Typical difficulties, at least in the initial period of activities, included problems with the definition of the role of RDAs in the overall state (regional) policy as well as relationships with the institutional environment. In many cases the concept of the RDA was, in a sense, imported from the European Union, which, in fact, was a universal phenomenon. At the same time, many RDAs were created by experts 'provided' by the EU, and most agencies were also originally financed by the EU. This mode of establishing RDAs had, as well as some favourable effects, some unwelcome ones; as a result, the early 1990s witnessed the import of institutions which did not fully correspond with their environment (in terms of economy, institutions and politics) in the countries of Central and, primarily, Eastern Europe. Frankly speaking, in some of these countries RDAs were set up prematurely, which adversely affected their functioning.

Although it is difficult to attempt dividing the process into stages, it seems justified to say that after 1992 the situation of RDAs became markedly varied. In the countries which consistently followed the course of economic reform, RDAs fairly quickly found their place in the circumstances more and more akin to the standards of democracy and a market economy, which generated the concept of the RDA. An atypical example in this respect is the agency in Ostrava, which constantly improved its performance until early 1995 when it was ignored by the government led by V. Klaus as an instrument of intervention contravening the doctrine of the free market.[1]

Generally, an opinion may be ventured that in the beginning of 1996 the state of RDAs in specific countries reflected the advancement of reforms, privatisation and the development of the private sector, and indirectly mirrored the state of the reform of the political system. Regional development, and by the same token opportunities for the functioning of RDAs, are particularly affected by the decentralisation of power. In this respect, Poland has definitely the most impressive record. About 90 per cent of all RDAs established in post-communist countries operate in Poland. Polish RDAs are more and more visible on the European forum, highly effectively undertaking joint projects with their partner organisations in the EU.[2]

Regional development agencies in Poland – basic facts

Legal framework

The majority of RDAs in Poland have the form of joint stock companies, which has distinct advantages since the Commercial Code imposes stringent criteria of financial effectiveness on the management of companies. This is undeniably a controlling factor which allows the measurement of the company's performance on the basis of the size of profits. At the same time, functioning in the form of a joint stock company has both advantages as well as disadvantages. In the first place, the Commercial Code does not recognise the concept of 'not-for-profit' activity, which implies that it is rather difficult to reconcile the requirement of earning profit with activities promoting development (e.g. subsidies for other entities). The Code grants the right to

---

1 According to the data from mid-1995, the agency has managed to overcome this barrier and there are hopes for its inclusion in the implementation of Czech government policy.
2 For example, in the exchange programme organised by EURADA, Polish agencies participated in 12 projects while the second next country, Great Britain, in only six.

forgo participation in profits and to assign profits to other types of activity (i.e. non-profit ones) only to the general meeting of shareholders, not allowing for any other mode of taking such a decision (Article 335). Additionally, the non-public status of joint stock companies affects their relations with the state administration.

This also applies to limited liability companies (whose activities are regulated by the Commercial Code as well), which are easier to establish because the lowest required capital is relatively small, and this makes such companies an attractive formula for RDAs. In this formula, however, the general meeting of partners cannot forgo their right to distribute profits if such a right is not included in the contract of partnership.

Some of the regional (local) development institutions were established as foundations; that is, on the basis of the Act on Foundations of 6 April 1994. This formula seemed to be particularly attractive in the years 1991–93, since it allowed avoidance of problems related to the infamous hypernormative remuneration tax (tax on excessive payroll, which penalised enterprises for growth of wages higher than the average growth in the sector). On the other hand, however, entities acting on the basis of commercial law were more willing to participate in a company than in a foundation, which does not produce profit to be distributed. Undoubtedly, the limitation in the number of existing RDAs is due to the practices of registration courts, which, owing to their sluggishness and frequently questioned requirements regarding the drafts of the foundations' statutes, forced the founders to abandon their plans.[3] Whether they liked it or not, many of them wholly abandoned their plans or established commercial partnerships.

Nevertheless, it seems that unlike in some neighbouring countries, Polish law offers a wide selection of legal formulae for establishing development agencies. In order to optimise regulations, the notion of not-for-profit activity should be introduced, which would confirm the public character of RDAs.

Territorial range and formal status of RDAs

At the central level, there are three institutions which are important for the functioning of RDAs:

1. The Polish Agency for Regional Development (PARD), closely cooperating, on the basis of signed agreements, with agencies operating

---

3   The courts may be partly justified because of the fact that the registering of all foundations in Poland rests in the hands of three judges.

in the regions covered by complex financial aid for the sake of restructuring and growth.

2. The Industrial Development Agency (IDA), which is a shareholder in many regional and local agencies.

3. The National Association of Regional Development Agencies, which functions as an association, but is also an organiser of a number of training programmes and other projects. Most RDAs belong to the Association as supporting members.

IDA and PARD are institutions established by the government, serving to implement its policies. PARD is the only government agency specialising exclusively in the implementation of the regional programmes.[4] It should be added that support for regional development programmes and institutions is also provided by numerous other institutions and organisations both at home and abroad, governmental and non-governmental ones alike. A particularly valuable contribution has come from the PHARE programme, financed by the EU. In our further discussion of RDAs we shall disregard central level institutions.

Apart from these three central level institutions, in Poland there are currently 66 agencies and foundations generally referred to as 'regional development agencies'. RDAs do not exist in the voivodships[5] of Nowy Sacz, Pila, Siedlce, Sieradz and Wroclaw (in Sieradz there is an agency under preparation).

Local agencies (foundations) restrict their activities to the areas of their communes (*gminas*, which usually comprise a town) or groups of communes. Local self-government authorities are their primary partners. Regional agencies (foundations) normally operate within the boundaries of one voivodship. There are a few exceptions to this rule, such as the Mielec RDA, which comprises part of the Rzeszów voivodship, just as the Nowa Ruda RDA in the voivodship of Walbrzych. The pattern of the territorial scope of the operations of RDAs is presented in Table 6.1.[6]

4   The largest regional programme is the STRUDER, financed through PHARE. In the years 1993–96 it has operated in five regions (comprising six administrative regional units). The programme's aims were to support structures and activity on the regional level; to provide financial assistance (grants, guarantee funds, regional investment funds); to ensure provision of training and advisory services; to support small infrastructural projects. For the years 1996–99 the programme has been extended to further regions and its 'sister programme' RAPID has embraced rural areas.

5   The regional administration in Poland.

6   The data presented in this study, unless specified otherwise, come from the survey sent out to 66 regional development agencies; 42 responses (two-thirds) were sent back. The survey was conducted as part of the ACE 'Institutional Background for Regional Development' project that comprises Germany (Rheinich-Westfälisches Institut für Wirtschaftforschung e.V. in

Table 6.1 Territorial scope of RDA operations

Range of operations	Percentage of cases
One voivodship	45
Region/several voivodships	31
Several neighbouring communes	15
One locality	9

Source: Survey.

The first institutions using the name of regional development agencies came into being at the beginning of 1991; the agency in Suwalki was registered in January 1991. Generally, most agencies were set up in 1993, and the lowest number was established in 1995.

In most cases (85%) the establishment of RDAs was initiated by the voivods, local government or the Polish Agency for Regional Development. In several cases the idea came from other entities (e.g. chambers of commerce and industry, research institutions – see Table 6.2).

Table 6.2 Initiators of the RDAs

Initiator	Percentage of cases
Voivode	43
Local self-government	23
PARD	20
Local committee	7
Other	7

Source: Survey.

As a rule, the closest cooperation concerns organs of administration and state and self-government authorities. At the regional level (i.e. in 49 voivodships), however, there is visibly no regional entity which would determine and finance development policy in a given area. The communes have full

Essen), Great Britain (European Policies Research Centre, University of Strathclyde in Glasgow), Hungary (Centre for Regional Studies, Transdanubian Research Institute of the Hungarian Academy of Sciences in Pécs) and Poland (European Institute for Regional and Local Development, University of Warsaw).

sovereignty and control almost 20 per cent of the state's revenues and expenditures. It was possibly this strong position of the local government authorities in Poland, coupled with unrestricted growth of the private sector, that constituted the decisive factors in such a dynamic development of regional and local institutions there.

In one out of four RDAs surveyed some external entity contributed to their creation; in most cases those entities were research institutions, foundations or private persons, and, in a few cases, the Industrial Development Agency.

Among the surveyed RDAs, almost 80 per cent had problems during their creation stage. The basic problem they encountered was primarily the shortage of financial resources and difficulties in winning support for the idea of establishing an agency among the authorities and local elites alike. Relatively fewer problems were connected with legal and organisational issues, and with the finding of suitable personnel.

Shareholders and financing

In 1994, the total capital of RDAs was assessed at about 50 million PLN (about 20 million USD). The most affluent agency represented initial capital of approximately four million USD,[7] while the financially smallest agency (though not the weakest one) – of about 2000 USD. Initial capital of a typical RDA amounts to 500,000–1,000,000 PLN (200–400 thousand USD).

The finances of RDAs should be examined from two angles: first, from the perspective of the structure of initial capital, and second, from the perspective of their annual budgets.

The volume of initial capital for the surveyed RDAs oscillated between 2000 PLN and 11,200,000 PLN. On average, the initial capital of an RDA was 927,000 PLN. However, the median value, which has the advantage of being unaffected by the impact of the highest capital, is considerably lower and amounts to 381,000 PLN for the surveyed agencies.

Almost half of the surveyed agencies was additionally co-financed by the Industrial Development Agency.[8] The average amount of IDA co-financing for a single RDA was 304,000 PLN. Among the co-financed RDAs 40 per cent received a sum not exceeding 100,000 PLN. The share of IDA co-financing of the volume of capital varied, and oscillated between 0.4 per

---

7 The Upper Silesia Agency for Enterprise Restructuring is an exception since it specialises in cooperation with state enterprises.
8 IDA had the biggest shares in the agencies in Suwalki (48%), Walbrzych (47%) and Bielsko-Biala (46%).

cent and 69 per cent; 18 per cent on average. This means that the rest, that is over half of initial capital, came from a given region. Recently, IDA has reduced its share in newly founded RDAs to 10 per cent. On the whole, an extremely positive contribution of IDA in the financing and promotion of RDAs in the initial period of their operation should be emphasised, even though IDA is a shareholder only in some agencies (foundations). As a rule, the most significant shareholders are voivods, IDA and local self-governments (see Table 6.3). Although an enterprise is mostly the main shareholder, in the majority of cases the quantity of its shares is small, less than 25 per cent.

Table 6.3 Main shareholders at the moment of RDAs' establishment

Main shareholder/stockholder	Percentage of cases
Enterprise	21
Local self-government	19
Voivode	14
Bank	12
IDA	12
Foundation or private person	11
Chamber of Commerce & Industry	4
Other	7

Source: Survey.

The differentiation of the ownership structures is so enormous that we can find agencies in which 95 per cent of shares were taken over by IDA and the voivode – more or less half of the shares for each party, as in Suwalki, and those in which a prevailing number of shares is owned by local self-government (Olsztyn). The agency in Szczecin has an exceptional structure of capital since all its shares were taken over by the state treasury, that is the voivode. Majority blocks of shares usually belonged to the voivodes and self-governments, while the blocks owned by enterprises, although greater in number, were much less significant.

In more than half of the surveyed agencies the number of shareholders/stockholders has changed since their establishment. In almost 40 per cent of cases their number increased, and in almost 20 per cent of cases it was reduced. This seems to prove better understanding of the fact that the success of agencies largely depends on reaching an optimum dispersion of stocks which can guarantee a significant share of the key regional players, that is, the voivode, self-governments and financial institutions; naturally, this does not apply to local agencies which operate on a limited scale and therefore seek alliances at the strictly local level. The number of shareholders grew in those agencies in which it was originally high. Those RDAs which had few shareholders at the moment of their establishment underwent few changes later. The changes that occurred in the structure of shareholders/stockholders in the period between the creation of RDAs and the survey are shown in Table 6.4, which implies that new shares/stocks were mainly purchased by enterprises and the IDA, while the role of local self-government became gradually reduced.

Table 6.4 Changes of shareholders

New shareholders/stockholders	Percentage of cases
Enterprise	48
IDA	20
Voivode	16
Local self-government	4
Bank	4
Foundation or private person	4
Other	4

Source: Survey.

Initial capital was not always brought in the form of financial means. Frequently it was a contribution in kind, such as buildings and other fixed assets that were left over after the liquidation of state enterprises. As a result, RDAs could seldom enjoy actual financial liquidity. It goes without saying that the discussed differences in the capital of agencies from the very outset determined real opportunities for action on the regional (voivodship) scale, and often reflected the condition and wealth of particular regions.

Many RDAs, over 40 per cent, were able to raise their initial capital significantly. Agencies raised their capital, with amounts ranging from 24,000 PLN to 12,005,000 PLN, which represents from as little as 2 per cent to as much as 96 per cent of the values of initial capital. Those agencies which raised capital increased it by 45 per cent on average. Those agencies which reduced their capital on average decreased it by 50 per cent.

Unlike many agencies in the European Union, Polish RDAs received, as a rule, a one-time 'dowry' and were left to themselves. Neither voivods nor local self-governments grant subsidies for their operations and activities. This is partly due to legal obstacles, and partly to insufficient understanding of the benefits that a well-managed agency can provide for a region or locality. We often witness a vicious circle: the environment poses constantly new expectations for the agency, the agency often has to refuse due to the shortage of funds, and this, in turn, invites the question '*what do we need the agency for?*'

Should the RDAs therefore be subsidised from public funds? As usual, such a decision is of a political character. Nowadays, it is more and more difficult to envisage the formula of direct subsidising. However, in recognition of the positive role RDAs play, and an even more positive role they could play, they could be proposed to execute some tasks commissioned by the state administration or even offered tax rebates, which would increase RDAs' financial resources.

As it has been stressed, financing of development activities from their own resources – profits – is a necessity for most RDAs, and these funds are, necessarily, limited. In this situation, even small funds from foreign aid programmes, such as those earmarked for training programmes, study visits, exchange of staff, significantly increase the scale and range of agency activities. It is so not because those aid funds are so huge, but because usually RDAs' own funds are so humble.

Additional financial resources were secured by the majority, over 70 per cent, of the agencies surveyed. The percentage of RDAs which used external sources of financing grew systematically every year, from 16 per cent in 1992 to 50 per cent in 1995.

The financial means donated usually came from institutions and agencies financed or set up by the British government – 40 per cent of cases of using the aid – and by the EU – 34 per cent. RDAs were also financed, though on a much smaller scale, from Polish funds (8%). Table 6.5 illustrates also the average and median values of sums donated by particular sources.

Two-thirds of RDAs used the funds donated for the implementation of specific projects, and 26 per cent for their own needs.

Ten agencies have budgets for development activities amounting to 2–3 million USD per year.[9] These are the RDAs that operate in voivodships covered by complex development programmes financed by foreign aid funds. Two such programmes are of major importance: PHARE-STRUDER (Programme for Structural Development in Selected Regions, coordinated by the Polish Agency for Regional Development) and the Polish-British Programme for Enterprise Development. It should be stressed that if foreign

---

9   This applies to the agencies in Olsztyn, Suwalki, lódz, Rzeszów, Mielec, Katowice, Walbrzych, Nowa Ruda embraced by STRUDER, and the foundations in Lublin and Bialystok that collaborate with the Know-How Fund.

Table 6.5 Sources of additional funds

Sources of funds	Percentage of cases	Average sum in PLN	Median in PLN
Cooperation fund, Know-How fund	30	335,000	92,700
PHARE (PLI, STRUDER, CROSSBORDER)	30	1,016,000	940,000
British government (British Council, Polish-British Programme for Enterprise Development)	10	702,600	360,000
Polish funds (PARD, Labour Fund, MFR)	8	16,000	16,000
USAID, TOR-10, Japanese government	7	765,000	26,300
Other EU programmes (EURADA, Counterpart Found)	5	172,000	100,000
Other sources	10	208,000	105,000

Source: Survey.

aid in financing the programmes is curtailed, which is highly unlikely, it would not mean an automatic downfall of the agencies. The vast majority of those RDAs are efficiently managed and have sufficient of their own resources at their disposal to continue activities for the sake of their regions, though maybe on a smaller scale. Their unique achievement is the creation of a sustainable mechanism for the mass transfer of funds for the needs of regional development which remains at the disposal of the government, but is also compatible with EU mechanisms and practices. This is an undeniable accomplishment in the dimension of European integration.

It has to be conceded that the volume of the available capital of RDAs is not a good criterion and can be confusing.

Employment

The number of staff in RDAs normally matches their capital, and varies considerably from 1 to 83 employees; the average for all agencies being 19 people and the median 14 people. The number of office staff oscillates from 1 to 32 people, and the average is ten people (median − 7). The number of employees who do not work in the agency office amounts to approximately one-third of all staff, and in some agencies exceeds 90 per cent (Table 6.6). Among professional personnel the most significant groups are engineers and economists, and frequently lawyers. However, their professional worth is not determined by their formal education acquired in universities but by profess-

Table 6.6 Employment in RDAs (per cent of cases)

Number of employees	Total	Office only
1–5	14	34
6–10	27	29
11–15	17	12
16–20	10	12
21–25	10	10
26–30	7	-
31–50	10	3
51–83	5	-

Source: Survey.

ional experience and training taken in Poland and abroad. There is no doubt that RDAs managed to hire the best available staff, particularly in weaker regions. If only such a trite criterion as command of foreign languages is taken into consideration, RDAs outdo many other regional institutions. Undeniably, the 'human capital' is one of the strengths of the RDAs.

Some publications on the employment in agencies can create a lot of confusion. For instance, it has been reported that the agency in Rzeszów has 80 staff. Technically it is true, because this is the number of personnel on the payroll. Actually, however, more than 65 people are employees of a design enterprise brought in as a contribution in kind by the voivode (incidentally which at the moment of takeover was going bust, but now yields profit). The number of staff actually employed in the agency and for the implementation of its statutory goals is less than 15 people. Other agencies are in a similar situation.

The definite majority of the RDAs surveyed, almost two-thirds, has had one president since the moment of their establishment, 26 per cent of agencies have had two presidents, and 12 per cent three presidents. These data well prove the *stability* of the management of RDAs.

Objectives and goals

The definition of objectives and goals implemented by regional development agencies is rather difficult. This is because they depend not only on the environment of their operations but also on the expectations of the shareholders and available financial resources, not to mention the qualifications and vision of the managing staff.

Basically, there exist no fully satisfactory characteristics, and this applies to both Western studies and the few Polish attempts. EURADA defines the tasks of a regional development agency in the following way:

> ...each organisation realising a mission which lies in the common or general interest of a given territory. From this point of view, a development agency has to maintain significant relations with local or regional authorities in terms of management, financing or setting tasks. Furthermore, it has to operate in a sufficiently large area of activities, yet smaller than the area of the whole country.[10]

This definition seems to illustrate the definition problems a researcher of agencies and their operations has to encounter.

In Annex III to the Report on the Regional Policy, which is being prepared by the Central Office for Planning in Warsaw, it is said that:

> ...the regional development agencies are independent non-governmental organisations whose aims include primarily: development of regions, support to state administration in the implementation of tasks related to regional development, and creation of regional infrastructure for undertaken restructuring activities.[11]

Almost each Polish RDA pursues the following types of activity:

- business activity conducted according to general principles of competition and undertaken for profit

- activity undertaken according to the 'break even' principle, without producing profit

- strictly development activity, financed from the agency's own resources or donated resources, domestic or foreign programmes such as co-financing of analyses, fairs, events, promotions, training projects.

The proportions between the types of activities listed above differ for specific agencies. Unlike numerous agencies in the European Union, most Polish RDAs are bound to conduct profit-oriented activity, which is forced by the Commercial Code and other factors in the legal and institutional

---

10 In a study prepared by the European Association of Regional Development Agencies (EURADA) the common features are defined as undertaking activities for the improvement of endogenous development potential of a given territory or, sometimes, as attracting inward investment. See 'Regional development agencies in Europe – who are they? what are their objectives'. In EURADA EEN, Bulletin No.3, 1994.
11 Central Office for Planning (1995) *Report on Regional Policy*, Annex III, p.1. Warszawa: Central Office for Planning.

environment. Fortunately, agencies do not restrict themselves to such activities only.

In the opinion of most RDAs, business is their least important activity, the most important being the promotion of the region among potential investors and tourists (see Table 6.7).

Table 6.7 Significance of specific types of activities of RDAs

Types of activity	Very important	Important	Not important	Does not occur
Promotion of region among investors and tourists	86	14	0	0
Business consulting	45	45	10	0
Training programmes	57	31	10	2
Setting up of business incubators	36	36	24	5
Securing and granting loans	41	21	36	2
Organising fairs and commodity exchanges	24	38	33	5
Forming companies and partnerships, bringing in shares to companies	21	45	26	7
Own business activity (production, trade)	31	19	45	5
Other	36	5	0	60

Source: Survey.

Operations

It has already been said that at the moment of their establishment RDAs were in varied financial situations. Those differences also manifest themselves in the functioning of agencies (see Table 6.8). Due to the fact that the sample surveyed included agencies created in different years, the table shows the results for RDAs existing in a given period. Moreover, it should be stressed that some agencies are non-profit organisations. This table implies that along with a rapid increase in yielded profits in 1994, the number of RDAs gaining profits grew systematically: in 1992 there were about 20 per cent of such agencies, in 1993 over 25 per cent, and in 1994 over 35 per cent. Over half the agencies which yielded profit did not invest it.

**Table 6.8 Agencies according to financial profit/loss in given years
(percentage of all RDAs)**

Loss/profit in PLN	1992	1993	1994
-75,000 to -25,000	–	7	3
-25,000 to -1,000	–	–	5
-1,000 to -1	11	7	3
0	66	59	53
+1 to +1,000	6	14	5
+1,000 to +25,000	6	10	11
+25,000 to +75,000	11	3	5
+75,000 to 75,000	–	–	15
Average financial profit/loss in PLN	24,260	1,460	96,870
Median finacial profit/loss in PLN	10,210	130	16,670

Source: Survey.

Seeking financial means, half of the RDAs conduct their own business in services, trade or production, thus entering into competition with other business entities, for example submitting tenders for the liquidation of state enterprises, or running trade or production companies. This is of no special significance in larger urban or industrial centres, but in poorly developed rural areas the business activities of RDAs ought to be carefully analysed due to a likely risk that the institution responsible for promotion and development may, in some sectors, effectively restrict potential competition by new entities, such as in the sphere of consultancy or training. On the other hand, it is difficult to overestimate the role of many agencies in the creation of a network of business-related institutions such as business incubators, special economic zones, fairs and exchanges, centres for business support and technology parks.

There are agencies which run their own shops or rent commercial premises to private businesses. Some have their own printing facilities. Other RDAs have opened brokerage bureaux, virtually all agencies conduct lending activity, and some manufacture specialised microscopes.

As yet, introducing new financial instruments is a novelty for many regions, though it might help to fill in a distinct gap in the financing of many enterprises. Interestingly enough, unlike most Polish banks RDAs have a very low percentage of unrecoverable debts. Highly profitable lending and guaranteeing activities of many RDAs enhanced investments and, as a result, increased employment and profits. Similarly, quality specialist training programmes for entrepreneurs have something valuable and new to offer. Nonetheless, should trade, profitable as it is, be conducted by agencies? Would it not be better to leave retail trade to small and medium-sized private companies?

Ideally, RDAs should restrict their business activity undertaken for profit to those spheres in which local business entities cannot or do not want to function. It seems that following the introduction of an innovative, novel product (service) the agency should gradually give way to the private sector. This would open up interesting opportunities for financial engineering and capital activity in the local market. Strictly business activity ought to be clearly separated organisationally (profit centres) or even conducted by separate (though related in terms of capital) legal entities. The current situation, in which often a printer or a salesman is found next to a high quality expert on the agency payroll, causes many misunderstandings about the role the agency does actually play.

Obviously, activities undertaken primarily in the sphere of enterprise restructuring for the founding body, usually the voivode, arouse less controversy. The relation between the region's development and the restructuring of the economy is not disputed, and standards of services are normally high. It seems that the participation of RDAs and other non-state institutions in the execution of some tasks of the administration might be increased, benefiting all, particularly taxpayers. A classic example here is promotion – general, tourist and economic – as well as direct services to investors, especially foreign ones. Most communes are not able to do it single-handedly in a good or economical way. Besides, closer cooperation of state administration with RDAs would allow it to concentrate on strictly administrative functions.

The conflict between 'commercial' elements and pro-growth activity tackled here does not necessarily have adverse effects, for example for the promotion of competition and development of market relations in a given region. It can even serve as a stimulus for new actions and solutions, for instance for supra-regional and international expansion. The only dangerous moment is when profits become the sole criterion for the agency's evaluation by its shareholders and the existence of such a potential clash of interests is either ignored or concealed from public opinion.

It should be stressed that this dilemma is familiar to some Western RDAs. Although most of them are financed from public funds, some agencies, for example the majority of RDAs in Great Britain, were in fact privatised and at present are sustained wholly by their own proceeds. Generally speaking, well-developed countries with a liberal orientation strictly limit state

**Table 6.9 Evaluation of cooperation of RDAs
and other institutions (percentage of RDAs)**

	Very good	Good	Poor	Bad	No cooperation
Voivodship office	38.1	40.5	19.0	–	2.4
Private entrepreneurs	26.2	47.6	14.3	4.8	7.2
Territorial self-government	26.2	42.9	23.8	2.4	4.8
Consulting and advisory companies	23.8	45.2	14.3	–	16.7
Authorities of city/town – seat of RDA	26.2	38.1	28.6	–	7.2
Bank	19.0	45.2	23.8	–	11.9
Polish Agency for Regional Development	35.7	23.8	19.0	–	21.5
IDA	28.6	28.6	21.4	–	21.4
Universities, research institutions	21.4	31.0	16.7	–	16.7
Large state-owned enterprises	9.5	40.5	33.3	–	16.7
Other	31.0	16.7	–	4.8	47.6

Source: Survey.

subsidies for agencies. Countries which are less developed and which have a social-liberal orientation are more prone to subsidise, even though sometimes they fail to do so effectively. Besides, it seems that a similar

Table 6.10 Evaluation of RDA's independence

	Percentage of cases
Agency is fully independent, no one interferes with its activities	17
Donors financing specific activities strictly control the agency with regard to this activity, otherwise, agency is autonomous	45
Major shareholders control the agency's activities on a regular basis	38

Source: Survey.

tendency to restrict the intervention of public funds to underdeveloped regions will also appear in Poland.

The agencies operate in an existing institutional environment, which may influence both the directions and the means of their activities. In the opinion of the surveyed agencies, cooperation developed best with voivodship offices and private entrepreneurs, although the latter group at the same time received the highest number of negative marks (Table 6.9). The surveyed agencies maintain the weakest links with universities and research institutions.

Being financed by external sources the agencies are no doubt exposed to several influences. The surveyed agencies varied in the evaluation of their independence (Table 6.10).

Answers given to the question about the degree of independence reflect the findings of Table 6.10. Almost half of RDAs assessed this level as adequate, almost 40 per cent as rather adequate. Only slightly over 10 per cent regarded it as inadequate.

In the definite majority of agencies, the main shareholders agree as to the desired policies of operation. In a few cases only the main shareholders would like the agencies to change their profile. In a similar pattern, the main shareholders agreed as to the manner of allotting the profits of RDAs. In 5 per cent of cases the main shareholder (the voivode or an enterprise) disagreed with the agency's management and would like to pay out dividends on earned profits.

The agencies surveyed also pointed out barriers and obstacles hindering their operations (Table 6.11). Bad regional policy of the state or lack of it turns out to be the most serious barrier of all. Another is the shortage of financial resources. Additionally, inappropriate regulations and the legal system constitute strong barriers. Slight hindrances for RDA operations are internal factors such as too low autonomy of the managing board, lack of agreement between the main shareholders, and lack of conception of sensible functioning as well as external factors, including the inappropriate territorial division of the country and problems in cooperation with voivodship and self-government authorities.

The surveyed agencies also specified their greatest successes and failures. Most agencies (43%) regarded conducting sustainable regional activities – such as support in the creation of new companies, new jobs, participation in local economic initiatives (e.g. privatisation), organisation of such events as fairs, promotions and so on – as their successes. At the same time, equally frequently (41%) the improvement of the internal standing of the agency by way of raising sufficient funds for operations, maintaining good relations with the environment and building up a positive image of the RDA was regarded as a success.

Table 6.11 Perceived barriers to RDAs' activities
(percentage of RDAs)

	Very strong	Strong	Weak	Very weak	Irrelevant
Bad regional policy of the state or lack of it	50	33	7	–	10
Modest financial resources	50	31	5	12	2
Inappropriate regulations/legal system	38	36	12	–	14
Inactivity of local elites	5	55	16	12	12
Lack of external aid	10	40	31	7	12
Lack of adequately qualified personnel	2	26	37	14	21
Difficult cooperation with self-government	2	17	38	17	26
No conception of sensible activity	2	14	14	14	56
Difficult cooperation with voivodship authorities	5	12	29	14	40
Insufficient independence of the managing board	2	12	10	5	71
No agreement between main shareholders	5	5	17	13	60
Inappropriate territorial division of the country	7	2	21	7	63
Other	7	2	–	–	91

Source: Survey.

One out of three agencies participating in the survey believed it did not suffer a failure. The remaining RDAs most often indicated conflicts and lack of cooperation with the environment (almost one-quarter), and forsaken projects or renouncing part of their activity (24%). Inability to secure financial resources or financial loss were more seldom considered failures (almost 20%).

The surveyed RDAs have managed – in their opinion – to affect sustainably the growth of their regions; this is the opinion of almost three-quarters of the responding agencies. Among those RDAs which believe they permanently contributed to the improvement of the situation in the region, most did so primarily through the creation of new jobs (almost 30%) and through promotional or advisory activities (slightly above 25%). Somewhat lesser significance was attributed to the establishment of institutions serving the general public, such as business incubators or guarantee funds (20%), and to support in attracting or securing capital (10%). Those agencies which were not able to prove their contribution to the improvement of the situation in the region (town) pointed to the lack of funds, short period of operation and lack of conception of the agency's functioning as reasons for the inefficiency of their activities.

Plans and chances for the future

Among the agencies surveyed, almost 90 per cent had a plan of activities and a financial plan for the coming year. Table 6.12 shows the main policies of operation for the two years following the survey, 1996–97.

In the long-term future, after 1998 the profile of the operations of RDAs will change. Their role in capital and investment activities will significantly increase, just as will their participation in the restructuring and privatisation processes. At the same time, RDAs will completely discontinue their pursuits of external financial resources and will considerably restrict their creation of

Table 6.12 Main policies of RDAs in the years 1996–97

Policies	Percentage of cases
Training programmes	14
Promotion	13
Consulting, management, services to investors	13
Statutory activities, gaining independence	12
Establishing exchanges, incubators, technology parks	11
Attracting inward financial resources	11
Participation in investment projects, capital activities	10
Participation in ownership transformations and restructuring	10
Same as before	6

Source: Survey.

exchanges, business incubators and technology parks, an activity which is now conducted on a relatively small scale.

To a large extent, their plans for the future are not related to clear financial plans. More than half of RDAs (54.8%) could not specify the agency sources of financing after 1998. The other agencies intended to obtain financial resources mainly from their own business activities, such as production, trade, capital operations. Some of them will continue to hope for funds from foreign aid programmes, budget funds or local self-government resources. The lowest percentage of RDAs plan to contract loans for this purpose.

Conclusions

There is no doubt that in Poland since 1990 RDAs have been playing a major role in the transformation and restructuring processes of local and regional economies. They were some of the first, if not the only ones, practically to prove benefits originating from the overcoming of the traditionally 'soc-realist' division into the state-owned and the private-owned. By combining public and private capital, RDAs also combine the best properties of administration (predictability, routine, public accountability) and private companies (decision-making flexibility, undertaking calculated risk, measurable criteria of success). Overcoming those barriers at the meeting point of the state and the private is an outstanding achievement in itself.

Furthermore, it seems that most agencies were able to find their place on the institutional map. They avoided being transformed into yet another department of the voivodship office or a branch of special administration. On the other hand, RDAs basically did not go beyond the general guidelines set by the shareholders representing state capital, particularly the voivods, and respected their priorities. It does not mean, however, that seeking their own place was always devoid of conflicts. All the same, conflict is an inescapable feature of growth.

Undoubtedly, most agencies have established their identity. However, it is difficult to ignore the fact that at present RDAs, unable to hope for the systematic support of the state administration, have encountered a serious capital barrier which precludes their participation in the restructuring of the economy according to actual needs. Unless the status of RDAs is changed or unless the principles of their financing are regulated in the sphere of executing public tasks, their continued development will depend solely on their capacity to generate profit.

It has already been mentioned that any evaluation of the functioning of RDAs has to take into consideration the institutional and economic context of their activities. Agencies operating in developed urban centres with well-advanced transformation processes and vast economic, social and cultural capabilities can, and should, pursue other activities and goals than can realistically be achieved by agencies functioning in backward rural or industrial mono-culture areas. Despite this reservation there can be no doubt that the overall outcome of the functioning of regional development agencies in Poland is very positive. In every case, the overall evaluation depends primarily on the pro-innovative ability of RDAs. It should be noted, however, that the non-political orientation and stability of the staff of RDAs is also a considerable asset.

As organisations and structures in the business environment will become stronger, competition will become tougher along with the requirements to which RDAs will have to conform. Most probably, this will force the specialisation of agencies oriented to capital institutions, technology and innovations transfer, because in those spheres RDAs perform most naturally and most effectively. Specifically, in view of the lack of regional sovereignty – Polish regions are not self-governing bodies, but are directly subordinated to the central government – and therefore the lack of entity implementing intra-regional development policy, for the time being Polish RDAs cannot hope to become strong units of their own policies for the regions. In addition, since there is no state agency that would coordinate and implement government regional policy at the central level, the agencies cannot dream of becoming involved on any larger scale in the implementation of tasks of the state administration at the regional level. Those deficiencies in the institutional environment, which may bring about reduced cooperation with the authorities and public administration, will inevitably impel RDAs to pursue purely commercial activities. This tendency is bound to last at least until the political reform is completed, which is a pity, because agencies, as we have tried to show, apart from problems also have a great development potential, and, compared with many other alternative institutions, can perform both efficiently and effectively.

CHAPTER 7

Regional Development Agencies in The Czech Republic

A Future Solution to Current Problems

Jan Vozáb

Introduction

The socialist regimes in the Central and Eastern European countries were characterised by strongly centralised planning economies. Local and regional initiatives, independent opinions, as well as any attempts at bottom-up activities, were considered a danger to the central socialist power. Regional inequalities almost did not exist in official articles; regional disparities appeared as social rather than economic ones. In fact the territorial differences in the former Czech Socialist Republic were very small and insignificant compared with the differences within developed countries.

The social and economic transformation after 1989 has revealed the problems hidden in the socialist economy but the nature and the real scope of these problems are not yet clear. Certain areas have been expected to have transformation difficulties for a few years but the regional impact of these could be only roughly estimated. In addition, the political environment for solving regional problems has not been too friendly. Neither private nor public organisations in the regions have been prepared even to recognise the nature of future difficulties.

In the early 1990s the transformation has shown its basic orientation and the first steps have been taken. Two regional development agencies have been established in areas where major transformation difficulties seemed to be concentrated. Establishing RDAs was not in the main political stream of either central or local representatives, it was only one of the attempts to fill the gaps after the break-up of former political and administrative structures.

At the beginning none of the regional actors were quite sure what to expect from the RDAs, what their strategies and activities should be.

The RDAs have faced many problems in the first years of their existence. Their activities were very limited by the demand for their services and the lack of financial resources as well as by the absence of relevant projects among organisations within the region. In the last couple of years the situation has changed substantially and the RDAs have become reputable institutions. A shift in the motivation and expectation of clients, promoters and political sponsors was necessary to start new projects and to enlarge the market for the services of RDAs.

The aim of this chapter is to describe the process of developing RDAs in the Czech Republic and their changing roles and position in society. An important part will be a description of existing RDAs, their legal and financial background and their activities.

After the 1989 revolution – the transformation of society

If the role and position of various regional actors including RDAs are to be described and explained it is necessary to mention several main features of the socialist economy as well as the objectives, nature and consequences of the transformation process. It is only possible to understand the evolution of regional and local policies within this framework. In addition, shifts in the attitudes and behaviour of many local organisations as well as central government can underpin or threaten the activities and successes of the RDAs.

The socialist economy can be characterised by two main attributes for the purpose of this article. First, an equalisation/levelling of society, and second, strong centralised hierarchical structures of economic, administrative and political powers.

The equalisation was attained by a massive redistribution of financial resources. It had three dimensions:

- the equalisation/levelling among people, particularly the total regulation of wages
- the equalisation/levelling among companies (economic bodies) made by extensive central redistribution of subsidies within the national economy
- the equalisation among regions, districts and cities caused partly by central redistribution of public financial resources and partly being a side effect of previous equalisation policies.

If there were some imbalances among regions or territorial units, they were mostly differences in social quality of life and in social structures of the society rather than differences in economic conditions of regions.

A vertical hierarchical structure was typical for communist regimes and the whole life of society was organised this way. There was no self-government, no independent public or private institutions. Dominant links within society were vertical ones where lower organisational level or smaller organisational subjects were directly subordinated to the higher ones. Subordination meant that there was very little room for independent decision making by individual organisations and any decision could be changed by higher authority.

Horizontal relationships within regions or local and regional cooperation were politically undesirable and considered to need to be repressed. The political environment discouraged independent or individual activities. The only regional groups with some influence on the central government were several specialised industrial lobbies which were organised as sectorial lobbies with almost no interests in the region whatsoever.

After the breakdown of the regime in 1989 former relationships survived, and the change of the system conditions, such as legislation and economic rules, was quite quick. However the establishment of new relationships and new attitudes of people, institutions and economic subjects have lasted until now.

A new system enabled a rise of differences in society, which were positive results of the first steps of the economic transformation; they were often understood as a failure of central government policy. Moreover, the orientation of the economic reform was subject to political disputes. As a consequence, the social and political environment was somewhat chaotic for the first few years.

The slow, continuous adjustment of institutional relationships has been ongoing since the beginning of this period of transformation. After initial difficulties, when the people as well as institutions tried to orient themselves to the new emerging structures and rules, some positive results were brought into economic and regional interactions. Vertical links were interrupted and new horizontal networks began to be created, although some necessary steps of transformation, such as administrative reform and the establishment of regions, have not yet been finished.

The first important problems for individuals as well as for the private and public sectors were not of a regional nature; the impact of transition was similar throughout the country, and any regional inequalities were hidden in the changing society as a whole. After the initial period, which lasted approximately until 1992, certain regional differences could be recognised, although at that point, it could not be assumed that the conditions had already settled down. Social and economic problems appeared in several small areas, but they were localised.

Regional disparities emerged because the economic reform/ transformation revealed varying specific conditions usually determined by the historical development in individual regions and localities. The role of the state diminished. Central redistribution and equalisation decreased as privatisation began. As the market economy slowly appeared, the natural differences among regions, previously repressed, started to grow.

The rise of regional inequalities had three phases which overlapped each other. This process was territorially differentiated. Moreover, various industries and individual companies or public authorities also went through the process at a different pace and in a different time. Hence it is difficult to connect the phases described below with particular time periods.

Phase 1   Regional differences are small, not well developed and unclear. Central–local relationships are top-down orientated, and cooperation within regions is very rare. The massive redistribution of financial resources still survives.

Phase 2   Slow rise of differences which are understood by regional actors as a failure of central government. Redistribution processes in the national economy begin to diminish rapidly. Bottom-up actions aimed at strong demand for larger support from the centre are revealed.

Phase 3   More pronounced and partially stabilised regional disparities (stabilised in terms of earmarking 'good' and 'bad' regions, differences are possibly increasing). Stabilisation of redistributive flows of finance focused mainly on the public sector. Regional imbalances to some extent are accepted by the public administration and private sector. The first coordinated attempts to look for regional solution of problems take place.

It could be generalised that the increase of differentiation among regions and localities was only a small part of the transition to a market economy. On the other hand it was an important part where the development of regional horizontal networks is concerned.

These differences have been acceptable for several years. At the same time, support from central government has proved limited and insufficient, leading to the creation of horizontal networks and the introduction of regional and local actions.

To complete the picture of the society during the first years of economic and social transformation it is appropriate to mention public administration reform. In 1990 independent self-government municipalities were established, from which time we can speak about local government in the Czech Republic. Higher levels of the administration were either transformed – the district offices, which are the upper tier of local administration, are not self-governing – or abolished without compensation at that level, such as the former regional state administration (regional national councils). Hence there is no regional level of government in the Czech Republic and local government is at the lower/municipal tier only.

The results of the current situation are the diversified and non-conceptual activities of public organisations. Decisions and actions of various local authorities at sub-regional level are often counterproductive or competitive. Another consequence is the non-satisfactory and complicated communication between private and public organisations.

Regional policy of central government

The main goal of transformation, clearly stated by central government, was to decrease radically the participation of the state in the economy. The aim was also to transform state ownership into private ownership and to keep macro-economic stability. Another important goal was to reduce financial redistribution among regions, industries and companies.

Within this framework there was no room for specific regional policy, at least in the first phase of transformation. Reasons for not having any regional policy programmes were as follows:

- regional differences were poorly developed
- a rapidly changing economy did not allow for the prediction of the needs of regions
- emerging problems were specified locally and had very limited regional scope
- inequalities among regions or even among smaller areas (districts and municipalities) were not so important compared with the overall transformation changes
- the pace of transformation was different in different territories.

For all these reasons it was difficult to set up goals and criteria for top-down regional policy actions.

The actions of the government were mostly focused on sectoral industrial policy, and their regional impacts were only indirect ones. Central government gave direct support either to the specific companies/industries or to the specific problems in selected areas – mostly to environmental improvements. Central government support was predominantly characterised by specific sectoral subsidies, a situation which did not change much until 1996. Only some small changes are to be expected in 1997.

In fact, central government has undertaken several actions and has run one truly regional programme during the last few years. However, the government activities were only short-term reactions, generally aimed at narrowing the worst regional impacts of the steps of transformation; mostly they aimed to decrease unemployment and to establish new businesses. The main forms of support have been the subsidy on the interest on entrepreneurial credits and various specific investment subsidies focused on building a new technical infrastructure.

The only regional programme has been focused on the small and medium-sized enterprises in selected 'problematic' districts and micro-regions, the majority of which into the North Bohemia or North Moravia regions. This programme – called REGION – is only an additional one for the participants of another, non-regional programme, and its form has also been a subsidy on the interest on entrepreneurial credits.

The results of these programmes and their success are at least questionable. Having been applied for several years, the programmes have not prevented conditions from worsening in the regions. They have a poor image amongst target groups. The total amount of money given to them each year is very limited and the access to them too complicated. Generally, the measures used to promote selected regions probably approach the problem in the wrong way.

Existing regional differences in the Czech Republic

It took a few years of transition before regional differences developed and reached a more stable level. During these years two larger areas of economic and social difficulties appeared in both old industrial regions and there were more small areas/micro-regions affected by the economic transformation, although their problems were limited territorially and the individual characters of the problems have been very diversified and possibly short-term.

The two larger problematic regions – North Bohemia and North Moravia – have had typical features of transition, such as locally high and slowly increasing unemployment (which means from 6% to 8% in the Czech Republic,[1] underdeveloped SMEs, a heavily polluted environment and a low

1   The Czech Republic has the lowest rate of unemployment among transitional countries. The causes are still a matter of discussion among economists.

quality labour force. These regions depended on a few very big factories, mostly operating in heavy industries such as coal mining, power generation, metal production and basic chemicals. Many of these industries and individual companies became either uncompetitive or subject to restructuring after 1989 and the regions in which they were concentrated were severely affected; the prospects are not optimistic.

Although an attempt at changing the sectoral structure has been made and central government has been subsidising improvement in the competitiveness of these industries, there are still many companies in trouble. As the transformation process proceeds and the economy opens to the normal European market conditions there is a strong possibility of various kinds of increasing difficulties in the affected regions.

The establishing of RDAs in the early 1990s

The position of the RDAs after their establishment has changed substantially, as have the needs of the regional actors, the economic relationships and local-regional-central links during the transformation of the society. The changing environment modified the motivations and attitudes of companies and public authorities, which consequently opened new opportunities for their development and for local and regional cooperation. The establishment and evolution of the RDAs have been very closely connected with prevailing ideas and the orientation of top managers and public representatives in the regions.

The first stage following 1990 was characterised by the non-coordinated effort of individual companies and public authorities at the rehabilitation of vertical links and redistributive financial flows from the centre. This effort was led particularly by large manufacturers before privatisation, and was not very successful because of a strong and quite opposite policy of central government at that time. In this early phase some attempts to coordinate or to institutionalise/formalise these lobbying pressures have been made. In spite of this no important or visible results have been reached.

RDAs in both the regions of North Bohemia and North Moravia were established in 1993. Rather uncertain conditions of unfinished privatisation and the beginning of the new state of the Czech Republic still characterised processes and relationships in the regions. The origins of the first RDAs were different but their goals and the expectations of their founders and potential clients were very similar. It was assumed that they would be able to obtain subsidies, grants and so on for regional development which consequently would be used by individual organisations for their own purposes. Regional actors had not been able to get sufficient financial support from the centre, so they established RDAs in the hope of diversifying the possibilities of obtaining financial resources from anywhere outside the region. The majority of these activities have failed, and as a result the political support for the RDAs from within the region has diminished.

The RDAs were in a difficult situation shortly after their establishment. There were almost no accessible resources at central government level; if central government and its agencies provided any support, it was in the form of specific subsidies under their direct control. To get support from other possible resources – such as from the PHARE programme – either some conceptual programmes or projects with greater regional impact were required. However, there were no such programmes and the regional actors themselves were individualistic, and therefore the RDAs were rather unsuccessful in their early years. An additional reason why the RDAs failed in their aspiration was due to their inexperience with the preparation and implementation of regional projects and with the coordination of various local actors. Being totally new institutions they have had to try to find their position/niche in the regions and to translate their goals and objectives into activities.

The next phase, which continues at the present, has been characterised by a gradual reorientation of public and private organisations to a bottom-up approach to the regional problems. Initially, functional regionally coordinated courses of action have slowly been revealed and initial horizontal networks have appeared.

This stage of the RDAs has meant a development of strategies and conceptual approaches to planning. This probably could not be possible without the massive support of the PHARE programme which has provided technical assistance in the planning stages as well as financial support for carrying out regional projects. As a general effect of this process the first regionally developed and financed projects have emerged. The market in which the RDAs can take part has opened, and the RDAs have gradually taken a role which could enable them to influence at least some partial activities at the regional level.

The PHARE programme played a key role in establishing the RDAs in the Czech Republic. While the RDAs have not simply been established only to get PHARE support – for example the RDA in Most, North Bohemia, existed as The Foundation Renaissance of Most more than one year before the PHARE funds became accessible – the PHARE programme was a strong encouragement for their activities, and both RDAs are still heavily dependent on the PHARE programme's financial support.

PHARE financial support in an environment of doubts, lack of state regional policy and shortage of both public as well as private financial resources did enable the RDAs to survive in their initial phase. Technical assistance and consultation services within the PHARE programme has helped the RDAs prepare and execute various projects, develop and promote their own activities and adjust to the changing economic environment. An important part of the PHARE support is the participation of foreign professionals and consultants in developing strategic plans for the future, both for the RDAs themselves as well as for the regions.

Description of the Czech RDAs

Regions covered by the activities of RDAs

The RDAs in the Czech Republic are located in two old industrial regions which were severely affected by extensive coal mining and the development of heavy industries during the socialist times. Both of the regions are the most urbanised in the Czech Republic, after that of the capital city, Prague. They include from 20 to 40 towns and cities and several hundred small municipalities, and have a population of about 0.8 million inhabitants.

Although the activities of the RDAs formally cover whole regions, individual projects are more or less focused on much smaller areas, usually towns and cities and their hinterlands. But there is a difference between the North Bohemian and the North Moravian agencies in the number and size of clients. In North Bohemia the majority of the services are provided for smaller cities and towns and cooperation with private companies is limited, the likely reasons for which are the multi-central character of the North Bohemia urbanised area and the very early phase of creating a horizontal network in the region. On the other hand the North Moravia has one strong centre, Ostrava (about 330,000 inhabitants), and the most important projects are connected with the development of this city. But both RDAs try to adhere to the policy that any project undertaken by an RDA has to have impact on a larger area.

Legal status and ownership of the RDAs

An important feature of the Czech RDAs is their legal status, which determines their operational freedom and the general orientation of their policy. The RDAs have been established as joint-stock companies with shareholders from both the private and public sector. This means that they are at least partially separated from various political pressures, and it also allows them to select and support projects according to professional rather than political criteria. But it also brings some obstacles into their work. Since the RDAs are formally independent companies they have to be financially self-reliable, which limits their freedom to work on projects to some extent; the number of projects carried out on contract for regional clients will play a more important role in future. Another problem of this legal status, particularly in the initial years after their establishment, was the lack of or insufficient political support from the founders. The early stage of both RDAs was very problematic and this was mainly caused by both the lack of interest of the establishing organisations and the low demand for their services of the RDAs at the regional level.

**Table 7.1 Current structure of shareholders
in RDAs (percentage of total)**

North Bohemia RDA, Most		North Moravia RDA, Ostrava	
Cities	30	Ministry of Economy	30
Banks	14	Association of Municipalities of Upper Silesia and North Moravia	35
Big industrial companies	40	Association for Reconstruction and Development in North Moravia and Silesia	35
Trade unions	12		
The Foundation Renaissance of Most	4		

Source: Regionální rozvojová agentura Most, Výroční Zpráva 1995 *(Annual Report).*

Current structure of shareholders of the RDAs

As regards North Bohemia the structure of owners is more diversified, which causes some difficulties in terms of political support. The North Bohemian agency is more dependent on a market approach in its work, and the amount of funds accessible for this RDA is much lower because it is not the administrator of PHARE funds but only the manager of some projects. Non-direct and more complicated access to funds for political sponsors can also be the reason for lower political support.

In North Moravia political sponsorship is more likely from the shareholders and also their interests in RDA activities have been much higher. This has been a big advantage. The Project Management Unit (PMU) role of this RDA could be a significant reason for the good participation of the political sponsors – it means that the RDA in Ostrava is not only the manager of projects but also the administrator of PHARE funds, and hence is responsible for the distribution of funds. Besides this, the very strong role of the City of Ostrava and the organisations based here accounts for the importance of this RDA.

Objectives and activities

The objectives of the RDAs in the Czech Republic are very similar although their particular activities are different. Important objectives in both cases, since RDAs are quite new organisations, is to develop a professional attitude for the RDA itself, to get sufficient technical equipment for providing clients with high quality services, to develop specific regional know-how and to become respectful organisations for the coordination of regional development programmes.

The main external objectives of RDAs are:

- the promotion of public-private partnership
- the coordination of regional development activities
- identifying common needs of various organisations at the regional level and supporting the creation of a regional network
- attracting inward investment
- the improvement of the regional image and its promotion outside the region.

RDAs carry out many activities to fulfil the objectives described above. These activities are mostly consultancy, information support and providing technical assistance to organisations realising various projects that are supported by the RDAs. The range of activities is wide and the RDAs are still in the stage of settling their position in the regions; they are open to various kinds of activities that are in accord with their main objectives.

The majority of the projects are in some way connected with support for SMEs. Many ways to support these businesses are either used or are being prepared by the Czech RDAs such as:

- the creation of regional information centres and business innovation centres in bigger cities to provide public and private representatives/organisations with comparative information on the status and current changes of social, economic and legislative issues
- information, consultancy and financial support in infrastructure development projects
- information on national and international programmes focusing on financial and technical aid to local and regional projects
- creating and updating regional databases (i.e. databases of premises, investment opportunities, etc.) for enterprises within and outside the region as well as for public authorities.

Other activities are focused on the general support of development effort:

- coordination and assistance in cross-border cooperation programmes
- establishing or supporting tourist information centres and publishing various promotional materials/brochures for different target groups
- participation in common activities of other regional subjects (coordination and information exchange)
- providing information support to government agencies and foreign institutions.

Only from 1995 have the RDAs in the Czech Republic had some viable political support and as a result their activities have been developing continuously since then. Currently it is not easy to distinguish 'core activities and objectives', i.e. the most important ones. On the other hand it is supposed that the activities described above will become inter-related in the near future, which will help the RDAs in improving their services.

Because the RDAs in North Bohemia and North Moravia work in different conditions, their activities also vary to some extent. The North Bohemian RDA in Most focuses on consultancy, technical assistance and information support in smaller projects for a number of clients, and its activities are more spread out across the whole region. Although a general development strategy for North Bohemia has been worked out, the projects are rather separated and they rarely have an impact on the whole region. In North Moravia, meanwhile, the activities are concentrated at the heart of the region, and the agency works for a limited number of clients and on a limited number of larger, long-term projects.

Financing

Both RDAs in the Czech Republic are part of the PHARE programme, although they each have different relationships to it. However they were established on the basis of the programme to react to the expected needs of regional actors, and hence the programme has a dominant role in the activities of RDAs and in the early years has also been their main financial resource. After all, this financial dependence on foreign supporters decreases only very slowly.

The origins of RDAs in the Czech Republic were very modest. As described above, initial difficulties caused a lack of projects and substantially limited the scope of activities. In the first period of existence of the RDAs their budgets ranged in tens of thousands of ECU. The real extension of their activities started in 1995 and continues up to now. There is a still big difference between two RDAs, for only one of them (North Moravia – Ostrava) has the status of a PHARE PMU, which it allows them direct access to European Union PHARE finance. The turnover of this RDA reached about 700,000 ECU in 1995. The North Bohemia RDA has to be more modest but has also expanded its activities and its budget substantially, with a turnover in 1995 of about three million CZK, or 90,000 ECU.

While the Ostrava RDA is focused on using PHARE financial resources predominantly and on executing a limited number of larger projects, the Most RDA was forced to look for local/national finance as although it also depends on PHARE support, but its financial resources are more diversified. Both RDAs however have tried to enlarge the number of projects carried out on a commercial basis and are probably being successful.

The role of RDAs in the regions of the Czech Republic

Instability is the most important characteristic of the RDAs in the Czech Republic. Changing economic and social conditions make them adapt to the specific and variable needs of public institutions and private companies, and they often have to modify their approach to solving regional problems. Within this framework it is therefore difficult for RDAs to pursue long-term strategies. The main causes of this are the enormous number of regional actors (hundreds of municipalities and thousands of businesses) together with the lack of functional, unifying institutional structures as well as limited and non-diversified financial resources. It is not difficult to develop a regional strategy, but it is extremely difficult to convince the regional organisations to accept it.

Despite this unstable environment the RDAs play a considerable role, especially in filling the gaps in the Czech economic and the public administration system and in changing the motivations and habits of Czech representatives at regional level. The main features of this role are described in the following paragraphs.

Despite the fact that the RDAs are aimed predominantly at promoting regional economic development they have to try to supply some functions usually undertaken by regional government. Unfortunately that level of government does not exist in the Czech Republic. Due to this situation several problems have persisted since the early 1990s.

First, central–local communication between cities and central agencies is very complicated because of the large number of municipalities. The RDAs try to act as a representative of the region in some cases where economic development is concerned. The effort to channel opinions of municipalities to the central level of public administration is accompanied by attempts to coordinate the activities of municipalities within the region. Hence the role of RDAs as mediator has two dimensions: a vertical one in mediating the bottom-up and top-down exchange of information and opinions, and a horizontal one which is aimed at getting a certain compromise among the interests of cities and towns: a compromise that could serve as a common or leading position for the region as a whole.

Second, due to the lack of regional government in the Czech Republic there is no regional partner on the Czech side for foreign regional bodies – governments, agencies and so on. The RDAs of course cannot fulfil the role of regional government representatives, but they do try to promote the common interests of the region. Again it is necessary to facilitate some general consensus among regional actors that could be presented outside the region.

The above-mentioned mediation role of the RDAs within the region among various individual organisations as well as between private and public sector in general is a very important one. There is almost no common understanding among public and private institutions for the regional dimension of policy and economic development. As a result the activities of individual organisations are often either counterproductive or at least non-coordinated. In this situation the role of the RDAs is to support the exchange of information, to develop a regional strategy acceptable for a majority of the regional subjects and finally to put in accord the various development activities of many individual actors. This is not an easy task and they are still at the beginning of a long process, but the first success has been achieved as the RDAs have been accepted in this role by the most important companies and public institutions.

An integral part of the facilitation role of the RDAs is the promotion of public–private partnership. The mistrust persisting between the private and public sector is a considerable obstacle to economic development, and the RDAs again act as a mediator, trying to support projects from which the private as well as the public sector can benefit.

The final role undertaken by the RDAs is the implementation of modern skills, knowledge and information concerning regional development. It includes the transformation of foreign methods to the Czech economic and legislative environment, the opening of access for selected projects to foreign financial aid, the promotion of various ways of development to SMEs, and consulting and implementing specific measures of local economic policy.

The future

The position of the RDAs has not yet been settled, but they have found a number of activities and roles that they can carry out better than any other institution. Their activities are likely to extend from mediation and support of small projects to getting involved in larger infrastructural developments, in which the RDA in Ostrava is more advanced. The RDAs will probably not become an important provider of financial support in terms of having their own money for granting projects or getting considerable financial support from their shareholders and political sponsors. On the other hand they have an increasing role in the coordination of local government development projects as well as in the coordination of private sector activities in accord with general regional interests.

The RDAs have introduced strategic planning methods to regions and have become respectable consultants in this field. This allows them to help the regional actors with the preparation of projects and development programmes which are necessary in order to apply for any financial support from outside. Because of their mediation role, the RDAs are the leading bodies in the planning approach to regional and local development and it is assumed that their professional experience will help them to stabilise their position.

There is still considerable uncertainty as far as the creation of regional government in the Czech Republic is concerned. Regional government is included in the Czech Constitution but has not yet been created. This issue is subject to political disputes which have been ongoing since 1991. There is a probability that a regional government tier will be created in 1998, however, at the time of writing, nothing certain can be said about the number of regions, their responsibilities and powers and so on.

The expected creation of regional government can help secure the position of the RDAs as important regional consultants and coordinators. At the same time there are some expected changes regarding the financial flows between centre, regions and localities that can extend the amounts of money spent on regional projects. The RDAs are the best prepared and most experienced organisations to implement this change to the benefit of the whole region.

Conclusion

The RDAs in the Czech Republic are part of the economic and social transformation process within society. They may not have been a too large or important part, especially at the very beginning of the process, but their significance has been increasing. They have found methods and strategies to respond to the needs and expectations of local and regional institutions, both private and public. But not only the RDAs have changed; the society itself has developed new approaches and modified its view of local-central relationships, and all the changes have caused a slow rise in the demand for services of RDAs.

The current situation of the RDAs in the Czech Republic is not yet a stable one but the prospect seems to be good. Their role becomes more important as they provide services for increasing the number of clients and work on larger projects.

Further Reading

Agentura pro regionální rozvoj, a.s. (1996) 'Výroční zpráva 1995'. Ostrava: Agentura pro regionální rozvoj, a.s., Ostrava.

Andrews, R.N.L., Paroha, L., Vozáb, J. and Šauer, P. (1994) 'Decentralized environmental management in the formerly communist states: a case study of Děčín, Czech Republic.' *Environmental Impact Assessment Review 14*, 111–136.

Bennet, R.J. (1993) 'European local government systems.' In R.J. Bennet (ed) *Local Government in the New Europe.* London: Belhaven Press.

Dostál, P. and Hampl, M. (1993) 'Territorial organization of society: Czechoslovak developments.' In R.J. Bennett (ed) *Local Government in the New Europe.* London: Belhaven Press.

Ministerstvo hospodářství CR (1996) 'Podpora podnikání v České, republice'. Praha: Ministerstvo hospodářství CR.

Perlín, R. and Vozáb, J. (1996) 'Public administration and territorial and administrative divisions in the Czech Republic.' In B. Krčová (ed) *Effective Democratic Development Through Cross-Sectoral Cooperation: The Case of the Czech Republic.* Prague: Institute for EastWest Studies.

Regionální rozvojová agentura, a.s. (1996) 'Výroční zpráva 1995'. Most: Regionální rozvojová agentura, a.s., Most.

Tomeš, J. (1996) 'Vývoj regionálních rozdílů nezaměstnanosti jako indikátor transformacních změn.' In M. Hampl (ed) 'Geografická organizace společnosti a transformační procesy v České republice'. Praha: Přírodovědecká fakulta University Karlovy.

CHAPTER 8

Transition, Institutions and Regional Development in Hungary, BAZ County

Anne Lorentzen

Introduction

The post-command economies of Central and Eastern Europe (CEE) are faced with a wide range of challenges, and regional development problems have become significant. The process of transition socially and geographically has had a very uneven impact in the CEE countries and Hungary is a case in point. The regional disparities represent a potential factor for political destabilisation, nationally and internationally, and therefore both national governments and the European Union have focused on the development of regional development strategies in CEE since 1992–93.

The deep crisis in the industrialised Borsod-Abaúj-Zemplen (BAZ) county (as well as in the neighbouring agricultural Szabolc-Szatmár-Bereg county) is the point of departure for experiments with the creation of new regional developmental institutions. For research, the experiences now being made in Hungary are of particular interest, because they widely reflect important new approaches to regional and industrial development.

It is of course too early to assess the impact of the new institutions on socioeconomic development. The intention of this article is much more limited. First, it will briefly characterise the economic crisis of BAZ in order to point out the major fields where action is needed. Second, it will analyse the institutional changes related to regional development in Hungary, with a focus on selected RDAs. The third and final part is an analysis of the first important output of the new regional development system, the development strategy for the BAZ county.

The article is based on ongoing research. Among other things it draws upon interviews with Hungarian enterprises and authorities made in 1993, 1994 and 1995. The present study is part of a wider research programme at Aalborg University, Denmark, on industrial change in Hungary after 1989.

The regional crisis of transition

The BAZ county is the area which has been most severely affected by the changes which have taken place in Hungary since 1989. This county contains 7 per cent of the Hungarian population (1994) or 744,000 inhabitants. It is an industrialised county which in 1990 employed 9.1 per cent of Hungary's industrial workers. Of particular importance is heavy industry. Thus 15.9 per cent of the Hungarian workers in the chemical industry, 17 per cent of the Hungarian mining workers and 23.5 per cent of the Hungarian metallurgy workers could be found in BAZ (BAZCDC 1995, p.4).

From 1990–92 industrial production dropped to 63 per cent of the 1990 level. The drop was most severe in engineering where the rate of decrease was 64 per cent, but even the strong chemical industry dropped by 30 per cent (BAZCDC 1995, p.4). The impact on employment is serious. The official unemployment rate in BAZ is 17.6 per cent, or about 60,000 persons (p.5). In other words: with 7 per cent of the population, BAZ has 11.5 per cent of the unemployed (the total number of unemployed in Hungary is 519,592 persons, Central Statistical Office 1995, p.64). The premises of prosperity in BAZ thus seem to have disappeared together with the planned economy.

Before World War I the industrial development of Hungary was mainly concentrated around Budapest, the capital. Its status as industrial centre was supported by a centralised railway network (Bernat 1989, p.109), and the rest of Hungary supplied raw materials from the mines, the forests and from agriculture. As a result, in 1949, 54 per cent of the industrial labour force was employed in Budapest.

The centralised model of development was challenged by the communists who came to power in 1949. The communist government wanted to reduce the dominance of Budapest and to eliminate regional disparities. In Hungary, as elsewhere, the development of backward areas at that time was synonymous with industrial growth, and the efforts of the government resulted in industrial development. An important premise of industrial and regional planning during the communist era was the amount and the structure of trade within CMEA (the Council of Mutual Economic Assistance).

Towards the end of the 1970s, industry was located more evenly than in 1950, as only 24.2 per cent of the people employed in industry worked in Budapest. The industrially developed counties were BAZ, Heves and Nógrád in the north, Komáron, Fejer and Veszprém west of Budapest, Györ-Sopron in the west and Baranya in the south. These counties accounted for 35.1 per cent of industrial employment in 1981.

After 1989 old regional disparities reappeared and new ones emerged. Budapest again became a magnet of investment, western Hungary prospered and the formerly flourishing BAZ was caught in a vicious circle of underdevelopment. Four factors seem to have triggered the downturn of BAZ.

The *international setting* was an important precondition for the industrial development of Hungary during communism. Regional specialisation and the strong concentration of industry within some branches which had proven successful until 1989 were in fact based on the large and stable demand within CMEA. BAZ benefited particularly from closeness to the Soviet Union, which bought a large part of the products from the heavy industry. CMEA trade broke down soon after the change in 1989, mainly because of the severe crisis of the Soviet Union. Shortly after, CMEA was formally dissolved.

Faced with Western competition the *industrial structure* of the heavy industry, characterised by large, vertically integrated companies, proved very inefficient and unable to compete on equal terms. One reason was their technology: equipment was out-dated, and product quality was low. (Lorentzen 1993, 1994a and 1997).

The *role of geography* is related to production culture and closeness to markets. Visits and interviews in Hungary suggest that in the eastern part of Hungary CMEA standards and ways of doing things prevail, whereas in the west of Hungary the proximity to Austria and Germany has made the enterprises acquainted with Western production culture through export-import relations. After 1989 the western Hungarian relations to the West accelerated, not only in terms of export, but also in terms of direct foreign investment (Losoncz 1994, p.106). Györ in western Hungary soon became the most prosperous and dynamic provincial town in Hungary with practically no unemployment. BAZ county, which has only attracted 3 per cent of the foreign capital going to Hungary (BAZCDC 1995, p.5), became the centre of industrial crisis. This 'east–west disparity' can also be found in other CEE countries. Poland in particular resembles Hungary in this respect (Downes 1995, p.3).

The global *crisis of metallurgy* hit BAZ particularly hard because of the mono-industrial structure of the county. Since 1980 metallurgy has been characterised by global restructuring and recession, and in Hungary employment fell from 50,000 in mid-1980 to 22,000 (1996). Planned modernisation is going to reduce the number of employed further, and it will not be economically viable to try to maintain its earlier magnitude (OECD 1994).

Engineering, closely connected to the needs of metallurgy, is now hit by the recession of metallurgy, by the general drop in investment, by foreign competition and by the end of the cold war. The latter has closed the production of armaments which has been important in BAZ.

Until now the market economy has been detrimental to the development of BAZ, and therefore BAZ is a case for public action. This implies a new role for national and local government in economic development.

Technological capacity and institutional capability

It is now widely acknowledged that the social dynamics of technological change are present at the sub-national level. Each sub-national region may possess characteristics which are not shared by other regions in the same nation. Thus Scott and Storper (1992, p.4) argue that today's economic geography can be conceptualised as a mosaic of specialised production regions, which are not autonomous, but dependent on other regions, not only within the nation, but also globally. The implication for development politics is that these should be tailor-made for the individual regions. Porter (1990, p.157) has found that entire clusters of internationally competitive industries are often located in a single town or region; and that it is the combination of national and local conditions that fosters competitive advantage. Therefore both state and local government can play a prominent role in industrial development.

Against this background it seems justified to approach the development of BAZ in terms of the change of its *regional technological capacity* (Lorentzen 1988 and 1994b). And consequently it becomes fruitful to discuss government action with a focus on the regional level.

A focal point in the change of technological capacity is a *change of technology* at enterprise level. Technology is embedded in socioeconomic structures (markets, production structure and infrastructure) which determine the path along which it is changed. However actual technology change is based on decisions taken and implemented by social agents or '*social carriers of technology*' and here the role of *institutions* is crucial.

Generally speaking institutions give encouragement to technological change and thereby to economic development, and they influence the direction of change.

According to North (1990) institutions are the rules of the game in society. They affect the performance of the economy by their effect on the costs of exchange and production. Institutions may be *general* (e.g. the market) or *specific* (e.g. a training institution) (Lall 1990). According to Ostrom, Schroeder and Wynne (1993) the institutions produce *incentives* (competition or openness towards new technology) and moreover, the social agents respond in a rational way to the incentives they meet because they want to optimise their benefit. However, rationalities may differ or conflict (e.g. environmental versus economic rationalities).

Both general and specific institutions and incentives may change, but it takes time, as they are rooted in history and in culture. Old and new institutions may coexist and produce counteracting incentives (Nagy 1994; Lorentzen 1996a). Therefore, when new institutions are installed, the outcome in terms of changed behaviour of the social agents is far from certain, as the social agents may respond to other institutions and incentives in ways other than the planners thought they would.

The actual impact of institutions on technological and economic development depends on the *capability of the individual institutions* (Lorentzen 1996b, p.7) and on the *institutional thickness in society* (Amin and Thrift 1994, pp.14–15).

In the present context institutional capability is regarded as the ability of institutions to produce incentives which are relevant in that they motivate the wanted change of behaviour, i.e. the introduction of new technology or investment in new productive activities. This capability tentatively can be seen as dependent on the legitimacy of the institution and of the extent to which it is embedded in society (Braathen 1996). Further, the capability is based on the resources at the disposal of the institution and the influence of the institution on their distribution, in brief, its power (Halkier 1996).

By institutional thickness is understood a plethora of institutions of different kinds with high levels of interaction among them, clearly defined roles and shared overall goals (e.g. regional industrial development) (Amin and Thrift 1994, pp.14–15).

The concept of institutional capability is applicable to specific institutions and may serve as a point of departure for an evaluation of their efforts to change the behaviour of the social (i.e. economic or technology) agents. The concept of institutional thickness is useful in the assessment of the relations between different institutions as well as in the societal analysis of the region.

Regional development institutions and RDAs

In the context of this paper a regional development institution is understood as a specific institution, the purpose of which is to produce incentives in favour of regional economic and technological development.

A recent stream of literature focuses on one particular part of the regional development institutions, namely the so-called regional development agencies (Halkier and Danson 1996, p.9). They have come particularly in focus in connection with EU regional development programmes. An RDA can be characterised as 'a regional, semiautonomous body, the purpose of which is to increase regional competitiveness and economic growth. Their instruments are to supply venture capital, advisory services, technical infrastructure and training. They consider regional development in an integrated way, their support is selective, discretionary and proactive' (p.9). It seems that traditional institutions and RDAs may exist side by side, the tasks of RDAs being to carry out certain aspects of the regional development policy in close contact with the target groups. The creation of RDAs and other regional development institutions may be both a means and an end in regional policy.

Under the planned economy the state and its branches was the prime economic and technology agent. In a market economy the role of government seldom is direct, and particularly today, due to liberal political winds both in Eastern and Western Europe, indirect public measures have gained momentum. A crucial task today in the development policy of BAZ is therefore to create institutions, including RDAs, which motivate the potential private entrepreneurs and enterprise managers to become social carriers of new technology in production and infrastructure.

The question is now how the emerging regional development institutions in Hungary and BAZ can be characterised in terms of institutional capability and institutional thickness.

Regional development institutions before 1989: a lacuna

The regional administration in Hungary for obvious reasons reflects the trends of change characterising the national administrative system (Sóvári 1995a, p.49).

Until 1920 Hungary consisted of 25 counties with traditions of widespread, although not democratically based, autonomy. In 1920 as part of the Treaty of Trianon, the number of counties was reduced to 19. This is the number of counties found in Hungary today.

At community level democratic national committees were established after the end of World War II. A certain degree of local and regional institutional autonomy thus belongs to the Hungarian tradition before 1948.

As part of the centralised planning system which was established in Hungary from 1949, the national committees were replaced by Soviet type councils. These councils were branches of the centralised state administration. In 1971 a new Act on councils allowed for some degree of self-government, however with no room for communities and civic organisations. Most ministries had – and still have – a regional department in charge of the sectoral development in the counties.

Regional administration in Hungary during the centralised planning period can be characterised as centralised and sectoralised. This was a general characteristic of Eastern European regional administration before 1989 (Artobolevskiy 1994, p.93). Decisions and initiatives concerning the economic development of the regions were taken at government or ministry level and 'all state plans were the sum of spatial proposals of the various ministries' (p.95), for example the ministry of labour, the ministry of industry and so on. Consequently the plans did not consider the regional socioeconomic development as independent goals and economic development of the regions did not take place in an integrated way.

After 1989 things started to change. In 1989 a new act on local governments replaced the 1600 local soviet-type councils with 3100 local governments, while the counties, under attack for being the fortress of the communist party, were assigned a more limited role (Farkas 1995; Sóvári 1995a, p.49). The local governments had been strengthened, but lacked resources in terms of money, experience and clear guidelines for their work. The counties had been weakened and lacked money and formal competence. Hungary was in lack of efficient regional and local units of self-government.

In sum, at the eve of transition, there were no institutions in Hungary, neither at central nor at the decentralised levels, with a capability to stimulate regional development. This lacuna turned into a great problem, as the crises of BAZ and other Hungarian regions made themselves felt after 1989.

The PHARE programme

The crisis and the resulting political pressure caused concern both in the Hungarian government and in the EU. Chronologically the EU was the first to produce results through the so-called PHARE regional programme. The role of PHARE is therefore the first point in the following description of the new regional development institutions in Hungary.

PHARE is the European Community's support programme directed towards the countries of Central and Eastern Europe (Commission of the European Communities 1992). The intention behind the programme is to help the governments to create the conditions of a market-oriented economy.

The most important focus of PHARE is not investment but institution building, and the focus has developed along with the rapid changes in the CEE countries. Originally the focus was to support the creation of structures or institutions of a market economy and the development of democracy. Since 1994 an additional goal has been to help the countries prepare themselves for their future membership of the EU (PHARE 1995, p.6).

The total activities of PHARE amounted from 1990 to 1994 to 4,248.85 mio ECUs (PHARE 1995, p.3). Poland, Hungary, Rumania and Bulgaria were the main receivers of PHARE funds between 1990–94. Together they received 59 per cent of the aid. Hungary alone received 12 per cent during this period, the largest amount in 1991 (based on PHARE 1995).

The involvement of PHARE starts with a dialogue between the Commission and the national government, who agree on annual 'indicative programmes' where priorities are set. On the basis of that, specific sectoral, regional or multilateral programmes are identified, and the necessary funds are committed. The subsequent implementation phase is managed by the national authorities (Commission of the European Communities 1992, p.9), which may receive technical assistance, through PHARE, to help them in this task. PHARE support thus implies the involvement of the recipient countries during all phases of the programme at different administrative and political levels. This brings about a learning process and a gradual approach to EU procedures.

PHARE and the regions

In 1993 a regional programme was approved in Brussels in the framework of the general PHARE programme (Farkas 1995, p.7). The regional programme of PHARE aims at developing EU compatible institutions and the creation of the basis for a regional development which can solve the crisis of depressed regions, mainly through a growth of the private sector.

In Hungary, the PHARE regional programme has consisted of three sub-programmes for the period 1994–96. Together these could spend 10 mio ECUs. One sub-programme should assist the Hungarian government in developing new legislation on regional development and planning. The aim was to decentralise decision making and to mobilise resources for the development of depressed regions. The new law was approved in March 1996. Another sub-programme was the Pilot Action Programme, which started in 1993 in the depressed areas of Hungary, Borsod-Abaúj-Zemplén county and Szabolc-Szatmár-Bereg county. A third sub-programme was to promote a new type of cooperation between small local governments, of which there are 3100 (Sóvári 1995b, p.52 and interviews). This phase of the PHARE regional programme ended in 1996. The continuation of the PHARE involvement now takes place as participation in development projects.

The Ministry of Environment and Regional Policy is the main Hungarian coordinator of the PHARE activities. In addition PHARE has got several representations in Budapest in relation to the programmes. But coordination has probably been the weak point of the first three years of the PHARE activities, which mainly took place at the decentralised level.

The pilot action programme

As mentioned PHARE chose two counties, namely BAZ, an industrial region, and Szabolc-Szatmár-Bereg, an agricultural region. The two counties should host pilot projects in institution building in relation to regional development. In that way an investment in a limited geographical area should have an impact in the whole of Hungary, as well as in other countries of CEE. Experiments were started with new institutional forms and procedures. This work started long before the contours of the regional development law were ready.

PHARE set up a new fund, the Pilot Action Fund (PAF), of 4.5 million ECUs for the period 1994–95. As it was formulated in 1994 the philosophy of this fund was to contribute to the economic development of the county and to explore the contribution of different types of local initiatives to that process as an alternative to the prevailing centralised approach to regional development. The PAF was intended to develop local/regional skills in project management and collaborative work in order to enhance the capability at county and local level to undertake regional development projects.

An important premise was the change of attitude of people by building confidence at the direct levels of regional decision making. During the programme period it should be possible to demonstrate the feasibility of a regional strategy and of local decision making. An overall intention was that in the end the law would be changed so that national regional development funds could be decentralised, and both resources and responsibility handed over to local authorities (PHARE 1994, p.1).

After three years of existence PAF has resulted in the creation of the County Development Council and its executive body, the County

Development Agency (since 1994). Many different institutions and individuals at county level have been involved in the development and the formulation of an integrated reconversion and crisis management programme for BAZ county.

In the following section the new institutions will be presented and analysed.

The new legislation on regional development and planning

The above-mentioned PHARE objective concerning new legislation went hand in hand with the intentions of the Hungarian governments (under prime ministers Antall and Horn) to do something about the development of poor regions. PHARE experts were involved as advisers, and finally in March 1996 the Act XXI of 1996 on regional development and physical planning was approved.

The new law represents a change in focus as it turns regional development into an issue in itself, as an alternative to the earlier sectorised and centralised approach to economic development. It represents an effort to change the top-down tradition in Hungarian regional development policy into a dynamic bottom-up movement of both initiative and resource mobilisation. By the law the responsibility of the central government is reduced, but made more precise than before. Correspondingly the responsibility of the decentralised institutions and of the private sector, represented through the chambers, is increased.

Coordination is a key word of the new law, not only in the overall aim of the law, but also in the detailed instructions concerning who is going to coordinate what with whom. The law draws up a system of regional development institutions, which implies a continuous mediation of interests, a coordination of aims and tasks, and a coordination of funds. Coordination takes place between the different administrative levels as well as between the participants at the same level.

In brief the objective of the law is to assist the development of a market economy in every region of the country and to create the necessary conditions for sustainable development. Further, the law aims at reducing significant differences between the Hungarian regions in terms of living conditions, economic, cultural, and infrastructural conditions, to prevent the formation of new crisis areas, and to ensure equal social opportunities. The institutions to be involved in this task are many, as follows.

Parliament must ensure that the government has a regional policy and that funds from the central budget are allocated for regional development purposes. The *government* must develop a regional policy in terms of a 'nation-wide regional development concept and principles' and propose the funds that can be used for regional development. The government must decentralise the funds and encourage the establishment of regional development associations, for example among local municipalities or between counties. Two coordinating bodies are to assist the government, namely a *National Council for Regional Development* which coordinates the national interests in regional development, and the *Ministry of Environment and Regional Development* which coordinates the regional tasks of the ministries.

Many institutions at different decentralised levels are by this law given a responsibility in relation to regional development. Thus *local governments*, of which there are 3100 as mentioned above, may enter into agreements to establish regional development associations in order to draw up joint development programmes and set up joint funds for such programmes. The *county self-governments* must coordinate the decentralised development activities, cooperate with the economic actors of the county, and approve the decisions of the county development councils.

The *county development councils* (CDCs) are envisaged to be the driving force behind the local development efforts. The CDCs are known from the pilot projet in BAZ and Szabolc-Szatmár-Bereg county. Now CDCs must be established in every county within 30 days of the announcement of the law. Participants in such CDCs are representatives of the private sector (the chambers), the County Self-Government, the national government and the County Labour Council, among others.

The task of the CDCs is to develop and approve the long-term regional development concepts and the regional development programmes of the counties, as well as the individual sub-programmes. While the operation of the CDC will be paid by the member organisations, the implementation of the development programmes and projects is to be financed by different sources. These include ministries and the EU, and financing must be negotiated each time a programme is planned. The *County Development Agency* (CDA) is the executive body of the CDC. The CDA will be discussed in detail in the section below on development institutions at the county level.

Like the local governments, the CDCs may cooperate and set up *regional development councils* which include several CDCs in order to be able to undertake common regional (cross county) development tasks, for example big EU-financed projects.

This combination of newly established and redefined institutions constitute the new integrated regional development system in Hungary. Along this, the old sectorised regional institutions still exist, like for example the regional department of the ministries. They are to implement the regional development tasks of the government, and they shall provide technical assistance, information and supervision.

While initiatives and decision making thus are decentralised, *funding* is basically centralised. The financial sources mentioned in the law all originate in the central budget, that is from the Regional Development Fund and the ministries, although 50 per cent of the money from the Regional Development Fund will be subject to decentralised decisions. The decentralised level may mobilise supplementary resources in terms of grants and loans (from international organisations) and voluntary contributions, whereas decentralised taxation is not mentioned as a possibility.

No doubt the law represents a great leap forward for regional development policy and development in Hungary. It allows for a more locally rooted regional policy and for flexibility. The regional policy ideas and initiatives will be better coordinated and the expenses will be subject to more control and evaluation through the programme and project forms.

The weak points of the law seem to be the unclear distribution of responsibility, both horizontally and vertically. The coexistence of old centralised and sectorised institutions and new decentralised and integrated institutions represents a contradiction which may blur goals and legitimacy in regional development. Further the unstable stream of financial resources may represent a barrier to action at the decentralised levels. Finally there seems to be a contradiction between the decentralised responsibility on the one hand and the centralised funding on the other.

As a whole, the overall institutional capability and the thickness of institutions related to regional development is increased by the law. Below the institutional changes at county level will be assessed.

Development institutions at county level

Three of the new regional development institutions have been chosen for an in-depth study, based on interviews, literature and official documents. The three institutions can be considered RDAs. The chosen institutions are the local enterprise agencies, the chambers of commerce and the county development agencies. These institutions emerged at different points of time, their goals differ, but their tasks are interwoven with each other, and they all operate in the field between the private and public spheres, with private sector development as a major objective.

Local enterprise agencies

The so-called local enterprise agencies (LEAs) were the first new regional development institutions in Hungary, and a network of LEAs thus has been established since 1991 by the initiative of PHARE, as part of the programme on SMEs (PHARE doc 1993). In the context of LEAs small businesses are here understood as enterprises with ten employees or less. The 19 LEAs have a coordinating body, the Hungarian Foundation for Enterprise Promotion. This is an independent institution, which was set up in 1990. In 1994 a LEA had been established in every county (interview, Nov. 1995).

The LEAs serve entrepreneurs who are just about to start, and newly established firms during their first two years of existence. During the first phase PHARE financed the whole programme; the Hungarian Foundation for Enterprise Promotion has direct contact with PHARE and channels the money to the LEAs. Today PHARE only finances part of the daily operations. The idea is that, in a few years, the LEAs shall raise their own funding, for example by selling their services and applying for funds. The activities consist of financial support, courses and consultancy directed towards the local community. In addition the LEAs participate in defining regional development goals and projects.

BAZ had already established its LEA in 1991 (interview, Nov. 1994). The main office is situated in Miskolc, there are five sub-centres in other locations in the county and 17 information offices. A total of 24 people work in the LEA in BAZ county, of which five are in Miskolc, namely an economist, three engineers and a secretary (interview, Nov. 1994). Most people connected to LEA BAZ have been entrepreneurs themselves, so they know the world of the target group quite well (interview, Nov. 1995).

The formal focus of LEA BAZ, like any LEA, is quite narrow and precise, but neither LEA Györ nor LEA BAZ stayed within the limits. They also participated in the formulation of regional development goals and projects.

Compared to the LEA in Györ where small and medium-sized enterprises blossom, the task of LEA Miskolc is much more to participate in the change of the enterprise structure of the county and the creation of an enterprise culture. Thus apart from training, consultancy and the micro-credit programme, which presupposes the existence of small enterprises, LEA Miskolc together with other local partners is involved in the creation of an industrial park and in the development of a technology centre at Miskolc University (interview, Nov. 1994), and of course it has been involved in the development of the integrated crisis and reconversion programme for BAZ county (interview, Nov. 1995).

The strength of the LEA as a regional development institution is related to its network and to its knowledge. This network consists of the direct contacts with private enterprises and entrepreneurs, contacts with public authorities at county level and, at national level, through the Hungarian Foundation of Enterprise Promotion, the contacts with other LEAs and with national authorities. Another resource is the practical entrepreneurial approach of the staff.

The weak point of the LEA BAZ is related to resources and goals: it is difficult to find sponsors for the activities, so that, for example at least for the first four years, the LEA BAZ did not have any computers. A general weakness is that the LEAs tend to do parallel work with the other two regional development institutions, the Chamber of Commerce and the Regional Development Agency, which may lead to a waste of resources. The future impact of the self-financing model on the goals and operations of LEA has to be seen. Finally the use of LEA services by part of the private sector seems to depend on the general economic climate and the entrepreneurial culture. On this point BAZ county is a difficult place for a LEA to operate.

The chambers of commerce

The chambers of commerce are new in Hungary. A law on economic chambers was passed in March 1994 (Dunai 1995, p.18) according to which chambers should be established before October 1994. The role of chambers as regional development institutions is due to the fact that they are organised on a regional basis. The permanent staff and their activities may be considered an RDA. In each county plus in Budapest three chambers have been established, one for agriculture, one for artisans and one for industry and trade. The regional chambers together form three national chambers located in Budapest. The county chambers are, according to the law on regional development and physical planning, represented in the county development committees.

The number of staff of the chamber in Győr is six persons (1994), while in BAZ it is 17 (1995). The goal of the chambers is to promote economic activities in the county. The first task of a chamber is to register the members, the enterprises, in order to collect fees and to establish a mailing list for newsletters, and to correct the old information about the enterprises. In BAZ there are now (1995) 22,000 members in the chambers, in Győr 21,000 (1994). The key words in the work of the chambers are information and advice, matchmaking, cooperation and, of course, representation. For example the chamber was represented in the development of the 'integrated reconversion and crisis management programme'.

The strength of the chambers is the network of information and cooperation, locally, nationally and internationally. But while the chambers have been welcomed and accepted in Győr this is not so much the case in BAZ. Therefore main weaknesses in relation to the chamber in BAZ are the lack of money, and the lack of confidence and legitimacy among the members. Without these it is difficult to promote any change in the target groups, in spite of the many incentives produced by the chamber.

The county development agencies

The County Development Agency (CDA) is a result of the pilot action programme of PHARE in Szabolc-Szatmár-Bereg and in BAZ. The CDA is the secretariat of the County Development Council. A CDA was established in Szabolc-Szatmár-Bereg in October 1994, and in BAZ in November 1994 (interview, Nov. 1995). After the establishment, the PHARE experts continued to work rather intensively with the CDAs. The intention was to enhance the institutional capability of the CDAs in terms of local decision making, cooperation with other partners, recruitment of personnel and development of qualifications. The ends and means of the process were to develop a development strategy of the county. The pilot action programme ended in June 1996, and PHARE support to regional development is now continued in the form of programme support.

The general task of the CDA is to be in the centre of local decision making and in the centre of local development initiatives. More specifically the main task of the CDA in BAZ until now has been the coordination of the 150 experts, divided into 15 subgroups covering eight sub-programmes, who developed the county development strategy. The CDA staff members participated in every subgroup. People from the sector ministries also participated.

Through this process an increased awareness of the problems and the potentials of the county was produced, a regional network of experts was created, and the participants learned new forms of cooperation. Finally, new forms of implementation were introduced, which were operational in terms of responsibility and funding (interview, Nov. 1995).

The position of the CDA is, in the intention of PHARE, a *coordinating* one. The CDA must thus keep contact with the other organisations in the county, for example the LEA, the Chamber of Commerce, the university, the regional job-centre and the different representatives of the ministries in the county who are working on aspects of regional development. While the mentioned institutions all have direct contact with the enterprises, with the unemployed, and so on, the CDA should integrate the ideas and experiences and propose development initiatives and strategies to the County Development Council. The latter then allocates the money (interview, Nov. 1994). In this way the CDAs should operate at a higher, more aggregate, level than the LEA, the Chamber of Commerce and the other regional development institutions (interview, Nov. 1994).

The staff of the CDA in BAZ consists of a general director and four managers, all with academic backgrounds and experiences from industry. These four managers have in principle four different tasks but cooperate a lot. In 1995 one major concern was to expand the staff, but at that time future funding of the agency was not secured. Daily operations were paid by a fund then consisting of government money, PHARE money and support from 13 local governments (interview, Nov. 1995). The new law decentralises the national Regional Development Fund, and this will probably stabilise the financial situation of the CDAs.

The CDAs are thus given a crucial role in the new system of regional development institutions as the new integrating level of regional development initiatives.

A major strength of the CDA in BAZ is the newly established external network and the qualifications as well as the attitudes of the staff. The CDA is probably the institution where the new concept of integrated, 'bottom-up' regional development is most strongly represented.

The weakness of the CDA is among other things related to the relatively scarce resources in terms of a small number of staff. The success of the CDA is extremely dependent on the 'fiery souls' who are employed at present. Another weakness is related to the institutional context of the CDA. This context is characterised by potential competition from other county level and state level institutions, and by conflicting attitudes (top-down, sectorised versus bottom-up and integrated development concepts). This may lead to problems of legitimacy. Finally the CDA owes resources and legitimacy to PHARE, which will be phased out.

The integrated reconversion and crisis management programme of BAZ

The preparation of the 'integrated reconversion and crisis management programme' started in 1994, when a draft development strategy was made in the county with the help of PHARE. The further elaboration of the programme was the first task of the newly founded CDA. The formulation of the programme was finished in June 1995. The County Development Council approved the programme soon after, and the government approved it with some modifications towards the end of 1995.

The objective of the strategy is to increase the county's economic potential in a long-term perspective, based on the mobilisation of economic actors from the private, the state and the communal sectors; the county must adapt to the new capitalist environment. Environmental concerns are also included as a main priority (BAZCDC 1995, p.9).

Table 8.1 Summary of the financing of integrated reconversion and crisis management programme for Borsod-Abaúj-Zemplén county (1995–98, millions)

Sub-programme	State		PHARE		Self financing		Grand total		Distri- bution
	HUF	%	HUF	%	HUF	%	HUF	%	%
1. Business consulting and business services	60	12	299	58	158	31	517	100	2
2. Provision of capital	6514	40	1635	10.1	7967	49	16,116	100	53
3. Business intrastructure	728	52	494	35	176	13	1398	100	5
4. System of sub-regional institutions	25	18	95	68	20	14	140	100	0.5
5. Macro-economic conditions	–	–	–	–	–	–	–	–	–
6. Training	64	25	188	74	2	1	254	100	1
7. Measures for special groups	639	58	204	19	257	23	1100	100	4
8. Physical conditions of economic development	9247	85	635	6	957	9	10,839	100	36
TOTAL	17,277	56	3550	12	9537	31	30,364	100	100

Source: BAZCDC, June 1995.

The sectoral priorities of the strategy are, in this order, the development of tourism, the modernisation of agriculture, and the development of the processing industry. A particular focus is on the development of agro-industries. In brief, other priorities are a development of the business sector, increased competitiveness, greater social and economic cohesion, a development of the workforce in terms of qualifications, and an improvement in the physical environment of the enterprises (BAZCDC 1995, p.17).

The total costs of the programme are 30.363 mio Hungarian Forints of 202 mio ECU for the three-year period 1995–98. The distribution of funds among eight proposed sub-programmes can be seen in Table 8.1.

The specific development activities resulting from the programmes are related to projects. Projects will be proposed by different applicants in the county. These could be, for example, enterprises, registered civic organisation and self-governments and universities (PHARE 1994, p.7).

It is of course much too early for an evaluation of the 'integrated programme', but it invites a few comments concerning the priorities, the sub-programmes and their implementation in terms of budget and organisation.

The sectoral development priorities reflect an *alternative technological capacity* to the one existing in BAZ today. Both tourism and agro-industrial production, which have high priority, are today very small sectors in the BAZ economy. On the other hand there is no explicit point of departure in the existing engineering and chemical industries, which in spite of structural problems, represent important economic and technological potentials. Other priorities are generally designed to stimulate the emergence of SMEs, while there is no consideration about the future of the existing big and privatised enterprises. The discontinuity between priority and reality in the sectoral priorities is likely to make the development efforts difficult and expensive.

The sub-programmes can be seen as designed to create an infrastructural basis for private business development. Judging from the budget there is a clear bias in favour of *financial infrastructure* (provision of capital, 53%), and *physical infrastructure* (programme 3 and 8, 41%). *Social infrastructure* training and measures for special groups is small (5%), while *technological infrastructure* (programme 1) is negligible with 2 per cent. *Institution building* will continue with only 0.5 per cent of the budget. While it seems justified to focus so much on the provision of capital, the dominance of physical infrastructure is not justified. It does not seem to match the development priorities, and if the technological capacity of BAZ is going to be developed or radically changed, the development of the social and of the technological infrastructure must have a high priority.

The role of PHARE in relation to financing can be seen as the mobilisation of Hungarian resources at government and at county level. In the financing plan PHARE is thus going to contribute about 12 per cent of the costs between 1995 and 1998. The Hungarian state will contribute 56 per cent and the self-financing share of the county will be 31 per cent. PHARE thus through the limited contribution is able to exert a pressure both on the priorities and on the mobilisation of the Hungarian resources, because of the threat of withdrawal of PHARE support.

The success of the programme depends on the number of projects worthy of support. This again depends on the awareness of the general public about the programmes. It also depends on the ability of the applicants to elaborate relevant and realistic projects. While the many regional development institutions may produce sufficient PR, it is still a hurdle to produce good applications, including to fulfil the degree of self-financing which is a precondition for support. The future will show whether the number of relevant projects matches the expectations. The wider socioeconomic development effects of the programme for the BAZ depends on that.

Summary and conclusion

The crisis in BAZ is due to the loss of Eastern markets, cultural and geographic distance to new markets, the global crisis of traditional industries, the mono-industrial character of the regional economy and the outdated technology. A precondition for renewed wealth and employment in BAZ is the development of competitive industries. This again requires new market possibilities and new supportive infrastructures. In order to motivate the economic agents to become involved in the development of industrial production, institutional change is crucial.

Through national and international initiatives a movement towards integrated and decentralised development institutions has begun in Hungary, which is of great importance for the development of the regional economy of BAZ. A new law formally establishes a new system of regional development institutions. The actual impact of the new institutions will depend on their *legitimacy* and *resources* as well as on their *thickness*. With a particular focus on three newly established RDAs the following tentative conclusion can be drawn.

Within a very short timespan many regional development institutions have been established in Hungary. They cooperate quite closely and share important views and goals, although they operate at different levels and with different target groups. Thus a considerable thickness of new regional development institutions has developed.

However, the new institutions co-exist with old centralised and sectorised institutions, and there is therefore an inbuilt contradiction in the present regional institutional system in Hungary, which is likely to weaken the new RDAs in terms of resources and legitimacy. In addition, two of the three RDAs studied here owe resources as well as legitimacy to the EU's PHARE programme. As PHARE's regional programmes run out the new RDAs must work both for their legitimacy and resources as a precondition for the production of incentives for the target groups. So far incentives for overall private sector development as well as for industrial technological change have been produced, but it is too early to assess the wider socioeconomic impact of these incentives.

The regional development strategy of BAZ is the first important outcome of the new regional institutional system. The process has in itself contributed to the institutional thickness through the shared insight and the consensus which has been obtained by the participants. Each sub-programme represents incentives for private sector development. An analysis of the strategy reveals the very wide gap between the goals and priorities of the strategy and the present situation, as well as a lack of balance in the proposed measures, where the creation of social and technological infrastructure is practically ignored. In any case the better provision of capital may represent an important incentive to small investors, but not necessarily in industry or in new technology.

References

Act XXI of 1996 on regional development and physical planning. Hungary.

Amin, A. and Thrift, N. (1994) 'Living in the global.' In A. Amin and N. Thrift (eds) *Globalization, Institutions and Regional Development in Europe*. Oxford, New York: Oxford University Press.

Artobolevskiy, S.S. (1994) 'Regional policy in Western and Eastern Europe: two approaches.' In Z. Hajdú and G. Horvath (eds) *European Challenges and Hungarian Responses in Regional Policy*. Pécs: Center for Regional Studies, Hungarian Academy of Sciences.

BAZCDC (Borsod-Abaúj-Zemplén County Development Council) (1995) *Integrated Reconversion and Crisis Management Programme for Borsod-Abaúj-Zemplén County*. Miskolc, June 1995. Mimeo.

Bernat, T. (1989) *An Economic Geography of Hungary*. Budapest: Akadémiai Kiadó.

Braathen, E. (1996) 'The Relationship Between State, Institutions and Organisations.' Lecture at the PhD seminar *International Technology Transfer*. Aalborg University, Denmark, 5–7 June.

Central Statistical Office (1995) *Statistical Yearbook of Hungary*. Budapest: Central Statistical Office.

Commission of the European Communities (1992) *PHARE. Assistance for Economic Restructuring in the Countries of Central and Eastern Europe. An Operational Guide*. Luxembourg: Commission of the European Communities.

Downes, R. (1995) 'Regional Policy Development in Central and Eastern Europe.' Paper presented at the Regional Futures Conference, Regional Studies Association, Gothenburg, Sweden, 6–9 May.

Farkas, B. (1995) 'Regional Policy in Hungary: Tendencies in the Transition Period.' Paper presented at the Regional Futures Conference, Regional Studies Association, Gothenburg, Sweden, 6–9 May.

Halkier, H. (1996) 'Institutions, power and regional policy.' *European Studies 16*. Aalborg: Aalborg University, European Research Unit.

Halkier, H. and Danson, M. (1996) 'Regional development agencies in Western Europe. A survey of key characteristics and trends.' *European Studies 15*. Aalborg: Aalborg University, European Research Unit.

Lall, S. (1990) *Building Industrial Competitiveness in Developing Countries*. Paris: OECD, Development Centre Studies.

Lorentzen, A. (1988) 'Technological capacity. A contribution to a comprehensive understanding of technology and development in an international perspective.' *Technology and Society Series 5*. Aalborg: Aalborg University Press.

Lorentzen, A. (1993) 'Industrial Technological Change and the Scope for Industrial Policy in the Process of Transformation: The Case of Hungary.' Paper presented at the EADI 7th general conference, *Transformation and Development in Eastern Europe and the South*. Berlin 15–18 September.

Lorentzen, A. (1994a) 'Technological Change in Hungarian Industry – Is There a Way?' Paper presented at the conference *East Europe: Between Western Europe and East Asia*. Aalborg University, May 19–21.

Lorentzen, A. (1994b) 'Teknologi og udvikling i den nordjyske maskinindustri (Technology and development of the machine-building industry of Northern Jutland).' *Technology and Society, Series 10*. Aalborg: Aalborg University Press.

Lorentzen, A. (1996a) 'Regional development and institutions in Hungary. Past present and future development.' *European Planning Studies 4*, 3, 259–277.

Lorentzen, A. (1996b) 'Crisis, Institutions and Technological Change, in BAZ County, Hungary.' Paper presented at the EADI 8th general conference *Globalisation, Competitiveness and Human Security. Challenges for Development and Institutional Change*. Vienna, 11–14 September.

Lorentzen, A. (1997) 'Technological change in Hungarian industry – is there a way?' In A. Lorentzen and M. Rostgård (eds) *The Aftermath of 'Real Existing Socialism in Europe' Volume 2: People and Technology in the Process of Transition*. Basingstoke: Macmillan.

Losoncz, M. (1994) 'Hungary and the European integration.' In Z. Hajdú and G. Horváth (eds) *European Challenges and Hungarian Responses in Regional Policy*. Pécs: Centre for Regional Studies, Hungarian Academy of Sciences.

Nagy, A. (1994) 'Transition and institutional change.' *Structural Change and Economic Dynamics 5*, 2, 315–328.

North, D.C. (1990) *Institutions, Institutional Change and Economic Performance*. Cambridge: Cambridge University Press.

OECD (1994) 'Synthesis report on the seminar: The Steel Industry in Transition. Financial and Privatisation Issues.' *OECD Working Papers, No. 77*. Paris: OECD.

Ostrom, E., Schroeder, L. and Wynne, S. (1993) *Institutional Incentives and Sustainable Development*. Boulder, San Francisco, Oxford: Westview Press.

PHARE doc (1993) *Cooperation Programme between the European Union and the Republic of Hungary. PHARE Indicative Programme 1994–95, annex 2: Review of Main PHARE Programmes 1990–1993*. PHARE. Mimeo.

PHARE doc (1994) *The Criteria and Application Procedure of the Pilot Action Fund in Borsod-Abaúj-Zemplén County*. (HPH-1372/94). Miskolc: Regional Development Council, Miskolc. Mimeo.

PHARE (1995) *PHARE Årsberetning 1994 (PHARE Yearly report, 1994)*. Bruxelles 20.7.95Kom.95(366).

Porter, M. (1990) *The Competitive Advantage of Nations*. Basingstoke: Macmillan.

Scott, A.J. and Storper, M. (1992) 'Regional development reconsidered.' In E. Huib and V. Meier (eds) *Regional Development and Contemporary Industrial Response*. London, New York: Belhaven Press.

Sóvári, G. (1995a) 'Less money, more tasks.' *Hungarian Economic Review 24*, February, 48–49.

Further reading

Dunai, Péter (1995) 'Chamber report. Chambers in a new role.' *Hungarian Economic Review 24*, February, 18–19.

European Bank for Reconstruction and Development (1994) *Transition Report*. London: European Bank for Reconstruction and Development, October.

Sóvári, G. (1995b) 'Regional development: a country split in two.' *Hungarian Economic Review 24*, February, 51–52.

Van Zon, H. (1994) 'Towards regional innovation systems in Central Europe.' In Z. Hajdú and G. Horváth (eds) *European Challenges and Hungarian Responses in Regional Policy*. Pécs: Centre for Regional Studies, Hungarian Academy of Sciences.

PART IV

RDAs, Regional Governance and Accountability

A perennial question in the assessment of the delivery of policy at the sub-national level concerns governance, and in particular the extent to which RDAs are accountable and to whom. Also, recent years have witnessed a restructuring of the relationship between agencies at the regional level with, increasingly over the last decade, the EU playing an important part in encouraging the delivery of Structural Funds support through partnerships of public and semi-public bodies, political authorities and other organisations. The question of accountability has become more complex, therefore, with RDAs having to address not only their own and their political sponsors' agenda but also the priorities and programmes of other institutions operating in the area. Many of these new partnerships have been established, often specifically, to deliver strategic planning and integrated programmes, so impacting directly on the core responsibilities of the RDAs.

Developing such a framework for organising local and regional economic development has ensured that RDAs have been presented with complementary and alternative roles in the governance of public policy and resources. Decentralising decision making to local and regional organisations in the context of multi-annual, region-wide programmes it is believed would improve coordination and synergy between projects. Yet this partnership approach also represents an alternative form of governance over national and supra-national expenditure to the traditional arm's length quango. In many areas partnerships have been dominated by central government and its regional offices, with other economic and social partners, especially the private and voluntary sectors and the trades unions, effectively marginalised. There is some evidence to suggest, however, that they have allowed the main sub-national institutions to collaborate in strategic and innovative ways. In some parts of Europe, Scotland, Wales and Belgium for instance, experience with a series of bottom-up partnerships and contractual agreements between local and regional economic development institutions has promoted the evolution of a more coherent and cooperative form of regional governance structure.

This section draws on the lessons of RDAs in such areas to explore the issues of regional governance and accountability more deeply, with four chapters concentrating on differing aspects of the debates. In discussing the emerging characteristics of regional development agencies in Flanders, Rik Houthaeve focuses on the importance of interactions between institutions. This allows a better understanding, within an historical, social, political and economic context, of their evolving role in regional development and strategic spatial planning. He demonstrates that differences in current policy regimes often arise from past experiences of policy making and implementation, economic structures and cultures of economic development. So, Houthaeve illustrates that forms of regional governance of RDAs cannot be divorced from the environments which have created and developed such institutions.

Jim Hughes addresses the particular role of rural agencies in his discussion of regional development institutions in the UK. Drawing on his extensive academic and practitioner background expertise, he uses his own experience of the first multi-functional RDA in the British Isles, the Highlands and Islands Development Board, to explore the differences in culture between the 'research' and the 'executive' communities. He argues that awareness of these differences is essential if research analysis and conclusions are to influence real policies. Inevitably questions of the forms of governance, strategy, leadership, and management are investigated, because formal structures provide the framework and channels through which development and planning forces operate. Critically, Hughes also argues that the 'spirit of the organisation' determines how the agency works, and so how efficient and effective it is in the pursuit of its objectives. As 'learning organisations' they are dependent on the resources devoted to research in meeting the challenges of rural development.

The significance of the lessons and successes of the Scottish regional development institutions in the wider UK context should not be underestimated. Initial plans for RDAs in the English regions, as drawn up by the 1996 Millan Commission into regional policy options, are largely based on the Scottish Development Agency model of the early 1970s. John Fairley and Greg Lloyd contribute a chapter on an evaluation of the philosophy, policy and programmes of Scottish Enterprise, partly based on their roles as specialist advisers to the Scottish Affairs Committee of the UK Parliament. Building on both theories of regional strategic planning and public sector management, they parallel Houthaeve's study by emphasising how the essential governance and corporatist tendencies in Scotland differ from the rest of the UK. They support the proposition that tradition and political culture are critical elements in the determination of the success of the RDA model of regional economic development, wherever it is located.

The increasing tendency for RDAs to be operating in partnership environment with other agencies and authorities is addressed by Jan Olsson in his account of planning regional development in a European Structural Funds policy context. Discussing democratic accountability specifically, he focuses on aspects of regional governance in EU single-programme documents. The planning process has evolved into a partnership framework in Sweden, with the involvement of local and regional politicians, business organisations, trades unions and other social partners as well as the regional bureaucracy. As argued above, how the latter network, cooperate and interact with their partners will be significant in the future success of many regions and RDAs, not only in Sweden but across Europe. Olsson applies himself to such issues in a refreshing and systematic manner so that the analyst of RDAs can understand more fully the evolving role of these agencies in the democratic planning process. At the hub of this debate lies a potential conflict between accountability and political control on the one hand, and administrative efficiency and effectiveness on the other. Whether it is more advantageous to leave the prioritisation of plans and strategies to the bureaucrats or to the unspecialised elected members remains unresolved at this stage.

CHAPTER 9

Changing Aspects of the Role of Regional Development Agencies in Flanders (Belgium)

The Case of West Flanders

Rik Houthaeve

Introduction

This paper examines some aspects of the role of regional development agencies in Flanders (Belgium) in regional development policy making. Flanders, Wallonnia and the capital region of Brussels are the three regions into which Belgium has been 'federalised'. Flanders lies in the densely populated and urbanised centre of the European Union. It has a surface of about 13,500 square kilometres and a population of almost six million people. The province of West Flanders is the most western of the five Flemish provinces and borders on the North of France. The district of Kortrijk is highly urbanised and industrialised and situated in the south of the province, near the French town of Lille.

This report is based on observations made during an ongoing research project on recent processes of strategic spatial planning at the regional level in Flanders. Indirectly this research has yielded knowledge on the role of regional development agencies in plan making and decision making about regional spatial organisation. The basic research focused on the process of elaborating a 'spatial structure plan' for the province of West Flanders and the revision of the West Flemish sector plans (sub-regional zoning plans), in which the regional development agency of West Flanders (the Gewestelijke Ontwikkelingsmaatschappij (GOM) West-Vlaanderen) played an influential role. We then analysed the role of the inter-municipal development agency (Leiedal) in the district of Kortrijk in a project in which 12 local authorities are formulating a common 'general local development plan'. We paid special attention to the role of the regional development agency and the inter-municipal development agency in steering the debate on the spatial and economical development of their (sub)region, thereby setting the agenda for regional planning. We have observed that these agencies established key positions in plan-making processes concerning spatial organisation and development. This key position was a favourable factor in generating the main concepts of the spatial organisation and development of each (sub)region and consequently in influencing the perception of other actors and framing the decision-making processes.

We can relate this role to the historical development of these agencies. In this report we describe these institutions in a broader (historical, social, political and economic) perspective in order to understand some aspects of their actual role in regional development and strategic spatial planning. The regional development agency of West Flanders was particularly active, for instance, in reional economic research, direct interventions in the economic field (supporting investments in infrastructure, industrial zoning, the facilitation of private and public investments) and the conception of spatial planning. The role of this development agency can be examined in relation to the evolution of concepts and practice of regional policy in general and spatial planning for the purpose of economic development in particular.

We will also pay special attention to changing elements in the context in which the agencies operate, in order to deduce some changes in their role in policy-making processes on spatial organisation. The role of regional development agencies in regional development policy making is influenced by changes in their institutional context and conceptual changes in policy-making. The latter refers for instance to the policy making in and around European programmes for regional development, the devolution process of Belgium, the emergence of a government for the Flemish region and consequently the elaboration of Flemish regional policy. The former refers to the transformation of the role of state intervention, the emphasis on local and regional partnerships, endogenous economic development, inter-regional competition and policy changes in Flemish strategic spatial planning.

Within the ongoing institutional developments in Flanders the changing role of the regional development agencies can be seen most particularly in their activity on the intermediate level of policy making as until very recently no statutory intermediate spatial planning level existed.

The unfolding of regional development policy in Belgium

The post-war conception of regional development policy

Since the middle of the 1950s a programme of 'regional development' has been instituted in Belgium to deal with so-called 'backward' regions. This policy was formalised in the General and Specific Expansion Legislation (1959). In comparison with other Western European countries the establishment of such legislation came rather late. In the early post-war period economic life could be restarted almost immediately, since the industrial capacity and infrastructural potential of Belgium were not so badly damaged (Albrechts 1992). The slowing down of economic growth during the 1950s, such as the decline of coal mining in Wallonia, stimulated this legislation (Gay 1989).

The general objectives of the regional economic development policy were a more balanced economic and social development and welfare, and consequently a better distribution of the allocation of the production structure. For that purpose 'development areas' were established. The programmes of economic incentives concerned with these areas provided, on the one hand, subsidies to support investments by private enterprises and, on the other hand, support by the national government for the construction of infrastructural accessibility, the development of 'industrial estates' or the implementation of a 'reconversion' programme for declining regional industrial structure. The legislation of 1959 also gave public authorities the power to encourage firms to move into 'development areas'. Parallel to the development of the economic planning system a process was started to work out a spatial planning system.

The relationship with strategic spatial planning

The Belgian spatial planning system was largely based on legislation passed at the end of World War II, which provided municipal spatial planning. The need for greater intervention in local planning resulted in the eventual Planning Act (1962). Its objective was the provision of a system of hierarchical statutory plans on the regional, sub-regional and local levels.

The elaboration of the post-war planning system started, parallel with the parliamentary preparations for the Planning Act as soon as the 1950s, when 20 regional studies were commissioned. The outcome of these studies (proposals for strategic spatial organisation and regional (economic) development) were of great conceptual influence, for instance in regional development programmes, but they did not result in statutory regional plans. The discussions and conflicts between the two Belgian communities (the Flemish and the French-speaking communities) were, among other things, reasons why no agreement could be reached on how to define the 'regions'. As the discussions on regional planning could not be held, the attention shifted from the regional to the sub-regional level. The issue of land-use management replaced the unfinished proposals for strategic planning. So-called sector plans, detailed zoning for land use, were elaborated for each sub region, and covered the whole of the Belgian territory.[1]

The main aim of the Planning Act was to renew the old economic machinery (Saey 1988). In that period of rapid economic growth, authorities were frequently confronted with the need to assign industrial sites. Concepts of regional development were advocated and there was a general understanding that Belgium should not lag behind other industrialised countries in adopting some machinery for planning (Anselin 1984). The tools for that purpose were a better location of enterprises and the construction of an efficient traffic network. The regional economic development policies, programmed since the 1950s, merely saw spatial planning as an instrument for a more rational and efficient spatial organisation, in reaching goals for economic development and growth of welfare. In that perspective the sector plans offered tools for a broader allocation of economic activities. Strategic planning was incriminated as merely a functional coordination of space, the sector plans were tools for economic development, for instance the design of industrial zoning (one of the main tools of the 'expansion legislation' for regional development).

The erosion of the Belgian state's 'regional development policy'

In the 1960s the socioeconomic and historical cultural differences between the two Belgian communities resulted in divergent models for social organisation and political strategies towards the formulation of economic development policies and according to the concepts for national and regional planning (Albrechts and Swyngedouw 1989). Gay (1989) explained this reality in a clear way as he described the difficulties to devise a regional policy that was other than 'a costly compromise acquired at the State's expense'. Indeed, from the start in the 1950s, Belgian regional development policy was focused on the balanced division of the budget for regional aid between the Flemish and Walloon parts of the country. In 1966 special measures to revitalise the local economies of coal mining and

1   'Gewestplannen', 'Plan secteurs' for territories which one can compare with an
    'arrondissement' ('district'). Only for a procedural objective in the approval process of these
    sub-regional plans the 'regions' were defined according to the administrative boundaries of
    the 'provinces'.

textile-producing areas reinforced these policies, and in 1970, after new criteria were introduced together with the recognition of the political necessity of balancing aid between Flanders and Wallonnia, a set of very extensive 'development areas' were marked, to include one-third of the country (Gay 1989).

This was a hindrance for objective regional development policy. Even so, these regional policies have indeed achieved a measure of success, for instance in the establishment of numerous industrial estates. In Flanders the industrial estates (developed and equipped by the state, port authorities, regional development agencies, inter-municipal development agencies and private firms) have, as a non-negligible factor, allowed the region to speed up its rather slow rate of early industrialisation. Investments of foreign capital during the 1960s were to a large extent located in the northern part of Belgium (Gay 1989).

This development and the internationalisation of capital that brought the traditional Walloon industry into crisis, deepened the socioeconomic differences between the northern and southern parts of the country. The Flemish politicians perceived the Walloon adaptation of regional development policy merely as state dirigisme and interventionism, especially at the expense of the now more prosperous Flemish part of Belgium. Eventually it facilitated the process towards devolution and the breaking down of Belgian 'regional development policies'.

The unfolding of the role of the European Commission in cohesion policy in general and the start of the European Regional Development Fund (ERDF) in 1975 in particular interfered with Belgian regional policy. The influence of the European Commission on Belgian policies regarding regional development affected the broad spectrum of regional support in the Walloon and Flemish regions. Gradually the Belgian government became more selective in the division of regional support. So the unfolding of the European regional development programmes in the 1970s and 1980s gradually diminished the impact of the Belgian regional development programmes. This evolution ran parallel with the ongoing devolution process of the Belgian state, and so the inter-regional competition for Belgian public financial aid decreased, only to decrease the inter-regional struggle for European financial support.

The 'federalisation' of regional development and the establishment of the regional development agencies

The decentralisation of economic planning

The developments described above had already resulted in the 1970s in a Framework Law concerning the organisation of economic planning and decentralisation. This law expressed a firm political acknowledgement of the regional diversity between the north and south of the country. Its announced purpose was to secure, through a general economic policy, a maximal and balanced economic expansion and continuous social improvement together with a fair division of the advantages of growth and cultural development of the Belgian people nationally and regionally (Albrechts 1992).

A national planning bureau and, more important, consultative regional economic councils for the Flemish, Walloon and Brussels regions were made operational. The former had the task of elaborating the national five-year plan (of which none was ever approved), the latter could give recommendations on regional economic matters. Nevertheless this law marked an important step in the decentralisation process of planning competence. In the 1980s, during the further devolution process of Belgium, competence on matters such as spatial planning and regional economic policy was withdrawn from the national level and transferred to the level of the Flemish and Walloon regions. It has to be noted that the emergence of more liberal principles in the 1980s also contributed to the abandonment of this type of national economic planning.

The law of 1970 also institutionalised an active regional development policy. Regional development agencies were established for each Flemish province, within a legal framework offered by the central government. The statutory role and structure of the RDAs in Flanders have been regulated, since 1990, by the Flemish government. These agencies, in particular the West Flemish, produced studies on the socioeconomic needs of the area, formulated proposals and promoted economic activity, spatial planning, and improvements in the social and economic infrastructure. They also undertook concrete action to facilitate or expand private and public investment (e.g. by expropriating land, buying and selling premises, providing infrastructure). Briefly, they played an active role in the definition of concepts of regional planning and its operationalisation.

Within the context of the eroding 'central state' regional policy and with initially only a minor transfer of competencies to the level of the regions (e.g. Flanders and Wallonia) the RDAs (operational on the level of the Flemish provinces) in general gained an influential position in terms of decision making and implementation in the domains of regional and economic development and consequently on the planning of spatial organisation and infrastructure. These factors were common to all Flemish regional development agencies (RDAs). But in the case of the West Flemish RDA, and its counterpart the Inter-communal Development Agency Leiedal in the district of Kortrijk, some specific factors encouraged the strong position of these agencies at the intermediate level, i.e. the province of West Flanders and the district of Kortrijk respectively.

The growing autonomy of Flemish regional policy

In general the evolution during the 1980s resulted in an erosion of traditional Belgian regional development programmes. In this changing context of the growing importance of the Flemish government, the RDAs tried to consolidate their positions.

Although the Flemish government in 1990 reconfirmed the role of the RDAs as the major public institutions with responsibility for the different aspects of regional development of the territory, the Flemish government increased its own impact and control on regional development: for instance, with respect to the division of resources in general, gate-keeping regarding European funding, and steering and conceiving policy making in diverse sub-regions, in particular.

In the late 1980s a discussion on the relevance of an additional Flemish regional programme took place. There was a general feeling in leading socioeconomic consultative committees that the Flemish reconversion and expansion policy which at that time was focused on the (now closed down) coal basin of Limburg ('Kempense Steenkoolmijnen') could be widened to other areas in Flanders. The monitoring of the socioeconomic situation of the (sub)regions in Flanders was carried out by the Socioeconomic Council of Flanders (Sociaal Economische Raad voor Vlaanderen) and resulted in a general understanding that there were, beneath the problem areas recognised by the European Commission, still some smaller sub-regions that could be given special attention in terms of their development. The outcome was that eight sub-regions were selected. They were referred to as 'impulse regions' in the programme.

The establishment of consultative committees in the impulse regions encouraged the forming of a social network and intermunicipal cooperation and a more comprehensive way of thinking about the region. Partnerships between local and regional authorities and (inter)national authorities became more and more the rule (Cabus 1995). This process of regional networking and comprehensive thinking can be considered an important innovation in regional development practice. From a purely regional economic viewpoint, greater attention was paid to non-economic factors that were important for regional development, such as social cohesion, territorial and environmental quality.

The policy and implementation evaluation of the impulse region policy by the Socioeconomic Council of Flanders led to the overall institution-alisation in 1995–96 of comparable 'standing regional committees' (Streekplatformen) by the Flemish government in almost all sub-regions of Flanders (at a scale comparable to the scale of 'districts'). To these committees, conceived within the philosophy of local and regional partnerships, the task was commissioned of formulating a vision of the territorial development and the selection of strategic projects of the sub-region. The assignment of the members of these committees was nevertheless partially balanced politically at the level of the Flemish government and its political cabinets. This increased even more the growing importance of the Flemish government in steering (local) sub-regional development. The policy of the Flemish government concerning the establishment of 'impulse regions' and 'standing regional committees' is perceived as counteracting the strongholds of RDAs (which are perceived as provincial).

Although this policy illustrates the broadened perspective of a new regional policy (partnerships between public and private actors and between local and central authorities), the more tactical goal of the Flemish government of controlling regional development, and attempts at bypassing the power networks of the RDAs, cannot be neglected.

Aspects of the role of the regional development agency of West Flanders

The establishment of the role of the West Flemish RDA

In the period of the first awareness of regional development policy in Belgium in the 1950s, provincial economic councils were established in order to study and advise regional economic development. In 1954 the West Flemish Economic Council (WER, West-Vlaamse Economische Raad) was established by the province, the communities and social partners (trade unions, employers' organisations and so on). The industrial elite was also represented in this council. The bad economic situation of West Flanders at that time (especially the rural and relatively isolated western part: the Westhoek) and the general perception of marginalisation of the region, encouraged this establishment. The WER was a forerunner in the conception of regional economic development as there was no tradition in that field at that time in Belgium, and it established a strategic position in a field that would be of increasing importance. It not only had a dominant influence on concepts and ideas of the regional economic development of subregions of the province of West Flanders, but they were also influential in Belgian policy making on regional economic programmes (De Rynck 1995, p.143). When in 1959 the Regional Expansion Legislation was established, the province of West Flanders was immediately ready to establish its own economic research agency (WES, Westvlaams Ekonomisch Studiebureau) (Vanhove 1994).

As was explained above, the ideas of regional planning and balanced development, as they were developed in the policies and programmes described above, have been of great importance for the planners who were working, in the 1950s and 1960s, on the establishment of the spatial planning system in general and on regional studies in particular. The conceptual link between spatial planning thought on regional levels and the concept of regional development was expressed in the work of regional economic researchers within institutions of the WER and WES and later the RDA.

The regional economic researchers of the WER and WES at that time played an important role in the 'regional study' for the province of West Flanders. As was the case for the regional studies, the preparations for the drafts of these sector plans were also commissioned from private research groups. The West Flemish regional economic researchers played an important role in the preparation of the West Flemish sector plans.

It is within this tradition that, since its establishment in 1975, the West Flemish RDA has held its firm position as the institution for the economic development of the province of West Flanders with a major influence in decision making on spatial organisation. Especially with respect to the specific Belgian regional development programmes for the Westhoek, the agency established its key position in the province, remaining relatively autonomous from local and central government. The RDA was and is embedded within the context of provincial decision-making structures and networks. It derived its legitimacy largely from the cooperation of local authorities, local and provincial social partners and intermunicipal cooperative organisations, in short by forging an elite consensus on the local and intermediate levels (De Rynck 1995). As the strategic institution on these issues it gained a large influence in the Belgian administrative and political structure. This network and political legitimisation of the RDA of the province of West Flanders are based on contingent historical, political and economic factors which resulted in a broad public/private cohesion on territorial policies at that time in the province of West Flanders.

As De Rynck and De Rynck (1992) observed, the West Flemish RDA also established direct contact during the 1970s with the European administration. Their key position with regard to strategic territorial planning and management for the province of West Flanders led to a favourable and influential position during negotiations with the European administration. In defending their own agenda, they bypassed the central government and reinforced their position in territorial management in the province.

The influence of a changing institutional context

From that period on, as a result of the growing importance of the Flemish government, the relative autonomy of the West Flemish RDA was more and more thwarted in the 1990s by the Office of the Minister-President responsible for regional economic development, for instance with respect to the European programme. Negotiations shifted more towards the level of the new Flemish government, which now became a dominant player in dividing policy interest and financial support (cf. De Rynck and De Rynck 1992).

The new government of the Flemish region gradually succeeded in establishing its competence for regional economic development and territorial management during the early 1990s. This situation led to continuous struggles for the domination of these fields of policy and decision making concerning sub-regions in the province of West Flanders. The way the Flemish government creates and institutionalises its own, parallel circuits for (sub)regional development and strategic territorial management was illustrated above.

The installation, in the first half of the 1990s, of a 'regional manager' for each 'impulse region' (with a budget to create and implement projects over a period of three years (1991–94)), caused tensions with the RDA concerning the management of these 'impulse regions'.

The relationship with spatial planning

The historically active role of the West Flemish RDA and its twin institution the WES in the conception of spatial organisation and its performance in plan making and decision making processes about the statutory plans has already been mentioned. Recently the current planning system in Flanders has become the object of a major revision. A new Planning Act was passed by the Flemish parliament in July 1996 and a spatial structure plan for Flanders is in the making and is intended to play a role as a substantive overall framework for the revision of the 'outdated' sector plans.

Within this changing context of spatial policy, in which the Flemish government tries to establish its newly gained political authority, the provincial decision makers and the 'provincial' institutions, the RDA and the WES, quickly anticipate these developments. Already in 1991 the province of West Flanders had commissioned a provincial spatial structure plan, the elaboration of which was executed by the WES. Through the close links with their staff and management the RDA was (in)directly involved (De Rynck 1995; Houthaeve and De Rynck 1996).

The provincial structure plan aims at the formulation of a substantial framework for the revision of the sector plans. With this planning process the provincial authorities and the management of the WES/RDA clearly try to stay ahead of the comparable plan-making and decision-making process generated in 1993 by the Flemish government. This pre-investment of the province in planmaking proved to be valuable as the new Planning Act (1996) recognised the province as the intermediate level of planning.

The West Flemish RDA, confronted with the growing need for new industrial estates, initiated a second decision-making process, the revision of the sector plans. This is a parallel effort to influence spatial policy making. The West Flemish RDA could rely on its formal competence to propose partial revisions of the current sector plans in order to design new industrial estates. This strategy is advantageous in persuading leading political and economic actors in this strategy, influencing their perception of spatial organisation, and securing once again the managerial position of the RDA.

Aspects of the role of the inter-municipal development agency in Southern West Flanders

A contingent situation

The Intercommunale Leiedal, a cooperative association, was established in 1959 as a result of regional expansion legislation in Belgium. After the approval of the 1962 Planning Act, Leiedal became the first fully inter-municipal development agency in Belgium. The consensus at that time between the economic and political elites of the region regarding economic development stimulated this establishment. It illustrates the sense of common interest of the local authorities, the province and private actors (trade unions, the financial sector, the Chamber of Commerce and Industry, the employers' association and individual entrepreneurs) in joining the cooperative association Leiedal (Houthaeve and De Rynck 1996).

Musyck (1995, p.626) indicates that the traditional flax industry in the district of Kortrijk has been a perfect breeding ground for the development of a solid entrepreneurial culture in the south of West Flanders.[2] The

2   According to Musyck this economic structure, in which a relatively large number of economic actors were competing with fairly similar products in the same international market, led to a strong sense of individualism and a local industrial mentality in which rivalry and competition played a leading role.

reconversion of the flax industry towards a diversified textile industry and its evolution into various industrial sectors was perceived as an ability to adapt to alternating boom and recession periods in an ever-changing economic environment. Leading economic actors in the region for that reason have a strong common perception of their entrepreneurial culture and business achievements and a collectively shared confidence in their ability for economic adaptation. This was evaluated by Musyck by means of the model of 'endogenous development'.[3]

Specific elements of social and political cohesion favourably affected the existence of social and political agreement and the development of the district as a whole. The district of Kortrijk has always been dominated by the Christian Democratic Party. The organisation of the Christian Democratic Party was by itself an instrument for social stability as the party was (is) built on the basis of a coalition of the unions, the association of employers and the organisation of farmers. The Kortrijk region has always been described as a relatively harmonious and stable region in terms of labour relations. The presence and direct involvement of the unions in regional institutions such as Leiedal, illustrate the integration of the unions in local and regional policy making.

The Kortrijk region (around 278,500 inhabitants in 1991) is a densely urbanised region. The functional-spatial structure of the region is not dominated by a central urban focus point and the economic and consequently the morphological growth was divided over several centres. Industrial development was not limited to urban conurbations; on the contrary, the dispersed economic activities induced a widespread urbanisation. The perception of the agglomerated urbanisation pattern indicates that they had little in common with the administrative municipal boundaries. This was a facilitating element for the (now) 12 municipalities of the district of Kortrijk towards the recognition of the importance of a common approach of territorial management (Houthaeve and De Rynck 1996).

Expertise in spatial planning

The inter-municipal development agency differs from the RDA because of its close link with local authorities and its major role as a consultative and design

---

3 It implies in effect the capacity to transform the socioeconomic system; the ability to react to external challenges; the promotion of social learning and the ability to introduce specific forms of social regulation at local levels which favour the aforementioned points. Endogenous development is (according to Garofoli (1972, p.7), quoted after Musyck 1995) the ability to innovate at a local (and regional) level.

agency on local urbanisation and planning issues. Leiedal obtained, compared with other intercommunal development agencies in Flanders, a unique position and established itself as a factual regional policy-making institution.

Since the late 1930s the interwoven urbanisation process in the Kortrijk region has resulted in a growing belief in an inter-municipal approach. In the 1950s this finally led to the elaboration of an 'intermunicipal general development plan' for the municipalities of the district of Kortrijk, a unique example in Flanders. Although the plan never gained statutory power, because the preparations for the 1962 Planning Act were in their last phase, it had a large conceptual influence on the sector plan for the Kortrijk district.

In 1991 the further urbanisation of the district and the gradual outdating of the current sector plans generated a specific intermunicipal project of spatial planning and development policy in the Kortrijk district. In accordance with a forgotten article of the 1962 Planning Act, the twelve local authorities are working together with the inter-municipal development agency in order to formulate a common general local development plan (the GAPAK project).

The GAPAK project can be described as an intensive thought and bargaining process between diverse interest groups and local authorities with the inter-municipal development agency Leiedal as the initiator and coordinator. The project follows a cooperative method in the definition of the planning situation and plan proposals, and aimed at a shared understanding of the common spatial development of the region.

The approval of this GAPAK plan could result in the replacement of the current sector plan for the district. The planning process has comparable aims, therefore, to that of the provincial structure plan. In both planning processes development agencies play an important role.

Concluding remarks on the changing aspects of the role of the regional development agencies in West Flanders

The key position of the West Flemish RDA in setting the agenda for territorial management can be explained by the relatively weak position of Belgian central economic planning and traditional regional policy. Concepts of regional development, with, for instance, its emphasis on the (physical) distribution of industrial capacity, explain the important role the RDA played in plan making and decision making on spatial organisation, i.e. the sector plans.

The influence that the provincial policy makers and the local network of the provincially based WES and GOM, gained on the decision-making process for European programmes is in some contrast to the general observation by Hart and Roberts (1995, p.105) that 'there was insufficient consultation with local and regional authorities in the preparation of the regional plan...and the Community Support Frameworks were prepared without any direct intervention of local and regional authorities'. As an example Hart and Roberts indicate the unsupportive, or in some instance overtly hostile attitude, of many national governments to local and regional authorities' efforts to establish effective cross-frontier cooperation. This is in contrast to the relatively autonomous and active role of the provincial decision makers and public officials in West Flanders in negotiating, for instance, the Interreg programmes.

The role of the West Flemish RDA illustrates the way regional and local circuits of decision making can conquer a specific niche or domain in policy making. The RDA filled up a relative regional gap' in Belgium. The legitimacy of the West Flemish RDA was based on a strong local and provincial (personal and institutional) network, day-to-day access to local information and a long tradition of conceiving and implementing regional development policy.

In the district of Kortrijk contingent historical, political, economic and even interpersonal factors led to a strongly autonomous perception of regional identity by the local and regional elites. These factors were favourable to cooperation and agreement on spatial planning and regional development. The level of the region (supra-local level) formed the context for the social construction of this policy.

Economic and urban development was the basis of a cooperative approach with a long-standing tradition between the socioeconomic and political elites of the region: an inter-municipal approach to the urbanisation process of the region (growth management) and a common understanding of regional economic development (growth coalition).

In the district of Kortrijk the inter-municipal development agency gained an identically key position to the West Flemish RDA, although its legitimacy was and is to a great extent based on local authorities and the local economic elite. Since the unfolding of the regional development policy in the 1950s and 1960s, the authority of the provincial RDA has also been continually challenged in the southern part of West Flanders.

It is clear that a project such as GAPAK is embedded in the general and contingent structure and culture of society, and additionally in its policy practice and power relations. On the one hand, the traditionally large degree of social cohesion and common sense of cooperation within the Kortrijk region were favourable factors for this collaborative approach to planmaking. But on the other hand, dominant stakeholders, such as the Chamber of

Commerce and Industry and the economic elite, still rely on their own traditional circles of influence with respect to the decision-making process.

Although the GAPAK project is relatively innovative in Flanders, as it contains some elements of a determined collaborative and sociocratic attempt to plan making and to influencing the stream of decision making over the social production and organisation of space (Houthaeve and De Rynck 1996), it nevertheless illustrates the pragmatic handling of the institutional heritage of these previous eras to control growing divergent interests in the region. The recognition of 'environmental groups' and 'agricultural associations' as cooperative members in the GAPAK project and even as formal members of the council of representatives of the inter-municipal development agency, is an illustration of these changing patterns of social interaction.[4]

Changing aspects of the policy environment of the West Flemish RDA and the inter-municipal development agency of the district of Kortrijk, such as the more dominant position of the Flemish government in the re-emergence of regional development policies and spatial planning, redesigned the role of these institutions.

The changing patterns of regional development strategies clearly come to the fore in recent initiatives such as the 'standing regional committees' for (sub)regional development. In contrast with earlier periods of regional policy, these development strategies in general are more oriented towards the recognition of endogenous potential. Development strategies and programmes such as those developed by and with the West Flemish RDA therefore become strongly aware of the necessity of cooperation with diverse public and private partners. The West Flemish RDA anticipates these changing patterns of policy making through the initiation of planning processes. Also the practices of the inter-municipal development agency Leiedal in the district of Kortrijk reflects an innovative way of policy making through the building of consensus (Houthaeve and De Rynck 1996).

Recently, planning with respect to the spatial organisation of the region has once again become an important issue through which these institutions articulate and adapt their positions and reinforce their influence in the local and regional decision-making network within a changing context. As the West Flemish RDA is closely linked with the provincial economic research agency (WES), it gained on the one hand an influential position in the planning of the provincial spatial structure plan while trying to be very

4   Also Erneste and Meier (1992, p.264–265) emphasize on the importance of communication and negotiation in contemporary regional development. Policy making and implementation calls for negotiations rather than for command.

closely involved in the design of the plan itself, while on the other hand it holds a privileged relation with provincial decision makers and initiated at the level of the Flemish government, a revision of the sector plans.

Nevertheless, the relationship between the RDA, as a factual 'provincial' institution for regional development – but formally working within a legal framework offered by the Flemish government – and the elected provincial 'council' is changing. The province is more and more aware of its potential leading role in planning issues.

The inter-municipal development agency in the Kortrijk district has put greater emphasis on the control of the changing context of decision making in the region. The practice of building consensus is used as a method of creating arenas for mutual agreements between various partners. The agency nevertheless holds a key position as the main contributor of planning concepts and plan proposals. Both institutions collaborated at the same time in a joint effort to change the existing sector plan for new industrial zoning, whereby they launched a joint strategy to influence central decision making on these issues; which was partially successful as the Flemish government proposed to change the sector plan in July 1997.

References

Albrechts, L. (1992) 'Changing aspects of Belgian public planning.' In A. Dutt and F. Costa (eds) *Perspectives on Planning and Urban Development in Belgium*. Dordrecht/ Boston/ London: Kluwer Academic Publishers.

Albrechts, L. and Swyngedouw, E. (1989) 'Regionale planning en ontwikkeling: exponenten van maatschappelijke ontwikkeling.' *Ruimtelijke Planning Afl. 23*, 1–40.

Anselin, M. (1984) 'Belgium.' In R.H. Williams (ed) *Planning in Europe. Urban and Regional Planning in the EEC.* London: George Allen & Unwin.

Cabus, P. (1995) Vlaanderens Regionaal beleid op nieuwe wegen. In Cabus, P. and Houthaeve, R. (eds) *Planologisch Nieuws 15*, 2, 175–201.

De Rynck, F. and De Rynck, S. (1992) 'Europese steun voor de Westhoek: analyse van de bestuursverhoudingen.' *Ruimtelijke Planning Afl. 28*, 1–23.

Erneste, H. and Meier, V. (1992) 'Communicating regional development.' In H. Erneste and V. Meier (eds) *Regional Development and Contemporary Industrial Response*. London: Belhaven Press.

Garafoli, G. (1992) *Endogenous Development and Southern Europe*. Aldershot: Avebury.

Gay, F.J. (1989) 'Benelux.' In H.D. Clout (ed) *Regional Development in Western Europe*. London: David Fulton Publishers.

Hart, T. and Roberts, P. (1995) 'The Single European Market. Implications for local and regional authorities.' In S. Hardy, M. Hart, L. Albrechts and A. Katos (eds) *An Enlarged Europe. Regions in Competition?* London: Jessica Kingsley Publishers.

Houthaeve, R. and De Rynck, F. (1996) 'Het GAPAK: samen de streek sturen.' In L. Goossens (ed) *Ruimtelijke Planning 4*, 1, 65–99.

Musyck, B. (1995) 'Autonomous industrialisation in South West Flanders (Belgium): continuity and transformation.' *Regional Studies 29*, 7, 619–633.

Saey, P. (1988) 'Ruimtelijke planning als onderdeel van een groenstrategie: een sociaal-wetenschappelijke standpuntbepaling.' In Vereniging voor Groenvoorziening v.z.w. (eds) *Ruimte voor Groen*. Gent: Vijfde Vlaamse Wetenschappelijk Congres over Groenvoorziening.

Further reading

Allaert, G. and Houthaeve, R. (1996) *Ruimtelijke Plannen op Regionaal Niveau*. Gent: Academia Press.

Houthaeve, R. (1996) 'Spatial planning in Flanders. Looking for strengths and weaknesses through its regional approach.' In J. Alden and P. Boland (eds) *Regional Development Strategies. A European Perspective*. London: Jessica Kingsley Publishers.

Vanhove, N. (1994) 'Veertig jaar WER-GOM-West-Vlaanderen.' *West-Vlaanderen Werkt 36*, 4, 176–633.

CHAPTER 10

Regional Development Institutions
Rural Development in the UK
Jim Hughes

Introduction

Although the role and importance of regional development agencies have been neglected in the study of regional policy, the range of papers and subjects in this volume shows that the gap is being filled. However, two aspects of the study of development institutions – indeed of any institutional structure – have been difficult to achieve. They are:

- the gap between external presentation and the actual (I am tempted to say real) balance of work and resources in the organisation

- setting the organisation in a holistic context of its origins, political and policy framework.

To fill this gap and create this broader and deeper picture is a very tall order and this paper certainly does not do so. Rather, it draws upon three strands of personal work which may be described as follows:

1. an academic background in regional theory, planning and policy

2. a practitioner in rural development agencies in the UK

3. a brief intensive research study of one organisation, the Highlands and Islands Development Board 1965–91.

There has been considerable, if somewhat intermittent, literature on the relationship between research and policy. One of the principal conclusions is that an important obstacle to the acceptance and implementation of research findings is the difference in culture between the 'research' and the 'executive' communities. If we aim to have our work influence the real world of regional development for the better, we must be aware of this gap in the way we structure the research and present the findings.

First, there are problems of access. Organisations tend to commission studies on a particular aspect of their work, usually on some external set of questions. They are seldom interested in an examination of themselves, except under the guidance of an unusual leader. Second come difficulties of publication. There are often unforeseen sensitivities to criticism. Even cases when a fact-finding visit has been publicised ('The RDA is currently being studied as a model by a high-powered group from … pictured here with the Chief Executive') it has often been followed by acrimonious disputes about conclusions. Publication by academics is many times more likely to run into such problems.

A central problem is that the questions which interest researchers and practitioners, while overlapping, are different. Without the cooperation of the RDA it is difficult for researchers to develop a fruitful project. By this I do not mean that researchers need a 'soft' relationship with the RDA they are looking at. They need to introduce rigour by the usual methods available to the social scientist. Unfortunately comparison with a 'model', either organisational or developmental, runs into the problem of comprehension by management. To the criticism that an RDA is falling short of or deviating from a model, the reply is likely to be:

- *either* the model won't work (even if we understood it)
- *or* the current position is a whole lot better than it used to be.

In rural development one of the most powerful concepts is the distinction between the Centre and the Periphery. The central argument is that the Centre, however defined, has had at best a position of indifference or at worst a neo-colonial and exploitative relationship. Not only is this literature highly conceptual, but it is counter-intuitive to development practitioners (Howe 1996). The fact that historically new industries have wrecked the stability and long-term prosperity of local rural economic systems is not a convincing argument to practitioners who clearly see that additional jobs will not be generated by traditional industries.

There are two practical ways to structure research which can help to distinguish between the influence of external, exogenous and internally controlled variables: longitudinal or comparative studies. This paper examines UK rural development agencies in a comparative context but it will also reflect the difficulties and weaknesses of the research course which has just been indicated, in particular the risk that historical analysis is perceived as irrelevant to current and future decisions (e.g. Rich 1981).

Historical policy context

The four rural development agencies in the UK have markedly different origins.

- The Development Commission was established before World War I after the Liberal government had imposed new taxes on capital, which it was expected would lead to the break-up of landed estates with resulting problems for surrounding rural areas. As a Standing Royal Commission it had limited executive powers and largely operated through other agencies such as the Council for Small Industries in Rural Areas (CoSIRA) and county-based programmes in close collaboration with local authorities (Development Commission 1984). Its successor body, the Rural Development Commission, was established in 1987–88 with greater executive powers, but continued its general approach and the structure of many programmes. Having once covered all of Great Britain, it now operates in England, especially in its designated rural development areas.

- The Highlands and Islands Development Board (HIDB) was set up in 1965 at the height of enthusiasm for regional policy. It had followed 30 years of proposals for an RDA dedicated to the unique problems of the Highlands of Scotland. The Secretary of State for Scotland, when introducing the Bill to set it up, described it as correcting the neglect and mistakes of the previous 200 years. This history led to an important strand of the Board's work on major development projects, although it was also a handicap through the expectation that the Board's policies would be much more radical, for example in changing the pattern of land ownership.

- The Development Board for Rural Wales (DBRW) came from a different stable. The development of Mid Wales from the middle 1960s was to be based on the rationalising and stimulative effects of a new town. The scheme was in fact modified to expanding an existing town, called (confusingly) Newtown. A development corporation was set up which drew upon the personnel and services from an established new town corporation in Wales, Cwmbran. The DBRW was established in 1977 when it was given a much wider and explicit brief for the development of rural Mid Wales. However, its continued investment in housing and factories has meant that its programme continues to have a 'property bias' which

is reflected in its activities and budget compared to other rural
RDAs.

- The Rural Development Council in Northern Ireland was created in
  1991 from a very active and effective community development
  movement. The trigger, apart from the reputation of the projects,
  was the LEADER Initiative, an EU programme to stimulate more
  bottom-up projects in rural development.

Thus, although there is much discussion of optimal development strategies,
the plans and programmes of rural RDAs have been fundamentally
influenced by the historical framework and the context of their
establishment. This influence continued for many years, indeed decades into
the life of the organisations. Carter (1975) maintains that the first
appointments to HIDB shaped its strategy in the first decade; the first
chairman was given a prediction of his future difficulties by a colleague
within days of the announcement of the full list of HIDB board members
(interview with author). We need, therefore, to take a look at the
organisational structure and dynamics of the organisations.

Relationship to government

All of these bodies encounter a high degree of control by the government,
normally through the sponsoring department through which the budget is
provided and which will have a section whose responsibility is to supervise
the development of policies and operation of programmes.

In interpreting the language used by people in the RDA sector and by
commentators on it, there is a need to understand an important schism:

1. Ministers and senior members of quangos will overstate the degree of
   independence which they have.

2. Opposition members and the press will use any failure or apparent
   deviation from the official version as an occasion to criticise government
   policy or claim a conspiracy.

The two are, of course, interrelated. RDAs are part of the governmental
machine. Not only do they operate within government policy, but they are
also an important source of ministerial publicity. Public announcements
about new programmes or successful projects are not occasions to introduce
any note of frankness about the frustrations of working together. Quite apart
from being an unforgivable breach of confidence, if not of official secrets, it
would reduce faith in the scheme as a carefully designed development tool.

The principal formal means of control are:

- the provisions of the Act of Establishment

- a corporate plan looking forward 3–5 years, supplemented by a business plan and annual budget
- often an annual review visitation by the responsible minister
- a financial management policy review (FMPR), approximately every three years.

The Acts often contain provision for a Direction or instruction to the RDAs by the Secretary of State but these are seldom, if ever, used. It should be clearly understood that the balance of power is heavily weighted to the government department (see Grassie 1982). The 'informal' weapons are various:

1. power of reappointment to the board – and also influence over staff appointment in reorganisations
2. expressing views 'in the name' of the minister, even when it is not clear what the ministerial view will be
3. indirect threats to future budgets
4. threat of less active support on other issues
5. a cautionary memo (however mild) which could leave the quango carrying not only the full responsibility but also the burden of 'ignored advice', if things go wrong.

Since one of the justifications for the creation of RDAs is independent action, how can that be possible in the light of the relationship described in this section? There are a number of aspects of independence.

1. The largest programme run with least reference to the sponsoring department was grant and loans awarded by the HIDB to the private sector. This amounted to between £15 to £20 million per year from the 1970s through much of the 1980s, amounting in some years to almost half the Board's budget. The limits below which the Board could make its own decision allowed around 1200–1500 cases to be decided with only a small number being referred for departmental approval. The development and protection of that programme can be attributed to a strong director of finance, who later became the Board's chief officer.

2. The Rural Development Commission (RDC) has probably been the most outspoken about the impact of other government policies on rural areas. This has included planning policy, housing and more national policy events such as privatisations and changes in defence. There is extreme sensitivity to criticism, however indirect, of other departments. The RDC statements have been careful not to bring into question the principle of a policy, but to concentrate on its operation. The power to do this stems from a recognition of RDC's role to 'speak for' rural areas (which to

some extent reflects its relatively small budget for the area to be assisted) reinforced by a chairman and senior commissioners (board members) of high independent standing.

3. The independence of the boards presents some contrasts. In its first five years a senior Scottish Office civil servant sat in on HIDB board meetings. When ministers found out about the practice, it was stopped; thereafter board minutes were sent to Edinburgh. On the other hand, in the case of DBRW there was no regular passing of board deliberations to the Welsh Office, indeed an expressed reluctance to know by at least one official. Although there may be some advantages in asserting that no civil servant is going to read our decisions over our shoulder, the dependent position of quangos make it desirable to have a reasonably firm grip on the maternal hand.

4. The most fundamental test of independence is the ability to develop innovative programmes. One of the common features of all of the bodies is that they contain staff capable of developing original and relevant ideas, to think 'outside the box' in current management jargon. The extent to which they are translated into practical programmes depends also upon: a) their skill in proposing *and sustaining* the case; b) the initiative of the sponsoring department to approve and, if necessary, argue the case (bearing in mind that 'innovative' can be a very prejudicial word in the civil service); c) the existence of a 'product champion', ideally the chairman or senior board member. For sheer density of initiatives, especially in fisheries and community development, the decade from around 1972/73 in HIDB, was a 'golden age'. However, the Highlands and Islands Telecommunications Initiative in the late 1980s demonstrates a major project initiated and implemented under Conservative rule.

5. There are other notable examples when the RDA acted to protect the interests of its region from the effects of related policy changes. During the review of regional policy in 1982/83, when most rural areas lost designated status, DBRW negotiated the power to administer the Mid Wales Development Grant: a major achievement in the ethos of the surrounding policy changes and also because it had to persuade Welsh Office to use the powers of the Welsh Development Agency by acting as its agent.

In summarising the independence of RDAs, it is clear that the weakest position is one of defying or challenging the sponsoring department. It needs only the slightest of indications to ensure that the annual audit turned up at least some awkward questions for the body in question. The relationship tends to be comparable with a small or satellite country dominated by a powerful neighbour. The RDA will choose certain areas in which to exercise greater freedom at the expense of others. However, it is always possible for a minister to reach down and overturn any established equilibrium.

Strategy

Most analysis of RDAs focuses around the changing expressions of strategy. Certainly strategy, as published and in public statements by senior staff and board members is significant. However, it needs to be understood against two other factors.

1. Strategy statements are often partial in two senses: a) they tend to be more concerned with 'high profile' activities, often politically popular; b) they do not identify trade-offs and opportunity costs.

2. There are often significant areas of work within the 'real' organisation which are only briefly referred to, if at all. The question of the nature of the organisation and how it works is developed later.

The following are summaries of key strategic issues for rural RDAs. Any serious review of them would have to address most of these questions. Within the organisations themselves there is a running dialogue on many of them, although the difficulty in creating a forum for a comprehensive review means that they are seldom fully addressed (Hughes 1979).

Inward investment

There is a clear distinction between the two 'regional' RDAs – HIDB and DBRW – and the RDCs in England and Northern Ireland which have a wider rural remit. Although, given the generally greater resources of the two regional RDAs, their concentration on inward investment need not be at the expense of indigenous growth, in practice it attracts much of the strategic publicity and creates less scope for positive discrimination to less developed areas. However, the dividing line between external and indigenous can be very disputatious; is an arrival in the region 'local' when it applies for assistance with its next development stage? In the minds of many people in the region the 'outsiders' seem to receive more than a fair share, in part because local firms are more reticent about publicising their assistance.

Proactive or reactive

This dichotomy has been a constant issue in rural development. A strong case can be made for not relying upon business opportunities coming forward to be supported, but rather placing emphasis upon improving the conditions for development in rural regions. The most comprehensive programme of proactive projects was in HIDB. At any one time there were sectoral projects which developed new species for fish farming, tested new methods of sea fishing, promoted the development of timber resources, deer farming, new entrepreneurs, in addition to planning studies on integrated development – even oil and gas refining. In the 1980s greater emphasis was placed upon encouragement and support of private sector-based groupings, for example in Mid Wales a regional export association and group of manufacturing employers.

Community or business

All rural RDAs have social programmes, although the main DBRW programme of social grants was removed by the review carried out by the Secretary of State for Wales, Mr John Redwood, in 1994–95. In England there has been a greater concentration upon acting through the community as an engine of change; this approach has also extended to support of socially desirable services, for example passenger transport projects. Shifts in this balance is one of the most interesting study points in the field. In 1976–77 the HIDB embarked upon an ambitious programme of multi-functional community cooperatives under leadership from the chairman and secretary and in the 1980s on support for Gaelic. DBRW promoted the building of local recreation centres as part of tourism infrastructure, although eventually were not allowed to contribute funding. The Rural Development Council in Northern Ireland is almost wholly focused on community development, although many of the other rural development programmes are delivered through the main government department.

Growth or disadvantaged areas

It is much less acceptable in a rural development strategy to concentrate on areas of high growth potential and to expect that development will spread or trickle down. The effect of both HIDB and DBRW has been to help create highly prosperous zones in the Moray Firth and East Montgomeryshire respectively. Research in England also shows that accessible rural areas have high rates of business growth and a record of business achievement which compares favourably with any other type of region. The emphasis placed on priority to disadvantaged areas is frequently limited by lack of scope to improve the long-term conditions for development, as described above, and by the choice of performance measures, in particular employment creation. The English Rural Development Commission has developed the most formal mechanism for designating rural development areas, but these have been in effect sub-regions comparable (at least in terms of population) to Mid Wales or the Highlands.

Assessment

The principal difficulty in assessing comparative strategies among current RDAs is to verify the stated strategy with the allocation, preferably the changing allocation, of resources. Even from the summary in this section it is clear there are so many policy vectors that it is almost impossible to be clear on the trade-offs. Also, where identifiable, they do not correspond with administrative or financial categories.

In summary, all four RDAs would claim that they are pursing a balance between these strategic choices, but it is very difficult to verify the differences in allocations in relation to the needs of the region. A far more dominant predictor of, for example, next year's allocation of resources is the existing structure of programmes. This reflects their staffing and structure; also the extent to which major shifts are discouraged by the system of departmental control. It may be argued that variations in impact are more dependent upon management effectiveness.

Leadership and management

This aspect must be studied in a longitudinal way. In part it is dictated by the resources required to study inside an organisation and also because most of the more convincing theories of organisations stress the importance of tradition, informal structures and self-image, all of which involve continuities. Even when an organisation is radically restructured much of the old remains.

So far as existing records are concerned, there is a tendency to follow the 'public' story, often through the sequence of chairmen appointed to head the agency. This is often a simplistic interpretation of the statements of the political party in power and the personal background of the chairman. Chairmen play an important role in creating and sustaining direction and morale, but it is impossible to tell the story of the RDA through the 'keyhole', as it were, of the chairman or even the whole board.

To take as an example the HIDB, the popular phases were: (I)1965–70 – first chairman appointed by Labour party, planner and academic: period of testing new and innovative programmes; (II) 1970–76 – second chairman appointed by Conservatives, retired diplomat: dull period of consolidation; (III) 1976–81 – third chairman appointed by Labour, academic economist on record as favouring a radical approach (Hetherington 1990). Despite the popular interpretation of phase (II) that it was a dull period sandwiched between two more visionary ones, there was considerable progress during that time, in particular a substantial growth in budget (personal interviews). Yet it is not contended that chairmen have no influence. Taking the case of the third chairman, two initiatives during his term depended upon his intervention: (1) the creation of community development cooperatives; (2) a proposal to take direct action to improve landuse. Neither action would have been taken into Board policy without the chairman's lead and were particularly significant as the agency entered its second decade.

The corollary of this direction of attention is that important contributions of other board members are overlooked. Two deputy chairmen had an important role in shaping the organisational structure of HIDB. One founder board member by general acknowledgement led the re-establishment of fishing in the Outer Hebrides. The untold story is the role of two men who were secretary and chief official, of the HIDB between 1965 and 1990. Much of the interaction with the sponsoring department, upon which much of the independence of the RDA depended, came across their desk.

Many commentators write of RDAs as if they were coherent organisations. As in the case of businesses, a 'behavioural' explanation (e.g. Cyert and March 1963) lays emphasis upon the role of parts of the organisation with differing goals and priorities. This not only flows from the differing/conflicting criteria of success, which lead the inward investment team to accuse the property department of frustrating their efforts. There is always a number of 'orphan functions' or 'agendas in waiting' which may operate on a substantial scale seeking a place in the sun or happy to avoid attracting board or public attention.

The overall strategy of an RDA will normally be the result of a compromise among board members and directors. Individuals will lead within their chosen areas and at least temper their criticism in the parallel fields of their colleagues. As an illustration of the steps taken to avoid internal conflict, the new chairman of an RDA was asked what colour of pen he would use to comment on memos and papers. One of the consequences of these collective agreements is an unwillingness to criticise former colleagues, at least while they are alive. This also makes life difficult for researchers.

Against this realistic background, is it possible to generalise on the factors likely to create success in an RDA? There are three key roles: 1) managing itself; 2) managing support programmes; 3) managing change.

1. *Managing itself.* The chairman and chief executive must be a
   complementary team since usually the former is part time. The HIDB
   was a unique exception in that the chairman, and a majority of board
   members were full time. Although this position created some ambiguities
   about the role of staff, there were advantages in that structure, especially

for the role of 3) below. The chief executive must be able to structure and manage the organisation, to maintain liaison with partners and, most importantly, manage the relationship with the civil service. EURADA (1996) sets out many of the management issues.

2. *Managing support programmes.* Business advice and support programmes, including financial assistance, require continuity and smooth management to clear response times and targets. Publicity and marketing are necessary but schemes which attract a high take-up in rural areas require trust and recommendation from business to business, even if it is in seeing a competitor gain a grant. Inward investment schemes are similar in the need to be customer-focused and driven.

3. *Managing change.* The whole *raison d'être* of RDAs is to respond to and create change. However, there is an especially important role in creating the conditions for longer term shifts in the competitive position of the region. This is a crucial issue in rural areas if their needs are not, as many people assume, 'modernising' but a strategy which is not disruptive of local social, economic, as well as cultural, patterns. The benefits from these projects extend well into the future and are often dependent on sequential steps. For example, the first step to encourage improved breeding of sheep and cattle on Scottish islands was to build up local marketing organisations. The RDC has predominantly developed programmes of community strengthening through protection of services in the expectation that stronger communities will produce development proposals. DBRW assisted railway improvements and local recreation centres as a means of increasing 'friendly' tourism. Virtually the whole programme of the Northern Ireland RDC was designed to build upon community-based initiatives.

Successful projects to foster long-term change require:

- *Ideas:* most importantly the sieving and development of ideas; we all know that opinions on what rural areas need can be ten-a-penny.

- *Planning:* projects which are going to change the structure of linkages are going to involve complex concepts and relationships; they need to be fitted into a proposal which, while presenting the case as broadly as possible, should be focused on a clear decision from the board and permission from the sponsoring department

- *Implementation:* important both to launch the project with realistic targets and expectations but also to sustain it through periods when difficulties arise and there is an appetite for a new idea (the fourth-year itch!).

- *Empathy*: the new projects must not dismiss the existing practices but understand their full significance (e.g. agricultural markets are not merely buying and selling events, but have many other social roles) and fit the new activities into as holistic a model of the region as possible.

- *Faith*: the new, as Macchiavelli said, has many more enemies than the *status quo*; the chairman has a particular role in resisting the complaints of those who believe their interests to be damaged and sustaining the project against the uncertainties.

- *Realism*: there is equally a need to maintain a realistic assessment of progress and to exit from a mistaken decision.

The 'spirit' of the organisation

In summary, an analysis of rural RDAs requires coverage of the formal structures outlined in the sections above. A study will have to take account of this framework, but more important it will have to uncover the forces which operate from and through these channels. For example, the historical context in each case includes strong forces imposing a distinct pattern on RDAs. However, although challenging, there are examples of research on the following issues.

1. Statutory powers
2. Historical context
3. Relationship with government
4. Strategy
5. Organisation structure

However, in the last section it was necessary to indicate questions beyond the objective categories and to consider much more subjective qualities.

In this respect RDAs are not different in kind from many other organisations. There is increasing emphasis upon the 'personal qualities' in looking at the effectiveness of businesses and organisations. Peters and Waterman (1982) introduced a very woolly concept in their search for 'excellence' but one which won almost instant recognition. The same sort of limitation on the success of a formalised analytical approach was recognised even earlier in public administration. Lindblom (1958) in a seminal article picked out the 'muddling through' of even successful public bodies – so much so that he termed it a 'science'. This was a very pertinent problem for the author in introducing policy planning to the HIDB. The available experience did not 'produce much evidence that decision-making by following a difficult model is an inescapable requirement for success in the life of a public administrator. There is even less evidence that the superimposition of their models on most acts of decision-making should be a conscious process, except in retrospect.' (Jones 1964, p.159).

In fact the HIDB board reacted quite warmly to the idea that they had been as successful in the past by 'muddling through' (Hughes 1982). Staff were more inclined to set the justification for their programmes in more rational terms. However, one of the most experienced and senior members, K. Farquharson, Director of Industrial Development, said that promoting industrial development in an area such as the Highlands and Islands depended to a considerable extent on eccentricity (of developers) and serendipity (interview with author).

There are a number of approaches to the understanding of successful organisations. The ones most relevant to RDAs are where there is a need for innovatory thinking, response and planning. They must include the right conditions in at least three stages:

1. *climate*: a set of expectations which encourages innovatory behaviour and not simply 'delivery' of routine targets

2. *ideation*: the effective generation, communication, development and interplay of ideas

3. *enabling*: implementing and managing the innovation process.

Experience suggests that it is difficult to generalise about these conditions other than (obviously) rigid departmental and hierarchical structures either do not allow the process to flow or raise the transactions costs to levels which threaten the success of innovation ('We told you it would not work'). A more contemporary term for these successful conditions is to describe the result as creating a 'learning organisation'.

Reference is also made to the need for 'strategic vision'. The following comments are not meant to deny, only qualify, that need. I would add the desirability of 'strategic unvision'. I have two things in mind. For remote rural areas opportunities can be taken up in the most unexpected and original ways; thus development results can be too specific and limit the benefits. Second, in a long interview the first chairman of HIDB told me that he watched with anticipation what form the organisation would eventually take (interview with author).

In a relatively new contribution to this field Morgan (1986) stresses the importance of how organisations perceive themselves, including what metaphors they use about themselves and the importance of corporate personality (Douglas 1987). RDAs tend to imitate private sector commercial undertakings for a number of reasons, including the interchange of staff and the perceived importance of the 'confidence' factor referred to above. This drive can lead to unique potential but, coupled with a need for constant innovation, has its pitfalls. It can lead to feelings of excellence which are not deserved and a resistance to external ideas or recognition of relevant changes in the external environment.

Conclusions

The paper quickly left behind the idea that four rural RDAs in the UK should follow similar or marginally differing strategies. Therefore a straight comparison of their strategies or analysis against a 'model' would not take the study far. The discussion had to include issues about the context, establishment and evolution of the agencies.

Above all their record will have to be compared against an understanding of how they worked as organisations. The interpretation of phases coinciding with political appointments to the chairmanship or change of government is also too simple, although certainly a relevant factor. A fuller understanding depends upon analysing both the formal and informal structures of the organisations. Many of these factors can only be researched fully from inside. If accepted this is a daunting prospect for researchers of RDAs.

There is no single resolution to the research problems and the long-standing persistence and ingenuity of the academic research profession will no doubt discover, by means of reasoning and serendipity, many solutions. Success will be more likely in the following circumstances:

1. a group specialising in regional economics
2. access to political science and organisational studies disciplines
3. regular attraction of RDA staff to postgraduate or professional courses
4. encouragement of practitioner research or participation by current or ex-executives
5. long-term contact to accumulate and encourage the creation of contemporary records of RDA issues and argument
6. access to and dialogue with RDAs without becoming either 'tame' or a perpetual critic
7. above all, an ability to learn from the RDA about the nature of decisions required in regional development.

However, there are concepts and leading examples in the study of organisations in both the public and private sectors. Because of their challenging task and the quality of staff in them, rural RDAs are *prima facie* 'learning organisations'. A small diversion of the research effort from the field of business and institutional management to RDAs would find far more fertile ground and produce many more benefits not only for rural society, but for the whole nation. The hope must be that the sort of research advocated here will assist the creation of effective rural RDAs which will meet the changing challenges of rural policy in Europe, in particular the importance of integrating the environmental dimension into development planning.

Note

The author is Director of the Wales European Centre, Brussels; none of the conclusions or views expressed should be attributed to the centre nor any of its sponsors. He is also Honorary Professorial Fellow, University College of Wales Aberyswyth, and gratefully acknowledges a Fellowship Grant from Leverhulme Trust to undertake research on the HIDB in 1991.

References

Carter, I. (1975) 'A socialist strategy for the Highlands.' In G. Brown *The Red Book on Scotland.* Edinburgh: Edinburgh University Student Publications Board.

Cyert, R.M. and March, J.G. (1963) *A Behavioral Theory of the Firm.* Englewood Cliffs: Prentice-Hall.

Development Commission (1984) *Guidelines for Joint Development Programmes.* London: Development Commission.

Douglas, M. (1987) *How Institutions Think.* London: Routledge and Kegan Paul.

EURADA (1996) *Creation, Development and Management of RDAs.* Brussels: EURADA.

Grassie, J. (1982) *Highland Experiment: The Story of the Highlands and Islands Development Board.* Aberdeen: Aberdeen University Press.

Hetherington, A. (1990) *Highlands and Islands: A Generation of Progress.* Aberdeen: Aberdeen University Press.

Howe, J. (1996) 'A case of inter-agency relations: regional development in Mid-Wales.' *Planning Practice and Research 11,* 1, 61–72.

Hughes, J.T. (1979) 'Evaluating the work of a regional development agency.' Paper presented at the Regional Studies Association (Scottish Branch) *Conference Aspects of Development in a Peripheral Region.*

Hughes, J.T. (1982) 'Policy analysis in the Highlands and Islands Development Board.' *Journal of the Operational Research Society 33,* 1055–1064.

Jones, R.W. (1964) 'The model as a decision maker's dilemma.' *Public Administration Review 24,* 158–160.

Lindblom, C.E. (1958) 'The science of "muddling through".' *Public Administration Review 19,* 79–88.

Morgan, G. (1986) *Images of Organisation.* London: Sage.

Peters, T.J. and Waterman, R.H. (1982) *In Search of Excellence.* New York: Harper & Row.

Rich, R.F. (1981) 'Can evaluation be used for policy action?' In R.A. Levine, M.A. Solomon, G-M. Hellstern and H. Wollmann (eds) *Evaluation Research and Practice: Comparative and International Perspectives.* Beverly Hills: Sage.

CHAPTER II

Enterprise in Scotland

A Mid-Term Assessment of an Institutional Innovation for Economic Development

John Fairley & Greg Lloyd

Introduction

Regional planning is a specific form of intervention by government in the spatial and institutional economy which attempts to provide an integrated approach to the management of economic, social and physical change in defined geographical areas. In general, regional planning operates at a sub-national scale of administration thereby providing a strategic framework for agenda setting, resource allocation and decision making at the local level by local authorities, public sector agencies and the private sector. In practice, however, regional planning is caught between the national policy agenda for the management of industrial restructuring and economic change and the local outcome and response to that change. In part as a consequence of this and the changing political context, the experience of regional planning in Britain has been a relatively chequered one (Glasson 1993). It has been described as representing 'an enduring but inconstant feature of public affairs' in post-war Britain (Wannop and Cherry 1994, p.52). Furthermore Diamond (1979) has asserted that it is important to acknowledge that a strategic planning approach is capable of assuming a variety of forms which may be deemed appropriate to prevailing circumstances. In this context, planning refers to a form of intervention which may be achieved through different institutional forms or policy instruments which seeks to address market failure in land, labour and capital markets in order to create the conditions for sustained economic development.

In Scotland, for example, there is a long-established tradition of regional planning which has attempted to reconcile the priorities and concerns of a national political agenda for economic growth and development with local needs and circumstances, and opportunities for the management of change. This has resulted in a diversity of structures and cultures. Regional planning in Scotland is facilitated through a complex network of organisations and agencies which are dedicated to different aspects of the managed change of defined localities, such as the Highlands and Islands, and the central belt. As a consequence the bodies involved have defined responsibilities, jurisdictions and resources and include central government departments, local authorities, semi-autonomous agencies and local public and private interests. Binding the institutional structure together, however, is a culture of intervention which is generally described as corporatist (McCrone 1994).

In the late twentieth century a distinctive corporatist tradition of intervention in economic matters has evolved (Fairley and Lloyd 1995). This reflects a number of factors, including Scotland's poor economic performance relative to that of Britain, a divergence of Scottish politics from those in the rest of Britain (Brown, McCrone and Paterson 1996), and a convergence of interests of the governing elites in Scotland which resulted in a consensus for development intervention (McCrone 1994). This context encouraged broad political support for the creation of powerful regional development agencies (Damesick and Wood 1987; Fairley and Lloyd 1995).

As a result, Scotland is noted for its distinctive forms of regional development agency such as the Highlands and Islands Development Board (HIDB) and the Scottish Development Agency (SDA) (Danson, Lloyd and Newlands 1990). These bodies, together with their successors – Scottish Enterprise (SE) and Highlands and Islands Enterprise (HIE) – have attracted considerable attention. SE, HIE and their local enterprise companies (LECs) have now been operating for five years and have been subjected recently to parliamentary scrutiny and quinquennial review. The Scottish Affairs Committee for example, which sits to examine, *inter alia*, the expenditure, administration and policy of the Scottish Office and its associated public bodies undertook an investigation, of the enterprise networks in the country (Scottish Affairs Committee 1995).[1]

In the context of public policy the complexity of deciding upon appropriate forms of evaluation cannot be overstated. These will be determined in the light of the underlying assumptions, the outputs and the outcomes involved. In the context of SE and HIE there are a number of theoretical issues to be addressed not least because the operational paradigm of the two agencies is founded on the neoclassical concept of market failure.

---

1   The authors were specialist advisers to this enquiry.

In practice however the outcomes of the work of the enterprise agencies may involve wider notions of social benefit which may not be included in more conventional assessments. Furthermore, SE and HIE involve wider constitutional and accountability issues together with considerations associated with policy, programme and performance. Compounding this position are the differences between the SE and HIE networks, the latter having a statutory responsibility for community and social development. And, as was the case with their predecessor organisations, there has been a tendency for the programmes implemented by the individual LECs in the SE and HIE networks to evolve in the light of emerging circumstances thereby making any attempt at evaluation difficult. Over and above this range of questions there are the broader, more speculative challenges of assessing what difference the networks have made to localities throughout Scotland and the counter-factual issues of what might have happened in Scotland had SE and HIE not been established.

Scottish Enterprise and Highlands and Islands Enterprise: the context

In 1991, the arrangements for the regional development agencies in Scotland were dramatically overhauled. SE and HIE replaced the SDA, the HIDB and the Training Agency – formerly the Manpower Services Commission (MSC). SE and the HIE assumed the responsibility for the integrated delivery of economic and business development initiatives, the provision of training and the implementation of measures to secure the improvement of the environment in Scotland. They represent a radical development in the Scottish tradition of regional planning for economic development by bringing more closely together the key factors of capital, labour and land. The institutional restructuring involved may be considered representative of the general shift in economic policy making and governance from managerialism to an approach based on entrepreneurialism (Harvey 1989). This process of change in approach on the part of the agencies had already started with respect to local and regional development by the SDA and the HIDB and the creation of SE and HIE took this process of introducing market principles further forward (Danson *et al.* 1990).

SE and HIE are charged with the specific responsibilities of stimulating self-sustaining economic development and the growth of enterprise, securing the improvement of the environment, encouraging the creation of viable jobs, reducing unemployment and improving the skills of the Scottish workforce. The delivery of the integrated enterprise and training services is sub-contracted by SE and HIE to a network of 22 LECs. These are not statutory bodies *per se* but are private companies constituted under the companies legislation 'to bring a direct knowledge and understanding of the needs and opportunities of the local economy to the delivery of the government's enterprise, environment and training programme, and to engage the commitment, experience and entrepreneurial flair of senior members of the private sector' (Scottish Affairs Committee 1995, p.v). In practice, the LECs provide a delivery framework for the specific services associated with training, enterprise and business development and environmental improvement. The training programmes comprise the delivery of national schemes and the design of customised measures to reflect local circumstances throughout Scotland. The LECs implement government-funded training programmes in their individual areas; assess local requirements for industrial property and for environmental improvement or land renewal schemes and investigate and recommend new local initiatives in respect of training and economic and social development. The LECs operate in defined geographical areas and within the strategic context established by the parent organisations.

The Scottish arrangements are distinctive: they differ considerably in their remit and their potential for securing an integrated development framework when compared with the institutions in England and Wales. The new bodies have a much broader role to play than their predecessors (Fairley and Lloyd 1995). In practice, SE and HIE provide strategic policy guidance and expert advice to the LECs on individual economic sectors; undertake major projects or research activities which extend beyond the areas of individual LECs; provide individual LECs with a range of central support services which will initially include administrative, accounting and property services; undertake marketing and inward investment programmes for the areas in question; undertake major environmental improvement and land renewal programmes, in consultation with the LECs involved; and monitor the progress of the LECs in implementing their plans and achieving their objectives. Crucially the LECs are contracted to SE and HIE to secure the provision of economic development and training services.

Operational and theoretical issues

The rationale for the enterprise agencies' operations is important. For example, Haughton and Peck (1991) point to the neo-classical rationale that underpins the training and enterprise councils (TECs) which operate in England and Wales. The same principles underpin the enterprise networks in Scotland. The principle of market failure underpins the regional and local enterprise bodies.

A market failure may exist where the market does not work efficiently because of a number of factors, including the existence of public goods (which, because of their inherent characteristics, are likely to be under-provided or not provided at all by the market) and the creation of external effects (often in the form of costs, which are referred to as spillovers, which are not compensated for through the normal market processes). The existence of a market failure is bad insofar as it represents a misallocation of resources, which detracts from the overall level of welfare in a given society. However, market failure does not mean that nothing good has happened, only that the best attainable outcome has not been achieved. Market failures are generally structurally embedded in the economic system itself. The market failure 'has to be seen as something that is extensive and endemic to economic systems, not as a peripheral deviation from an ideal' (Pearce 1977, p.127). Yet the view of market failure as a 'peripheral deviation of an ideal' has engendered a view that market failures are essentially *ad hoc* occurrences which can be corrected either by the market or, where strictly necessary, by limited public sector intervention. This is evident in that the LECs are intended by government to get involved in their local economy only where there is 'market failure', and to know their 'exit strategy' from intervention at the outset. In their evidence to the enquiry conducted by the Scottish Affairs Committee, SE made it clear that 'market failure' may be widely understood. Indeed the labour market is often viewed by economists as a 'market' which is characterised by 'failure'. Within this reasoning there are probably very few forms of action which are likely to be considered by the enterprise networks which would be ruled out by the 'market failure' doctrine.

The market failure debate has triggered an interest in the related concept of government failure. It has been argued that in recent years, 'there has been a resurgence of faith in the welfare generating properties of the market mechanism and growing disillusionment with the ability of government to improve on market outcomes, even where markets are working imperfectly' (Roper and Snowden 1987, p.48). Ashford (1985, p.44) has argued that 'when the reality of government failure is measured against the reality of market failure, the former is much worse'. This suggests that intervention, where justified by the market failure argument, would best be limited so as to avoid any perceived negative effects of intervention and displacement of the market mechanisms. Fairley (1991, 1996a), for example, points to the continuation of the 'voluntarist' traditions in the training roles of the LECs where the strategic objective is to reduce state funding and gradually effect a transfer of responsibility to the private sector. This is an ambitious objective given the historic and well-documented reluctance of many employers to fund employee training.

Whether any real progress towards minimalist intervention and voluntarist solutions is being achieved is difficult to determine. SE (1995), for example, has claimed very high levels of 'leverage' in training, with the private sector: public sector funding ratio standing at about 3:1. It is not clear how this ratio was calculated, but if SE's view is accurate then it would seem to suggest substantial progress in limiting the extent of intervention by enhancing the contribution of the private sector. Further progress in this respect could lead to a questioning of the very necessity of the public sector input. At programme level, however, matters look different. There is no evidence that the private sector is willing to take the main responsibility for the unemployed, who remain the principal beneficiaries of state-funded training. And some employee-focused programmes appear to be the antithesis of voluntarism. The new 'modern apprentice' programme puts public money into employing enterprises with apparently little thought being given to deadweight and substitution, or to equality of opportunity.

The constitution and governance of Scotland

In England and Wales, the TECs have been acclaimed as a constitutional innovation: 'There is nothing quite like them anywhere in the world' (Marquand 1991, p.12). Furthermore, it has been suggested that the TECs enjoyed considerably greater powers than the private industry councils in the USA on which the institutions were loosely modelled. These points are valid also for the Scottish LECs. But two additional points need to be stressed.

First, the LECs are considerably more powerful than the TECs (Fairley and Lloyd 1995). LECs have responsibility for the provision of specific services associated with training, enterprise and business development and environmental improvement. These involve the delivery of national schemes and the design of customised measures to reflect local circumstances. Further, LECs are engaged in industrial property, business development, environmental improvement and land renewal. The LECs are distinguished by the potential of an integrated development framework in bringing together the key foundation stones of local economic development. In comparison, TECs are essentially focused on training but the LECs go much further in effectively being able to manage the planned renewal of local economies by the integration of the constituent services. It would appear that there is much more coordination than previously, particularly where training is linked to business development. The power of the LECs is considerable, but it is also constrained, particularly by the terms of the operating contract with SE or HIE.

In the key areas where the LECs are active there is a considerable degree of institutional fragmentation. This is not of the LECs making, but it affects the environment in which the LECs seek to be effective. In business development, for example, the LECs, local authorities, enterprise trusts, chambers of commerce and others are active. In the training area there is such a plethora of agencies at work that one commentator has suggested that it may be impossible for strategy to emerge (Fairley 1996a).

Second, as a form of 'constitutional innovation' the LECs present the paradox that they have been introduced and championed by a government which has set itself strongly against democratic constitutional reform for Scotland. This aspect of the LECs cannot be left out of any assessment of their performance. Paterson (1994, p.171) has argued that the formation of the LECs reflected a nineteenth-century belief 'that the essence of the nation lay in its people's autonomous and private activities'. This reflects the over-riding economic ideology which prompted the initial design of the SE and HIE arrangements and which provides a wider context within which the organisations operate. Much of government policy in Scotland is predicated on the notions of market forces, individualism, self-help and partnership. In the wider constitutional context, however, the very nature of the LECs may lead to a degree of politicisation of the previously technocratic area of economic development, particularly if LEC performance is believed to be weak.

Despite the partisan nature and controversial aspects of the 1990 reforms, however, the SE and HIE networks seem to have established a firm consensual support for their activities. As advocated by the Scottish Affairs Committee, the Scottish Office (1996) has urged them to work more closely with the local authorities. This will assume more importance in light of the changing arrangements for local governance in Scotland. The main opposition political party proposes broadening the management boards and strengthening accountability to an elected Scottish parliament. But the fundamental nature of the networks is not now seen as a matter of controversy.

A management revolution?
Marquand (1991) hints at the huge management change required in moving from centralised civil service-driven programmes to delivery through local companies. In this respect the LECs have brought the language of the business sector to their area of public policy. Public sector policies for economic development and training are controlled by contracts and

monitored for performance. Some funding is output related and this is perhaps the most radical management change.

However, two major doubts have been expressed about the nature of the management change which has occurred. The first is that the system of contracts and performance management is more designed to bolster central control than to support local autonomy. In Power's (1994) terms the LECs are ensnared in a 'low trust' management system which leaves them little policy freedom. The second is that the performance management system relies on targets and indicators some of which are likely to encourage 'short-termism' while others will have 'displacement' effects similar to those associated with centralised Soviet economic planning (Gray 1996). The LECs will work to meet their targets whether or not these are what the local economy most needs. The irony is clear for reforms which intended to bolster local enterprise!

Employer empowerment?

The establishment of the networks has brought the private sector much more into public policy making at national and local level. This was widely held to be desirable, particularly in training policy. SE, HIE and the LECs are required to have two-thirds of their boards drawn from the private sector. Some LECs also employ other devices such as advisory committees to widen employer involvement. Grampian Enterprise, for example, has a membership scheme which is shared with the local Chamber of Commerce. While the private sector is much more involved than many would have considered possible in the 1980s, important questions remain about the level and quality of that involvement.

The procedures for filling board vacancies were criticised by the Scottish Affairs Committee (1995). The problem is that once established a LEC board will tend to become a self-selecting and self-perpetuating group. In this scenario far from a general empowering of the private sector the reform could be seen as privileging a small business elite in each LEC area. And most of the activity of the LECs remains centrally determined either by the parent body or by the Scottish Office. They have little policy autonomy. In training provision, for example, more than 95% of their expenditures remain tied to national programmes (Scottish Enterprise 1995).

The concept of the LEC as the property of a small elite seemed to be given some support by a 1996 survey of small firms commissioned by the Federation of Small Business (1996, p.12). It found that 72% of small firms in the SE area could not name the appropriate LEC and that there was widespread confusion between enterprise trusts and LECs.

Decentralisation?

The earlier institutions, the SDA, the HIDB and the MSC, were perceived to be quite centralised organisations. The MSC in particular was seen as remote, bureaucratic and powerful by its partners. While the SDA's operational efficiency was widely respected, many local authorities found it remote, bureaucratic and over-bearing, particularly in instances where the organisation entered into partnership with local authorities and other public agencies in the pursuit of area-focused economic regeneration.

Within the SE and HIE framework the LECs were set up in part to refocus attention on local economies and local labour markets. Paterson (1994, p.172) observed that the LECs 'are almost bound to be more embedded in local Scottish society' than their predecessors. The involvement of local people at board level ensures that. Even if the board becomes something of a clique it is still local in character, with the interests of the locality at the centre of its thinking.

However, doubts remain about the extent of the decentralisation which is taking place. What degree of autonomy do the LECs really enjoy? To what extent are the LECs merely local agencies for implementing policies determined elsewhere? Perhaps responsibility and elements of accountability are being devolved to the local level rather than any ability to tailor policy to local need.

Improving accountability?

The SDA, the HIDB and the MSC were only weakly accountable to Parliament – the SDA and the HIDB through the Scottish Secretary, and the MSC through the Employment Secretary. The MSC had no real accountability at Scottish level for its operations in Scotland. None of the organisations was accountable at the local level. One aim of the 1990 reform was to improve institutional accountability, in its regional and local dimensions, and to make operational matters more transparent. The principal concern of the Scottish Affairs Committee was whether the new accountability arrangements were working satisfactorily.

There can be little doubt that accountability has been changed. On the financial side, for example, there is a clear upward line of accountability from LEC to SE and HIE to the Scottish Office and to the Treasury. Accountability is secured also through the contracts between SE and HIE and their LECs and the strategic guidance and operating instructions given to SE and HIE by the Scottish Office. The LECs are subject to the audit requirements on private companies and may be separately held to account for any expenditure financed by the European Union. The lines of financial accountability are more clearly in place, even if some of the LECs do complain of being 'audited to death'.

The recommendations and conclusions of the Committee reflected this concern with the need to enhance accountability of the enterprise network particularly in the context of the relationships between LECs and their respective communities and localities. The Scottish Affairs Committee recommended that the geographical coverage of the LECs in the Scottish Enterprise network be reviewed to ensure coterminosity between their boundaries and those of local authorities. Further, the Committee wished to see local authorities and others in the public sector being involved fully with the development of the LECs' training strategy. The theme of accountability was pursued also through a recommendation that there be greater openness in the letting of contracts by LECs to local contractors – a policy already developed by HIE. Finally, the Committee drew attention to the importance of better consultation between the LECs and the new local authorities, a point subsequently supported by the Scottish Office (1996).

Whilst the principal attention of the Committee was directed to the issues of accountability and of securing a greater legitimacy for the enterprise networks in Scottish local governance and communities it stressed also the need for a strategic perspective to be developed with regard to a comprehensive skills strategy for Scotland which could be linked to sectoral targets in partnership with industries. The point here is that an aspect of accountability is the way in which the enterprise networks are responding to the problems of the Scottish economy as a whole (Fairley and Lloyd 1995).

In certain respects, however, accountability may also have been weakened. MPs asking questions about their local LEC in Parliament have been told to take the matter up directly with the chief executive or chairman. Some have complained about the quality of the LEC response and have contrasted this with the carefully researched answer which they would have expected from Parliament in the old system. And there remains an 'accountability gap' at local level. LECs are simply not accountable to their local communities. It is not easy to change this state of affairs; the LECs' legal status as limited companies provides a formidable obstacle. However there may be scope for some improvements in the relationships which the LECs develop with the new unitary local authorities. In Edinburgh, for example, the LEC and the city council are working to a joint economic strategy. This could lend to the LEC some of the legitimacy of the democratically accountable local authority. However it would still be a weak form of local accountability.

Governance and the regional planning agenda

It is evident that the established regional planning tradition in Scotland continues to evolve in response to emerging and changing circumstances. Within the wider constitutional debate about the future governance of Scotland the nature of regional planning will play a major role (Paterson 1994; Bell and Dow 1995). The regional development agencies are already being confronted with political pressures and concerns about their accountability to the communities for which they have responsibility. At the same time, other forces for change are emerging. The issues associated with the operation and accountability of the enterprise networks are thrown into sharper relief because of the process of local government reorganisation in Scotland.

In 1996, a new system of 32 all-purpose local authorities was introduced. These have responsibility for securing the delivery of a number of services such as education, structure planning, local planning and development control, social work, housing and economic development (Lang 1994). The reorganisation ended the regional character of Scottish local government through the fragmentation of many of the previous administrative units (Alexander and Orr 1994; McFadden 1996). Thus in place of the nine regional councils which had discharged a strategic role for the management of change within relatively large geographical areas there are now 29 councils which required special arrangements for joint working to be put into place to secure a coordinated perspective of the strategic issues. This fragmentation and erosion of space is not even across Scotland but it will impact more heavily on certain areas such as Strathclyde and Tayside. Where the fragmentation is greatest, the LECs may assume ownership of the regional strategic perspective on the management of change. Thus in the former Tayside region the LEC, Scottish Enterprise Tayside, which covers the area of three smaller unitary authorities, now has the strategic overview for planning the region. This brings the debate back to the accountability of such arrangements.

Interestingly, there is also scope for competition and even conflict within the new arrangements. Between 1975 and 1996 local authorities had weak, cash-limited powers for economic development (Fairley 1996b) and were able to use the planning framework to improve the local economy (Rowan-Robinson and Lloyd 1987; McQuaid 1992). Local government reorganisation introduces an interesting balance of change. The 1994 legislation gives Scottish local authorities the clear legal mandate to conduct local economic measures (Fairley 1996b). As a result, economic development will become a more legitimate sphere of activity for the unitary authorities notwithstanding the discretionary nature of the powers and the fact that such activity will have to compete within general resource parameters of the authorities. The power will certainly place economic development as an item on local authority agendas and it may serve to act as a 'glue' to the other general developmental activities (Lloyd 1995). More local authorities are recognising the importance of economic development and many are making it a strategic priority. These councils are seeking to maximise their overall impact on their local economies, and to work in partnership with the LECs and others for this purpose.

Conclusions

SE and HIE represent the most recent manifestation of the regional planning tradition in Scotland. Intervention by such regional institutions is clearly a highly political activity in that it rests on the relationships and power linkages between the different interests in society in defined geographical areas (Delafons 1995). This is borne out by the experience of the bodies and the issues encountered in attempting a provisional evaluation of their contribution to the Scottish economy. It has been argued that attempts to find universal solutions to problems have 'at times failed to understand the needs of the locality and its regional context' (Morphet 1995, p.203). This is the case in the context of SE, HIE and the LECs. The design of these bodies reflects a prevailing ideology which, as with any set of such ideas, serves a dual function: first, to explain, justify or contest the prevailing political arrangements within a community and, second, to provide plans for action for public political institutions (Freeden 1990). SE and HIE reflect a changing relationship between the public and private sectors with greater involvement by the private sector in public policy. Within the public sector there is a greater emphasis on the central than the local (Wapshott and Brock 1983; Harden 1987).

This makes for a complex and volatile mix of influences, assumptions and parameters to action by the organisations. It also makes any assessment very difficult as the effect of SE and HIE on the Scottish economy transcends narrow concerns with economic development, employment generation and skill enhancement. Rather, the impact of the institutional innovation raises a series of fundamental questions about the evolving nature of governance and accountability in Scotland today.

References

Alexander, A. and Orr, K. (1994) 'The reform of Scottish local government.' *Public Money and Management 14*, 1, 33–38.

Ashford, N. (1985) 'The bankruptcy of collectivism.' In A. Seldon (ed) *The 'New Right' Enlightenment.* London: Economic and Literary Books.

Bell, D. and Dow, S. (1995) 'Economic policy options for a Scottish Parliament.' *Scottish Affairs 13,* 42–67.

Brown, A., McCrone, D. and Paterson, L. (eds) (1996) *Politics and Society in Scotland.* London: Macmillan.

Damesick, P. and Wood, P. (1987) 'Public policy for regional development: restoration or reformation?' In P. Damesick and P. Wood (eds) *Regional Problems, Problem Regions and Public Policy in the United Kingdom.* Oxford: Clarendon Press.

Danson, M., Lloyd, M.G. and Newlands, D. (1990) 'The role of development agencies in regional economic regeneration. A Scottish case study.' In R. Harrison and M. Hart (eds) *Spatial Policy in a Divided Nation.* London, Jessica Kingsley Publishers.

Delafons, J. (1995) 'Planning research and the policy process.' *Town Planning Review 66,* 1, 83–110.

Diamond, D. (1979) 'The uses of strategic planning: the example of the National Planning Guidelines in Scotland.' *Town Planning Review 50,* 1, 18–25.

Fairley, J. (1991) 'Scottish Enterprise, Highlands and Islands Enterprise and the local enterprise companies – some questions concerning vocational education and training in Scotland.' In S. Hardy and M.G. Lloyd (eds) *Business Development and Training: An Integrated Approach to Regional Policy?* London: Regional Studies Association.

Fairley, J. (1996a) 'Vocational education and training in Scotland – towards a strategic approach?' *Scottish Educational Review 28,* 1, 50–60.

Fairley, J. (1996b) 'Scotland's new local authorities and economic development.' *Scottish Affairs 15,* 101–122.

Fairley, J. and Lloyd, M.G. (1995) 'Economic development and training. The roles of Scottish Enterprise, Highlands and Islands Enterprise and the local enterprise companies.' *Scottish Affairs 12,* 52–72.

Federation of Small Business (1996) *The Enterprise Network in Scotland – a Survey of Members' Opinions.* Glasgow: FSB.

Freeden, M. (1990) 'The stranger at the feast: ideology in twentieth century Britain.' *Twentieth Century British History 1,* 1, 9–34.

Glasson, J. (1993) 'The fall and rise of regional planning in the economically advanced nations.' In R. Paddison, J. Money and W. Lever (eds) *International Perspectives in Urban Studies 1.* London: Jessica Kingsley Publishers.

Gray, A. (1996) 'Contract culture and Stalin's ghost: the distortive effects of output measures in local regeneration programmes.' Paper presented to the International Labour Markets Conference, The Robert Gordon University, Aberdeen.

Harden, I. (1987) 'Corporatism without Labour: the British version.' In C. Graham and T. Prosser (eds) *Waiving the Rules. The Constitution Under Thatcher.* Milton Keynes: The Open University Press.

Harvey, D. (1989) 'From managerialism to entrepreneurialism.' *Geografissker Annaler* *71B*, 3–17.

Haughton, G. and Peck, J. (1991) 'Evaluating TECs as effective labour market institutions: some theoretical and applied considerations.' In S. Hardy and M.G. Lloyd (eds) *Business Development and Training: An Integrated Approach to Regional Policy?* London: Regional Studies Association.

Lang, I. (1994) 'Local government reorganisation.' *Scottish Affairs 6*, 14–24.

Lloyd, M.G. (1995) 'Reorganisation and economic development.' In S. Black (ed) *The Impact of Re-organisation on Particular Services.* University of Edinburgh: Unit for the Study of Government in Scotland.

Marquand, J. (1991) 'TECS: a challenge for evaluators. The evaluation of training and enterprise councils.' In S. Hardy and M.G. Lloyd (eds) *Business Development and Training: An Integrated Approach to Regional Policy?* London: Regional Studies Association.

McCrone, D. (1994) *Understanding Scotland. The Sociology of a Stateless Nation.* London: Routledge.

McFadden, J. (1996) 'The structure and function of local government under a Scottish parliament.' *Scottish Affairs 17*, 32–42.

McQuaid, R. (1992) *Local Authorities and Economic Development in Scotland.* Edinburgh: COSLA.

Morphet, J. (1995) 'Planning research and the policy process.' *Town Planning Review 66*, 2, 199–206.

Paterson, L. (1994) *The Autonomy of Modern Scotland.* Edinburgh: Edinburgh University Press.

Pearce, D.W. (1977) 'Justifiable government intervention in preserving the quality of life.' In L. Wingo and A. Evans (eds) *Public Economics and the Quality of Life.* Baltimore: The John Hopkins University Press.

Power, M. (1994) *The Audit Society.* London: Demos.

Roper, B. and Snowden, B. (1987) 'The fall and rise of laissez-faire.' In B. Roper and B. Snowden (eds) *Markets, Intervention and Planning.* Harlow: Longman.

Rowan-Robinson, J. and Lloyd, M.G. (1987) 'Local authority economic development activity in Scotland: further evidence.' *Local Economy 2*, 1, 49–54.

Scottish Affairs Committee (1995) *The Operation of the Enterprise Agencies and the LECs. Volume 1, HC-339i.* London: HMSO.

Scottish Enterprise (1995) Evidence to the Scottish Affairs Committee.

Scottish Office (1996) *Report of the Scottish Affairs Committee on the Operation of the Enterprise Agencies and the LECs – Response from the Secretary of State for Scotland, the Rt Hon Michael Forsyth MP.* Cm 3036. Edinburgh: HMSO.

Wannop, U. and Cherry, G. (1994) 'The development of regional planning in the UK.' *Planning Perspectives 9*, 29–60.

Wapshott, N. and Brock, G. (1983) *Thatcher.* London: Futura.

CHAPTER 12

Regional Development
and Political Democracy

Jan Olsson

Introduction

The international political economy has been characterised during the last 20 years by an intensified competition of trade and investments. Large variations in business cycles cannot hide the fact that the Western countries have had difficulties in preserving high long-term levels of growth and employment. Newly industrialised countries (NICs) have efficiently challenged mature industrial countries in traditional manufacturing production, while the Japanese industrial success has increased the competition about advanced, knowledge-based production. The international struggle for good terms of trade has intensified and will be a decisive factor for the future levels of employment and welfare (Gilpin 1987; Walters and Blake 1992).

For several decades traditional industrial production has had a tendency to concentrate on peripheral geographical areas, while management and R&D functions have concentrated on central geographical markets. This means that the international competition is one between sub-national actors (regions and cities), rather than between nations. One theme in the literature is, for instance, the competition between big cities in the world economy (Savitch and Thomas 1991).

When it comes to actual responsibility for (economic) development, local and regional actors have become increasingly important during the 1980s and 90s. The traditional dominance of the state level has decreased, partly due to budget deficits and more complicated patterns of economic problems. During this time we have also seen a transformation of regional policies from an ambition to redistribute economic activity from prosperous to disadvantaged areas to strategies aimed at promoting the development of indigenous industries within individual regions. Regional policy has transformed to a more general development policy (Halkier and Danson 1995; Olsson 1995; Goetz and Clarke 1993).

One important aspect of this policy change can be called the 'marketisation' of industrial and regional policy. Public development actors adopted strategies and methods which better conformed with traditional market-based, entrepreneurial behaviour. Ideology and politics did not fit in well in this new epoch of public-private partnerships. (Public) policy was given larger degrees of freedom, often within private law organisations, making it possible to interact with private actors in a more pragmatic and flexible way. The new kind of development units were often set up to be able to operate at arm's length from politicians; development policies were rescued from politics (Halkier 1992; Halkier and Danson 1995; Olsson 1995). If we take this issue one step further, however, we may ask if rescuing policy from politics also means rescuing it from democracy? If we stand up for democracy do we anyhow put it on stake by safeguarding policy from politics? It is here important to make a distinction between the creation and implementation of policies. Much of the arm's-length argument basically refers to implementation, but in practice it is difficult to make a clear distinction between the two aspects. From a democratic point of view it seems reasonable that at least processes of policy formulation should to a large extent be handled and controlled by dominant political actors (parties and politicians) in an individual region.

However, research and experience do not provide much hope for a strong democratic influence in the processes of planning and decision making. Research has shown the tendency towards segmentation in different policy arenas, which are described and analysed as mixed administration, negotiated economics, iron triangles, corporatism and so on (Olsen 1978; Hernes 1978; Benson 1981; Pedersen 1988; Nielsen and Pedersen 1989). This tendency towards segmentation and problems of governance has increased due to internationalisation and EU integration. No longer is the agenda setting dominated by popularly elected parliaments, but rather by supra-national networks of authorities, international organisations and private companies (Petersson et al. 1996; Andersen and Burns 1996). In the EU integration, the Swedish state administration has increased its importance in Swedish politics due to its central role in both the creation (input) and implementation (output) of public policy (Olsson 1993); it has even been said that we now find ourselves in a post-parliamentary phase. Andersen and Burns argue that the parliament, the heart of the political systems of the Western world, is suffering from 'systematic erosion'. They state that: 'the system of post-parliamentary government tends increasingly to be one of organisations, by organisations and for organisations. Expert sovereignty tends to prevail over popular sovereignty or parliamentary sovereignty' (Andersen and Burns 1996, p.229).

Given that actual planning and decision-making processes seem to be deviating from the traditional textbook models of public decision making, it is particularly important to carry out empirical investigations into how policy is created and carried out in transnational contexts. The complex problems of democracy and development are especially interesting in relation to the EU-integrated regional policy field. In many different appointed regions hundreds of millions of crowns are allocated in a complex interplay between a number of different organisations from the local level right up to the European Commission. So, which actors influence the formulation of problems and goals in the regional development plans? Can one say that the planning processes are democratic in any reasonable sense?

Aim and method

The purpose of this essay is to analyse regional policy in relation to the EU and in which respects it can be said to be democratic. It is based on the results from an empirical investigation financed by the Federation of Swedish County Councils: *Regional Development in a European Context – a Democratic Analysis*. Four regions and their Structural Funds planning were analysed with regard to the following aspects:

- What concept of development is seen in their plans
- What actors have been influential in defining the problems to be faced in the plans, and in formulating the goals
- Whose interests are expressed in the plans.

The investigation was made in the form of comparative case studies, in which the cases varied in level of institutional complexity (Yin 1984; Merriam 1994). The following regions were investigated:

- Objective 2 Bergslagen in the middle of Sweden, which consists of parts of five counties, and includes a total of 24 local authorities.
- Objective 2 Blekinge in the south of Sweden, which consists of one county and four local authorities. (One of the county's local authorities is not included.)
- Objective 2 North Jutland in Denmark, which consists of 16 local authorities in the county of North Jutland. It is a region with long experiences of EU related regional policy.

- Inter-regional plan - Jämtland/Tröndelag which consists of one Swedish county and eight local authorities, two Norwegian counties and 49 local authorities.

We were searching for similarities within disparities and for unique conditions which, based on good grounds, could be explained by regionally determined conditions. A mix of different methods were used, the development plans were analysed (documentary studies), and the planning processes were studied with the help of an interview mapping technique (Hjern and Porter 1983; Olsson 1995). In the initial phase, when those who were most responsible were interviewed, interview visits were used, while in the later phase telephone interviews were primarily used to confirm and complement earlier results. The interviews were qualitative in character and characterised by a cautious and receptive attitude.

A democratic perspective

One way of analysing democracy is to start with a number of principles and values which should be present in a good working democracy. This approach is quite common in different types of evaluations of democracy (Beetham 1994; Petersson *et al.* 1996), and it is fruitful for analysis of complex contexts characterised by multiple actors and many levels of decision making.

The Council on Democracy is a group of Swedish political scientists who carry out regular audits on the actual operation of Swedish democracy. The Council has formulated an ideal of democracy which contains several different criteria or values. They see democracy not simply as a question of popular support and control, but also one of rule of law as well as capacity for effective action, which means that certain values can come into conflict with one another. Facing dilemmas and making difficult choices are therefore natural elements in the practice of democracy, not merely technical problems which experts can deal with. It is a question of fundamental, normative choices for which we all should seek reasonable solutions in public debate. Ideals of a perfect or optimal democracy are fruitless and, at worst, misleading (Petersson *et al.* 1996, p.12 ff). The theoretical approach of this article is partly based on the model of the Council on Democracy, and it is motivated as follows:

- *The regulation of powers.* A fundamental criterion of democracy is the regulation of political power so that any suspicion of arbitrary use of that power is removed. There should be no doubt about which actor has the right to exercise power in a given situation. This is a basic criterion in order to be able to hold politicians accountable. In this article the following question will be assessed: Is there a clear regulation on how the influence of different actors should be exercised in different areas, that is, who has the overall responsibility for production of Structural Funds plans, and who is allowed to be involved in the partnership?

- *Popular support and control.* Popular sovereignty is fundamental in democratic thinking and implies specific demands on political decision-making processes. 1) Which actors influence the agenda setting and problem definitions in the policy field? 2) Are there good preconditions for transparency and public debates that can contribute to an informed understanding of regional development issues? 3) Are there good preconditions for holding responsible decision makers accountable for their actions? If citizens in these regions are not satisfied, is it relatively easy to determine who is responsible and choose an alternative policy in democratic elections?

- *Capacity for effective action.* If a democracy lacks the capacity for effective action it risks losing its legitimacy regardless of how well its popular support and participation work. Every democratic system must be able to show results if its legitimacy is not to be weakened in the long run, although in this study we shall not discuss implementation and results since the aim is to study planning processes. Capacity for action is also studied in relation to planning and with regard to the question: are there preconditions and available resources so that the planning process can work efficiently?

Ideas of development

Development is a complex concept with many dimensions. There is no value-neutral definition of development, it means different things for different actors. In what follows we will analyse the idea of development in the plans of the four regions, and consider a number of dimensions within the concept of development.

In the first place one can speak of levels of development. Do we mean the individual's, the company's, the town's, the nation's, the EU's or the whole world's development? A deep understanding of development integrates many levels, while a shallow notion of it focuses on one or two levels. Second, development processes usually affect several types of problem areas. Are many or few areas affected? Is there a perspective which integrates the public and the private sector or is there the traditional dualism between them?

Third, the concept of development can be directed at quite different aspects of reality. Is it a question of economic/material or social/human development? A fourth aspect of this concept is change over time. When is the right time to measure and evaluate any particular effort? Should development be measured as a result or as a process, and should it be measured quantitatively or qualitatively?

The four Structural Funds plans have a very similar structure and lay-out. They are painted with a broad brush which gives the impression of their being the overall development plan for the region as a whole. All the plans offer a broad description of their region's problems, assets, weaknesses and possibilities. However, the actual aims show that their view of development is quite narrow and traditional, which negates their chances of being the key to an overall development plan for the region. For example, their views of development are characterised by traditional dualism between private and public; the private sector should solve development problems; the public sector constitutes an important prerequisite and support system for private business but is not a development object in itself. The plans are very structured, making top-down control possible. They seem to be a way of getting, distributing and controlling effects of economic support, rather than being the region's own visions and strategies for development.

All of the regions' development plans present themselves as being homogeneous units without internal or external conflicts of interest. There are, for example, no descriptions of current local development strategies and how these either coincide or conflict with the aims of the Structural Funds plans. Companies and individuals are regarded as target groups for the goals and efforts of the plans. There are no analyses in the plans regarding the degree to which companies, local authorities and individuals are interested in and capable of developing projects for application of economic support. The Structural Funds plans have an instrumental planning character, with the region seen as both a unitary area and actor. In other words there are no conflicts or conflicting interests in these development plans.

In all the Structural Funds plans examined it is the economic/material aspect of development that dominates. Development is to be measured and evaluated by increased employment, new companies, increases in hotel bookings in the region and so on. Of course, one could point to the goals of raising educational and skills levels within the plans as an expression of a more social/humanistic perspective, which would be correct in one sense. The problem is, however, that even social and human aspects are evaluated from a quantitative, output perspective, with economic/material goals in focus. They are about human beings as factors of production, not as complex social creatures with many and varying needs.

This view of development in the Structural Funds plans does not emphasise the qualitative processes in development but rather its quantitative outcome. A large number of indicators are formulated in the different plans and expected results are specified in detail. The structure of the plans facilitates control rather than development initiatives (Scott 1995).

It is remarkable that the expected results of all the plans are calculated without any specific analysis of developments of important external parameters. For example, no assessment is made on how important factors such as levels of taxation and its distribution of different factors of production and goods affect the outcome, which is curious considering that employment is such a central indicator in all the plans. We seem to have a paradox here, in that an instrumental and closed approach to planning dominates regional development in the new Europe without frontiers.

All in all the philosophy of the Structural Funds plans is rather shallow and narrow and emphasises the economic/material aspects which are then measured and checked quantitatively. The question is, what conditions and what actors have contributed to the formation of this view of development?

The planning processes

Formal responsibility for the planning processes varies in the Nordic countries. In Norway and Denmark popularly elected regional institutions have formal responsibility, that is the county councils called Fylke and Amt. In Sweden, it is the Swedish National Board for Industrial and Technological Development (NUTEK) that is formally responsible, but the government also appoints special operative officials often from different county administrative boards (*Lánsstyrelsen*), which are state administrations on the regional level (not popularly elected). Considering that the planning is an inter-organisational process (partnership) it is not surprising that popular support was not noticeably better in Denmark and Norway compared with Sweden. The democratic problem is more complicated than that. However, some differences could be found in the sense that popular support was considered more satisfying among politicians and officials in North and South Tröndelag (Norway) compared with actors in similar positions in Jämtland (Sweden). In Jämtland, there were representatives (politicians and officials) both from local authorities and the county council (*Landstinget*) that were critical to the fact that the board officials had controlled the process. One of the politicians in the county council said, in frustration, that we had to try to break into the planning process.

The Swedish government delayed several months before appointing operative officials to the new EU regions. This created uncertainty and stress among actors in the regions, especially since several were involved and no one was clearly responsible for the regional development issue, which resulted in competition and power games between different organisations. This was toned down when operative officials were appointed; the processes became more constructive but nevertheless remained stressful. Of course there is no guarantee that regional responsibility will be unambiguous through a 'long-term' central government decision, since several other actors are interested in regular involvement. In North Jutland (Denmark) for example, where the Amt has responsibility, there is a clear challenge from the Aalborg region which is made up of Aalborg itself and local authorities around it. This new regional body is interested in establishing a more formal role within the EU-related regional policy area, which can be interpreted as an open competition with the county council of North Jutland.

Even if the complexity of the policy area contributes to problems for democracy in form of uncertainty and unclear boundaries of responsibility, it appears, nevertheless, that the powerful role of unelected officials in all of the planning processes is an even more severe democratic problem. It is these officials, mainly at the regional level (Amt, Fylke and Länsstyrelsen), who have been the driving force behind the planning process; they have had a decisive influence on its organisation. They decide, among other things, who is to be invited to take part, for which there are no clear rules, only some advice and guidelines from the central government which are thought to be rather general and superficial. Furthermore, the unelected officials have dominated the formulation of problems and goals. The elected representatives, along with others have played rather the role of external advisors. The partnership has offered a certain legitimacy, since leading politicians and leaders in other fields have had insight but limited control, but in all of the new EU regions it was hard to have time to get external actors to commit themselves to such a working partnership. North Jutland's most recent planning process, an Objective 2 plan for 1997–99, has had a more developed partnership than in the three new EU-regions; there is more of a working partnership which, within the framework of a number of working groups, comes up with ideas and provides the basis for a plan. In particular, the world of business has been represented here to a far greater extent than in the new regions, where it has been principally actors from the public sector who have put together regional plans to develop private business.

In none of the regions has there been a strong presence of political parties, popular movements or a mobilisation of opinion in the planning processes. The conflicts which have taken place have not been ideological, such as green and small-scale versus large-scale industrial strategy. The policy area has been characterised by a low level of politicisation; more a question of trying to develop one's own region rather than scoring party political points.

As regards the content of the plans one could speak of consensus in the view of development. It is affected very much by the structure and lay-out demanded by the European Commission, which also explains the similar character of the four different regions. This policy area is imbued by what could be called an ideology of partnership that contributes to cooperation and the search for consensual solutions.

Divided interests in the planning process were rather between different authorities and concerned how to put together Structural Funds plans and, to some extent, what sort of organisation should perform the implementation. There were different interests concerning the form and method, rather than the content of the plans, that is to say, an institutional positioning game rather than an ideological struggle. Sometimes these aspects coincided in some actors' strategies. A good example of this can be seen in the planning process of Bergslagen. The five county councils had together hired a consultant who put together proposals which were in their joint interest. Among other things he emphasised the health aspect within the development, which would have meant a considerable expansion of the concept of development. This proposal was quickly the object of criticism by leading board officials who said that this lay outside the Objective 2 programme and would never be accepted by the Commission. A wider view of development was not to be allowed.

The dominance of appointed officials and the almost apolitical nature of the process are common to all the regions and, to a great extent, can be explained by the complexity of the policy field, involving many different actors (private-public and central-local). This complexity has increased considerably since the field began to be integrated with the regional policy of EU. Despite these common characteristics, however, we can discern, as regards the role of officials, considerable differences which can be linked to variations in the level of institutional complexity in the regions. The more complex the region is, the stronger the domination of appointed officials. Of the regions investigated Bergslagen is the most complex and Blekinge is the simplest, while the two other regions lie somewhere in between. Institutional complexity gives officials a degree of freedom which is increased when the time-frame is short: the faster the tempo of planning the fewer the actors involved. The role of officials seems far from the Weberian bureaucrat; a restricted number of officials who dominate the planning process in the more complex regions, particularly in Bergslagen, act more like entrepreneurial officials. This means that the nature of the work is creative and process-oriented, i.e. it is formed and changed during the process by their own contributions, often at a high tempo using fax and telephone. A communicative, consensus-seeking rationality is decisive for success when organisational structures and relations to the world outside are horizontal and 'boundless'. The planning process involves, furthermore, a real improvement in professional competence for this type of official, which in turn means that its influence increases over time. This is particularly noticeable if there is a change in the actors around them, not least in the elected representatives. The influential weight of this type of official tends to increase because his or her skills of competence are more in demand, especially in high-level negotiations.

Two officials (one in Bergslagen and one in North Jutland) had been practising at the Commission's DG XVI, which strengthened their market value and experience-based competence. According to people in their networks these officials are very influential. Their role indicates the basic organisational characteristics of the EU-related regional policy. Their influence is based on strategically important contacts of a horizontal as well as vertical character; they have lynch-pin positions in the intersection between complex horizontal and vertical networks. There are two basic driving forces in this complexity. The first is that the inter-organisational networks have a technocratic character, implying that policy formulation developed by way of a consensus-seeking, communicative rationality, rather than by a political-ideological one. Second, the planning processes have a top-down character, with the Commission as the dominant actor. It has a major influence over the agenda-setting and lays the ground for the regions' Structural Funds planning. In line with this, Joanne Scott concludes: 'It would appear that notwithstanding the rhetoric of partnership such discretion is severely limited and able to be exercised only within narrowly defined parameters which will inevitably conform to the dominant Community model of development' (Scott 1995, p.31)

Democratic planning?

In relation to our concept of democracy we can state that the policy area of regional development shows poor results.

Regarding the regulation of power we have seen that the formal responsibility has been poorly regulated; the frequency of negotiations in the policy area can be interpreted as an expression of a weak regulation of power. What does the subsidiarity principle mean in practice when regional development policy can be changed in negotiations behind locked doors between a few actors at different decision-making levels? The Commission's influence seems to be crucial. It decides the structure and form of the regional plans as well as approving them after negotiations.

The criterion of popular support and control is not fulfilled. It is a top-down system planning dominated by public officials. A limited number of leading politicians have had a minor influence, while political parties and popular movements have not been involved. The policy field is not politicised by politicians or parties. There are no conflicts along ideological lines that influence the atmosphere of the planning, which implies that public officials are given large degrees of freedom. This problem also concerns the difficult character of the regional policy field. It is about efforts today focused on the future. It is hard to judge the policies without good evaluations, which are expensive and rare. The development problem also seems to be more difficult today than compared with the situation 15 years ago. There is now a fundamental uncertainty about how public development initiatives can be made to result in new jobs (Ingelstam 1995). Furthermore, Structural Funds planning and democratic elections are not coordinated, and the large number of actors and frequent negotiations make it difficult for media and the public to assess who is really responsible. If a citizen is dissatisfied with the regional policy, what political options does he or she have in trying to influence and change it? In what election should one participate and which party and policy should one choose?

The third democratic criterion, concerning the capacity for effective action, is not unproblematic either. The time frame in the new EU regions was too short, implying that officials had to dominate in order to manage the time limit. A short time frame and lack of experience has made it impossible for the new EU regions to establish a working partnership like that in North Jutland. Beside these factors, fiscal austerity in public budgets is an important problem which reduces the capacity for effective action.

The argument of rescuing policy from politics is about giving stability and long-term conditions to development policies. This argument is particularly strong when it concerns the daily operation of development policy, that is the implementation. However, this study has shown that even the most basic political aspects of development policies (goals and priorities) are handled at arm's length from political parties and citizens of the regions. If development policies are not based on a strong and relevant democratic legitimacy, it may be difficult to rescue policy from short-term politics. Politicians with weak popular support and an unclear political mandate will probably be more sensitive to short-term initiatives from media and organised interests. If parties and politicians are experts on political visions and strategies of regional development, they will be better prepared for a democratic leadership. Democratic leadership in the post-industrial epoch, in fact, could contribute to more stable, long-term development policies. Thinking on development is needed on different levels of abstraction. Today, we see much concrete thought about marketisation and small firms. Which political visions and strategies do our political parties have when it concerns sustainable development? Which attitudes do they have to different conflicts and priorities that follow from a vision of a sustainable society? I would argue that our time of transformation is better understood as an ideological crisis or vacuum rather than a post-parliamentary phase. This means that important political work is waiting to be done; not short-term political action, but rather visionary and intellectual work.

References

Andersen, S.S. and Burns, T. (1996) 'The European Union and the erosion of parliamentary democracy: a study of post-parliamentary governance.' In S.S. Andersen and K.A. Eliassen (eds) *The European Union: How Democratic Is It?* London: Sage.

Benson, J.K. (1981) *Networks and Policy Sectors: A Framework for Extending Interorganizational Analysis.* Columbia: University of Michigan.

Beetham, D. (ed) (1994) *Defining and Measuring Democracy.* London: Sage.

Gilpin, R. (1987) *The Political Economy of International Relations.* Princeton: Princeton University Press.

Goetz, E.G. and Clarke, S.E. (1993) *The New Localism. Comparative Urban Politics in a Global Era.* New York: Sage.

Halkier, H. (1992) 'Development agencies and regional policy: the case of the Scottish Development Agency.' *Regional Politics & Policy 2,* 3, 1–26.

Halkier, H. and Danson, M. (1995) *Regional Development Agencies in Western Europe: A Survey of Key Characteristics and Trends.* University of Paisley: European Studies Working Papers, 7.

Hernes, G. (1978) *Forhandlingsokonomi och blandningsadministrasjon.* Oslo: Universitetsforlaget.

Hjern, B. and Porter, D.O. (1983) *Implementation Structures: A New Unit of Administrative Analysis in Realizing Social Science Knowledge.* Wien-Wurzburg: Physica-Verlag.

Ingelstam, L. (1995) *Ekonomi för en ny tid.* Stockholm: Carlssons.

Merriam, S. (1994) *Fallstudien som forskningsmetod.* Lund: Studentlitteratur.

Nielsen, K. and Pedersen, O.K. (eds) (1989) *Forhandlingsokonomi i Norden.* Köpenhamn: Jurist og Okonomforbundets Forlag.

Olsen, J.P. (ed) (1978) *Politisk organisering.* Oslo: Universitetsforlaget.

Olsson, J. (1993) 'Svensk statsförvaltnings EG-integration.' *Statsvetenskaplig tidskrift 4,* 332–358.

Olsson, J. (1995) *Den Lokala Näringspolitikens Politiska Ekonomi. En Jämförande Kommuntypsstudie.* Örebro: Högskolan i Örebro.

Pedersen, O.K. (1988) 'Den sönderdelte stat. Om interesseorganisationernes integration i den offentlige förvaltning og effekterna heraf.' *Statsvetenskaplig tidskrift* 2, 259–278.

Petersson, O., Hermansson, J., Micheletti, M. and Westholm, A. (1996) *Demokrati och Ledarskap.* Demokratirådets rapport. Stockholm: SNS, Förlag.

Savitch, H.V. and Thomas, J.C. (eds.) (1991) *Big City Politics in Transition.* London: Sage.

Scott, J. (1995) *Development Dilemmas in the European Community. Rethinking Regional Development Policy.* Buckingham: Open University Press.

Yin, R.K. (1984) *Case Study Research: Design and Methods.* Beverly Hills: Sage.

Walters, R.S. and Blake, D.H. (1992) *The Politics of Global Economic Relations.* Englewood Cliffs, New Jersey: Prentice-Hall.

PART V
RDAs and Public–Private Partnership

A major responsibility and objective of the European Union, national and regional partnerships increasingly has been perceived as the need to involve all the social partners in the design, resourcing and implementation of the policies, programmes and structures of regional economic development. In many areas there have been difficulties in involving the business sector in such processes, while others have embraced or developed existing networks and collaborations successfully. At the same time as partnerships are being extended into new policy areas, demonstrated in the previous section of this book, there has also been a reorientation of regeneration strategies towards endogenous forms of growth and development. This section addresses the ways in which these two major changes have impacted on RDAs, their roles, how they operate, their relative significance in these evolving regional environments, and on their accountability within these potentially more open structures.

Questions over governance issues, raised before, are therefore revisited, with critical assessments of the reduction of particular RDAs into mere facilitators or enablers, and of the advancing privatisation of power over public sector regional economic development resources. To what extent the apparent success of more progressive public-private partnerships, built on trust and cooperation, are real and are being upheld is addressed also. While there has been scepticism in the UK, and in England especially, over the value of growth coalitions and private sector-led regeneration, this section aims to put such debates into a wider European context. Similarly, the encouragement of competitiveness along lines promoted by Michael Porter and the adoption of the industrial district model of regeneration by many regional authorities, in the absence of a clear understanding of the underlying roles of trust and cooperation, are explored in the following chapters.

In Chapter 13 Kevin Morgan underlines the role of RDAs in the promotion of endogenous forms of economic development and argues that the role of RDAs is beginning to change. The RDA needs to move beyond its traditional role as a supplier of 'hard' infrastructure, such as land reclamation, factory building and inward investment, and also to become a *regional animateur* that promotes *social capital*, i.e. the networks, norms and trust which facilitate collaboration. These intangible factors are seen as crucial in helping or impeding the interaction between agents. In particular, he suggests that the networking capacity between firms in the supply chain and between private and public sectors is emphasised as this is increasingly recognised as one of the hallmarks of innovative regions in Europe today. Against the background of these theoretical considerations, the chapter then presents the Welsh Development Agency (WDA) as a case study and examines its changing structure, strategy and regulatory regime. The key lessons of the history of the WDA are in the significance of social capital and the question of securing public accountability in regional development institutions in order for them not only to be *in* a region, but also to be *of* the region.

The region of Emilia-Romagna in Italy is renowned for its approach to regional development.The distinctive features of its industrial policy are a structural, non-distributive, territorial and cooperative approach: giving rise to the internationally recognised label of 'the Emilian Model'. The Regional Board for Economic Development in Emilia-Romagna, ERVET, and its service centres, have played an important role in the participative approach and in Chapter 14 Nicola Bellini and Francesca Pasquini examine the performance of the ERVET system and make an assessment of the changes taking place. The district model and the service centres in Emilia-Romagna have traditionally been characterised by the active participation in management of a broad spectrum of actors such as businesses, universities, provincial and town councils, chambers of commerce, and industrial enterprises. Moreover, ERVET's traditional role in the building of consensus around the regional industrial policy in Emilia-Romagna is very much in evidence. A recent regional law specifically states the importance of a cooperative approach to regional development involving the regional government, ERVET and its service centres as well as other entities both public and private. Notwithstanding the networking arrangements in Emilia-Romagna, including inter-firm networks as well as the institutional support mechanisms, the ERVET system is facing a need to transform itself and develop new forms of collaboration and Chapter 14 discusses the present difficulties and the second-generation ERVET.

Taking a more theoretical point of departure, in Chapter 15 Daphne H. Kooistra examines the question of public-private collaboration in so-called urban growth coalitions. Growth coalitions are cooperative agreements between the local government and other local public, private and voluntary parties, where they come together in order to develop and execute a local economic development policy and to rejuvenate the city. In this connection, the chapter explains the local commitment and involvement of private actors by examining the question of motivation and linking it to a theory of place attachment. A better understanding of why private actors get involved in growth coalitions potentially could be of great practical value in identifying more efficient strategies for approaching these. However, empirical research into this subject is scarce and more basic research is needed to uncover the value and significance of the theory of place attachment. The chapter thus concludes by identifying the need for a research strategy.

The unifying factor of the chapters described above is their emphasis on the changing role of RDAs into mediators where the question of facilitating a partnership or network approach to regional and local development becomes central. The role of the RDA today goes beyond that of a multi-functional agency which takes sole responsibility for regional economic development. Increasingly, successful regional development requires the coordination and networking of many different regional actors and interests and RDAs have a crucial role to play here in facilitating the cooperation and building of trust between different partners: between firms as well as between private and public sectors. The key lesson of the following three chapters is therefore that what matters is no longer the different institutions as such, but their networking capacity in the locality as well as the mobilisation of the local community, broadly defined.

CHAPTER 13

Regional Renewal

The Development Agency as Animateur

Kevin Morgan

Introduction

Contemporary theories of regional development are beginning to attach more significance to institutions which lie between the central state and the market. These may be private institutions like chambers of commerce, trade associations and inter-firm networks or public institutions such as technology transfer centres, business service centres and training institutes (Cooke and Morgan 1993; Amin and Thrift 1995). In less favoured regions, where private institutions are often thin on the ground, public sector agencies invariably have to assume the leading role in animating economic development. Although regional development agencies are one of the key public institutions in these regions, our knowledge of how they operate in practice – how they are staffed and structured, how they design and deliver services, how they interact with firms and how they are regulated – leaves much to be desired. With a few notable exceptions academics have shown little interest in developing a better understanding of these agencies (Velasco 1991; Danson, Lloyd and Newlands 1992; Halkier and Danson 1995). This is surprising because as sub-central bodies these agencies are often better attuned to, and have a better knowledge of, their regional economies than central government.

Now that less favoured regions are under pressure to do more for themselves in economic development terms – not least because the fiscal crisis has forced central governments to reduce regional aid budgets – theorists and policy makers alike are exploring the role of endogenous factors in regional economic development. I shall argue here that RDAs deserve to be treated as one of these factors.

Taking the Welsh Development Agency (WDA) as an example, I shall also try to argue that the role of the RDA is beginning to change. In its traditional role the RDA was largely a supplier of 'hard' infrastructure, like land reclamation, factory building and inward investment; in its new role, which is driven by the need to promote innovation, it also needs to be a regional animateur, a role in which it seeks to develop a 'soft' *info*-structure of business services, skills and social capital. The concept of social capital refers to:

> features of social organisation, such as networks, norms and trust, that facilitate coordination and cooperation for mutual benefit. Social capital enhances the benefits of investment in physical and human capital…and is coming to be seen as a vital ingredient in economic development around the world (Putnam 1993, p.37)

Social capital, which highlights the role of intangible factors, is a key concept in recent evolutionary theories of innovation and regional development. At the heart of these theories is the notion that knowledge is the most important resource and that learning is the most important process. While evolutionary economists tend to focus on 'the learning economy' and 'the knowledge-creating company' (Lundvall 1992), regional analysts have used 'the learning region' as a prism through which to explore the regional aspects of innovation and development (Florida 1995; Morgan 1997). Whatever the unit of analysis the common thread in these theories is that intangible factors – like trust, networks and associational norms – have a significant role to play in promoting economic development (Hirschman 1986; Sabel 1992; Cooke and Morgan 1993; Storper 1995; Amin and Thrift 1995; Humphrey and Schmitz 1996).

The burgeoning theoretical literature on trust, for example, illustrates that this is an awesome economic asset *if* it can be secured. Trust – the confidence that parties will work for mutual gain and refrain from opportunistic behaviour – confers a number of important benefits: it saves time, reduces transaction costs, helps agents to cope with complexity, facilitates thick information exchanges and abbreviates the learning curve (Arrow 1974; Luhmann 1979; Powell 1979). The problem with trust, however, is that unlike most other assets it cannot be bought, rather it has to be earned by discharging one's obligations: trust is thus an asset which has a value but no price. Agents which have secured high-trust relations with their partner organisations have a comparative advantage over those agents – be they firms or regions – which have failed to do so.

The regional level is becoming something of a laboratory for both theory and policy because, as Storper (1995) argues, the region can be understood as 'a nexus of untraded interdependencies', that is, the intangible rules of action, customs and values which help or hinder interaction between agents. In the context of 'the learning economy' the regional level may be important for at least two reasons. First, it is small enough to sustain the regular interactions which are a necessary (though not sufficient) condition for trust-building activity and, second, it may be the most appropriate level at which to design and deliver economic development policies because central government is too remote from, and too ignorant of, local conditions. This is not to say that national and supra-national levels are unimportant, but simply to say that the regional level has potential advantages over these levels for certain activities, as the principle of subsidiarity suggests.

The concept of social capital also helps us to understand that what matters most from a developmental standpoint is not institutions *per se* but the *networking* capacity of institutions, that is their disposition to collaborate effectively for mutually benefical ends. Such networking capacity – between firms in the supply chain and between private and public sectors – is one of the hallmarks of innovative regions in Europe today (Cooke and Morgan 1993; Amin and Thrift 1995). The significance of social capital is now recognised by the European Commission, which seeks to promote networking capacity as a vital component of the new generation of EU regional policies, like the Regional Technology Plans and Regional Innovation Strategies, programmes which are principally designed to stimulate more robust interactions in less favoured regions and to encourage joint solutions to common problems (Morgan 1997).

While these new evolutionary theories stress the role which non-market institutions play in creating and sustaining social capital, they are deficient in two important respects. First, they are rather coy about engaging with real institutions, with the result that their theoretical propositions are built on an extremely slender empirical base. Second, they fail to address how these non-market institutions – such as RDAs – are regulated, and this is a significant omission because, in the UK for example, it is not too much to say that the lack of democratic accountability of these institutions has precipitated a crisis of governance.

This article aims to correct these deficiencies by focusing on the changing structure, strategy and regulatory regime of the WDA, one of the oldest and largest regional development agencies in Europe. Section two examines the changing character of the WDA as an institution; section three evaluates the key pillars of the Agency's economic strategy, namely inward investment and business support services; section four considers the crisis-prone regime under which the WDA is regulated; and section five tries to distil some wider lessons of the WDA's career.

The institutional character of the WDA

Created in 1976 the WDA was the product of an era when devolution was high on the political agenda in the UK. The Labour government was under intense pressure, from Labour and Nationalist parties, to devolve more political and economic responsibilities from London to Wales and Scotland. While political devolution failed to materialise, economic devolution in the form of regional development agencies offered some compensation to the awakening of national consciousness in the Celtic nations. With the exception of the Conservative party, which thought the proposed agency would undermine the market, all the other political parties favoured the creation of the WDA as a step towards a more devolved, locally-attuned form of regional policy.

Since its inception, the WDA has been fundamentally engaged in two activities: economic renewal and environmental improvement; both equally important for a region which has historically specialised in coal and steel. The contraction of these industries bequeathed a legacy of high unemployment and environmental degradation, a legacy with which the WDA has been grappling since 1976.

In terms of its structure the WDA has moved, since 1994, from being a highly centralised to a more decentralised organisation. As we can see from Figure 13.1, the centralised era of the 1980s was based on a functional division of labour in which six executive directors managed the Agency's main divisions. All these senior posts were concentrated on the same floor of the Agency's headquarters in Cardiff, an important point because this physical concentration of power frequently fostered a bunker-like mentality, leaving the Agency open to the charge that it was removed from the clients it sought to serve in the field.

What compounded this problem was the fact that the regional directors, who managed the outlying regional offices, suffered a progressive loss of power in the 1980s. This was unfortunate because these regional directors were the main ambassadors of the WDA in the field and, as such, were potentially well-placed to keep the Agency earthed in, and networked to, the communities in which it operated. What was equally demotivating for these regional directors was the perception that the local intelligence they had acquired in the field was not valued, or acted upon, by their superiors at head office. Indeed, reporting lines were such that the regional offices reported to different executive directors. It therefore became difficult to get an overall picture of what was happening in the field because horizontal channels of communication between executive directors owed more to serendipity than to structure.

Organisational issues like these are treated very seriously in the corporate sector because they affect a firm's innovative capacity, but in the WDA they were allowed to fester, so much so that they help to explain why the Agency gained a reputation in the early 1990s for being remote and unaccountable. These problems, together with the scandals which suggested that the Agency was 'out of control', meant that a reorganisation was inevitable. This finally came in 1994, when the Agency's six former regions were amalgamated into three larger and more autonomous regional divisions, each of which was to be headed by a person of managing director rank. These new 'super regions' are designed to operate as relatively distinct and self-contained units with the authority to design and deliver the full array of WDA services (WDA 1994).

As we can see from Figure 13.1, the new regional offices are now on a par with the prestigious international division, which is responsible for inward investment, and they report directly to the chief executive, a move designed

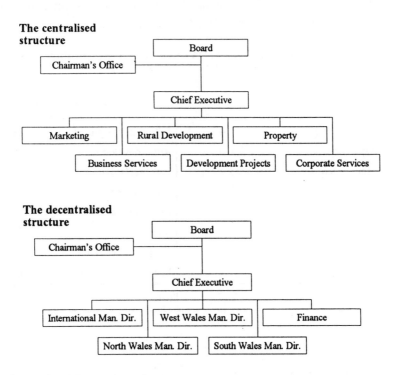

Figure 13.1 The changing structure of the WDA

to reduce the vertical and horizontal communication problems of the centralised structure.

Although the WDA was forced to cut its staff (from 440 to 330) as part of the reorganisation, the newly streamlined Agency is still beset by severe financial problems, indeed the current funding formula is simply not sustainable. As we can see from Table 13.1, the WDA's revenue comes from a number of different sources, of which internal income (that is, current and capital receipts) is the most important. Over the past decade the government has forced the Agency to fund an ever-larger share of its budget from internal income, which is largely generated through land and property sales. As a result of this government-imposed pressure, the Agency was responsible for generating 62 per cent of its £157.2 million budget in 1994/95. While this funding formula allows the Welsh Office – the WDA's sponsoring department – to reduce the level of grant in the short term, this strategy cannot be sustained because, by 1997, when the Agency will have disposed of its main property assets, it will have lost its principal source of internal income. Indeed, the WDA's financial crisis has arrived sooner than expected because its budget for 1995/96, originally set at £153 million, has been

Table 13.1 The WDA's income and expenditure profile, 1994/95 (£m)

Income		*Expenditure*	
HM Government	50.4	Urban development	31.5
European funds	11.0	Rural development	9.8
Current receipts	23.4	Land reclamation	39.7
Capital receipts	72.4	Business services	3.7
		International	4.1
		Marketing	7.3
		Corporate services	17.6
		Property	43.5
Total	157.2	Total	157.2

Source: WDA 1995.

reduced to £130 million because it failed to raise enough income from property sales (Barry 1995).

Having successfully reorganised its internal environment, the Agency now faces an external environment which is less stable from a resource standpoint than at any time in its history. Unless its funding formula is put on a more secure footing, the Agency will be unable to finance all the mainline services which it currently delivers, and this constitutes its key problem today.

The Agency as animateur: towards a new economic development strategy

The two main priorities of the WDA — economic regeneration and environmental improvement — are moving targets. For all the progress of the last two decades much remains to be done if Wales is to catch up with economic and environmental best practice in Europe. So while the WDA's goals are the same today as they were in 1976, both the strategy and the delivery mechanisms have changed quite significantly over this period. This section focuses on just two dimensions of the WDA's strategy, inward investment and business support services, even though its other activities — like land reclamation, property development and urban regeneration — clearly contribute to this economic agenda. These two areas constitute the most important pillars of the Agency's economic strategy.

Inward investment: towards the embedded branch-plant?

In 'place-marketing' terms the conventional wisdom suggests that the main locational attractions of Wales are its assisted-area status, its relatively low labour costs (and especially its low unit labour costs), a sound physical infrastructure, single unionism, proximity to London and the one-stop shop service of the WDA, which reduces transaction costs for potential inward investors. While these attributes have given Wales a prominent place in the UK inward investment league until now, they are no longer sufficient to attract (and retain) high quality investment in the future.

Wales of course benefits from the fact that the UK is the most favoured location for USA and Japanese investment in the European Union (EU). Among the UK's attractions as a business location the Conservative government went out of its way to stress the 'new realism' of the workforce and, in its overseas marketing campaigns, emphasised the 'non-union facilities' that are available to incoming investors (*Business Week* 1985). What is interesting about the Welsh marketing campaign, however, is that it eschewed this anti-union theme, preferring, instead, to stress the benefits of partnership between management and labour (Loughlin 1997). One WDA advert, entitled 'as a workforce the Welsh are anything but striking', summed it up in the following way:

> Hand in hand with silicon chips and fibre optics a new attitude has appeared. So what has changed so radically in Wales? Many companies

now form their agreements with one union and only one. Which doesn't mean that there are no disputes. But they do get settled without any of the paralytic seizures of full-scale industrial action (Morgan and Sayer 1988, p.186).

This contrast between the Welsh and UK inward investment campaigns can be partly explained by the fact that the WDA sets a high premium on having a good working relationship with the Wales Trade Union Congress, a body which acts as an ambassador for the 'new attitude' in industrial relations, and this is seen by the WDA as the best way to eradicate the traditional image of Wales as a region of 'militant miners'. Even the Conservative-controlled Welsh Office was party to this partnership approach to inward investment, tacitly endorsing the single-union as opposed to the anti-union line.

Turning to the actual inward investment record there can be no doubt that, until recently, Wales has been extremely successful on this front. In the period 1982–92, for example, Wales topped the UK regional league table with respect to both investment projects and jobs, so much so that a recent evaluation concluded by saying that 'in the early 1990s Wales remains the number one performing region, attracting around 20 per cent of total new foreign projects entering the UK annually' (Hill and Munday 1994).

If Wales has done well with respect to the *quantity* of foreign investment, what of the *quality* of this investment? The standard critique of the foreign investment in Wales is that it has been driven by the search for cheap labour, that it involves low-skill, low-paid activities and that the indirect benefits are minimal because of the weak local multiplier effect, all of which is said to be an inevitable result of the 'branch-plant syndrome'. Although these criticisms carry some force, they are too sweeping to capture the nuances within the foreign-owned manufacturing sector in Wales, and the cruder versions of the critique do not allow for the incremental changes that are underway in this sector.

The stereotype of the branch-plant in Wales is of a screwdriver facility which is wholly engaged in semi-skilled assembly functions. While this was certainly true in the past, many of these plants appear to be upgrading their facilities into fully fledged manufacturing operations with a growing brief for design and development and, in some cases, for research as well. It is surely significant, for example, that the rate of growth of managers and professional engineers in the electronics and automotive components industries – the most prominent inward investment sectors – was significantly above the UK average in the 12 years to 1990 (Lawson and Morgan 1990). Occupational upgrading of this kind is totally inexplicable if these plants are just assembly – or screwdriver – plants. What this means is that our understanding of the branch-plant economy needs to be revised to accommodate the possibility of upgrading, a point which has been reinforced by other studies of branch-plants (Amin *et al.* 1994).

While Wales performed well in the inward investment stakes until 1992, doubts have surfaced recently about the WDA's capacity to sustain this record in the future. These doubts centre around three issues: aftercare, over-regulation and the devaluation of assisted area status.

The issue of aftercare – which means servicing the changing needs of branch-plants in the hope of embedding them more deeply in the regional economy – has been propelled to the top of the agenda in development agencies largely because the mode of inward investment is changing. As we can see from Table 13.2, expansion at existing sites has supplanted the new start on a greenfield site as the most important mode of inward investment in the UK. This means that the initial attraction (like the one-off, up-front grant for example) offers no guarantee that the plant will continue to find its

**Table 13.2 Mode of foreign direct investment
to the UK, 1984–91 (percentage of cases)**

Expansion	45.6
New start	37.6
Acquisition	11.6
Joint venture	5.2

Source: Pieda (1993).

existing site sufficiently attractive to commit new rounds of investment at that site. Indeed, the grant factor may be less important to innovative firms than the quality of labour, the calibre of local suppliers and the networking capacity of the public and private sectors.

While the WDA feels that its aftercare programme is robust enough to capture additional rounds of investment from its existing stock of foreign plants, its conception of aftercare is too narrow, too focused on its own portfolio of services, a portfolio which does not include vocational skills for example. The problem with this conception of aftercare was exposed recently when some highly prestigious plants, including Panasonic and Sony, publicly criticised the poor quality of applicants to their apprenticeship programmes (Wood 1995). A recent study of vocational skills provision linked this to the aftercare issue, saying:

> If Wales is to capture the second and third rounds of inward investment it is imperative that local branch-plant managers are able to point to fac-
> tors, such as the vocational education and training (VET) infrastructure,

which help to sustain the competitive advantage of the plant over time. If branch-plants are to upgrade their activities in Wales they will require more sophisticated *aftercare* services, not just from the WDA, but from TECs and Further Education colleges as well. In our view the VET infrastructure will be expected to play a much more central role in the aftercare package and this, in turn, will require a more concerted, more professional form of multi-agency collaboration (Morgan and Rees 1995, p.21).

What this example illustrates is that responsibility for aftercare extends beyond the boundaries of the WDA and, as the key agent of economic development in Wales, the Agency needs to orchestrate all the services which have a role to play in economic renewal even if these services are provided by other organisations.

Because the issue of regulation will be addressed more fully in section four, suffice it to say that having been under-regulated in the past, the WDA is now being regulated by the Welsh Office in such detail that it is being over-burdened with bureaucratic controls, with the result that initiative in the Agency is being stymied. This problem of over-regulation was particularly acute when John Redwood, an ardent Thatcherite, was the Secretary of State for Wales. Redwood had little appetite for playing the inward investment game, for example, and this made it that much more difficult for the WDA to offer the best incentive packages to prospective inward investors.

The third factor which has adversely affected the WDA's recent performance was the devaluation of assisted area status in 1993, which penalised Wales relative to other UK regions because the government felt that Wales was now doing reasonably well. The key category of development area status, which triggers the maximum level of grant, was reduced in Wales from 35 per cent to 15 per cent of the working population, whereas in Scotland it remained at 46 per cent and increased from 9 per cent to 13 per cent in England. This devaluation of assisted area status, together with the WDA's managerial changes between 1992–94, which resulted in an entirely new management team, helps to explain why the Agency's share of UK inward investment projects declined from a peak of 21 per cent in 1991/92 to a low of 11.5 per cent in 1994/95 (Morgan 1997).

The WDA's recent inward investment performance clearly raises questions about its ability to market Wales as a premier business location. The key point to remember is that innovative inward investors are no longer content to operate in low-wage, semi-skilled locations; increasingly they are said to be looking for 'an educated, skilled and committed workforce, combined with a social and physical infrastructure capable of generating high productivity' (Unctad 1994). Wales, in other words, needs to reinvent its locational attractions if it wants to stay in the race for quality inward investment and a whole panoply of bodies, not just the WDA, has a role to play in this process, and this underlines the significance of inter-organisational collaboration.

Business support services: helping firms to help themselves?

All the truly dynamic regional economies in Europe are able to draw upon a wide array of business support services which is designed to keep firms abreast of new technologies, global markets and changing skill requirements. Although these services are particularly important for SMEs, many of which do not have sufficient in-house expertise, such services are not unimportant to foreign-owned branch-plants, indeed the latter often cite the local business support environment as a factor in their internal battles with sister plants for new rounds of investment.

Aside from the growing commitment to this activity one of the most important changes with respect to business support services concerns the delivery mechanisms. Drawing on the view that firms learn best from other firms – be they customers, suppliers or competitors – the Agency set about the task of designing and brokering inter-firm networks which tried to exploit the fact that firms are the most credible and effective tutors in the eyes of other firms (Dankbaar 1993). To illustrate this novel approach to enterprise support this article focuses on initiatives in three separate fields, namely, supplier development, technology clubs and training consortia.

In the *supplier development* field the WDA's main business support service is delivered through the Source Wales programme, the ultimate aim of which is to enhance the level of local sourcing in Wales. What distinguishes Source Wales from most other local sourcing schemes is that it is principally a supplier development programme; thus, instead of simply exhorting large firms to 'buy local', it seeks to raise the competence of local suppliers so that large customers have a genuine interest in forming partnerships with those that are able to meet demanding specifications. One of the main mechanisms through which these partnerships are promoted is the 'supplier association', in which a leading customer works with a group of local suppliers and, collectively, they seek to build up competences in such areas as joint product development, logistics, target costing and total quality management techniques.

The first supplier association to be set up in Wales – indeed the first in the UK – was the Calsonic Radiator Supplier Association, which was established in 1991 with the WDA playing the role of animateur. The Calsonic Association was initially restricted to just ten firms, a number which was felt to be small enough to begin the delicate trust-building process, the most challenging part of the whole exercise. Despite early scepticism on the part of each member of the Association, all the firms now concede that this was a valuable learning experience, not least because it was gleaned 'not from textbooks, but from people actually using the techniques' (Hines 1994).

There are now 31 such supplier associations in Wales, more than in any other UK region, and in each case the WDA has played the role of animateur, though the firms themselves provide the services. In principle these services could be secured from public or private service vendors; in practice, however, the firms set a higher premium on the knowledge of their partners, which reinforces the point that, wherever possible, firms prefer to learn from other firms (Morgan 1996). While it is still too early to assess the benefits of these supply chain mechanisms for regional development, the WDA's role has been decisive, so much so that without the Agency these inter-firm cooperation networks would never have materialised in the first place. Being an unobtrusive participant in these networks has allowed the WDA to acquire a better understanding of the conditions under which firms will cooperate.

A second category of business service is the technology support programme, which aims to promote the generation and diffusion of new technologies throughout the regional economy, especially to SMEs. There are three distinct aspects to this programme:

- *Technology audits*: as part of its effort to raise the innovative capacity of SMEs in Wales, the WDA conducts on-site technology audits of promising SMEs across a wide range of sectors with a view to identifying the strengths and weaknesses of each firm's technological capacity.

- *Centres of expertise*: in view of the fact that the higher education sector represents the largest concentration of technical expertise in Wales, the WDA has sought to tap these skills for the benefit of the wider economy. To date 22 centres of expertise have been created covering a wide range of new technologies and each centre is expected to take the initiative in forging collaborative links with local firms.

- *Technology clubs*: the most novel part of the technology support programme consists of technology clubs, the aim of which is to integrate the hitherto diffused expertise of key sectors to promote more innovative interactions.

The technology support programme has had mixed results to date, although, once again, it is too early to make a definitive judgement. While the technology audits revealed the key bottlenecks in the SME sector, as often as

not these were financial and management weaknesses rather than just tech-
nology-related problems and the WDA is not the most appropriate body to
address the former issues. With respect to the centres of expertise, one of the
key problems is that, being university based, they need to develop a more
commercial approach to the marketing of their services because, in some
cases, firms are simply not aware of their existence. In other words, a
supply-side strategy is not enough: if firms do not utilise the centres, then the
latter will be reduced to the status of 'cathedrals in the desert' (Cooke and
Morgan 1992).

But the concept of *technology clubs* has proved to be a highly valued forum
for exchanging ideas, pooling expertise and collective learning. The concept
was pioneered by the Welsh Medical Technology Forum (WMTF), a club
with over 500 members drawn from the healthcare industry, the National
Health Service (which represents highly informed users), the Welsh Office,
the WDA and others. The WMTF is essentially a networking device to
promote the interests of producers, users and regulators, with the WDA
acting as the animateur and with the agenda set by a representative steering
group drawn from the sector itself. The fact that the membership base has
grown so fast is perhaps the best index of the value which members attach to
belonging to such a club.

The third example of an associative form of business support is the use of
training consortia to raise the quality of skills in the SME sector. Although the
WDA is not directly involved in the skills development process – a task which
falls to TECs, further education (FE) colleges and private training vendors – it
does see itself as having an important role to play in the training policy
community, principally by acting as an intermediary between training
providers on the one hand and users (that is, firms) on the other. The best
illustration of this role is the way in which the WDA took the initiative in
designing a series of training consortia to try to overcome the barriers which
SMEs face in gaining access to affordable and customised training services. In
a partnership with the TECs and the FE colleges, the WDA identified groups
of SMEs in the automotive and IT sectors and encouraged the latter to define
their most pressing skill requirements, a procedure which helped to overcome
one of the traditional weaknesses of publicly funded training provision in the
UK, namely, a service menu which is predefined and driven by the interests of
providers rather than being defined in an interactive fashion with user needs
in mind (Morgan 1996).

The SMEs saw two advantages in the training consortia concept: they
could gain access to cheaper training provision, because the courses were
subsidised by the WDA/TEC consortium and, by using their collective
purchasing power to shape course design, they could get more customised

training courses from colleges which had hitherto been locked into a supplier-driven service culture. Although the training consortia concept was well received by the firms in principle, in practice it has had some serious teething problems. The most important teething problem stemmed from the fact that some firms were unable to release staff on the designated training dates, which meant that some of the courses were ill-attended, a problem which the WDA hopes to overcome by enlisting the support of more senior SME managers (Morgan and Rees 1995). Despite these problems, the training consortia exercise proved to be an innovative experience for all concerned: the firms came to see that they could achieve much more by acting in concert than by struggling alone; the FE colleges, obliged to be more alert to commercial pressures since incorporation, were forced to confront the shortcomings of their supplier-driven service culture and the WDA was better schooled in the skills involved in bridging the producer–user divide in training provision.

The common denominator in these three initiatives – supply chains, technology clubs and training consortia – is the use of collaborative networks as a device to promote collective learning and joint problem-solving capabilities at the regional level. The question as to whether these initiatives will be successful is easier to pose than to answer, not least because the benefits are so intangible. Here it is simply the intention to register the fact that these initiatives betoken a radically different approach to regional development policy compared with what has passed for such policy in the past, when regional policy was little more than a regime of subsidies for mobile capital.[1]

In evaluating the WDA's economic strategy – that is, its inward investment and business support services – the most charitable thing to say is that it has helped Wales to negotiate the transition from an economy dominated by declining coal and steel industries to a more buoyant manufacturing and services-based economy. The final section of this article will deal with the question of how we should evaluate the WDA's economic record.

Regulating the agency: the WDA as quango

Development agencies throughout the world have to contend with a fundamental dilemma: on the one hand they are charged with the task of

[1] The WDA's innovative approach to regional development was acknowledged when the European Commission chose Wales as one of the first tranche of 'pilot regions' for the Regional Technology Plan, a new generation of regional innovation policy in the EU (see Morgan 1997).

regional renewal, a long-term endeavour, but on the other they must satisfy the short-term interests of their political masters. Where there is a strong regional consensus, in which politicians and officials subscribe to a broadly agreed strategy, this problem need not be debilitating. Where there is no such consensus, this can be fatal. Agencies like SPRI in the Basque Country and ERVET in Emilia-Romagna have been unsettled by this problem recently, but few agencies have had to contend with as many political problems, both internal and external, as the WDA.

In this section I want to explore the regulatory regime under which the WDA has been governed because it highlights the conflict between public accountability on the one hand and efficiency on the other. These two issues need to be addressed together because it is an illusion to suppose that they are mutually exclusive; indeed, the political trials and tribulations of the WDA provide compelling evidence for thinking that public accountability, far from being a luxury we can ill-afford, is an essential condition of political legitimacy and this, in turn, creates the relative autonomy which is necessary for efficiency.

Having been created in the face of intense opposition from the Conservative party, the WDA was regulated by a Conservative-controlled Welsh Office between 1979–1997. What exacerbated the master–servant relationship between the Welsh Office and the WDA during those years was the fact that the political masters in the Welsh Office are Conservatives, a minority party in Wales with just six of the 38 parliamentary seats and a negligible presence in local government seats. In other words, the dominant political culture in Wales – Labourism – found itself totally divorced from the political party which controlled the Welsh Office.

Party differences, however, should not be exaggerated. At bottom Wales is a corporatist society in the sense that it sets a high premium on collaboration between the public and private sectors (Loughlin 1997). Previous Conservative Secretaries of State for Wales, like Peter Walker and David Hunt, felt able and willing to work within this corporatist culture because they were Disraelian Tories, a Conservative tradition which is akin to Christian Democracy on the continent. This tradition accepts that the state, in partnership with the private sector, has a positive role to play in social and economic renewal. This tradition of Disraelian Tories at the Welsh Office was shattered when John Redwood was appointed Secretary of State for Wales in 1993. An avowed Thatcherite, Redwood came to Wales with a pronounced ideological aversion to the public sector, and this further exacerbated the master–servant relationship.

Fallible servant: the failure of self-regulation

As a non-departmental public body (NDPB) the WDA is subject to the regulations which govern all NDPBs – bodies popularly known as quangos (quasi-autonomous non-governmental organisations). While quangos are not subject to day-to-day direction from their sponsoring department, in this case the Welsh Office, they must seek approval for their strategic aims from their political masters. In theory, therefore, quangos enjoy a large measure of freedom and it is the responsibility of the chairman, and of the board in general, to ensure that the organisation conforms to the standards expected of those who handle public finance, hence the first tier of regulation is *self*-regulation. In the case of the WDA, which is involved in a wide spectrum of activities, it is neither possible nor desirable for the Welsh Office to exercise detailed control over these activities, though this is not to say that it does not try to do so.

This convention of self-regulation makes it all the more important that the chairmanship of the WDA, arguably the second most powerful post in Wales after that of the Secretary of State, is occupied by someone who is alive to and respectful of the public service ethos of the Agency. Given the status of this post it seems astonishing that the Welsh Office could appoint a person without seeking a single character reference. Yet this is precisely what happened when Dr Gwyn Jones, a businessman from the computer industry, was appointed to the post in 1988 (Committee of Public Accounts 1993). While it is unfair to attribute all the WDA's internal problems to Dr Jones, who chaired the Agency from 1988 to 1993, when most of the problems occurred, it is fair to say that the flamboyant managerial style which he encouraged was at odds with the public service ethos of the WDA.

Projecting himself as a dynamic entrepreneur bringing private sector practices to a staid public sector bureaucracy, the new chairman seemed to the Tories to be beyond reproach. Indeed, in November 1989, Mrs Thatcher praised the 'marvellous chap they've got at the WDA'. Over the following two years, however, a series of scandals was uncovered which, taken together, spoke of a major internal crisis at the Agency (Committee of Public Accounts 1993).

Why did the system of self-regulation fail to detect and correct these irregularities? In the case of the redundancy payments and the car scheme it may be said that the WDA's board was simply unfamiliar with the rules and regulations. If this is the case then it exposes the limitations of a policy which extols the use of private sector personnel who are unfamiliar with the conventions of public sector bodies. Buying the silence of a key opponent of the chairman was an altogether more disquieting incident. And in the case of 'Operation Wizard' it was difficult for the board to take corrective action because the chairman and the then Secretary of State, Peter Walker, were both party to the project.

These and other issues were exposed to the full glare of public scrutiny in 1992 when the Public Accounts Committee (PAC) held an inquiry into the affairs of the WDA. In its report the Committee concluded by saying that it was particularly concerned:

> that the Agency have permitted poor management practices to develop, both for personnel matters and financial control. Overall, we consider that the matters covered in this report have demonstrated that the standards of the Agency have been well below what this Committee and Parliament have a right to expect... We regard it as unacceptable that the Welsh Office took no action against anyone in the top echelons of the Agency who presided over a catalogue of serious and inexcusable breaches of expected standards of control and accountability. (Committee of Public Accounts 1993)

Stung by this damning indictment, the Welsh Office quickly appointed a new, more mature chairman following the resignation of Dr Jones. With just one exception every senior manager of the Jones era was replaced after the PAC report, which constitutes one of the most radical managerial upheavals in the UK public sector.

Although this clean sweep was deemed necessary to re-establish the credibility of the WDA, it was also designed to demonstrate that the Welsh Office, under the newly installed John Redwood, was intent on taming the leading Welsh quango. While some new appointments were undoubtedly necessary, the decision to appoint a wholly new management team created its own problems when one considers that most of the new managers had little experience of regional development, little knowledge of the public sector and no experience of dealing with the Welsh Office. In short the new management team faced a formidable learning curve at a time when the WDA's stock of political capital was at an all time low.

Political master: the role of the Welsh Office

Founded in 1964 with a staff of just 225, the Welsh Office has grown to the point where, in 1995/96, it employed 2,200 permanent civil servants and controlled a budget of £6.8 billion. As a multi-functional territorial department, the Welsh Office has a somewhat schizophrenic role: while it is first and foremost an outpost of central government in Whitehall (London), it is also supposed to defend the interests of Wales in central government, where the Secretary of State has a seat in Cabinet.

Compared to the Scottish Office, which was created in 1885, the Welsh Office is often thought to be less autonomous and therefore more inclined to accept central government policy initiatives with just minor local variations (Rhodes 1988). While this view is broadly correct it tends to under-estimate the potential, however modest, for policy initiatives which are not part of the Whitehall template. In other words the stature and politics of the incumbent Secretary of State can make a difference. We might recall the way in which Peter Walker used the Welsh Office as a platform for his own brand of Conservative philosophy, which stressed the partnership approach over the free-market nostrums of Thatcherism. We should also remember that David Hunt, a committed Europhile, encouraged the WDA to forge links in Europe in a way that was unthinkable under John Redwood, a leading Euro-sceptic.

As a key member of the neo-liberal faction in the Conservative government, John Redwood had little in common with his two predecessors at the Welsh Office. His appointment, in May 1993, was received in Wales with a mixture of disbelief and apprehension: disbelief because it had been assumed that the Welsh Office was a sinecure for Disraelian rather than Thatcherite Tories; apprehension because he was seen as an ambassador of the free market in a corporatist society.

Redwood entered the post at a time when Welsh Office morale had never been lower. Like their counterparts elsewhere in the UK, civil servants in Wales felt battered by the cultural revolution sweeping through the service in the form of Next Step agencies, market-testing and redundancies. On top of these service-wide pressures, however, the Welsh Office had lost a good deal of credibility in both Whitehall and Wales for the fact that a number of quangos seemed to be 'out of control' (Perry 1993).

The political controversies surrounding 'quangoland' in Wales were compounded by the fact that some of the senior posts in these quangos were allocated to people who had been closely identified with the Conservative Party, fuelling speculation that that this minority political party was trying to further its influence through the unelected state (that is, through quangos) because it could not achieve power through the ballot box in Wales (Morgan and Roberts 1993). These problems fuelled a growing demand for more democracy and accountability in the governance of Wales, especially for a directly elected Welsh Assembly which would render the Welsh Office more accountable to the electorate in Wales (Osmond 1994).

What emerges from this sad catalogue of regulatory failure is that accountability and efficiency are now perceived to be absolutely inseparable attributes if the WDA is to be a sound and sustainable organisation. Nowhere is this view more deeply held than in the Agency itself, where managers are painfully aware of how much time has been wasted over the past few years by them having to attend to regulatory politics as opposed to regional development.

On a wider front this much is also clear: the more a government takes credit for the success of an agency – as the government did with the WDA in the 1980s – the more rival politicians will attack that agency as a surrogate for attacking the government. Because it is impossible to take the WDA 'out of politics' the second-best solution is for it to be somewhat more insulated from the hardy perennial of adversary politics through a new and broader consensus as to its existing role and future direction. But this is a challenge for the WDA's regulators rather than its beleagured managers.

The governance question assumed an added significance, when, in May 1997, a Labour government entered office committed to major constitutional change in Scotland, Wales and the English regions. In the Welsh case a referendum in September 1997 marginally favoured the creation of a directly-elected Welsh Assembly, and this prospect has induced a whole series of institutional changes. One of the earliest, and most important reforms announced by the new Labour-controlled Welsh Office was the creation of a so-called 'economic powerhouse', to be formed by amalgamating the WDA, the Development Board for Rural Wales and the Land Authority for Wales. This new agency will retain the WDA brand name and it will report directly to the economic development committee of the Welsh Assembly (Welsh Office 1997). In this new political environment one of the key challenges for the Assembly will be to prove that, as a regulator, it can ensure that the WDA is publicly accountable *and* operationally effective.

The lessons of the WDA

In evaluating the WDA we have to confront a curious paradox. The *external* perception, which is especially pronounced in the English regions, is of an Agency which has played an enormously successful role in regenerating the Welsh economy, particularly with respect to inward investment. The government, too, seems to have endorsed this view, hence its decision to reduce the level of assisted area status in Wales, a decision which was almost entirely based on the fact that the Welsh unemployment rate had moved closer to the UK average.

The *internal* perception, however, is more mixed and, perhaps, much closer to reality. Within Wales it is common knowledge that the Welsh unemployment rate obscures large areas, like the South Wales valleys for example, where unemployment rates are at least double the UK rate and where the male unemployment rate remains stubbornly high, at 30 per cent in some areas. No less troubling is the fact that the official unemployment rate is not the only index of deprivation: in the valleys low economic activity rates, very low wages and the growing proportion of young people who no longer appear *anywhere* in the official statistics may be better indices of the scale of socioeconomic problems (Instance, Rees and Williamson 1994). But since these problems are not confined to Wales we cannot expect the WDA to have resolved them through unilateral action at the regional level alone.

Even so, the fact remains that the areas that have chiefly benefited from inward investment have been outside sub-regions like the valleys. This illustrates the extent of *divergent development* in Wales, which in turn helps to explain why it is possible to entertain different, and seemingly contradictory, perspectives on the performance of the WDA. In short, while Wales has performed relatively well with respect to employment and unemployment trends over the past decade, relative to the UK at least, these benefits have been tempered by low activity rates, low wages, changes in industrial structure and an unfavourable occupational structure, factors which shed further light on the paradox of Welsh economic performance (WDA 1992).

Notwithstanding this paradox it seems reasonable to argue that the economic situation in Wales would have been that much worse were it not for the endeavours of the WDA over the past 20 years. In the context of a less favoured region with an inauspicious industrial inheritance on the western periphery of Europe, that might not seem like an illustrious achievement, but it more than justifies the decision to create the WDA, indeed no one in Wales has ever seriously suggested otherwise.

On a wider front, the history of the WDA carries at least two key lessons for the current debate on economic development. The first concerns the significance of *social capital*, the networks, norms and trust which facilitate collaboration for mutually beneficial ends. The attributes of social capital are part of the so-called 'intangible factors' which are deemed to play such an important role in corporate and regional development today (Putnam 1993; Scott and Storper 1995).

In section three, 'the Agency as animateur', I argued that the WDA has begun to develop an approach to enterprise support which seeks to overcome some of the weaknesses associated with traditional forms of state intervention. The main weakness is that public agencies are ill-equipped to engage with the corporate sector because they have 'low tacit knowledge of business, few specific business skills and thus a very weak capacity for learning by doing' (Bennett 1995). On a modest scale the WDA has tried to overcome this problem by acting as the animatuer of *self-organised* networks in the corporate sector. The growth of supplier associations, training consortia and technology clubs signals a new approach to state intervention at the regional level, an approach which is predicated on the principle that firms learn best from their peers, that is, from other firms (Morgan 1996). Because these inter-firm networks are valued by the firms as a device for collective learning the latter have begun to appreciate the distinctive skills of the WDA, skills which the firms themselves did not possess. In helping to craft these high-trust networks the Agency's unrivalled local knowledge – of firms, their practices and their personalities – played no small part.

What this suggests is that trust and other forms of social capital are perhaps most feasible at the regional level because this is the level at which regular interactions, one of the conditions for trust-building, can be sustained. It also suggests that, under the right conditions, social capital can be created through a combination of corporate need and judicious public policy.

The second lesson concerns *public accountability*, a condition which has eluded many public institutions in the UK in recent years. In a drive to make government and quangos more 'businesslike' in their goals and operating procedures we have witnessed an unprecedented epidemic of mal-administration, to the point where these failings are seen to represent 'a departure from the standards of public conduct which have mainly been established during the past 140 years' (Committee of Public Accounts 1994). Furthermore, the first report of the Committee on Standards in Public Life, a body created in 1994 to allay fears about 'sleaze' in public life, soberly recorded the fact that, in the public standing of key occupational groups, government ministers came bottom of the league, with politicians generally being the next least trusted by the public (Nolan 1995). Clearly, the WDA's management failings were a symptom of a much more generic institutional malaise.

A key component of this institutional malaise was the lack of public accountability, not upwards to central government, but downwards to the regions in which quangos are based. Because quangos are neither elected by, nor answerable to, the communities in which they operate their roles are rendered more difficult because they are hampered by *too little* political legitimacy. This was precisely the position of the WDA between 1979 and 1997: widely perceived to be the agent of a Conservative government in a Labourist region, the Agency became a surrogate for political attacks on the government, and this diverted it from its developmental agenda and demoralised its staff at the same time.

Against this background it is perhaps understandable that the debate about the future of the WDA is now inextricably linked to the Welsh Assembly, which will open its doors in May 1999. When the WDA is regulated by the Assembly the problem of public accountability will be finally resolved. But at this point another issue begins to emerge – an issue which is barely acknowledged let alone debated – and that is whether *excessive* political control would undermine the technical expertise of quangos like the WDA. In other words, while elected representatives would redress the deficit in public accountability, would other professionals in the economic development community – business people, educationalists, training experts and the like – be prepared to offer their expertise if the new regulators of the WDA were mostly politicians?

What this suggests is that the key issue here is *not* public accountability *per se*, but how best to secure this without compromising the need for economy, efficiency and relative autonomy on the part of bodies like the WDA. Unfortunately, when politicians enter office after a long spell in opposition, forbearance is usually not the most prominent item on their agendas. Even so, striking a balance of this sort is today one of the most important challenges if we wish to design institutions which are innovative and accountable. It is no longer enough for agencies to operate *in* a region, to be effective and sustainable they also need to be *of* the region. This is the most salutary lesson of the WDA's recent career.

Acknowledgements

This paper forms part of an ESRC research project funded under the Local Governance programme. I would like to thank the ESRC for its financial support and I am grateful to my research colleagues, Shari Garmise and Gareth Rees, for their comments.

References

Amin, A., Bradley, D., Gentle, C., Howells, J. and Tounaney, J. (1994) 'Regional incentives and the quality of mobile investment in the less favoured regions of the EC.' *Progress in Planning 41*, 1, 1–112.

Amin, A. and Thrift, N. (1995) 'Institutional issues for the European regions: from markets and plans to socioeconomics and powers of association.' *Economy and Society 24*, 41–66.

Arrow, K. (1974) *The Limits of Organisation.* New York: Norton.

Barry, S. (1995) 'WDA holds talks over cutbacks in projects.' *Western Mail*, 17 November.

Bennett, R. (1995) *Engaging the Business Community: Meeting Local Business Needs Through New-Style Chambers.* London: Association of British Chambers of Commerce.

Business Week (1985) *Labour Relations: We Have The Right Mix*, 28 January.

Caines, J. (1993) *Inquiry into the Findings of the Committee of Public Accounts Concerning the 1991/92 Accounts of the WDA.* London: House of Commons Library.

Committee of Public Accounts (1993) *WDA Accounts 1991/92.* London: HMSO.

Committee of Public Accounts (1994) *The Proper Conduct of Public Business.* London: HMSO.

Cooke, P. and Morgan, K. (1992) *Regional Innovation Centres in Europe.* Cardiff: Centre for Advanced Studies, University of Wales.

Cooke, P. and Morgan, K. (1993) 'The network paradigm: new departures in corporate and regional development.' *Environment and Planning D 11,* 543–564.

Dankbaar, B. (1993) *Research and Technology Management in Enterprises: Issues for Community Policy.* Brussels: European Commission.

Danson, M., Lloyd, G. and Newlands D. (1992) 'Regional development agencies in the UK.' In P. Townroe and R. Martin (eds) *Regional Development in the 1990s.* London: Jessica Kingsley Publishers.

Florida, R. (1995) 'Toward the learning region.' *Futures 27,* 527–536.

Halkier, H. and Danson, M. (1995) 'Regional development agencies in Western Europe.' *European Studies Working Paper 7.* Paisley: University of Paisley.

Hill, S. and Munday, M. (1994) *The Regional Distribution of Foreign Manufacturing Investment in the UK.* London: Macmillan.

Hines, P. (1994) *Creating World Class Suppliers.* London: Pitman.

Hirschman, A. (1986) *Rival Views of Market Society.* Cambridge: Harvard University Press.

Humphrey, J. and Schmitz H. (1996) *Trust and Economic Development.* Brighton: Institute of Development Studies, Brighton.

Instance, D., Rees, G. and Williamson, H. (1994) *Young People Not in Education, Training or Employment.* Cardiff: South Glamorgan TEC.

Lawson, G. and Morgan, K. (1990) *Employment Trends in the British Engineering Industry.* Watford: Engineering Industry Training Board.

Loughlin, J. (1997) 'Wales in Europe: Welsh regional actors and European integration.' *Papers in Planning Research 164.* Cardiff: Department of City and Regional Planning, University of Wales.

Luhmann, N. (1979) *Trust and Power.* Chichester: Wiley.

Lundvall, B. (1992) *National Systems of Innovation: Towards a Theory of Innovation and Interactive Learning.* London: Pinter Publishers.

Morgan, K. (1996) 'Learning by interacting: inter-firm networks and enterprise support.' In OECD (ed) *Networks of Enterprises and Local Development.* Paris: OECD.

Morgan, K. (1997) 'The learning region: institutions, innovation and regional development.' *Regional Studies 31,* 5, 491–503.

Morgan, K. and Rees, G. (1995) 'Vocational skills and economic development: building a robust training system in Wales.' *Occasional Paper 5.* Cardiff: Department of City and Regional Planning, University of Wales.

Morgan, K. and Roberts, E. (1993) 'The democratic deficit: a guide to quangoland.' *Papers in Planning Research 151.* Cardiff: Department of City and Regional Planning, University of Wales, Cardiff.

Morgan, K. and Sayer, R. (1988) *Microcircuits of Capital: Sunrise Industry and Uneven Development*. Oxford: Polity Press.

Nolan, Lord (1995) *Standards in Public Life, First Report of the Committee on Standards in Public Life*. London: HMSO.

Osmond, J. (1994) *A Parliament For Wales*. Llandysul: Gomer Press.

Perry, S. (1993) 'Quangos out of control.' *Western Mail*, 9 July.

Pieda (1993) *Inward Investment Trends and Prospects*. Glasgow: Pieda.

Powell, W. (1979) 'Neither market nor hierarchy: network forms of organisation.' *Research in Organisational Behavior 12*, 295–336.

Putnam, R. (1993) 'The prosperous community: social capital and public life.' *The American Prospect 13*, 35–42.

Redwood, J. (1994) *Strategic Guidance to the WDA*. London: House of Commons Library.

Rhodes, R. (1988) *Beyond Westminster and Whitehall: The Sub-Central Governments of Britain*. London: Unwin Hyman.

Sabel, C. (1992) 'Studied trust: building new forms of cooperation in a volatile economy.' In F. Pyke and W. Sengenberger (eds) *Industrial Districts and Local Economic Regeneration*. Geneva: IILS.

Scott, A. and Storper, M. (1995) 'The wealth of regions.' *Research Policy 27*, 5, 505–526.

Storper, M. (1995) 'The resurgence of regional economies, ten years later.' *European Urban and Regional Studies 2*, 191–221.

Unctad (1994) *World Investment Report: Transnational Corporations, Employment and the Workplace*. Geneva: United Nations.

Velasco, R. (1991) *The Role of Development Agencies in European Regional Policy*. Brussels: European Commission.

Welsh Office (1997) *An Economic Strategy for Wales*. Cardiff: Welsh Office.

Wood, L. (1995) 'Panasonic desperate for better recruits in Wales.' *Financial Times*, 17 March.

WDA (1992) *Industrial Decline and Recovery: The Welsh Perspective*. Cardiff: WDA.

WDA (1994) *Corporate Plan*. Cardiff: WDA.

WDA (1995) *WDA Corporate Plan 1995–1999*. Cardiff: WDA.

CHAPTER 14

The Case of ERVET in Emilia-Romagna

Towards a Second-Generation Regional Development Agency

Nicola Bellini & Francesca Pasquini

The regional level of industrial policy in Italy and Emilia-Romagna: the role of financial agencies and development boards

Historically Italy has been a country managed from the centre, with industrial policy no exception. According to the 1977 decree activating the institutionalisation of the regions, the 'ordinary statute' regions do not have the authority to handle industrial affairs, but only powers to deal with territorial development, the artisan sector and professional training.[1] Since then, but mainly in recent times, there has been a *de facto* extension of such powers, concerning issues whose impact cannot be limited to specific sectors of the production apparatus such as innovation, quality, export promotion, internationalisation and financial innovation. Furthermore, a limited but apparently progressive and far from irrelevant devolution of powers has been implied by a number of legislative acts and especially by the new Law No. 317 of 1991, supporting the innovation of small and medium-sized companies.

This is a fundamental element to be clearly understood in comparative analysis. Italian regions, with no exception, never started with a full range of policy options, never planned *a priori* overall industrial policy strategies, but rather went through a step-by-step learning process, picking up opportunities and reacting to political demands and interest groups'

---

1 The exceptions are the border regions (which face special ethnic problems) and the two islands (Sardinia and Sicily).

pressures that resulted in their progressive acquisition of policy tools and objectives (cf. Bellini 1996a).

Moreover, the availability of only very limited financial means on most industrial policy items has imposed a generalised shift from the direct transfers of funds, through subsidies to individual companies to structural interventions. Willy-nilly, Italian regions have then been turned into a laboratory for a kind of industrial policy essentially foreign to the national tradition (cf. Bellini 1996b).

Law No. 281 of May 1970 authorised the regions to set up financial agencies, which in some cases have been formally designated as 'development and promotional boards'. Thus the regions have intervened on many fronts, much beyond their formal jurisdiction, and by a variety of means which, while *de facto* under the control of the regional authority, have formally remained outside its scope, since they are legally considered subject to private law.

Financial agencies and development boards have been created in almost all Italian regions. Their activities, especially of those agencies operating in 'special statute' regions, have backed up government policies, being designed primarily to safeguard industry (including participation in the ownership of local companies, as in the case of *Friulia* of Friuli – Venezia Giulia Region) and, only secondly, to provide financial incentives.

In Emilia-Romagna a regional board for the 'economic valorisation of the territory' (*Ente Regionale per la Valorizzazione Economica del Territorio, ERVET*) was created by the region in December 1973 as a joint-stock company (*società per azioni, SpA*).[2] The task of ERVET is to carry out studies and to supervise specific projects, either directly or through participation in *ad hoc* companies.[3] The role of ERVET has been reaffirmed through the recent law which reformed it in 1993, pinpointing 'innovation, internationalisation, and finance' as the strategic priorities for the years ahead.[4]

The capital of ERVET is subscribed by the Emilia-Romagna region, which is the majority shareholder (75.5%), by banking institutions (22.3%), by the Federation of Chambers of Commerce (*Unioncamere*) (1%) and by entrepreneurial associations (1%). Registered stock is of 12.9 billions of lire; revenues amounted in 1995 to 16 billions of lire, as a result of efforts to overcome the negative results of the previous years (Table 14.1).

2   Regional Law No. 44 of 18 December 1973.
3   In other regions these are entrusted to specialised research institutes, like the internationally renowned IRPET in Tuscany. In recent years the research activities of ERVET have been down-sized and targeted to the actual operational needs of the agency.
4   Regional Law No. 25 of 13 May 1993 – the law renamed the agency '*ERVET – Politiche per le imprese SpA*'.

Table 14.1 ERVET's finances (millions of lire)

Year	Revenues	Net results of the year
1993	13.7	-741.4
1994	12.8	-410.6
1995	16.0	+7.8

Source: ERVET.

ERVET has three departments (Coordination of Centres and Resources; Special Projects; Administrative Offices) and employs 31 units, and its board is presently composed of seven members, including a president. The ERVET system as a whole, including the service centres, now employs 134 persons (Table 14.2).

Table 14.2 Employment (average units per year)

	1990	1991	1992	1993	1994	1995
ERVET	35	38	40	38	35	31
Total of service centres	78	82	89	81	80	103
Total of ERVET system	113	120	129	119	115	134

Source: ERVET.

In theory, the relationship between the agency and the regional government is one between the executor and the planner: a 'technical' tactical role vs. a 'political' strategic one. The 1993 law reaffirms such a division of labour by a number of statutory duties and constraints, including the formal, yearly reporting to the region on the activities and the budget. The law puts great emphasis on the transparency of the decision-making process. Two types of regional financing are allowed. According to Article 6 of the law, the actions aimed at implementing economic policy guidelines for the region – reference is made to the regional development plan and to the related sectoral plans – must be realised in a cooperative manner, together with ERVET's service centres and other entities, both private and public. They are financed by the region only up to 80% of the total budget. The law imposes a yearly resource allocation and control procedure based on a rigid system of project financing: indeed a somewhat cumbersome procedure, but – as far as the experience

Table 14.3 The region–ERVET relationship: the procedure *ex* art. 6 of Reg. Law 25/1933.

Region Emilia-Romagna	*ERVET*

Policy guidelines	
	Plan proposals, regarding partially self-financed projects, also based on proposals put forward by the service centres
Evaluation of the plan proposal → **approval and financing of the first (50%) tranche**	
	Implementation of the projects by ERVET and/or other subjects (esp. service centres) **reporting** (results, cost and revenues, evaluation indexes, documentation available at ERVET's archives)
Control on reporting → **financing of the remaining 50%**	

Source: Adapted from ERVET.

shows – it is actually working without excessive difficulties or delays (Table 14.3).

According to Article 7, the region may finance further projects, defined as 'special projects', that are of specific interest for the region and must be the matter of *ad hoc* agreements between ERVET and the regional government. In other words, the regional government buys ERVET services and pays them fully. In principle these services represent a further exploitation of the ERVET system's know-how, not necessarily limited to industry affairs but regarding infrastructures, the welfare system, the public administration and so on. The present balance between these two kinds of regional financing is described in Table 14.4.

As a matter of fact, ERVET has traditionally been a highly relevant contributor to the fundamental decisions of the regional industrial policy of Emilia-Romagna. In the past a great deal of the policy making itself was in

Table 14.4 Sources of ERVET's revenue (1995 budget year)

	Millions of lire	*Percentage*
Region *ex* art. 6	11,341	72.2
Region *ex* art. 7	2,314	14.7
Extra-regional sources	2,047	13.0
Total	15,702	100.0

Source: ERVET

the hands of ERVET, with the exception of the overall agenda setting and the final decision, but including the design and the implementation of the policy as well as the building of consensus around it. This was due to a number of reasons: the much greater flexibility of the agency, its technically qualified human resources, and the constitutional constraints hindering open regional policies. Often, politicians in charge of industrial affairs preferred to assign politically sensitive dossiers to ERVET rather than to the regional bureaucracy. Even recently, in the field of the international relations of the region, the regional government being formally constrained by the national 'monopoly' of foreign affairs, ERVET plays the most active role in weaving international relations and has even provided, through its technological agency, a representative office in Brussels.[5]

The 'Emilian Model' and the ERVET strategy

In a simple chronology of industrial policy in Emilia-Romagna, the 1970s represent the period where the region, as a newly-established institution, looked for a role in the promotion of the economy, consistent with the traditional, supportive role of local administrators, according to the so-called 'Emilian model'.[6] The main priority appeared to be the restoration of a

5 As a survey of the foreign economic policy of Emilia-Romagna shows, cf. Bellini, (1996c).
6 At least since S. Brusco's essay published in a 1982 issue of the *Cambridge Journal of Economics* (Brusco 1982), 'Emilian Model' has been an internationally recognised label to identify the peculiar, and perhaps unique, recipe for economic success of this beautiful, industrious, cultured and affluent Italian region, one with the highest standards in Europe. At the core of the 'Emilian Model' is the kind of integration between small firms according to patterns that are shared, although partially, by the rest of the so-called Third Italy. In short, we may single out as distinctive features of the economy of Emilia-Romagna the following: a highly fragmented production apparatus; nevertheless, a production apparatus that is often highly integrated in delimited territorial areas, in most cases 'pure' examples of Marshallian industrial districts (Pyke, Becattini and Sengenberger 1990); a deeply rooted tradition of balanced integration of agricultural and manufacturing activities and of different industries; an

territorial balance within the regional economy, by means of industrial sites and development zones. Early regional planning showed optimistic faith in the economic soundness of Emilia-Romagna, hailing the structural characteristics of the regional economy as the reason for its remarkable success in limiting the negative impact of the national crisis, especially with regard to unemployment.

Only at the end of the 1970s did Italian regions eventually receive the powers that allowed them to express some of their government potential, and the 1980s can be described as the 'golden years' of regional industrial policy. Most of the experiences discussed in this paper originated in that period.

Industrial policy assumed a major political significance in the strategy of the regional government: it allowed it to give a more clear-cut identity to the role of the new institution and to widen substantially the system of social alliances. Thus the business service centres, also due to their technical success, were progressively assumed as quasi-corporatist institutions at local level, to the extent that they recorded widening participation of all the different components of the entrepreneurial representation system, with the region's patronage. At the same time, the experience of Emilia-Romagna, more distinctively than that of other regions, appealed to scholars and politicians in Italy and abroad, strengthening the image of its 'positive diversity'.[7]

Since the beginning of the 1980s industrial policies have constituted a sort of 'grey area' of expanding regional jurisdiction. Here policy initiatives have assumed distinctively innovative features. By far the most important example is given by the ERVET system of business service centres. Emilia-Romagna can rightly boast of having played a leading role in this kind of initiative. This has had a marked impact on the shape of its regional industrial policy, which therefore has been characterised as mostly structural (i.e. with the aim of directly affecting the strategic variables in the structural

---

export-oriented industrial structure; the division of work within a single production cycle between specialised independent companies connected to each other by quasi-market production relations; the absence of a large metropolis and, on the contrary, the presence of many minor, territorially diffused urban areas; last, but not least, a remarkable stability in industrial relations, reducing the impact of conflicts and tensions linked to modernisation processes, together with the relatively efficient support of local authorities to economic activities as well as to the social welfare (list adapted from Bianchi and Gualtieri (1990). Cf. also Cooke and Morgan (1991)). In fact, the evidence of economic success gives only a partial explanation to the strength and influence of the Emilian Model. The Emilian Model was, and is, a highly fascinating combination of progressive government, social integration and entrepreneurial success. Not only success: to many, a pattern of economic development more authentically capitalist than that found in areas dominated by oligopolistic, large corporations (cf. again Brusco (1982)).

7   A more detailed discussion can be found in Bellini (1989), a reduced version in English is Bellini (1990).

adjustment of companies), non-distributive (i.e. not based exclusively on the transfer of financial resources), territorial and cooperative (with regard to the various actors and bodies that make up the local economic system). Such centres in fact envisage and require active participation in management of a broad spectrum of actors such as businesses, universities, provincial and town councils, chambers of commerce and industrial enterprises.

Basically, these centres act as collective agents whose task is to give a higher level solution to a problem that cannot be tackled by individual companies. Of course, this kind of solution is not neutral: to the extent that it suggests a certain path of adjustment, which can be accepted or refused by the individual companies for a variety of reasons, it promotes readjustment of the system as a whole and triggers selection processes among existing companies. Therefore it contributes to the reshaping of the existing networks and to the definition of new hierarchies and leadership positions (cf. Bianchi and Bellini 1991).

A celebrated and still extremely instructive example is offered by the activities of the Centre for the Textile and Clothing Sector (CITER) in Carpi (Modena).

At the beginning of the 1970s the Carpi industrial district was characterised by the presence of a very large number of small companies, highly exposed to competitive pressures. The idea of CITER (established in 1980) stemmed from a professional training experience. The crucial problem of the area was identified as the poor market performance of local companies: as market followers, they were operating in the low value-added segments of the market, with qualitatively poor products. A critical resource for a different market positioning was then identified in the availability of constant and reliable flows of information with regard to fashion trends. This information resource was essential to a strategy of increasing fashion contents of the products: the Centre provided it to local companies as a low-cost 'club good', together with related technological information, market information and, later on, opportunities for original innovation (a workstation for a stylist, developed by CITER, together with the complete database of the Centre's work). Of course, the Centre, whose qualified activity receives world-wide recognition, has not been a neutral factor in the development of the Carpi district. By providing such a flow of qualified information, it made explicit the common adjustment problems and triggered a selection within the area of a group of innovators and potential leaders.

In this field, it is important to stress the evolution in the strategy of ERVET. Initially, until the early 1980s, local public and private actors paid a great deal of attention to the emergent crisis of the industrial districts and the region basically cooperated with them to work out specific initiatives, acting through ERVET. The implementation of these initiatives, as in the case of CITER, was made possible or at least was facilitated by precisely that same territorial concentration of problems regarding the reorganisation of production. These problems help or have helped simultaneously to generate the necessary critical consensus and the financial and human resources to meet needs, whose collective importance is therefore concretely visible. In this 'bottom-up' way, the centre for the ceramics sector (*Centro Ceramico*) was set up in 1976 in Bologna, the already-mentioned centre for the textiles and clothing sector (CITER) in 1980 in Carpi, and the centre for the earth removal machines sector (CEMOTER) in 1982 in Ferrara.

Subsequently, the development board issued its own proposals and assumed a more protagonist, top-down stance with regard to the establishment of new structures, some of which were characterised by multi-sector services. 'District' centres – according to location and principal basin of activity – have been complemented, on different terms, by 'regional' centres – located in Bologna or in any case in areas not associated with particular districts and with users that are distributed throughout the regional territory. Thus the centre for the shoe sector (CERCAL) was established in 1983 in San Mauro Pascoli in the province of Forlì, the agricultural machinery centre (CESMA) in 1983 in Reggio Emilia, the metals centre (CERMET) and the regional agency for technological development (ASTER) in 1985 in Bologna, the construction sector centre (QUASCO) in 1986 in Bologna and the centre for subcontractors in the mechanical engineering sector (RESFOR) in 1987 in Parma. CERMET, ASTER and (much less successfully) RESFOR were the typical 'regional-horizontal' agencies and this trend appeared to be confirmed by the later establishment of SVEX, a centre for export promotion (1988), and FIT, an agency specialising in providing guarantees for the financing of technological innovations in SMEs (1989) (cf. Bellini, Giordani and Pasquini 1990).

Presently, the ERVET system, as described in Table 14.5, rests mainly on five 'pillars':

- two sectoral centres, i.e. CITER and QUASCO: both are performing remarkably well, but proved to be in many respects unique, unreproducible experiences;

- three horizontal centres, i.e. ASTER, CERMET, and the more recent DEMOCENTER. The special role of ASTER deserves a comment, both because of its increasing weight in the system and as a result of the wide range of its activities, covering, at least partially, the typical domain of a development agency.[8] In fact, notwithstanding a number of well-grounded reasons – both organisational and strategic – to maintain it as a separate entity, a fair comparative analysis of the role of ERVET as a development agency would require an integrated evaluation with ASTER activities.

Table 14.5 The ERVET system (Dec. 1995)

Centre	Location	Activity [employees*]	ERVET share (per cent)
Sectoral service centres			
CITER – Centro informazione tessile centre dell'Emilia-Romagna	Carpi (Modena)	Textile information Centre [19]	25.00
CESMA – Centro servizi meccanica per l'agricoltura	Reggio Emilia	Centre for farm machinery [4]	40.00
CERCAL – Centro emiliano romagnolo calzature	S. Mauro Pascoli (Forli)	Centre for the shoe industry [6]	46.67
QUASCO – Centro servizi qualificazioni e sviluppo delle costrruzioni	Bologna	Centre for the building industry [11]	44.09
Centro Ceramico – Centro di ricerca e sperimentazione per l'industria ceramica	Bologna (Branch unit: Sassuolo)	Consortium for ceramic research and testing	
CEMOTER – Istituto per le macchine movimento terra e veicoli fuori strada	Ferrara	National Research Council centre for earth-moving machines, works with ERVET under special arrangements	
Horizontal service centres			
ASTER – Agenzia per losviluppo tecnologicodell'Emilia-Romagna	Bologna	Agency for technological development	64.00

(continued)

---

8   These include: promotion and realisation of technology transfer and system innovation projects; specialised technical assistance to companies in the fields of technological innovation and management; partnership and business cooperation initiatives; customised informative services about technological innovation and the relevant regional, national and European funding; promotion of cooperative network arrangements among companies, local bodies, universities, research institutes, chambers of commerce, entrepreneurial associations etc.; assistance to companies and institutions (such as the Region itself, the ERVET system, etc.) in the relationship with international bodies and especially with the European Union; national and international transfer of ASTER know-how and expertise.

Centre	Location	Activity [employees*]	ERVET share (per cent)
Horizontal service centres (continued)			
CERMET – Centro per la recerca e le misure per la qualitá	S. Lazzaro di Savena (Bologna)	Centre for technology and certification for metal working	32.21
DEMOCENTER – Centro servizi per la diffuzione dell'automazione industriale	Modena	Centre for industrial automation	29.17
Financial services			
FIT – Finanziaria per l'innovazione tecnological	Bologna	Financial company for technological innovation. Is being taken-over by ER-VET [2]	75.27
Other (local development agencies)			
Agenzia Polo Ceramico	Faenza (Ravenna)	Promotion of ceramic district	8.75
Leonardia	Piacenza	Industrial/technological promotion	0.38
SIPRO	Ferrara	Industrial site promotion	4.43
SOPRIP	Parma	Industrial site promotion	10.00
SOPRAE	Piacenza	Industrial site promotion	18.76
PROMO	Modena	Industrial promotion	2.00

Source: ERVET.

* Average units employed, 1995.

The 1990s and the crisis of ERVET

The last 15 years of the Emilian economy have been marked by a good, but somewhat less than outstanding, economic performance. Restructuring and innovation in the 1980s apparently especially benefited large companies. The restructuring of large groups and the evolving competitive game, which has increasingly rewarded the globalisation of markets and the internationalisation of companies, has instead highlighted inescapable weaknesses of smaller companies. In addition to new achievements in specialisation and flexibility, size advantages emerged particularly for financial functions, research, marketing and direct presence on foreign markets. Thus the competitive positions achieved by smaller firms appeared to be unstable. In fact the remarkable performance of the Emilia-Romagna economy in the difficult 1970s was not repeated during the following decade. Italy as a whole and other important regions, such as Veneto and Lombardia, outperformed Emilia-Romagna.

Undoubtedly, the region's system of production is heavily involved in transformation; positive trends may even allow for renewed appreciation of the district formula, notwithstanding a growing criticism (although not an undebated one) about the supposedly too-weak innovative performances of Emilian companies. In fact, industrial districts' firms may remain small and even peculiarly successful, but actually belong to new, more hierarchical type structures.

Nevertheless the production system of the region continues to show a number of unresolved problems and difficulties that are related to a few fundamental issues:

- how to move away from traditional patterns of family capitalism
- how to manage productive internationalisation
- how to keep high innovation rates.

So debate once again revolves around the role of small and medium-sized firms and their need to grow. The policy objective (and dilemma) in Emilia-Romagna then becomes how to strengthen opportunities and increase resources for growth without upsetting the unique and delicate social and political equilibrium of the Emilian Model.

In the early 1990s, also due to the realisation of this less than brilliant performance of the regional economies in the 1980s, a somewhat simplistic pessimism diffusely substituted for the previous, unshakable faith in the soundness of the model. Ritual reference was made to the 'crisis' of industrial districts, supposedly implying a relative loss of validity of the territorial systems as such. Symbolically the Carpi-Reggio Emilia area ended up being included in the list of reindustralising territories according to Objective 2 of the European Structural Funds.

The appropriateness of the usual identification of Emilia-Romagna as belonging to the Third Italy had clearly weakened. To a growing number of scholars and practitioners the analogy with that pattern of development – the historic alternative to the mainstream of Italian economic development – began to appear less relevant for both policy's and analysis' sake than the complementarity with and the competitiveness within the Po Valley macro-region ('Padania') in indicating constraints and opportunities for continuing growth.

No one can dispute the contribution to economic growth made by the social and political stability of the area and by the relative efficiency of local administrations. Nevertheless the virtuous circle between civic culture and economic development has increasingly appeared as a relevant explanation for the past, but, as far as the future is concerned, cold comfort to the harshness of the new, emerging problems:

- the delayed modernisation of the infrastructural system, emphasising the limits of local/regional governance

- the serious environmental issue, showing that industrial districts are by no means less 'dirty' than large companies' areas

- the social problems linked to unemployment and – an absolute novelty in the history of Emilia-Romagna – to large immigration flows, especially from extra-European countries.

Political culture itself has changed. Values, myths and stereotypes of the Italian 'soft revolution' – including an ideology of superior market efficiency as opposed to the governments' inescapable inefficiency – were imported, with a noticeable degree of generalisation and quite irrespective of the achievements of the tradition.

Unsurprisingly, industrial policy has been the target of a series of polemical remarks concerning both the management of established policies and the balance between different policy tools. In fact both critical and defensive arguments have been characterised by the almost total lack of a serious evaluation of the existing and proposed policies, except for – not irrelevant, but marginal – considerations about bureaucratic efficiency in processing applications for public funds and simplistic analogies between budget indicators in service centres and private firms. Notwithstanding several previous discussions, proposals and attempts, the regional government itself lacked any serious evaluation process and therefore missed the opportunity to supply the debate with factual references.[9]

Yet, industrial policy has kept changing in recent years. In particular, a new generation of incentives has emerged.[10] It is especially worth noticing their thematic, rather than sectoral, character and the linkage between the transfer of funds to individual enterprises and the other policy tools, such as the service centres. The regional government has also been involved for the first time in the planning of an EU Objective 2 intervention for the period 1994–99. Both geographically and financially it is a limited experience, yet

---

9   The lack of adequate evaluation procedures (if any) is not at all a characteristic feature of Emilia-Romagna, but is shared by the public administration in Italy as a whole, at both national and regional level.

10 The two instances that best fit into this 'new generation' concept are the regional law on the promotion of industrial quality (1992) and the regional law on new innovative enterprises (1994). These laws do not mark a totally original experience in Italy, Lombardia having played a pioneering role in this respect, and are not without contradictions and severe limitations, especially regarding the amount of available funds.

highly instructive and influential in terms of organisational models and planning techniques.

Also based on the expectation of growing powers, a general trend can be identified that apparently leads to a more assertive role for the regional government (bureaucracy and agencies) in the support of SMEs and to a more conscious and systematic approach to the structural problems of the regional industry. This trend includes innovative actions such as the initiatives for inter-regional networking, with the explicit aim of fostering structural economic interdependencies with Southern Italy. Only partially contradictory with such a trend has been the low-profile commitment of Emilia-Romagna in those few tasks that the national law on small and medium-sized enterprises (No. 317 of 1991) has attributed to the regions.

The crisis of ERVET was the most significant event of the industrial policy of Emilia-Romagna during the 1990s. It was a long and troublesome process, formally triggered by the severe criticism voiced by the regional branch of the industrialists' association *Confindustria*, but patently driven by the local political struggle within a changing scenario and very often unconcerned with the 'technical' requirements of industry. In appraising the arguments and the outcome of the debate, many 'disturbing' factors should be taken into account: the neo-liberal mood spreading wide in the country and in Emilia-Romagna; a new generation of leaders, even within the Partito Democratico della Sinistra (heir to the dominating Communist party), significantly less dependent on the stereotypes and rites of the Emilian model's 'consociated politics'; the shifting balance in the representative power of entrepreneurial associations; last but not least, ERVET's exposure to charges of unfair business practices. For the last few years, astonished foreign scholars have compared the continuing international perception of the ERVET system as a positively paradigmatic experience with the local image of ERVET as an inefficient, money draining *'carrozzone' (caravan)*.

Based on the new regional law, eventually approved in April 1993, a reform of ERVET has actually started.[11] A fully renewed board has patiently and successfully rebuilt the image of the agency, removing from the scene the hypothesis of bringing to a definitive end the ERVET experience and de-emphasising popular, pseudo-ideological issues (like the demand for rapid 'privatisation' of the centres). This was made possible by a swift and unambiguous implementation of the new transparency rules, by a reduction of ERVET's dependence on regional funding and by bringing about several

---

11 The reform of ERVET was, however, part of a more general revision of the region's holdings, as outlined in the report of an *ad hoc* committee (Regione Emilia-Romagna 1992).

rationalisation actions.[12]

Evaluating ERVET's past, building ERVET's future

The above-mentioned evaluation deficit has been even more serious as it is objectively difficult to attribute to policies implying so limited resources a clear-cut impact on the economy, never mind to measure it. As a consequence, the evaluation of the industrial policy of Emilia-Romagna and of the ERVET experience needs to rely mostly on qualitative arguments, i.e. on the apparent tuning of individual initiatives with the main trends of structural adjustment of the economy. Notwithstanding a few disappointing initiatives, such fine-tuning was mostly realised with service centres. It is important, though, to isolate the historical appraisal of these experiences, which is undeniably positive, from a judgement on the potential development of these experiences in the future.

First, this judgement certainly leads to new efficiency requirements of the centres themselves and of the system as a whole. Of course, the differentiation of centres (different in the sectors to which they make reference, in the timing of their establishment, in the organisational choices, in the sociopolitical conditions in which they operate…) makes simplified comparisons of their performance, such as those based on self-financing ratios extremely difficult and possibly arbitrary.[13]

In an even more fundamental way, a judgement concerning a centre may vary depending on whether it has been assigned 'conservative' or 'innovative' tasks in respect of the existing forces. In fact, many of the initiatives were implicitly or explicitly intended to introduce new functions and information while maintaining the balance and system of relationships present in a district. However, the very development of the economic structure of the districts brought to light a contrast between a strategy

12 The experiences of SVEX that openly overlapped well-consolidated export-promotion activities of the chambers of commerce and industry, of RESFOR and of two other minor initiatives (CETAS, a centre for the training of LDC's technicians, and SPOT, for the promotion of metal-working industry) failed to meet their objectives and have been brought to an end. FIT has been progressively taken over by ERVET itself. Non-strategic holdings were also cancelled, as in the case of IDROSER, which was transformed into an agency for the environment.

13 Quite naively – and, in our opinion, mistakenly – Article 8 of Law No. 25 on ERVET's reform states that the agency should 'endow itself with univocal (!) criteria to measure and evaluate the effectiveness and efficiency of its activity'. ERVET itself has for some time tended to consider the self-financing of the centres as a basic parameter. Initially, this was found to be a positive incentive to make the centres more efficient and aggressive with regard to the market of potential service users. Subsequently, however, it proved to be an incentive not to opt for innovative and, from the financial point of view, inevitably risky activities, which would upset the overall self-financing level of the centre.

designed primarily to maintain the status quo and one that accommodated and even reinforced the drives for change and the emergence of new hierarchies within the districts, even though this meant relinquishing some political consensus.

Second, any judgement should be related to the issue of the supposedly scarce innovative character of the industry in Emilia-Romagna. In recent years, this belief has given supportive arguments to science and technology parks initiatives. However the main experience, the 'science and technology pole' in Bologna, has clearly missed the linkage with the regional production structure, although the impact on SMEs was a great part of the misled expectations of the participating actors (the region, local governments, associations, the university).

The system of service centres has given only a partial answer to this problem of the 'missing link' in technology transfer, but there are significant opportunities for development also with regard to other themes: quality systems; standardisation and certification; internationalisation. In general we may outline a possible line of development of the service centres as evolving from the one-sector, one-area, one-theme character of the origins to an 'open' role of intelligent networking for local industrial structures, where a complex and diversified (but inter-related) range of information flows and service activities can be conveyed to companies.[14] In this respect service centres may offer a credible compromise between the global and local dimensions of technology policy: the former pushes toward a technocratic, at least regional, kind of structures; the latter toward further 'territorialisation' of service activities as a means to be 'close' to companies and therefore effective.

The prospects for development of the business service centres and of the role of ERVET are at present marked by four types of difficulties.

The *first* relates directly to the characteristics of the economic system and its evolutionary tendencies: the limits within which the district model can be used to interpret a regional economic system which is characterised by strong differences; the restructuring of relationships within the districts accompanied by the emergence of new hierarchies among companies; the opening-up of the local economic system, which is heading towards a strategy of increasing internationalisation, but also experiencing the significant phenomenon of take-overs.

---

14 A very recent and illuminating example is provided by some of DEMOCENTER's activities, such as the laboratory for rapid prototyping, where up-to-date technology is made available to SMEs.

Most of these new needs of the economy of Emilia-Romagna require apparently more than a mere adjustment in ERVET's organisation and structure, as it has been realised so far.[15] Its strategic positioning must be questioned at least with regard to issues such as the modernisation of infrastructures, the further diversification of the regional economy, and the national and international networking of service activities.

The *second* category of problems concerns the relationship with local authorities – town and provincial councils, which increasingly act as protagonists in the field of economic development and over which the regions have very weak powers of control.

Recently, several local initiatives have led to the proposed or actual establishment of science and technology parks or 'poles'. The local character of these initiatives, i.e. their being not dependent on ERVET or other regional agencies, must be emphasised. Only in one case has the region openly played a supporting role, issuing an *ad hoc* regional law, and ERVET itself was involved. This was the case of POSTER (Emilia-Romagna Science and Technology Pole) in Bologna, a local initiative that presented itself – although it never managed to be in reality – as regional rather than local in scope and objectives. POSTER was eventually wound up; the proposals of a regional law, strengthening the region's powers, were abandoned. However, the issue of the subsidiarity relationship between ERVET, as regional level development agency, and these 'poles' remains on the agenda.

The *third* set of problems concerns the need for greater coordination of a full 'toolbox' of industrial policy: from technology transfer to export promotion and internationalisation assistance, from training and education to financial services etc.[16] Coordination implies both integrating the supply of services *within* the ERVET system[17] and integration between ERVET and other entities, including entrepreneurial associations, chambers of commerce, universities and those national entities whose operations are increasingly regionalised.[18]

---

15 A similar perception can be found in a recent strategic document of ERVET itself (ERVET 1995). Cf. also Cooke (1996).
16 FIT being canceled, ERVET has taken over not only the activities of that centre, but also the task of designing innovative financial tools to support regional industrial policies: cf. ERVET (1995).
17 This is now attempted especially for the mechanical industry, through joint operations of CERMET, CESMA and DEMOCENTER. On the contrary, old suggestions about straight mergers between existing service centres have been dismissed.
18 Two recent agreements with the national institute for foreign trade (ICE) and the national research council (CNR) seem to indicate that this direction may be especially relevant in the near future. The agreement with the CNR explicitly outlines the idea of establishing a new regional agency for technological development and technology transfer, based on the CNR research centres operating in the regional territory and on ASTER.

The *fourth* set of problems comes into play as a consequence of a foreseeable institutional discontinuity. Can a major devolution of powers to the Region, implying a dramatic increase of its tasks and resources, be managed simply by playing the old game on a larger scale? In this perspective, a thorough revision of the industrial policy toolbox, *including organisational resources*, building a future that cannot be just the fine-tuning of the past, would be a wise concern for regional decision makers.

It is probably early to judge the degree of maturity and consistency of any new orientation within Emilia-Romagna; of course, this indicates that the movement toward the second-generation ERVET has not reached an end: transition goes on.

References

Bellini, N. (1989) 'Il PCI ed il governo dell'industria in Emilia-Romagna.' *Il Mulino, 5,* 707–732.

Bellini, N. (1990) 'The management of the economy in Emilia-Romagna: the PCI and the regional experience.' In R. Leonardi and R.Y. Nanetti (eds) *The Regions and European Integration. The Case of Emilia-Romagna.* London: Pinter.

Bellini, N. (1996a) 'Regional economic policies and the non-linearity of history.' *European Planning Studies 4,* 1, 63–73.

Bellini, N. (1996b) *Stato e industria nelle economie contemporanee.* Roma: Donzelli.

Bellini, N. (1996c) 'La politica economica estera delle Regioni d'Europa: soggetti, contenuti, strategie.' *Federalismo e società 3,* 1, 53–80.

Bellini, N., Giordani, M.G. and Pasquini, F. (1990) 'The industrial policy of Emilia-Romagna: the business service centres.' In R. Leonardi and R.Y. Nanetti (eds) *The Regions and European Integration. The Case of Emilia-Romagna.* London: Pinter.

Bianchi, P. and Bellini, N. (1991) 'Public policies for local networks of innovators.' *Research Policy 20,* 487–497.

Bianchi, P. and Gualtieri, G. (1990) 'Emilia-Romagna and its industrial districts: the evolution of a model.' In R. Leonardi and R.Y. Nanetti (eds) *The Regions and European Integration. The Case of Emilia-Romagna.* London: Pinter.

Brusco, S. (1982) 'The Emilian Model: productive decentralisation and social integration.' *Cambridge Journal of Economics 6,* 2, 167–184.

Cooke, P. (1996) 'Building a twenty-first century regional economy in Emilia-Romagna.' *European Planning Studies 4,* 1, 53–62.

Cooke, P. and Morgan, K. (1991) 'The intelligent region: industrial and institutional innovation in Emilia-Romagna.' *Regional Industrial Research Report, No. 14.* Cardiff: University of Wales.

ERVET (1995) *Il Progetto ERVET: evoluzione del Sistema ed orientamenti strategici.* Bologna, June 1995. Mimeo.

Pyke F., Becattini, G. and Sengenberger, W. (eds) (1990) *Industrial Districts and Inter-Firm Cooperation in Italy.* Geneva: International Institute for Labour Studies.

Further reading

Regione Emilia-Romagna (1992) 'Le società, le aziende e gli enti regionali.' *Documenti studi e ricerche, No. 10.* Bologna: Assessorato programmazione e bilancio.

Relevant internet resources

http://www.aster.it
http://www.ervet.it
http://www.regione.emilia-romagna.it

CHAPTER 15

Entrepreneurs and Business People in Urban Growth Coalitions

Place Attachment and Active Participation in Urban Economic Development

Daphne H. Kooistra

Introduction

One of the most pressing problems of today is the essential regeneration and continuing rejuvenation of urban and regional economies. As a result of global economic restructuring and the reorganisation of governing, cities are increasingly forced to develop their own local economic development (LED) policies in order to cope with their dwindling economies. During the past 20 years a shift has taken place in the governance of cities. Instead of a managerial attitude focused on the provision of services and benefits to the local population, urban governance has, particularly in the USA, taken on an increasingly entrepreneurial approach (Harvey 1989). 'Local public policies in American cities have been characterised by a shift in emphasis away from provision of social services and public goods towards accelerating growth or reversing decline in local economies in order to create jobs and improve the tax base' (Leitner 1990, p.147). As a result, competition between localities and growth-promotion now dominate urban policy making.

Competition between cities is a relatively new phenomenon. Whereas many locational advantages were previously of a local nature, nowadays cities are to a large extent able to steer their own development by creating and advertising their own locational advantages. This active attitude towards advertising and attuning urban supply and industrial demand is called city marketing. Apart from being able to adopt a more active approach voluntarily, cities are pushed by their national governments, particularly in the United States but increasingly in Europe, to develop a more active approach towards the management of their economies. The heart of this shift from central to local politics is formed by the concepts 'commitment' and 'involvement'. Financial cutbacks, shifts in responsibilities and the focus on indigenous expertise are meant to stimulate local actors' commitment to the local economy and community, for example by becoming active in a growth coalition. These cooperative agreements between public and private actors originated during the 1970s and 1980s in the United States as spin-offs from the Reagan period and spread to the United Kingdom during the Thatcher era. They are now slowly being adopted throughout Europe.

Corporate community involvement and corporate social behaviour, well known in the United States, mainly focus on social causes. A parallel, however, can be drawn between getting involved in social issues and participating in a growth coalition. Both types of behaviour link organisations to their physical and social context. Although it seems generally accepted that companies become more footloose, the trend towards local commitment and involvement provides proof to the contrary. It is this link between actor and context that forms the focus of attention for geographers and which is central to this chapter.

One of the main questions to be answered when considering this new urban situation is whether securing national economic growth through public-private cooperation is similar to building on quicksand. Can we rely on the willingness of companies, universities, chambers of commerce and other local actors to pick up these new tasks and be successful? When cooperation between local actors is going to be the prospect for economic development policies, the question of motivation is not an unimportant one. In order to get more clarity about the feasibility and the future value of these bottom-up initiatives, the motivation of private parties is explained.

After addressing the concept of urban growth coalitions in the following section, and the theoretical approaches and explanations developed in the USA in the succeeding one, we will discuss some examples of research into motives. The following section will focus on the macro context in which individuals function. Individuals are part of a larger context or society which determines norms and values about the roles and functions of government and business in society. In the next section, we will develop an approach to the problem of putting the individual in his local social and physical context. Additionally, we will look into the potential link between actors and their context and relate this link to the question of motivation. The possible explanatory value of this relationship between motivation and place relation is examined by using the theory of place attachment.

Urban growth coalitions

Many local and regional governments try to stimulate potential local actors to become involved in urban development. Commitment to this cause can result in the founding of a so-called growth coalition. A growth coalition is a cooperative agreement between the local government, the business community and other local actors in aid of formulating and carrying out an LED policy. Coalition building as such is defined as '…a complicated task of bringing together the people whose particular interests are served, allaying the concerns or isolating those whose particular interests are threatened, and presenting one's actions as being consistent with the good of at least a majority' (Stone 1987, p.8).

Cooperation between public and private parties has received much attention. This body of research, the bulk of which is carried out in and applies to the United States, is of an extremely complex and diverse nature. Although at first glance studies seem to deal with the same subject of urban development, one seems to be able to divide this topic into at least a dozen related issues. Part of this complexity results from the operationalisation of the term 'urban development policy'. It '…can be defined as consisting of those practices fostered by public authority that contribute to the shaping of the local community through the control of land use and investments in physical structure' (Stone 1987, p.6). Confusion is created by using two different aspects of urban development. Whereas one branch of research focuses on downtown economic (re)development, physical renewal and investment initiatives, another branch focuses mainly on creating economic growth by attracting companies from outside the region and keeping local companies inside. These two bodies of research, although strongly related and originating from the same source, have developed into two separate fields.

Both branches of research have formed numerous twigs. When looking at downtown physical renewal for example, the consequences for downtown social housing are an important issue, as is agenda setting and the democratic value of decision making. The branch of research focused on local economic development also falls apart in numerous sub-topics. The investigation and classification of initiatives to attract and retain companies (like tax abatements, development bonds, governmental subsidies of business activity) and the study of the effectiveness of and rationality behind these measures forms an important part of research, as do topics like fiscal austerity and urban fiscal stress.

In many of these articles the research topic is not named specifically. Only after lengthy study of the article in question does it become clear what type of public-private cooperation is intended. In order to improve clarity, the growth coalition is distinguished from another type of public-private cooperation, the so-called Public-Private Partnership (PPP) or 'development coalition' (Table 15.1). The PPP, a frequently researched topic, focuses on urban (usually downtown) building projects. Cooperation is based on consultation and negotiation between parties. The growth coalition is much more modest in the sense that it has not received the bulk of attention and it is not focused on large-scale image improving real estate projects. The development of a large-scale real estate project, by a public-private partnership, however, can be part of the LED policy formulated by the urban growth coalition.

Table 15.1 Characteristics of the growth coalition and the development coalition

Characteristics	Urban growth coalition	Development coalition
Main incentive	Idealistic	Financial
Private parties involved	Every possible actor involved	Real estate developers, investment trust, companies
Range of coalition	Collective policy formulation	Concrete project
Common interest	Collective policy	Collective financing
Initiatives	Local amenities	Property development
Dominant party	Balance	Private investor
Duration of the coalition	Longer term cooperation	Cooperation only for the duration of the project

A local actor should not think too lightly about joining a growth coalition. Unlike the development coalition it demands long-term commitment to the cause of economic regeneration – a long-term process – by collective policy formulation and execution. The ambition of a growth coalition is to create economic growth and employment, for example by improving local amenities. Growth coalitions can be classified as special kinds of regional development agencies. Instead of being publicly financed, or institutionalised and started up by the central government like regional development agencies in the United Kingdom, their existence partly depends on financial contributions by business sector or other private parties. Also, institutionalisation is not an essential factor, as long as the public and private parties involved are dedicated to long-term commitment.

As a result of a missing definition and the *ad hoc* use of the term 'growth coalition' in existing studies, it has remained a very vague concept. In several theories the growth coalition concept is used to define a situation where local public and private parties come together in pursuit of urban development. The fact, however, that these theories look differently upon the concepts of urban development and urban growth, and that each focuses on different aspects of the relationship between public and private parties, turns the growth coalition into an empty concept that is filled in according to need. By using the growth coalition in contrast to the development coalition or PPP, it becomes distinguishable, and it can develop into a genuine research topic.

Theoretical frameworks and academic explanations of urban growth coalitions

Several theories deal with explaining public-private cooperation, and all of them are based on the USA situation. In the UK several attempts have been made to adapt these USA theories to the UK situation, but an acceptable compromise has not yet been found. In this section the four most important theories will be discussed. The first three are generated by the field of urban politics, and depart from the assumption of 'global economic restructuring', and the resulting economic crises of cities and regions.

Peterson (1981), in his *City Limits*, supports a neo-classical approach to public-private cooperation. He assumes that cities function similarly to companies in a marketplace and looks upon them as corporate entities engaged in maximising economic productivity. This neo-classical approach departs from the assumption that the city as a whole has one unitary interest. As a result of this provocative deductive approach, two reactions developed within the body of the American Political Science Association.

Logan and Molotch's (1987) political economic theory of the city as a 'growth machine' builds on the assumption that local companies dependent on local economic growth, like local developers, retail stores or newspapers, will try to use the city as a generator of financial growth. When a city grows, for example in number of inhabitants, their profits will rise accordingly. As a result of this reasoning, local governments are more or less forced to give in to the requirements of local companies, as the obstruction of economic activities is thought to hinder growth.

Stone's 'regime politics' (1987, 1993) departs from a different conceptual framework. He reasons that as a result of the increasing complexity of society, governments are no longer able to make a difference. In order to increase their range of influence, cooperation with and commitment of local actors like the business elite has become a necessity. Instead of treating a city, as Peterson does, like one single entity, Stone stresses the fact that a governing coalition exists of many different actors who each have their own interests. It is therefore important to consider which interests compose a coalition and by what rules they play. The common good, which Peterson takes for granted, is according to Stone not simply something that happens. 'It is something that must be brought into being, albeit imperfectly, by a set of political actors. However defined, the common good is mediated through the agency of political leadership' (Stone 1987, p.11). In short '...regime theory treats policy as a product of the struggle over a community's political arrangements' (Stone 1987, p.17).

The fourth theory is developed by the geographer Cox (Cox and Mair 1988; Cox 1991; Cox 1995). Cox does not depart from the assumption of global economic restructuring. According to him, companies are still highly locally dependent. This 'local dependency' is to a large extent based on the irreplaceable commitment of the local workforce and on the fact that the workforce is not as hypermobile as the factor capital. This mutual dependency of local employers and employees leads to a larger concern for local economic welfare and social well-being.

Although these four theories explain the functioning of growth coalitions by using the motives of participants, assumptions are made about the behaviour of actors. These postulates are easily detected in Peterson's neo-classical deductive theory, but are also present in the other theories; they all adopt a structural approach to the behaviour of participants by reasoning that local actors are pawns in an economic structure that does not give them much opportunity to behave voluntarily.

In order to really understand behaviour, an individual (behavioural) approach has to be adopted. At this micro level it will become clear whether postulates are justifiable or not. There are generally two ways to focus on the individual. First of all, personality traits like character, interests, religion, upbringing and personal norms and values form actor-centric explanations of behaviour. Second, the focus on the network of economic, social and cultural structures within which the individual has to function forms the structural approach to explaining behaviour.

An inductive or exploratory research method, however, makes it possible to approach the individual from a different angle. A qualitative inductive research method is particularly useful to uncover and understand what lies behind any phenomenon about which little is yet known. When using for example the grounded theory procedures and techniques, theory '...is discovered, developed, and provisionally verified through systematic data collection and analysis of data pertaining to that phenomenon' (Strauss and Corbin 1990, p.23). Complex matters, like in this case the relationship between the actor, their context and their motivation, are made approachable. In the following section a closer look is taken at some examples of research into motives using an individual approach.

Motives

Corporate social behaviour and corporate community involvement are important research topics in the United States. USA business schools have adopted the subject of 'business and society' and the formal community of managers in the United States, the Academy of Management, has established a division for 'social issues in management' (Berthoin Antal 1992, p.21). Business sciences have taken a practical approach towards prosocial behaviour by focusing on individual motives. Davis (1973, in Berthoin Antal 1992) recognises ten categories of reasons behind corporate social behaviour: 1) long-run self-interest; 2) enhancing the public image; 3) viability of business; 4) avoidance of regulation; 5) socio-cultural norms; 6) stockholder interest; 7) let business try; 8) business has the resources; 9) problems can become profits; 10) prevention is better than curing. Berthoin Antal recognises three additional reasons in her research on the social performance of German and British companies: 11) social conscience, or 'the right thing to do'; 12) personal satisfaction; and 13) why not? (1992, pp.79–88). Although research by Berthoin Antal is based on responsiveness to social issues, in particular to youth unemployment, the results are probably equally relevant to explaining corporate response to economic issues.

Cook and Barry (1993) developed a decision-making model for small firms to become involved in public policy. The basis of their decision model is eight factors that play a key role in determining the outcome of the decision-making process. These factors are: bottom line (the effect of an issue on profitability); perception of government's attitude towards business (friendly or not); history of an issue (has the issue been on the agenda for long and is it likely be resolved in the near future); efficacy of the firm (the extent to which executives feel they can make a difference); involvement of others (and their competence); learning curve of the firm (sense of ability through experience); affordability of an issue (level of resources needed); and mobility of the firm (can it easily exit the area).

Rational, individualistic, self-interested behaviour cannot explain all of these above-mentioned motives. These types of non-economic, non-rational behaviour have always posed a problem, especially for economists. The economist Etzioni presents in his book *The Moral Dimension* (1988) a new paradigm and introduces normative commitment (N) and affective involvement (A) referred to as N/A factors (Etzioni 1988, p.93). The position he advances is:

> that *normative-affective factors shape to a significant extent the information that is gathered, the ways it is processed, the inferences that are drawn, the options that are being considered, and the options that are finally chosen.* That is, to a significant extent, cognition, inference, and judgement – hence, decision-

making – are not logical-empirical endeavors but are governed by normative-affective (non-cognitive) factors, reflecting individual, psycho-dynamic and…collective processes. (Etzioni 1988, p.94, italics in original).

Although Etzioni adds a vital factor to the explanation of behaviour and tries to develop a new paradigm to oppose the classic economic explanation, not many researchers follow his example or develop a method to measure normative and affective factors in order to establish their importance.

From the above examples, it can be concluded that there are many more motives than purely economic ones. In the following section, norms and values at the macro level and their effects on decision making are considered, by looking at the roles of government and business in society. Individuals are influenced by the reigning ideology. 'A broad definition of ideology means that the term is not necessarily opposed to the concept of rational action. It is rational for an individual to base her actions upon some set of beliefs and values about the nature of society; indeed it would seem irrational not to do so' (Self 1993, p.54).

The macro context: the role of the government and business in society

Staub (1972) uses the following definition of norms: 'Norms are expectations generally held by members of a social group that people will behave in a certain way. They are rules which tell a person what behaviour is expected of him in various situations, based on agreement or consensus among members of the group' (Thibaut and Kelley 1959, quoted in Staub 1972, p.131). Trends in the macro context of society make up the setting in which individuals function and which influences their norms and values. This macro context consists of three fields: the relationship between government and society; the role of business in society; and the relationship between government and business (Figure 15.1).

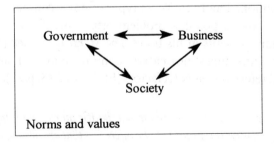

Figure 15.1 The macro context

From 1945 until the late 1970s the national government expanded in almost every Western industrialised country. Keynesianism provided the reasoning behind this intervention of the state in the capitalist economy. The ideology of the Keynesian welfare state is based on the belief in the many limitations and failures of the market and on the ability of the state to stimulate both social welfare and economic prosperity (Self 1993, p.55). The increase of fields and tasks of government involvement led to the expansion of government personnel, the increase in the number of procedures and their complexity, and the rise of government expenditures. During the 1970s, it became clear that the all-encompassing government could no longer keep up with developments and the rising expenses of the welfare state.

Welfare economics were replaced at the beginning of the 1980s by the ideology of supply-side economics or monetarism (Thomas 1994). Instead of stressing political interference in market forces '(t)he new ideology …argues the general beneficence of markets and the many failures of politics' (Self 1993, p.55). This belief in the merits of the market was adopted by the conservative leaders Ronald Reagan in the USA and Margaret Thatcher in the UK. It resulted in the retreat of the central government by casting off government tasks, decentralising government tasks to lower (local) governments, introducing market forces, financial cutbacks and deregulation. Instead of equity, social policy and basic responsibilities, the argument of 'efficiency' is now given maximum attention (Self 1993, p.61).

The willingness of entrepreneurs and business people to behave in a socially responsible way and to become involved in society is not a new phenomenon. During the end of the nineteenth and the beginning of the twentieth century many large entrepreneurs for example built bridges, founded museums and laid out parks. More large-scale initiatives by entrepreneurs consisted of providing housing and services to their employees. In many cases these kinds of prosocial initiatives, which seemed more or less social and altruistic, were based on short- or long-term, economic self-interest, and it is not known what role altruistic, social or economic motives played in them. The expression 'enlightened self-interest' is often used to explain this behaviour; McGuire tried to measure the profit effect of enlightened self-interest and came to the conclusion that it at best represents 'a crude blend of long-run profit and altruism' (McGuire 1963, in Galaskiewicz 1991, p.302).

The growing number of tasks carried out by the central government after 1945 resulted in the withdrawal of companies from local community affairs. As a result, business focused increasingly on internal functioning and efficiency. Since the 1960s, however, there has been a growing interest in the role of business in society, which began with initiatives to control business behaviour. 'Workplace health and safety regulations, equal opportunity legislation, and consumer protection laws are examples of this approach' (Berthoin Antal 1992, p.17). During the 1970s 'systems theory' was introduced. The most significant aspect of this shift in organisational theory was the reconceptualisation of the interdependent relationship between business and society. The focus on partnerships, networks and other collaborative approaches marks the beginning of the new paradigm. The 'transition is founded on a different principle of order – socioecological as contrasted with hierarchical, interdependence rather than dominance-submission' (Trist quoted in Berthoin Antal 1992, p.20).

The relationship between government and business is also subject to change. Lately the government has started to play a more enabling and a less regulating role towards business by giving them more responsibilities and freedom through, for example, deregulation.

The local context

In the previous section the roles and activities of government and business in society as a whole were discussed on an abstract macro level. By transferring the above-discussed developments to the local scale actors can be put in their local context. This change from macro to micro level comes down to changing the concept 'society' in Figure 15.1 into '(local) community' (Figure 15.2).

At the micro scale the local government and the business sector have numerous connections with, and are part of, the local community. 'Community' is, however, a very complex concept. A community can be a group of people living together in a geographically defined area. This relates community to the concept of 'place'. Apart from a mainly locational concept, a community is also a social concept; a group of people with strong social ties is also considered a community. The third meaning of community entails a locally accepted morally valued way of life. Norms and values determine to a

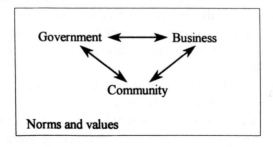

Figure 15.2 Government and business in their local context

large extent who can and cannot be a member of the community. These different meanings are not mutually exclusive. Communities of place are often also characterised by strong social ties and a specific type of local ideology.

When wanting to study the relationship between business people and their physical and social context the problem arises that geographical theories generally do not deal with the factors time or context. They are based on theories in mainstream natural or social sciences. These compositional theories break down human activities into general categories based on principles of similarity. They are then recombined to form an explanation of (part of) social life. These parts of social life, however, cannot be traced back to their specific time and space. The concept of compositional theory has been developed by the geographer Hägerstrand, as a contrast to his contextual theory (Hägerstrand 1984). He developed the term contextual theory to represent his famous time–space geography by which aims to make phenomena 'locally connected'. In the dictionary of human geography the difference between contextual theory and compositional theory is described as follows: 'Contextual explanations…depend upon identifying relations of coexistence, connection or "togetherness", rather than the relations of "similarity"' that characterise compositional theory' (Johnston, Gregory and Smith 1994, p.90). In the following section the factor place attachment is developed to investigate the link between the actor and his or her context and to use this concept to develop a contextual theory based on phenomena or people being locally connected.

Place attachment

Actors' links with their contexts can be determined by their 'attachment' to 'place', in short, by measuring their place attachment. The concept 'place attachment' is subsumed by a variety of analogous ideas like topophilia (Tuan 1974), place identity, insidedness, genres of place, sense of place or rootedness, environmental embeddedness, community sentiment and identity. Place attachment is a very complex subject matter, not a discipline. It is studied by a number of disciplines all functioning in their own worlds and therefore with little knowledge of each other's developments or findings (Riley 1992). Altman even suspects that the concept may be so complex that place attachment may not be a single phenomenon (Low and Altman 1992, p.3). 'Few fields in inquiry are so interdisciplinary in nature as the study of human feelings about places. This theoretical complexity is inevitable, for the emotional bonds of people and places arise from locales that are at once ecological, built, social, and symbolic environments' (Hummon 1992, p.253).

Aspects of decision making or reasoning

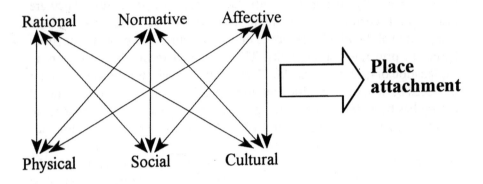

Figure 15.3 The relationship between an actor and his context

In order to keep this complex matter transparent, the factors place and attachment are explained. 'Place' consists of physical (build-up and natural), social and cultural aspects of a context, whereas 'attachment' applies to economic, normative (e.g. philanthropic) and emotional aspects of decision making or reasoning.

As visualised in Figure 15.3, nine types of place attachment can be recognised. A person can have a:

- rational link with the physical aspects of the context
- normative link with the physical aspects of the context
- affective link with the physical aspects of the context
- rational link with the social aspects of the context
- normative link with the social aspects of the context
- affective link with the social aspects of the context
- rational link with the cultural aspects of the context
- normative link with the cultural aspects of the context

An entrepreneur who is mainly interested in the quality of local amenities like, for example, infrastructure has a rational link with the physical aspects of his or her context. A normative link with the physical aspects of the context comes down to feelings about the necessary preconditions for settlement, development and urban growth. Someone who is led by affection for the physical aspects of the context loves the environment in which he or she is located. A rational approach to the social aspects of context is characteristic of someone who is involved in the local social network because of possible spin-offs. An entrepreneur or business person, however, who has normative ties to the social aspects of place has certain ideas about how society should function and plays an active role creating this ideal situation by, for example, investing time and/or money. Someone with affective ties towards their social context usually has historic ties and their family probably still lives in the area. An entrepreneur or business person who has rational ties with the cultural aspects of the context is someone who financially supports local and regional traditions and celebrations. By showing this kind of commitment they try to improve their image, and become part of the network of people who have a more normative or affective approach towards the local culture. Normative ties with this cultural context are displayed by people who reason local culture is valuable, creates identity and should be protected and supported. An entrepreneur or business person with emotional ties with the cultural aspects of the context feels at home. He or she identifies emotionally with the local and regional culture and traditions.

A famous case by Galaskiewicz into corporate contributions to charity in Minneapolis-St.Paul, can be used to illustrate a situation of normative reasoning applied to the social aspects of the context. Through time, this condition changed to a situation where rational ties dominate. Galaskiewicz stresses that although corporations – as opposed to natural persons – are immune to social controls, have no conscience, are amoral and therefore able to behave irresponsibly, there are many cases where corporations show they are able and willing to act in the interest of, for example, the local community. '…(T)here are cases where business corporations have joined together and developed new governance structures which imposed normative controls upon members' (Galaskiewicz 1991, p.297). The corporate grants economy, characterising Minneapolis-St.Paul, was first based on informal old-boy networks. The functioning of this philanthropic elite was based on the spread of norms and values. Several developments such as the increasing footlooseness of corporations, companies becoming more corporate and less dominated by natural persons with loyalties to the area, and the disinterested new generation of elites, posed a threat to the survival of this community. By bureaucratically institutionalising their roles and organising formalised award systems, the community made sure local elite structures and corporate social involvement would survive.

Although global developments in transportation and telecommunication have increased the action spaces of organisations, the links between actors and their contexts are, as seen in Figure 15.3, of such a diverse nature that these processes will only have a limited effect on place attachment. This argument supports Cox's theory of dependency in which he also argues that there are still many ties between companies and their context.

Place attachment and growth coalitions

The theory of place attachment is developed in order to get a better insight into what motivates people to become involved in urban development, and to get more clarity about the feasibility and future value of these bottom-up initiatives. The reasoning behind linking place attachment to motivation is articulated by the hypothesis that the characteristics of the link between actors and their contexts will reflect in the motivation to become involved in

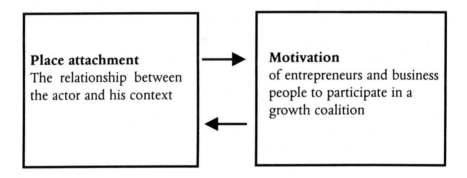

Figure 15.4 The relationship between place attachment and motivation

local development (Figure 15.4). This relationship between place attachment and motivation is of a two-way nature. Actors involved in local development are also likely to develop more and different relations to their context. This side of the relationship, however, will not be discussed.

It has yet to be empirically analysed how strong this relationship between place attachment and motivation really is. The explanatory value of place attachment can turn out to be of major or only minor importance. Apart from answering these more fundamental questions, empirical research into place attachment and motivation can also be used to get a better understanding of more practical problems. Insight into the types of actors in growth coalitions and their place attachment can lead to a better understanding of how to get these people involved. Findings could, for example, point out that actors in a growth coalition show an over-riding type of place attachment. A conclusion of this kind can lead to the development of a strategy to approach actors with this type of place attachment who are not yet involved, or to a focus on actors with a different type of place attachment. This insight into place attachment makes it possible to approach individual actors in a more efficient way.

Geographically, the theory of place attachment can be used to explain spatial variation in the founding and functioning of growth coalitions. For example, when a place or region is characterised by a lack of cultural features, and only has a very loose social network, actors with place attachment sensitive to these factors will probably be absent from the growth coalition. Empirical explorations and findings concerning place attachment could eventually lead to the explanation of success and sustainability of individual growth coalitions. However, before place attachment can be used in such a functional way, more basic research is needed to uncover its value and significance.

An issue not yet addressed is the practical approach to empirical research. In this initial stage, still much is unclear about the relevance and strength of place attachment. Therefore, it is important to use an inductive or exploratory qualitative research approach. As mentioned before, an inductive research method makes it possible to study complex matters without having to resort to simplifications or postulates about behaviour. In-depth and broad interviews about all sorts of aspects of a person's life (personality, norms, values, and motives) will make it possible to determine place attachment and to confirm the link with motivation.

Conclusion

Shifts in governing from managerialism to entrepreneurialism and from Keynesianism to government by the market have made bottom-up urban development or economic regeneration increasingly important. Local and regional governments have become prominent parties in determining their own future. As the problems of society are becoming increasingly complex, private parties have to become involved in generating local economic growth. The willingness and motivation of entrepreneurs and business people to play an active role in local or regional well-being has turned into an important research topic. The answer to the question of what motivates these people using the theory of place attachment that links actors to their context could become a tool to stimulate potential local actors to become actively involved in a local growth coalition.

References

Berthoin Antal, A. (1992) *Corporate Social Performance: Rediscovering Actors in Their Organizational Contexts*. Frankfurt am Main: Campus Verlag/ Boulder Colorado: Westview Press.

Cook, R.G. and Barry, D. (1993) 'When should the small firm be involved in public policy?' *Journal of Small Business Management 1*, 39–50.

Cox, K.R. (1991) 'Questions of abstraction in studies in the new urban politics.' *Journal of Urban Affairs 13*, 3, 267–280.

Cox, K.R. (1995) 'Globalisation, competition and the politics of local economic development.' *Urban Studies 32*, 2, 213–224.

Cox, K.R. and Mair, A. (1988) 'Locality and community in the politics of local economic development.' *Annals of the Association of American Geographers 78*, 2, 307–325.

Etzioni, A. (1988) *The Moral Dimension: Toward a New Economics*. New York: The Free Press.

Galaskiewicz, J. (1991) 'Making corporate actors accountable: institution-building in Minneapolis-St. Paul.' In W.W. Powell and P.J. DiMaggio (eds) *The New Institutionalism in Organizational Analysis*. Chicago: The University of Chicago Press.

Harvey, D. (1989) 'From managerialism to entrepreneurialism: The transformation in urban governance in late capitalism.' *Geografiska Annaler 71B*, 1, 3–17.

Hägerstrand, T. (1984) 'Presences and absences: a look at conceptual choices and bodily necessities.' *Regional Studies 18*, 373–380.

Hummon, D.M. (1992) 'Community attachment: local sentiment and sense of place.' In I. Altman and S.M. Low (eds) *Place Attachment. Human Behaviour and Environment, Vol. 12*. New York: Plenum Press.

Johnston, R.J., Gregory, D., and Smith, D.M. (eds) (1994) *The Dictionary of Human Geography, 3rd edition*. Oxford: Blackwell Reference.

Leitner, H. (1990) 'Cities in pursuit of economic growth: The local state as entrepreneur.' *Political Geography Quarterly 9*, 2, 146–170.

Logan, J.R. and Molotch, H.L. (1987) *Urban Fortunes: The Political Economy of Place*. Berkeley: University of California Press.

Low, S.M. and Altman, I. (1992) 'Place attachment: a conceptual inquiry.' In I. Altman and S.M. Low (eds) *Place Attachment: Human Behaviour and Environment Vol. 12*. New York: Plenum Press.

Peterson, P.E. (1981) *City Limits*. Chicago: University of Chicago Press.

Riley, R.B. (1992) 'Attachment to the ordinary landscape.' In I. Altman and S.M. Low (eds) *Place Attachment: Human Behaviour and Environment Vol. 12*. New York: Plenum Press.

Self, P. (1993) *Government by the Market? The Politics of Public Choice.* London: Macmillan Press Ltd.

Staub, E. (1972) 'Instigation to goodness: the role of social norms and interpersonal influence.' *Journal of Social Issues 28*, 3, 131–150.

Stone, C.N. (1987) 'The study of the politics of urban development.' In C.N. Stone and H.T. Sanders (eds) *The Politics of Urban Development.* Lawrence Kansas: University Press of Kansas.

Stone, C.N. (1993) 'Urban regimes and the capacity to govern: A political economy approach.' *Journal of Urban Affairs 15*, 1, 1–28.

Strauss, A. and Corbin, J. (1990) *Basics of Qualitative Research: Grounded Theory Procedures and Techniques.* Newbury Park, California: Sage Publications.

Tuan, Y. (1974) *Topophilia: A Study of Environmental Perception, Attitudes, and Values.* Englewood Cliffs, New Jersey: Prentice-Hall Inc.

Further reading

Thomas, N.C. (1994) 'Institutions, interests, and ideology in economic policy in Canada, the United Kingdom, and the United States.' *Environment and Planning C: Government and Policy 12*, 165–176.

Part VI

Policies and Evaluation of Endogenous Development

Leading on from the broad discussion of endogenous development models in the previous section, this section analyses the role of RDAs in enhancing regional growth through the promotion and encouragement of new and small enterprises. A significant expansion in the mainstream economic literature in the 1980s saw theories of endogenous development brought to the fore in not only academic circles but also in popular political economic discourse. Faced with deindustrialisation in many old industrial regions, as the traditional forms of regional policy became less effective and resourced in the post oil-crisis world and as the competition for internationally mobile capital investment became more intense, so there has been an increasing tendency for RDAs to address the needs of indigenous entrepreneurs and enterprises. The recognition that the invisible factors of economic development were often inexorably tied up with the civic culture of the region has come relatively late to several paradigms. Many areas have attempted to capture the essence of the industrial district, and Third Italy in particular, by adopting an aggressive policy towards networking and partnership. Others have sought to increase the business birth rate directly, through grants and subsidies or through policies of privatisation and the dismantling of large combines and conglomerates. In a number of regions across Europe, specialist development agencies have been established dedicated to the encouragement of new, and small and medium-sized enterprises. Indeed, apart from limited programmes to extend public procurement and, more significantly, local purchases by foreign direct investors with the objective of increasing the degree of embeddedness in the regional economy, most efforts at promoting endogenous development have focused on such activities. This section presents analysis from two areas which have pursued such a regional development strategy more vigorously than most: Northern Ireland and some of the regions of Spain.

As the endogenous development model is said to be characterised by an exhortation to abandon subsidies and protectionist policies which favour the small firm sector, to move closer to the competitive criteria advocated by its supporters, the experience of the Spanish regions is significant. Joaquín Guzmán-Cuevas, F. Javier Santos-Cumplido and F. Rafael Cáceres-Carrasco consider that, ironically, the prosperity of a region seems to have a direct bearing on the efficiency and effectiveness of its RDAs. The poorer endowed a region in economic wealth and potential, the less the development agencies appear to be able to operate consistently with the productive or entrepreneurial needs of the community. This seems to reflect the conclusions of the earlier sections on partnerships and governance; a region which needs the services of a successful RDA is perhaps least likely to accommodate one.

Maybe in contrast to these findings, the experiences in Northern Ireland are more mixed. As Marie Finnegan reports, this region has seen a similar change in policy regimes and philosophy. The largely interventionist approach of the 1970s and 80s, with substantial levels of public resources directly aimed at creating employment, gave way to a more selective and market-oriented programme, centred around the key objective of improved competitiveness aiming at increased long-term growth. Faced with a need to introduce a new competitiveness strategy, the five development agencies for Northern Ireland are investigated to assess their likely contributions to economic development in the region. In particular, and as with the previous chapter, Finnegan is interested in the coherence and consistency of the strategies of these development agencies in terms of their contribution to an integrated approach to regional economic development for a peripheral region of Europe.

The broad aim of the final chapter in this section, by Mark Hart, Ronnie Scott, Graham Gudgin and Eric Hanvey, is to assess the effectiveness of the agency in Northern Ireland dedicated to supporting the small firm sector especially, LEDU. Despite the change in policy over the 1980s, and the new focus on competitiveness, many small and new firm programmes aim to increase employment as the primary objective. LEDU is no exception and the analysis concentrates on this measure of its operational efficiency, alongside other methods of evaluating overall cost effectiveness.

CHAPTER 16

An Analysis of Regional Development Agencies in Spain from an Endogenous Development Perspective

Joaquín Guzmán-Cuevas, F. Javier Santos-Cumplido
& F. Rafael Cáceres-Carrasco

Entrepreneurship as a key factor for endogenous development

It is well known that in recent years regional politics have undergone considerable change not only in their objectives and strategies, but also in the diagnoses of the problems that characterise lesser-developed regions. The traditional regional policies prior to this decade were shaped around a central idea of 'assistance' to a region's economy. Yet, in contrast to this 'traditional' regional theory, a new policy approach focuses on endogenous development, i.e. development not dependent on external assistance (Table 16.1). In short, we could say that the model of development 'from above' starts to transform itself into one 'from below,' and, in a sense, abandons economics' penchant towards the allocation of resources, as opposed to their generation itself.

Yet, if we centre our attention on the modern approach to regional development, we can quite clearly appreciate that the diagnosis of the problems of economically lesser-developed regions strongly conditions our strategy, objectives and instruments; and the results. Indeed, with serious deficiencies in entrepreneurship, innovation, know-how and international economic relationships, it is difficult for self-sufficient development and for an acceptable level of international competitiveness to be achieved. But, within the specific context of these four problems, it seems obvious that the production of innovations, as well as of know-how and of a minimal level of internationalisation, ends up depending on a strong, consistent regional entrepreneurial base. The existence of an adequate and dynamic

Table 16.1 Traditional and new policies for lagging regions

	Traditional	*New*
Problems	Lack of capital	Lack of entrepreneurship
	Lack of qualified labour	Lack of innovations
	Exploit scale economics	Lack of specific know-how
		Lack of internationalisation
Strategy	Regional policy as a defence from international competition	Market-oriented regional policy
	Increase income transfers to the weakest regions	Regional policy based on economic efficiency
Objectives	Insure price competition	Decrease adjustment costs
	Reduce production costs	Decrease transaction costs
Instruments	Subsidies to firms	Supply of producer services
	Transfers to households	Territorial policies
		Inter-regional cooperation
Effects	No self-sustained development	Self-sustained development
	Increasing dependence	International competitiveness
	Contrast with the competition policy of the EU	Compatibility with the competition policy of the EU

Source: Cappelin 1991.

entrepreneurial tissue presupposes this necessary, but maybe not sufficient, condition, not only in order to overcome the rest of these problems, but also in order to develop strategies (economic efficiency) and instruments (supply of services to producers) that make us reach the intermediate objectives and final effects of competitiveness and self-sustained development. It seems evident that the current globalisation of financial markets has diminished the lack of capital, the principal problem in regional development, allowing another great problem that has not been sufficiently analysed to emerge: the lack of entrepreneurial activity.

To be honest, the entrepreneurial factor has always been present in regional policies. In fact, in the so-called 'traditional policies' the policy makers have aimed to defend the entrepreneur from international competition. More recently, regional development strategy has sought to attract firms to the least-favoured areas and regions with the hope of cultivating lasting growth. Nevertheless, in the majority of cases, this 'entrepreneurial attraction' strategy is showing limited results, and the lesser-developed regions' production, income and employment levels continue to be quite distant from those of the developed countries and areas.

Following this point of view, the empowering of the entrepreneur from within the local population, as opposed to the sole application of policies to attract entrepreneurs from other, more dynamic economies, appears as the key factor in endogenous development. In this sense, we can point out at least two reasons that justify this approach and that are evidently not related to a 'chauvinist' conception of regional production, or of a regional economy. First, the empowering of local entrepreneurs is becoming increasingly necessary for any take-off and subsequent preservation of economic growth, provided such growth basically consists of a sustained process of productive investments that include a large number of closely linked sectors and subsectors. Logically, external investments can generate important productive activity and even a high number of jobs; but only with difficulty, except in very small economies with many ties to international markets, can such exogenous investments dynamise the whole regional economy and not be reduced to creating productive 'islets' with scarcely any connection to the rest of the regional productive apparatus. Second, we should recognise equally that any productive activity that is principally founded upon foreign investment from large multinational groups is prone to be economically dependent and vulnerable to swings in national or international conditions. Whether faced with political changes, great changes in business focus, or changes in economic conditions, foreign investment finds itself in a notably less stable and less consolidated position than endogenous business investment.

Yet, the empowering or promotion of local entrepreneurship necessarily depends on the existence of its 'raw material': entrepreneurs. Evidently, if in a regional economy the entrepreneurial population appears to be weak or insubstantial, this economy will demand specific regional policy actions that go beyond traditional financial or material support or aid. In this sense, we have chosen four regions of Spain with different entrepreneurial traditions so as to determine how appropriate each region's regional development agency policies are for their different entrepreneurial bases, for their different realities.

The qualitative diversity of Spain's entrepreneurial base
The four regions we have chosen are Andalusia, Galicia, Catalonia and the Basque Country. As we can see in Table 16.2, the first two regions clearly fall below the Spanish averages in three principal economic development

indicators, whereas Catalonia and the Basque Country easily surpass those averages, even to the point of nearing the European Union averages. In addition to these developmental differences, the four regions' entrepreneurial cultures hold different traditions which can make a comparative policy analysis of their respective RDAs quite enlightening.

There is, however, another significant reason for selecting these four regions: they are considered to be the only four 'historic' Autonomous Communities in Spain's autonomous structure. They all possess, therefore, maximum levels of power and sufficient levels of political autonomy in order that the RDAs' functions do not respond necessarily to a national redistribution model. Consequently, one can say that there exists no tie or commitment that obligates them to establish joint organisations or common objectives, or even similar conceptual views.

Table 16.2 Regional development levels, 1994
(index 100 is EU or Spanish average)

Region	GDP at factor cost		Gross regional income		Household disposable income	
	EU	Spain	EU	Spain	EU	Spain
Andalusia	56.83	71.67	54.84	69.16	62.47	78.16
Galicia	66.09	83.34	65.06	82.04	74.78	93.57
Catalonia	97.47	122.91	97.13	122.49	93.64	117.17
Basque Country	86.75	109.40	87.78	110.69	86.16	107.81

Source: Fundación FIES.

Table 16.3 Proportion of entrepreneurs
among the employed

	Percentage
Andalusia	21.69
Galicia	31.51
Catalonia	20.05
Basque Country	22.25

Source: Encuesta Población Activa 1995.

Given these territorial differences, we shall try to relate the two variables we have been alluding to: the level of economic development and the entrepreneurial factor. At first, our intuition may lead us to think that the two more developed regions are so because of their populations' greater entrepreneurial tendencies. Both Catalonia and the Basque Country have a great entrepreneurial tradition, which can make us want to deduce a direct relationship between their economic development and a possibly larger number of entrepreneurs. Table 16.3, however, does not let us deduce such a relationship at all.

It seems, then, that if any possible weakness in these regions' entrepreneurial tissue influences the development process, it is not due to quantitative reasons, that is, to an insufficient number of entrepreneurs. Rather, this insufficiency may be qualitative and, as such, we shall examine some parameters which may reflect these qualitative questions. First, we shall centre our attention on the industrial sector.

From a macro-economic perspective and for several reasons, industrial activities generally contribute a stronger impulse, as compared with other economic sectors, to economic development. Manufacturing industries usually create a larger added value than, say, service activities, which usually operate closer to final demand and with a lower technological level than these industries. Second, manufacturing industries possess much denser inter-sectoral connections (relationships) than do services. This all adds up to an extremely significant multiplier effect on employment and production. Finally, in terms of international markets, it is necessary to remember that industries represent a fundamental component in developed countries' commercial exports and, therefore, directly reflect an economy's international competitiveness.

If we focus briefly on the industrial sector, we can observe (Table 16.4) that Catalonia as well as the Basque Country present a somewhat higher proportion of industrial firms than Galicia and Andalusia, which is a principle qualitative trait that differentiates the former, more developed regions from the latter, lesser-developed ones. Still, in calculating the number of industrial firms, one can include simple establishments, factories or work centres that do not necessarily constitute a formal enterprise. Furthermore, if one also includes the affiliate companies of national and international groups, the number of firms will differ notably from the number of entrepreneurs. Hence, in Table 16.5, we have collected the proportions of 'industrial' entrepreneurs over the total of entrepreneurs. As can be seen, the difference between the two more 'backward' and the two more advanced regions is clearly magnified, especially in the Basque Country, a land whose confined and

Table 16.4 Industrial firms by region
(share of total number of firms in region)

	Percentage
Andalusia	8.5
Galicia	9.3
Catalonia	12.8
Basque Country	9.9

Source: DIRCE 1995.

Table 16.5 'Industrial entrepreneurs' by region
(share of total number of entrepreneurs in region)

	Percentage
Andalusia	9.9
Galicia	6.7
Catalonia	15.9
Basque Country	21.4

Source: EPA 1995.

craggy character induces greater development of its primary and tertiary activities, which complements its great industrial tradition.

The fact that Catalonia and the Basque Country present much superior proportions of industrial entrepreneurs may indicate greater entrepreneurial quality, provided that industrial activity typically demands greater experience in and greater knowledge of the sector and its technological means. Indeed, a recent empirical study on entrepreneurial 'quality' pointed out several aspects of industrial entrepreneurs, as opposed to those in other sectors, and in particular their higher average quality (Arias et al. 1994).

Besides this positive correlation between the number of industrial entrepreneurs and economic development, another qualitative entrepreneurial element relates to the size (dimensional structure) of each region's firms. In this sense, we can distinguish three main groups:

- micro-enterprises: 1–5 employees;
- SMEs: 6–100 employees;
- large enterprises: more than 100 employees.

Using this classification, we have calculated the specific weight of each group for each region. As can be observed in Table 16.6, and across all sectors, large enterprises hold greater weight in Catalonia and the Basque Country (0.4%) than in Andalusia and Galicia (0.2%). On the other hand, the micro-enterprises are situated about 2 percentage points higher in the two latter, lesser-developed regions than in the former. In our opinion, this is significant inasmuch as in Spain these firms generally maintain either a role as 'satellites' of large companies or a strong isolation from general economic fluctuations. The first case can imply much vulnerability with respect to the large enterprises; and the second entails very small and excessively independent productive units whose reduced but loyal demand allows them to benefit from limited national and international competition (Averitt 1968). In any case, Spain's micro-enterprises, whether the first kind or the second, seem to respond merely to a survival motivation and not to any ambition to grow (Guzman 1994).

From an endogenous development point of view, the authentic SMEs end up representing the true nucleus of the productive apparatus itself. In facing the micro-enterprises' limitations and weaknesses and the large firms'

**Table 16.6 Firms according to size
(percentage of total number of firms)**

Region	Micro-enterprises	SMEs	Large enterprises	Total
All sectors				
Andalusia	92.7	7.0	0.2	100.0
Galicia	92.0	7.7	0.2	100.0
Catalonia	89.8	9.7	0.4	100.0
Basque Country	90.1	9.4	0.4	100.0
Industry				
Andalusia	80.2	19.1	0.6	100.0
Galicia	78.5	21.4	0.9	100.0
Catalonia	72.7	24.5	1.5	100.0
Basque Country	63.5	32.9	3.6	100.0

Source: Datos DIRCE 1995.

excessive dependence and even vulnerability, the SMEs, in their majority, possess a consistent and consolidated internal organisation and respond to local private initiatives that reflect the region's entrepreneurial capacity (Table 16.6).

Yet, if we centre our attention specifically on industrial activity, we can see significant differences between the industrial SMEs. In our opinion, the relatively high proportion of industrial SMEs in Catalonia and the Basque Country is another symptom of the qualitative difference that exists between those regions and Andalusia and Galicia. The case of the Basque Country is specially relevant because of its strong manufacturing tradition and its particular current situation of declining large industries, apart from them having reduced their size.

The quality of the entrepreneurial fabric can also be related to the type of industry that can prevail in the regional economy. It is not the same for industrial activity to be based in obsolete sectors as it is for it to be based in dynamic or forward-looking sectors. Hence, we have selected five industrial sectors catalogued by the European Commission (Ministerio de Industria 1994) as 'low-demand' sectors along with five 'high-demand' sectors, and we analyse the structure of the firms producing in these sectors. The five

Table 16.7 Firm size in 'low demand' and 'high demand' sectors (percentage of total number of firms in sector)

Region	Micro-enterprises	SMEs	Large enter-prises	Total
Low demand sectors				
Andalusia	82.4	17.0	0.5	100.0
Galicia	79.8	19.4	0.5	100.0
Catalonia	73.7	24.7	1.5	100.0
Basque Country	60.9	34.9	4.1	100.0
High demand sectors				
Andalusia	79.4	19.4	1.1	100.0
Galicia	79.1	19.7	0.8	100.0
Catalonia	63.0	32.2	4.6	100.0
Basque Country	53.9	41.3	4.7	100.0

Source: Calculated on the basis of data from DIRCE 1995 and the European Commission.

'low-demand' sectors are: textile, leather, wood, cork-plastics and metallurgy; the five 'high-demand' sectors are: chemicals, office machines and computers, electronics, electrical equipment and medical-optical equipment.

Table 16.7 shows the entrepreneurial distribution according to these sectors for the four regions. In our opinion, the SMEs' greater relative presence in the more dynamic sectors bolsters, yet again, the 'advanced' regions' greater qualitative level, given the regions' factors related to agglomeration, ties to innovation centres and so on have favourable effects on the economy.

The degree of networking among entrepreneurial agents can also reflect upon the quality in the entrepreneurial base, as networking and collaboration among entrepreneurs can lead to the use of productive, commercial, and other types of synergies. The available data do not allow us even minimally reliable information on this, but we can obtain some basic support by examining the firms' legal formulae, in particular: (1) individual (non-corporate) enterprises, which represent the highest level of individualism, regardless of the production level or whether they are family-owned or not; (2) (stock-issuing) business corporations, which represent the maximum degree of commitment among the firm's capitalist

Table 16.8 Types of ownership amongst firms
(percentage of total number of firms in region)

Region	Individual	Joint-stock corporations	Other
Andalusia	75.5	3.8	20.7
Galicia	75.7	2.9	21.4
Catalonia	69.3	8.7	22.0
Basque Country	71.4	9.8	18.8

Source: DIRCE 1995.

partners. According to Table 16.8, the low proportion of joint stock corporations makes manifest the lower degree of networking or, even, mutual trust among investors, and works to create solid and sizable business structures within Andalusia and Galicia.

All of these qualitative factors, then, hurt the competitiveness of the lesser-developed regional economies. The market globalisation of recent years has been fostering, one way or another, the increase in firm size and/or the growth in collaborations or alliances between firms. Some studies have brought out the correlation that exists between economic integration and firm size. Currently, the most competitive countries are the ones that have firms or conglomerates operating in world markets, though this does not nullify the necessity of small and medium size enterprises that 'attend local markets, that subcontract services or certain parts of the large companies' products, or that are super-specialized in a very specific product or service' (De la Dehesa 1995). As we pointed out earlier, the core of authentic SMEs in an economy represents the most important base of its productive apparatus, regardless whether or not they hold ties to large international groups. Still, the excessive predominance of individual micro-enterprises responds to a way of life which shows no ambition beyond mere survival.

In this sense, then, it is convenient to examine the role of the most used economic policy instruments to support business enterprises: the RDAs, so as to evaluate how well these agencies deal with their regions' entrepreneurial deficiencies.

The role of the RDAs in promoting entrepreneurship

Given that the differences between the entrepreneurial bases of regions in Spain are mainly qualitative, we have decided to approach the question with a qualitative methodology based on personal interviews, as in a case study. From there, and by means of an outline, we perform a comparative study of the four RDAs corresponding to the four selected regions: IFA (Andalusia), IGAPE (Galicia), SPRI (the Basque Country), and CIDEM (Catalonia).

The Institute for the Promotion of Andalusia (IFA)

Established in 1986 as a public entity subjected to private law, IFA's principle objective is to stimulate Andalusia's industrialisation through the improvement of the region's own entrepreneurial fabric and through the attraction of foreign investors. Beneath these main objectives lie the improvement of infrastructures and capital equipment, and the promotion of Andalusia in the rest of Spain and abroad.

Its organisation is based in several central offices and other peripheral offices in each of the region's six provinces and also in Madrid, Brussels and Tokyo. Seventy-five per cent of its financial resources come from the Andalusian Autonomous Community's general budget, mostly through the regional government's Council for Industry, Commerce and Tourism. It also receives financial support from Spain's central government (such as funds allotted to Spain's Centre of Industrial Technological Development) and from the European Union (SME support). Likewise, the Institute receives income from loans (that it makes and are repaid), from treasury bond yields, and from any other loans that are considered necessary.

IFA centres its activities around financial assistance to enterprises, allocating them up to 75 per cent of its expenditure, with 75 per cent of such aid being destined to manufacturing firms. This assistance consists of direct loans, subsidies, subsidised interest rates, capital participation and loan guarantees.

There also exists a preoccupation with technological support, which manifests itself as participation in projects and technological programmes (Euro-CEI, Malaga's Technological Park, programmes for SMEs) as well as the creation of the instrumental firm Andalusian Society for the Development of Computing and Electronics (SADIEL). Other activities, such as consulting, entrepreneurial training, and information have a very small or no role.

With regard to the implementation of the aid, IFA is passive; it waits to receive financial support requests from firms. These companies tend to be medium or small industrial enterprises, although there does not exist any specific standard based on size or subsectors. The aid is aimed towards existing enterprises. There is very little aid for new ventures.

The Gallegan Institute of Economic Promotion (IGAPE)

IGAPE was created in 1972 as a public entity and with the fundamental objective of business formation through the sectoral promotion of Gallegan enterprises. Likewise, it aims to attract foreign investment.

It is organised similarly to IFA, with both central and peripheral offices, although the latter are not located in every province. It also has offices in Tokyo and in Miami. Almost all of its financial resources (95%) come from the Gallegan Autonomous Community budget. The European Union and Spain's Institute for the Small and Medium Industrial Enterprise (IMPI) cover the rest. Overall, its general budget increased to 10 billion ptas. in 1993.

As regards its activities, incentives and financial aid, in the form of interest rate subsidies and other subsidies, absorb 80% of its budget, with industrial SMEs being its principle field of activity. Nevertheless, it also attends to some large firms, supports the Guarantee Loan Societies, provides grants to firms so that they provide training contracts, and collaborates with institutions oriented towards technological development. Attention to the information needs of firms also stands out among IGAPE's key activities. Similarly, though with less emphasis, it provides consultancy to firms, promotes Gallegan products, and works to attract foreign investment.

It also actively disseminates information and training to Galicia's entrepreneurs. Yet, it is passive towards incentives, as it waits for its financial aid to be demanded. A firm must want to invest more than 10 million ptas. for it to be able to attain financial assistance from IGAPE; this aid, however, cannot cover more than 70% of the investment. IGAPE generally focuses its aid on SMEs, and while it does promote the creation of firms by young entrepreneurs (mostly through their training), its financial aid is oriented overall towards existing enterprises.

The Society for the Promotion and Reconversion of the Basque Country (SPRI)

This corporation was founded in 1981 in reaction to the oil crisis. SPRI has now turned into the arm that administers the Basque government's industrial policy, with its main goal being the support of industrial SMEs and a secondary one being the attraction of large enterprises to the region.

It is organised as a holding company which unites central services, a society for the promotion of land for industrial use, and several municipal-level societies that provide some basic services to firms. Through this, it succeeds in integrating all the steps and processes of local development. In the same way its ties to loans and savings are very strong, which thus favours the placement of financial resources in Basque businesses.

Almost all of SPRI's financial resources come from the Basque government's budget. However, it receives additional funding for certain programmes from the European Union.

Its principle activities are aimed towards the dissemination of information to and assessment of new business ventures through its business and innovation centres. These act as incubators and offer all kinds of services, although they also make these services available, upon request, to existing firms. Support for technological innovation has special importance through SPRI's participation in two technological parks, where it aids SMEs focused on R&D. None of this means, however, that SPRI disregards entirely financial aid for new entrepreneurial initiatives.

The Society operates actively in consultancy and in the diffusion of information and financial aid for new projects, and aims its intervention towards certain industrial subsectors: the environment, software, automobiles, aeronautics and small appliances. That is, it works predominantly with 'high demand' industries.

The Centre of Information and Entrepreneurial Development (CIDEM)

The Centre was created by the Catalonian government in 1985 as a public entity subject to private law, and like SPRI, it works under the region's Industry Council. Its main objectives are to support Catalonian industries and to promote awareness of the importance of growth in productivity, quality and competitiveness. In addition, it pursues greater equality within its territory and the dissemination of information for the development and betterment of entrepreneurial activities.

Like the other RDAs, it is organised around both central and peripheral offices in each of the region's four provinces and outside Spain. It is financed almost entirely by Catalonia's general budget, with the rest being covered by charges for some of its services and funds from the European Union. Its main activities are to assess and provide information to industrial SMEs, especially in order to promote innovation and cooperation among firms. It also executes technology policies, fundamentally through its participation in technological centres and the Vallés Technological Park. All of these activities are linked to local development initiatives.

As regards any financial support for SMEs, CIDEM does not carry out any important activities, since another public entity within the Catalonian regional government has this role. CIDEM, however, does concern itself with finding potential investors and stockholders for regional firms, as well as with placing venture capital at their (the firm's) disposition so as to help them acquire more financial resources. All of these activities are governed by a single concern: to encourage the creation of industrial enterprises that produce high gross added value.

CIDEM operates proactively in making entrepreneurs conscious of networking and innovation, and reactively in its consultancy and information sharing. All of this is aimed, preferentially, towards the subsectors that produce high added value, within a global and long-term plan developed by the Catalonian government's Industry Policy Office.

Comparative analysis

We shall first focus on the common elements of the four RDAs so as to proceed, later, to our main analysis based on their differences. The following common traits among the agencies can be identified:

1. With respect to the legal form, and excepting the corporation SPRI, the RDAs are all public entities subject to private law. Both forms, however, allow the agencies much autonomy in their operations, as they are not directly integrated in any organism of the regional governments.
2. All contain a decentralised internal organisation, with both central and peripheral offices in most or all of their regions' provinces.
3. Almost all of their resources are provided by the regional governments.
4. The support and promotion of local industries are at least one of their objectives, though this objective varies subtly from agency to agency.

The agencies vary as follows:

1. In the first place, the strategies of IFA and IGAPE can be clearly differentiated from those followed by SPRI and CIDEM. While the

former have no clear long-term direction, the latters do. The Basque and Catalonian agencies outline their actions within long-range plans established by their corresponding regional governments. They also have selected certain priority subsectors upon which they focus their assistance. The Andalusian and Gallegan agencies have not done this.

2. Two different types of support tools can be differentiated, which again correspond to the Basque and Catalonian agencies, on one hand, and to the Andalusian and Gallegan on the other. IFA and IGAPE focus mainly on financial aid, showing no preference for size nor sector; the latter, SPRI and CIDEM, focus on assessing and providing information to entrepreneurs. SPRI and CIDEM are not identical, however, as SPRI works more through introducing innovations and promoting new initiatives, whereas CIDEM places emphasis on networking and inter-firm cooperation, which can create stronger entrepreneurial tissue.

3. IFA and IGAPE are passive in executing their respective activities; whereas both SPRI and CIDEM actively carry theirs out. In this sense, for instance, IFA and IGAPE wait to receive aid applications from firms. CIDEM organises seminars, expositions and meetings with entrepreneurs to stimulate a spirit of networking and to inform them of new technologies. Further, SPRI looks for and stimulates entrepreneurial initiatives through the development agencies at local level, even involving the town councils and private agents.

4. Neither IGAPE nor IFA operates in coordination with any local development agency, which generally are linked to municipal governments. CIDEM and SPRI, however, have and use such ties with the local development agencies in their regions.

Conclusions

Having analysed the quantitative and qualitative characteristics of the productive systems of the four areas, as well as the RDAs' role within them, we can now draw some conclusions which allow us to evaluate how well the agencies approach the entrepreneurial deficiencies and needs of the region.

Without entering deeply into purely organisational aspects, which do nonetheless betray the deficient coordination of IGAPE and IFA, basically because of the lack of local networks with their respective municipal governments and other local development organisations, we do observe that these agencies do not establish any coordination between the problems characteristic of their entrepreneurial tissues. Nor do they frame their actions well temporally, since their deficiencies can only be corrected in the long term. Yet, SPRI and CIDEM do seem to overcome these deficiencies, for not only do they operate more towards the long term, but they also tie their activities in with the business support operations of other public institutions.

Second, the activities of IFA and IGAPE are not appropriate given the qualitative, rather than quantitative, problems of their entrepreneurial fabrics. In this sense, their dominant use of financial aid, which generally is designed to 'assist' enterprises with problems, is not the best form of overcoming a lack of entrepreneurial quality; and this deficient quality is their main productive handicap. In contrast, SPRI and CIDEM, with their information and assessment focus, seem to be better oriented towards resolving these quality concerns.

SPRI and CIDEM work in accordance with the characteristics of their productive systems. The former, in a region with declining industries and dominated by large enterprises in crisis, favours, even with financial support, new business initiatives and has even selected 'high demand' subsectors to receive this aid. The second, in a region with a more consolidated entrepreneurial base, concerns itself with increasing the size of its firms and international influence. In short, it seems clear that the RDAs of less-favoured zones do not operate consistently with the productive or entrepreneurial needs of their regions, while the RDAs of the more prosperous zones foster and reflect the very development of their regions.

References

Arias, C., Basulto, J., Guzmán, J. and Santos, F. (1994) 'Un modelo explicativo de la calidad empresarial en Andalusia.' *Revista de Estudios Andaluces 20*, 49–64.

Averitt, R. (1968) *The Dual Economy.* New York: Norton & Company.

Cappellin, R. (1991) 'The new gravity centers of regional development in the Europe of the 90s.' Paper presented to the XVII Regional Studies Conference, Barcelona.

De la Dehesa, G. (1995) 'Competencia, competitividad y tamaño empresarial.' *El País*, 22 December, 45.

DIRCE (1995) *Data.* Madrid: Directorio Central de Empresas.

Fundación FIES (1995) Madrid: Fundación Fondo Investigación Económico y Social.

Guzm n Cuevas, J. (1994) 'Aspectos estructurales de las PYMEs. Las microempresas y los empresarios en España.' *Economía Industrial 300*, 197–204.

Instituto Nacional de Estadistica (1995) *Encuesta de Población Activa.* Madrid: Instituto Nacional de Estadistica.

Ministerio de Industria (1994) *Informe sobre la Industria Española.* Madrid: Ministerio de Industria.

Further reading

CIDEM (1995) *Memoria.* Barcelona: CIDEM.

IFA (1995) *Memoria.* Seville: IFA.

IGAPE (1995) *Memoria.* Santiago de Compostela: IGAPE.

SPRI (1995) *Memoria.* Bilbao: SPRI.

CHAPTER 17

Regional Development Agencies and Policy in Northern Ireland

Strategies and Implementation

Marie Finnegan

Introduction

Northern Ireland is a relatively depressed and under-developed region of both the United Kingdom and the European Union. Income *per capita* there is the second lowest in the UK, after Merseyside, and is 74 per cent of the EU average. Whilst unemployment has been falling, it represented 11.2 per cent of the workforce in July 1996, and Northern Ireland still ranks 158th out of the 174 EU regions. It has also suffered deep political conflict for over 25 years. Against this backdrop, economic development policy in Northern Ireland has undergone major changes in the 1990s; it has evolved from a largely interventionist approach in the 1970s and 1980s involving substantial levels of public resources with the direct aim of creating employment, towards one that is more selective, market-oriented and centred around the key objective of improved competitiveness with the ultimate aim of increasing economic growth. As such, Northern Ireland offers a good opportunity to look at the changing nature of economic development policy in a small, peripheral and relatively depressed region of the EU.

In Northern Ireland, economic development policy is overseen and coordinated by the Department of Economic Development (DED), and is implemented by five development agencies responsible for various aspects of policy: the Industrial Development Board (IDB) for the development of large indigenous firms and the attraction of inward investment; the Local Enterprise Development Unit (LEDU) for the promotion of start-up firms and small businesses; the Training and Employment Agency (T&EA) for addressing labour market problems; the Industrial Research and Technology Unit (IRTU) for the encouragement of technological innovation; and the Northern Ireland Tourist Board (NITB) for the promotion of tourism. While the DED sets the general parameters within which policy takes place, the individual agencies have a fair degree of autonomy to meet their specific remits within agency budgets.

This chapter attempts to examine the extent to which the policy shift towards increased competitiveness envisioned by DED has been implemented by its constituent agencies in the first half of the 1990s. The rest of this chapter is divided into three parts: the next section considers competitiveness as a basis for policy in Northern Ireland and elsewhere; the following section evaluates the implementation and monitoring of the competitiveness policy by the regional development agencies; the final section brings the main issues together.

Competitiveness as a basis for policy

Encouraging competitiveness has become a major policy theme in the 1990s in Northern Ireland and elsewhere. The DED has published two strategy documents on competitiveness (1990, 1995) while the UK government has published three White Papers on competitiveness (DTI, 1994, 1995, 1996). The European Commission has followed up its 1993 White Paper on 'Growth, Competitiveness and Employment' with the establishment of the Competitiveness Advisory Group, and the United States, Canada and Australia have published similar reports on competitiveness.

The concept of competitiveness has been dismissed as a basis for policy at the level of the nation by some leading economists. For example, Krugman argues that 'the obsession with competitiveness is not only wrong but dangerous, skewing domestic polices and threatening the international system' (1996, p.5). There are two main charges against the concept as a guide to policy. First, the competitiveness of a nation (and even more so of a region) has no agreed meaning in economic theory in that it means different things to different people. Second, using competitiveness as a synonym for raising productivity in the domestic production of goods and services may encourage protectionism by giving a misplaced emphasis to countries as rivals and to the role of trade in economic performance (Krugman 1994, 1996). However, the concept of competitiveness as a guide to policy remains useful for two main reasons: first, it emphasises international benchmarking, and second, it implies that the search for improved economic performance is never ending (Eltis and Higham 1995).

The policy approach to competitiveness is based on an empirical and theoretical analysis of competitiveness and economic growth, and, in general, four main determinants of competitiveness emerge from the extensive literature. These are:

- business support development which gives priority to technological development including innovation, research and development, information and technological transfer (Porter 1990; Best 1995; Romer 1994)

- human resource development including the education and training of the workforce to produce a high quality skills mix (Caves 1980; Reich 1991)

- infrastructure development including all modes of transport, different energy sources and telecommunications (Dunford and Hudson 1996)

- public finance and administration including ethos and commitment (Hutton 1995).

The literature also indicates that economists have not fully explained the process of economic growth and much depends on intangible factors such as social attitudes, for example, governance and institutional arrangements based on cooperation and trust (Fukuyama 1995).

Table 17.1 presents a framework for understanding competitiveness in terms of these primary determinants in the context of Northern Ireland. The table indicates that the DED and the development agencies have responsibility for factors such as human resource development and business support development, while both central and local government are responsible for infrastructure, the public finances and administration.

The DED's document *Competing in the 1990s* (DED 1990) formally introduced competitiveness as the main theme for economic development policy in Northern Ireland and this broad policy direction was consolidated in the Department's five year review, *Growing Competitively* (DED 1995). In concert with the UK-wide free market foundation for policy, the DED places primary responsibility for improving competitiveness with the private sector and limits the role of central government to the creation of a stable macro-economic environment and the role of DED and its agencies to intervention only in the case of 'market failure'. Since market failure is the central criteria for government intervention, it is important to be clear what the term means and how markets can be identified as working so imperfectly so as to justify government intervention. However, the Department fails to define the concept, or provide examples of its application as a criteria for

**Table 17.1 Framework for competitiveness
in Northern Ireland**

Key factors		Body responsible	Performance measurements
Human resource development	Education and training	DED	Employment trends
	Skills and productivity	T & EA	Labour costs
		DENI	
Business support development	Technological capabilities, including innovation and R&D	DED IRTU IDB LEDU	Input services costs Market share Trade & market dev. Investment levels
	Finance for development		Output growth
Infrastructure	Installed capacity in: Telecommunications	Central govt	Cost/range of services
	Logistics and transport	DED	
	Energy	DoE	
	Banking/insurance		
Public finance and administration	Ethos	Central	Public sector burden
	Commitment	govt	Regulatory burden
	Motivation	DED	Efficiency
	Experience and expertise		Responsiveness
			Inflation

Source: Adapted from Table S3.2 p.23 in Forfas 1996.

intervention in terms of the agencies' strategies. This serves to demonstrate the DED's limited ability to lead and direct the polices of its peripheral agencies.

The DED adopted the Department of Trade and Industry's (DTI) definitions of competitiveness and defines it at the level of the nation and at the level of the firm. Competitiveness at the level of the nation (and presumably the region) is defined as 'the degree to which a country can, under free and fair market conditions, produce goods and services which meet the test of international markets, while simultaneously maintaining and expanding the real incomes of people over the long term' (DTI 1994, 1995; DED 1995, p.3). It is defined at the level of the firm as 'the ability to produce the right goods and services of the right quality, at the right price, at the right time. It means meeting customers' needs more efficiently and more effectively than other firms' (DTI 1994, p.9; DED 1995, p.3). The DED goes on to assert that comparable working definitions have been adopted by the individual agencies in their corporate plans covering the period 1995–98.

Such working definitions of competitiveness and the initial appearance of uniformity across agencies are welcome. However, there are a number of problems with the generic definitions employed. First, the Department does not make the definitions relevant to a region in general or Northern Ireland in particular. It would seem that the definition of competitiveness at the national or regional level views it as the means to raise living standards. Living standards are generally approximated by real output per head measured at purchasing power parities. If output per head grows then living standards increase. Therefore, it can be assumed that the Department's targets for the economy over the period 1995–2001 for manufacturing productivity growth (4% per annum) and manufacturing output growth (6% per annum) are linked to its definition of competitiveness (DED 1995). In other words, it has to be assumed that growth in manufacturing productivity leads to improved competitiveness, which in turn, results in higher living standards.

Second, the Department fails to place the definitions of competitiveness in the policy context of the individual agencies. This ambiguous approach to competitiveness manifests itself in an inconsistent approach towards it both within agencies and across agencies. For example, LEDU displays inconsistency over time in its treatment of competitiveness while the other agencies have adopted a variety of stances in their approach to it as a basis for policy over their planning periods.

In 1991, LEDU defined competitiveness 'as the ability of a business to establish, maintain and then grow its market share profitably and without subsidy' (LEDU 1991, p.10). The Unit considered that encouraging companies to improve their competitiveness was central to LEDU's policy, while the promotion of jobs was dropped as a prime aim. However, the more recent corporate plan (LEDU 1995b) marks a clear departure from this stance, and instead stresses the need for increased economic growth and job creation while barely mentioning competitiveness.

Nor are the concepts of competitiveness employed consistently across the agencies. For example, competitiveness has remained at the core of IDB policy over its last two planning periods, employing its original definition of it. That is, 'IDB regards a company as competitive if it can continually secure profitable business against other companies operating in the same sector without recourse to public support' (IDB 1991, p.8). In contrast, the T&EA, though apparently committed to the concept of competitiveness, has made no attempt to define it at any stage. The IRTU identifies competitiveness with increased market share and stresses the non-price elements of competition such as product quality, marketing, selling and distribution.

The inconsistency both inter- and intra-agency highlights the need for the Department to fulfil its assigned role as a leading and centrifugal force in bringing the various agencies strands together into a coherent whole (NIEC 1994). The Department could begin such a process by clearly defining competitiveness in the context of Northern Ireland and the polices of its constituent agencies. Such an approach would facilitate greater understanding and thus lead to a more effective implementation of competitiveness policy.

Implementation and monitoring of competitiveness policy in Northern Ireland

Policy implementation

As already noted, the DED oversees and coordinates economic development policy while the development agencies implement policy. This section focuses on the activities of the primary agencies for delivering economic development policy, the IDB and LEDU.

The Industrial Development Board

The Industrial Development Board (IDB) is responsible for the encouragement and expansion of local companies with more than 50 employees in the manufacturing and tradable services sector and for the attraction of inward investment. The new policy signified a theoretical policy shift towards indigenous industry with little or no change in the approach to inward investment. The main instrument used by the IDB before 1990 was the allocation of Selective Financial Assistance (SFA) to individual firms, largely in the form of capital grants accounting for as much as 50 per cent of investment costs. The extent to which the policy switch with respect to indigenous industry has occurred can be assessed with reference to changes in the allocation of expenditure between different activities and the degree of selectivity in industrial aid, over the period 1992 to 1995.

ALLOCATION OF EXPENDITURE

The allocation of total IDB expenditure on different activities, broken down between established industry and inward investment where possible, is outlined in Table 17.2. Progress towards the IDB's competitiveness objective, defined as those that can 'secure profitable business against other companies operating in the same sector without recourse to public support' (IDB 1991, p.8), should be reflected in a decrease in expenditure on industrial aid towards established industry. However, if expenditure on new inward investment projects is excluded, the table shows that financial assistance to established industry as a proportion of total expenditure has actually increased in terms of grants, loans and shares since 1992.

Furthermore, a shift in assistance from that which encouraged capital investment (in particular through the allocation of capital grants) to the promotion of non-physical, knowledge-based investment (such as innovation, including R&D, and technological transfer) was implied by the changed strategy. Such non-physical and knowledge-based investment is deemed to be crucial to promoting non-price competitiveness (that is selling differentiated products based on design, quality, durability, after sales service and so on, rather than on prices) which is considered to be a major determinant of international trade (NEDO 1983). However, Table 17.3 indicates that there has been only a marginal change in relative expenditure across various types of grants over the period and, the majority of expenditure is still on capital grants (75 per cent in 1995–95). Moreover, the new feature of IDB assistance is described as 'other revenue grants', but no details of their purpose are offered. However, employment grants have been cut by over 25 per cent over the period.

SELECTIVITY

The increased exposure of firms to the market mechanism and the implied reduced dependence on subsidies which accompanies the competitiveness strategy also denotes greater selectivity in industrial aid. Increased selectivity in IDB policy would be indicated by a decrease in the level of SFA offered to companies, a decrease in its proportion of overall investment costs and a decrease in the number of offers made. However, it appears that the indicators are inconsistent with these expectations. Table 17.4 shows that the level of assistance, the number of offers made and the average size of the offers to established industry have all increased since 1992. In fact, the level of SFA offered has almost doubled over the period 1992–93 to 1994–95. Moreover, assistance as a percentage of total investment costs to established industry has remained largely unchanged since 1992.

In summary, there has been no marked change in the direction of policy officially announced by the Government in 1990. This is reflected in the increased relative allocation of funds in favour of grants (especially of the capital variety) and reduced selectivity in industrial aid to established industry. Furthermore, the annual reports continue to give priority to the promises of new jobs contracts signed. However, it must be remembered that grant-aid varies by industry, type of project, and general conditions and prospects in the economy. In the absence of a more disaggregated analysis,

Table 17.2 Actual expenditure and percentage share of total IDB expenditure to established industry and inward investment in various categories, 1992–93 to 1994–95 (£'000)

	Grants[1]			Shares[2]	Loans		
	Estab	Inward[3]	Both	Estab	Estab	Inward	Both
1992–93	47,597	21,130	68,727	2763	3700	4000	7700
	48.0%	21.3%	69.0%	2.8%	3.7%	4.0%	7.7%
1993–94	46,771	7131	53,902	2800	2120	360	2480
	58.8%	8.7%	67.7%	3.5%	2.7%	0.5%	3.1%
1994–95	44,040	7777	51,817	2878	3900	1250	5150
	53.7%	9.5%	63.2%	3.5%	4.7%	1.5%	6.3%

Source: IDB annual reports, various issues.

Notes: 1. The grants figure split over inward and established excludes marketing development grants and grants to agencies and research bodies as it is not possible to break them down on this basis.
2. Shares are only acquired in established industry
3. Grants are to new inward investment projects and vary depending on IDBs success in attracting projects and conditions in the international economy.

Table 17.3 Relative percentage allocation of IDB grant expenditure by various types, 1992–93 to 1994–95

	1992–93	1993–94	1994–95
Capital grants	74.0	73.5	75.3
Employment grants	14.6	13.8	10.7
Interest grants	2.0	1.3	0.1
Other revenue grants	–	2.4	7.6
Buying time grants	1.3	0.4	1.0
Marketing development grants	2.8	3.7	3.2
Grants to agencies and research bodies	3.3	2.0	1.2
Other grants	2.0	2.9	0.9
Total	100.0	100.0	100.0

Source: IDB annual reports (1994, p.69, 1995a, p.71).

the findings presented here are less than fully conclusive, though still probably indicative of a general trend in economic development policy.

Table 17.4 IDB offers of Selective Financial Assistance to established industry and inward investment companies and total investment costs, 1989–90 to 1994–95 (current prices)

	Number of offer		SFA offered (£m)		SFA as % of total investment		Average size of offer (£'000s)	
	Estab	Both	Estab	Both	Estab	Both	Estab	Both
1992–93	59	69	44	95	25.1	27.6	751	1377
1993–94	64	77	63	127	25.9	25.2	984	1649
1994–95	66	76	84	102	26.0	26.0	1030	1342

Source: IDB end of year statements, various issues.

Note 1. These figures refer to IDB offers of SFA to both established industry and inward investment.

Local Enterprise Development Unit

The Local Enterprise Development Unit (LEDU) implements government policy in relation to the promotion of enterprise and the development of small firms (generally defined as those with not more that 50 employees) in Northern Ireland, including new start-ups (DED 1992). For LEDU, the theoretical change in policy introduced in 1990 reflected a shift in focus away from capital grants and towards factors which influenced the competitiveness of firms such as marketing, quality and design. As with the IDB, the extent to which the shift in LEDU's approach to its task of supporting small firms has actually occurred since 1992–93 can be indicated by changes in the allocation of expenditure between different activities and the degree of selectivity in industrial aid over the period.

ALLOCATION OF EXPENDITURE
Progress towards improved competitiveness should be reflected in an increase of firms able to grow their market share profitably without subsidy (LEDU 1991), and be denoted by a decrease in relative LEDU expenditure on grants over the period 1992–95. However, Table 17.5 shows that the relative

expenditure on grants remains very high and represented 74 per cent of total expenditure in 1994–95.

As with the IDB, a shift in emphasis away from capital grants and towards other grants to induce competitiveness, such as marketing, would also be expected according to the recent policy shift. Table 17.6 shows that relative grant expenditure on capital grants remained high over the period (24 per cent in 1994–95) and such evidence would appear to be at odds with the intentions of the new strategy. However, LEDU has been reasonably successful in shifting grant expenditure towards modern competitiveness-oriented areas such as equity, management development, marketing, development and quality. In fact, relative grant expenditure increased in these areas over the period from just over 18 per cent to 27.2 per cent.

Table 17.5 Percentage share in expenditure by LEDU on various categories, 1992–93 to 1994–95 (current prices, £'000)[1]

	1992–93	1993–94	1994–95
Grants	25,781	24,016	24,849
	77.7%	75.0%	74.0%
Loans	–	130	345
		0.4%	1.0%
Investment in enterprises	426	820	1070
	1.3%	2.6%	3.1%
Administration	6956	7035	7373
	21.0%	22.0%	21.9%
Total	33,163	32,001	33,637
	100%	100%	100%

Source: LEDU annual reports (1994, p.46, 1995a, p.27).

Note 1. Includes expenditure on specific job creation initiatives.

SELECTIVITY

A decrease in financial support to business would be expected in line with the new strategy as more companies become profitable without subsidy. Table 17.7 shows LEDU's financial commitments to new offers of assistance and the number of offers issued direct to businesses. The number of offers has actually increased over the period, although the total amount of grants

Table 17.6 Relative percentage allocation of LEDU grant expenditure by various types, 1992–93 to 1994–95

	1992–93	1993–94	1994–95
Capital grants	27.7	24.5	23.7
Employment grants	9.7	11.4	12.8
Interest relief	5.9	4.7	4.4
Rent relief	0.9	1.1	0.9
Working capital	0.1	0.9	0.1
Self start	9.6	9.4	8.3
Loans	0.2	0.8	0.9
Equity	3.0	1.7	3.5
Management development	4.2	8.1	6.9
Marketing	6.5	9.9	11.3
Devlopment	3.7	3.8	4.1
Quality	0.7	1.5	1.4
Others	27.8	21.8	21.2
Total	100.0	100.0	100.0

Source: LEDU annual reports (1994, p.46, 1995a, p.27)

Table 17.7 LEDU new offers of support, 1992–93 to 1994–95 (current prices)

	Number of offers	Grants offered (£m)	Average size of offer (£'000s)
1992–93	2500	27.0	10.8
1993–94	2847	28.7	10.7
1994–95	2979	25.5	8.6

Source: LEDU annual reports (1993, p.10; 1994, p.10; 1995a, p.16)

offered and the average size of these offers decreased, which is what would have been expected.

In summary, LEDU has had some success in implementing the DED's competitiveness policy, although there needs to be greater evidence of a less interventionist policy. However, it worth noting that a recent study (NIERC 1996a) found that LEDU's performance over the period 1989–94 was favourable in terms of competitiveness measures. It was estimated that turnover increased by 40 per cent in real terms, external sales (sales outside Northern Ireland) increased by 63 per cent and export sales (sales outside the UK) doubled. However, no information on profitability is maintained. Moreover, such results should be interpreted with caution as they reflect only 10 per cent of all companies assisted by LEDU over the period 1989 to 1994.

Policy monitoring

Proper monitoring and evaluation procedures are important to ensure the effectiveness (i.e. that objectives are met) and the efficiency (i.e. lowest possible inputs to outputs) of competitiveness policy. However, the Department's five year review of policy, *Growing Competitively* (DED 1995), and the agencies corporate plans, were weak in a number of regards. In particular, there was no critical evaluation of the available instruments for the delivery of policy, inappropriate reliance on inadequate evidence on productivity, and proposals for an inadequate range of monitoring indicators.

First, the Department's review avoided one of the most critical questions: the effectiveness of the instruments of economic assistance provided by the agencies. This obscured one of the most important features that might have been in the review. Moreover, neither the IDB nor LEDU offer evaluative comments on the scale, range and effectiveness of the instruments at their disposal. Second, the ex-post evidence quoted on competitiveness relied on a NIERC study which argued that competitiveness had improved due to lower manufacturing unit labour costs and higher manufacturing productivity on average in Northern Ireland than in the rest of the UK. Such a conclusion might be valid but there also needs to be additional performance measurements to reflect a comprehensive review of competitiveness.

Third, the DED and its agencies have developed an insufficient range of *ex-ante* targets of competitiveness covering their planning periods. Table 17.8 outlines the performance targets of the DED and the agencies over their corporate planning periods 1995–98 in the context of the framework for competitiveness outlined in Table 17.1. The relative appropriateness of the different indicators for each of the agencies varies in relation to their respective remits. The table indicates that a number of relevant indicators of competitive performance have been developed by the DED and the agencies indicating the different definitions and understanding of competitiveness that have been used.

Following O'Donnell (1992), these measures can be divided into three categories of competitiveness: performance, potential and process. Competitive performance indicators include targets such as export sales,

Table 17.8 Performance indicators of competitiveness employed by DED, IDB, LEDU, T&EA, and IRTU

	DED 1995– 2001	IDB 1995–98	LEDU 1995–98	T&EA 1995–98	IRTU 1995–98
Competitive performance					
Employment trends (increase)	7950 manu. 12,000 services	7060 client co. [1] 12,000 inward investment	7000 client co.	Place 114,000 people into jobs	–
Market share	–	–	–	–	–
Trade & market development (growth pa)	7% exports [3]	16% external sales client co. [1] [4] 7% value of external sales	3.3% external sales	–	–
Output growth (growth pa)	6% manu. output	15% turnover client co. [1]	–	–	–
Competitive potential					
Labour costs	Wages per employee Unit labour costs	–	–	–	–
Productivity (growth pa)	4% manu. costs	–	–	–	–
Input service costs	–	–	–	–	Annual efficiency savings of 2.5%
Competitive process					
Skill levels	Value added per employee	Value added per employee		75% of co.s using NVQ within CDP 45% of Jobskill leavers with NVQs 25 Investor in People recognitions 80% satisfaction rating with MDPs	
Investment levels	–	–	–	–	Private sector R&D as % of GDP

Source: DED (1995, pp.47–53); IDB (1995b, p.15, p.20); LEDU (1995b, p.10); T&EA (1995, pp.42–43); IRTU (1995, pp.4–5).

Notes: 1. The IDB only collects measures of performance from home industry companies with accept SFA offers of assistance.

2. Due to the reclassification of inward investment in 1995, this figure has now been revised
   upwards to 18,000.
3. DED defines exports as sales outside Northern Ireland.
4. IDB defines external sales as sales outside Northern Ireland.
5. LEDU defines external sales as sales outside Northern Ireland.

turnover and output growth; competitive potential indicators refer to orthodox measures such as productivity and unit labour costs; and competitive process measures include indicators such as skill levels and value added per employee. Overall, however, such policy assessment is inadequate in a number of respects. In particular, there is an inadequate measurement of competitiveness and an absence of performance benchmarking.

First, a number of additional indicators could be developed which would be closer to measuring effective competitiveness. In particular, none of the agencies attempts to measure the export market share of their client companies. Such a competitive performance measurement may be defined as the ability of a firm to increase its market share in a given market. The advantages of such a results-based measurement are that it is widely accepted, it is easily understood, it is quantifiable and it would reflect improvements in competitiveness over time.

Second, the development of performance benchmarks is a useful way in which to convert the strategy of encouraging competitiveness into a practical method of measuring achievements at the level of the firm. Following Best (1995), the purpose of benchmarking is to ground a needs assessment in a strategic analysis. The performance indicators of target companies are contrasted with world class companies and the resulting gaps are used as targets for developing action plans. A recent report entitled *Performance Benchmarks for Developing Firms* (NIERC 1996b), which is the first report connected to NIERC's Competitive Analysis Model (CAM) project, is a constructive effort towards this end. In developing the CAM, NIERC has followed the concept of strategic bench marking as defined and practised by PIMS (Profit Impact of Market Strategy). PIMS define bench marking as 'learning from appropriate comparisons' and adopt a hierarchy of it starting at the level of the firm with strategic benchmarking. Within strategic benchmarking the major issues are productivity, profit potential and growth potential. The aim of CAM is to develop the means, determine the extent of the latent profit potential and identify the impact upon profit of those factors responsible for under performance. The publication of performance benchmarks allows firms to compare their performance and functional abilities against structurally similar firms in Northern Ireland and the Republic of Ireland. Such a development is to be welcomed, although the reference point for comparative companies could be expanded to include similar world-class companies to make the benchmarks more challenging.

Conclusions

This chapter has attempted to examine the extent to which the national policy shift towards increased competitiveness envisioned by central Government has been implemented by the regional development agencies in Northern Ireland in the first half of the 1990s. The evidence suggests that there have been deviations between theory and practice across the family of agencies and this dichotomy has been most evident in the IDB.

However, this dichotomy mirrors a much deeper division between rhetoric and reality that underpins the entire economic development strategy for Northern Ireland. The Department places primary responsibility for improving competitiveness with the private sector and limits its role to intervention only in the case of 'market failure'. This policy is informed by broader policy developments in the UK, such as the three White Papers on competitiveness (DTI 1994, 1995, 1996), and is based on a theoretical model of the economy that is neo-classical in essence. This model assumes that the market mechanism is the relatively superior way in which to allocate resources and is based on the assumption of perfectly functioning markets. However, in reality, the economy in Northern Ireland is not characterised by perfectly functioning markets but markets that are highly distorted. This is due to an interplay of complex factors such as, *inter alia*, the unstable political situation, the high and continuing levels of subvention, the peripheral nature of the economy, and embedded structural problems such as long-term unemployment.

The consequence of this deep-rooted duality between theory and reality manifests itself on a number of levels. First, the Department adopts the concept of competitiveness as the central strand of its policy, commits its constituent agencies to implement the policy, but fails to make the concept relevant to Northern Ireland generally or the work of the agencies specifically. In addition, the Department was not sufficiently committed to publishing the evidence of its competitiveness policy to date. Moreover, the Department adopts the term 'market failure', identifies it as a criteria for intervention by the agencies, but fails to define what the term means or even illustrate relevant examples of its application. Second, it has been shown that the agencies continue to operate a highly interventionist approach with high levels of subsidisation to industry despite their supposed commitment to free market principles. Third, the business community is receiving mixed policy signals as they are simultaneously exposed to and cushioned from the forces of market discipline (via the continuing receipt of generous grants). Such a contradiction between advocated and actual policy is neither conducive to optimal performance in the business community nor the subsequent effectiveness of the agencies in meeting their economic development objectives.

In conclusion, the competitiveness strategy in Northern Ireland needs to be based upon a realistic view of how the economy actually functions. Placing the prime responsibility for improving competitiveness on the private sector and on market forces while limiting the role of the government, not only denies the actual but also the possible potential role of the large public sector in Northern Ireland, in implementing the competitiveness policy. For example, the government could usefully foster the development of clusters of competitive industrial activities that draw on regional advantages (Porter 1990; Best 1995; EC 1993; Culliton 1992). A possible way forward is a systematic, coherent and integrated approach between the public sector and the private sectors that has characterised many successful regions in Europe (Dunford and Hudson 1996). This requires explicit policy choices for Northern Ireland, such as the respective roles to be given to market forces and non-market forces and the balance to be achieved between the public and private sectors. Whatever the case, policy must have its basis in a realistic and clearly communicated rationale if the benefits of regional economic development policy in Northern Ireland are to be optimised.

References

Best, M. (1995) *Competitive Dynamics and Industrial Modernisation Programmes: Lessons from Japan and America.* Report 115. Sir Annual Charles Carter Lecture. Belfast: Northern Ireland Economic Council.

Caves, R. (1980) 'Productivity differences among industries.' In R. Caves and I. Krause (eds) *Britain's Economic Performance.* Washington DC: Brookings Institution.

Corden, W. (1994) *Economic Policy, Exchange Rates and the International System.* Oxford: Oxford University Press.

Culliton, J. (1992) *Time for Change: Industrial Policy for the 1990s.* Report of the Industrial Policy Review Group. Dublin: Stationary Office.

DED (1990) *Competing in the 1990s – The Key to Growth.* Belfast: Department of Economic Development.

DED (1992) *Local Enterprise Development Unit: Relationships Document.* Belfast: Department of Economic Development.

DED (1995) *Growing Competitively – A Review of Economic Development Policy in Northern Ireland.* Belfast: Department of Economic Development.

DTI (1994) *Competitiveness – Helping Business to Win.* London: HMSO.

DTI (1995) *Competitiveness: Forging Ahead.* London: HMSO.

DTI (1996) *Competitiveness: Creating the Enterprise Centre of Europe.* London: HMSO.

Dunford, M. and Hudson, R. (1996) *Successful European Regions: Northern Ireland Learning from Others.* Belfast: Northern Ireland Economic Council.

EC (1993) *White Paper on Growth, Competitiveness and Employment: The Challenges and Way Forward into the 21st Century.* Luxembourg: Official Publications of the European Communities.

Eltis, W. and Higham, D. (1995) 'Closing the UK competitiveness gap.' *National Institute Economic Review 154,* 71–84.

Forfas (1996) *Shaping Our Future: A Strategy for Enterprise in Ireland in the 21st Century.* Dublin: Forfas.

Fukuyama, F. (1995) *Trust: The Social Virtues and the Creation of Prosperity.* London: Hamish Hamilton.

Hutton, W. (1995) *The State We're In.* London: Jonathan Cape.

IDB (1991) *Forward Strategy, 1991–93.* Belfast: Industrial Development Board.

IDB (1993) *Annual Report and Accounts 1992–93.* Belfast: Industrial Development Board.

IDB (1994) *Annual Report and Accounts 1993–94.* Belfast: Industrial Development Board.

IDB (1995a) *Annual Report and Accounts 1994–95.* Belfast: Industrial Development Board.

IDB (1995b) *Developing Greater Competitiveness, Industrial Development Strategy, 1995–98.* Belfast: Industrial Development Board.

IRTU (1995) *Corporate Plan, 1995–98.* Belfast: Industrial Research and Technology Unit.

Krugman, P. (1994) 'Competitiveness: a dangerous obsession.' *Foreign Affairs 73,* 2, 28–44.

Krugman, P. (1996) *Pop Internationalism.* Cambridge Mass: MIT Press.

LEDU (1991) *Forward Thinking, 1989–94.* Belfast: Local Economic Development Unit.

LEDU (1993) *Annual Report 1992–93.* Belfast: Local Economic Development Unit.

LEDU (1994) *Annual Report 1993–94.* Belfast: Local Economic Development Unit.

LEDU (1995a) *Annual Report 1994–95.* Belfast: Local Economic Development Unit.

LEDU (1995b) *LEDU Corporate Plan, 1995–98.* Belfast: Local Economic and Development Unit.

NEDO (1983) *Standards, Quality and Competitiveness.* London: National Economic Development Council.

NIEC (1994) *Autumn Economic Review.* Report 113. Belfast: Northern Ireland Economic Council.

NIERC (1996a) *Measuring The Difference, 1989–94 LEDU Performance and Impact Study.* Belfast: Northern Ireland Economic Research Centre.

NIERC (1996b) *Performance Benchmarks for Developing Firms.* Belfast: Northern Ireland Economic Research Centre.

O'Donnell, R. (1992) 'Ireland's Competitive Advantage: Conceptual, Definitional and Theoretical Issues'. Seminar Paper. Dublin: Economic and Social Research Institute.

Porter, M. (1990) *The Competitive Advantage of Nations*. London: The MacMillan Press.

Reich, R. (1991) *The Work of Nations*. New York: Vintage Books.

Romer, P. (1994) 'The origins of endogenous growth.' *Journal of Economic Perspectives 8*, 1, 3–22.

T&EA (1995) *Corporate Plan 1995–98*. Belfast: Training and Employment Agency.

CHAPTER 18

Value for Money?

The Effectiveness of Regionally Based Small Firm Development Agencies

Mark Hart, Ronnie Scott, Graham Gudgin & Eric Hanvey

Introduction

As a consequence of the increasing importance of the notion of a 'Europe of the regions' and the underpinning concept of regionalism there has been a resurgence of interest in regional development agencies. However, too often the justification for specific regional institutional structures, such as RDAs, is presented solely in terms of the need for greater regional autonomy and democracy in the economic development process. Whilst these political considerations are essential it is also important to have some idea of the effectiveness of RDAs. What do they actually achieve in terms of economic and social benefits as a result of the resources committed to them? Do they represent good value for money?

The aim of this chapter is to address this issue by presenting an evaluation of the activities of the Local Enterprise Development Unit (LEDU), the public sector-funded small business agency for Northern Ireland. The reasons for this are twofold. First, Northern Ireland has had a long history of regionally specific business development agencies and it is therefore appropriate to assess what lessons arise with respect to the broader question of the effectiveness of regional development agencies. Second, the evaluation of LEDU utilises a methodology to arrive at the net additional effects of government assistance which will be of value to other researchers engaged in assessing the contributions of RDAs.

At the outset it is important to state that LEDU is one of a number of industrial development agencies under the umbrella of the Department of Economic Development (DED) for Northern Ireland which is responsible for economic development policy in the region and establishes the policy framework within which the industrial development agencies operate.

The DED has five main agencies or businesses responsible for delivering industrial and labour market programmes in Northern Ireland: the Industrial Development Board (IDB), the Local Enterprise Development Unit (LEDU), the Industrial Research and Technology Unit (IRTU), the Training & Employment Agency (T&EA), and the Northern Ireland Tourist Board (NITB). LEDU's cumulative budget for the five-year period 1989/90 to 1993/94 was £170 million and accounted for 6.6 per cent of total expenditure on the Industry, Trade and Employment programmes in Northern Ireland (£2570 million).

LEDU's remit includes firms with less than 50 employees in the manufacturing sector and those service sectors with activities potentially tradable beyond Northern Ireland. LEDU is also responsible for the promotion of enterprise in Northern Ireland, including the encouragement and fostering of self-employment and micro-businesses. LEDU's activities in this area include the establishment of a regional network of local enterprise agencies, which largely provide workspace and services to small firms in their locality, and the provision of training, financial assistance and advice to individuals considering entering self-employment.

The policy context

The 1984 review of industrial policy in the United Kingdom and mounting research evidence that traditional approaches to industrial development in Northern Ireland were less effective and efficient than previously believed resulted in a number of policy initiatives in the late 1980s.

In 1990 the emphasis of industrial development policy in Northern Ireland was radically changed. The DED (1990) document *The Key to Growth* laid out a new strategic framework for industrial policy to be adopted by its various agencies including LEDU. The essential components of the government's new approach were stated as:

- ensuring that government assistance, while not displacing private sector finance, is focused on the obstacles to growth and will help improve the competitiveness of Northern Ireland industry
- intensifying the drive for inward investment
- building up management and workforce skills

- stimulating the development of entrepreneurs and the growth of an enterprise culture
- targeting growth areas through detailed sectoral studies.

The main implication for the industrial development agencies was the requirement to ensure that all potential sources of private finance had been adequately explored before any offer of financial assistance was made. Moreover, any assistance should be focused on improving the competitiveness of industry rather than just maintaining or creating employment. While the overall long-term aim was to create employment and reduce unemployment, the strategy emphasised that this should be achieved through a strengthening of the economy rather than subsidising inefficiencies. As a result the focus on assistance was expected to move away from capital and employment grants and towards schemes which would address perceived weaknesses in areas such as marketing, research and development, and management and workforce skills. As part of its aims the DED also gave a commitment to 'ensure...targeting of programmes where necessary on areas of social and economic deprivation and on the needs of the long term unemployed' (DED 1990, p.35).

LEDU strategy 1989 to 1994

In their strategy for 1989 to 1994, *The Single Market and Beyond* LEDU's principal aim was stated as 'to maximise enduring employment for Northern Ireland by continuing to stimulate directly and indirectly all stages of the formation, survival and growth of enterprise'. LEDU planned to set targets in terms of productivity, profitability, liquidity, the number of exporters and export sales growth. To achieve these targets LEDU was to promote the growth of existing businesses by encouraging competitiveness and supporting export development and achieve a substantial increase in new starts and in enterprise growth.

The change in emphasis in the DED strategy in 1990 required LEDU to rethink their strategy and in 1991 it issued *Forward Thinking* (LEDU 1991), a revised strategy for the 1989 to 1994 period. LEDU adopted a new mission statement 'to strengthen the Northern Ireland economy by encouraging enterprise and stimulating improvements in the competitiveness of new and existing businesses with defined markets'.

The principal aim which derived from the mission statement was 'to increase the number, turnover, profitability and hence employment potential of competitive small businesses in Northern Ireland'. Promoting jobs was no longer the primary aim. The focus of the new strategy was to strengthen the

Northern Ireland economy in anticipation that additional enduring employment would result.

To achieve these new aims and objectives LEDU radically changed the approach to assisting small firms. The new approach involved two main changes. First, LEDU segmented client companies into 'Growth' firms and 'Established' firms. Growth firms were identified on an analysis of a firm's strengths and weaknesses using a Business Analysis Model (BAM) developed by the agency. Growth firms were identified as those having the potential to double turnover over a three- or four-year period. Assistance to these firms was to be focused on overcoming any barriers to growth they faced. The remainder of LEDU's existing clients were classified as established clients and assistance to them would be geared to raising their ambitions and competence for growth in the future.

Second, the form of selective financial assistance offered to most firms changed. Capital and employment grants were only to be offered in exceptional circumstances. New investments were largely to be supported through loans, equity and interest relief grants. 'Softer' forms of assistance such as grants for strategic planning, marketing, research and development, quality certification and management salary grants were the preferred forms of support since they were in most cases geared to identified constraints on growth within the firm.

The broad aim of this chapter is to assess the effectiveness of LEDU's impact on small firm performance in Northern Ireland over the 1989–94 period. The results presented in the paper are based on a more detailed analysis and evaluation of LEDU's activities undertaken by a research team at the Northern Ireland Economic Research Centre (NIERC). The major focus is on the additional employment generated by LEDU's activities and some assessment of overall cost effectiveness. Other aspects of the evaluation which consider the impact of LEDU in terms of the growth of sales and exports among assisted firms can be found in the full NIERC report (NIERC 1996).

The structure of the chapter is as follows. First, a brief discussion of some methodological issues is undertaken. The following section then analyses the comparative employment performance of LEDU firms compared with the control groups and provides estimates of the degree of deadweight associated with LEDU assistance. The next section provides estimates of the net additional employment effect of LEDU assistance, and the final section examines the extent and nature of financial assistance offered and paid to LEDU firms over the period and assesses the value for money of LEDU assistance. The chapter concludes with a discussion of some of the policy issues arising from the analysis.

Methodology

The methodology adopted by the research team at NIERC is similar to that used in previous evaluations of the activities of LEDU and, therefore, will not be presented in detail here (see Hart *et al.* 1993; Hart and Scott 1994). Selective financial assistance is the major category of assistance dispersed by LEDU. Due to the delay between offers of assistance and firms undertaking the agreed activities receiving grants the analysis investigates job creation and sales/export growth among firms which received an offer of selective financial assistance between 1988 and 1993. This is consistent with the previous NIERC study for the 1984–89 period (Hart *et al.* 1993).

For those firms and individuals assisted under the enterprise programme to start up in business the lag between offer and payment is less marked. For the most part grant is paid out in the twelve months following the offer of assistance. In these cases it seems more reasonable to assume that the relevant cohort is those which received an offer in the 1989–94 period.

Because of the change in LEDU strategy in the middle of the study period the results reported here cannot be interpreted as an evaluation of the current strategy. The current LEDU strategy only began to be reflected in letters of offer in 1992 and the study period which ends in 1994 is too short to allow for impacts to emerge. Nevertheless, since the general direction of policy began to change, in terms of a greater focus on competitiveness and export-led growth in 1989, some indication of the effectiveness of the change in policy may be discerned.

An important question in any evaluation of the effectiveness of industrial development assistance is what would have happened in the absence of assistance. This is usually referred to as the base or counterfactual case. To produce an assessment of the base case involves considering the concepts of deadweight and displacement.

In the absence of assistance all or part of the employment created by LEDU client firms might have occurred anyway. For example, some firms may have started up or expanded in the absence of LEDU assistance, although they may have done so at a later date or on a smaller scale. The extent to which firms in receipt of assistance would have gone ahead anyway is called 'deadweight'. Deadweight is difficult to measure since there is no exact way of estimating what would have happened if assistance had not been made available.

The approach adopted here is to use control groups in an attempt to measure what might have happened in the absence of assistance. The three control groups used are:

1. non-LEDU assisted small firms in Northern Ireland

2. small firms in Leicestershire

3. small firms in the Republic of Ireland.

There is the possibility that assistance given to one firm may displace output and employment in other Northern Ireland firms. An assessment of 'displacement' therefore involves estimating the extent to which assisted firms displace the sales of other firms. The assessment of displacement in this study involves an investigation of the market orientation of LEDU-assisted firms and the degree of direct market competition with other Northern Ireland firms.

Estimates of 'additional employment' created by LEDU are therefore generated by firstly estimating what employment would have been in assisted firms in the absence of assistance. The difference is the employment created among assisted firms after allowing for deadweight. The level of displacement of employment on other Northern Ireland firms is then subtracted to give an estimate of the additional employment generated by LEDU assistance.

Employment performance 1989 to 1994

Components of employment change

Over the evaluation period 1989 to 1994, full-time employment among LEDU client firms increased by 10,264 or 54 per cent (Table 18.1). By comparison, employment in the Northern Ireland economy as a whole increased by 2.6 per cent. LEDU clients in the manufacturing sector were responsible for just under half of the net increase in employment with the remainder concentrated in private service activities. LEDU manufacturing employment increased by 33 per cent at a time when total manufacturing employment fell by 5 per cent. Employment among LEDU service sector clients more than doubled compared to a 14 per cent growth for the sector as a whole.

There are, of course, two obvious caveats that need to be made with respect to the performance of LEDU clients. First, most firms with growth potential can be assumed to apply for LEDU assistance and as a result some of the subsequent assisted growth might have occurred in the absence of assistance. Second, and perhaps more important, the selection of companies with growth potential is a key aspect of LEDU's strategy. Therefore, using the difference in growth between assisted and non-assisted as an estimate of the impact of LEDU assistance is likely to exaggerate the true impact of that assistance. The difficulty cannot be completely overcome, but it is addressed in the analysis reported below by comparing non-assisted companies in Northern Ireland with those in other areas. For example, if non-assisted firms in Northern Ireland perform similarly to those elsewhere we may reasonably presume that the Northern Ireland non-assisted firms provide an indication of what could be expected in the absence of assistance. This approach is far from foolproof since general economic conditions can vary between areas. Particular interest thus rests on the comparison with Leicestershire since small firms in this area are normally subject to most of the same national macroeconomic influences as those in Northern Ireland.[1]

Between 1989 and 1994 employment created in surviving LEDU assisted firms was sufficient to outweigh employment lost through closures significantly. However, employment created among new firms starting up between 1989 and 1994 was the major source of employment gains.

Of the 2164 LEDU-assisted firms in existence in 1989, 543 companies had closed by 1994, with the loss of 2475 jobs. However, the 1621 surviving firms expanded generating an additional 3679 jobs by 1994. Hence, the net increase in employment in firms which were in existence at the start of the period was 1204 jobs. The number of jobs lost in closures (including the self-employed) was 13 per cent of the total employment in 1989 within companies or individuals assisted during the period. Employment growth among assisted firms which survived throughout the period was 22.4 per cent. The resulting net employment change for existing assisted companies (i.e. net of closures).

Just under 4500 new firms started up with LEDU assistance between 1989 and 1994. The vast majority of these were one or two person businesses assisted through the Enterprise Grant Scheme (EG) or Business Start Programme (BSP). However, a significant minority of new businesses were assisted through the Home Start and Export Start schemes which were designed for larger start-ups and those new firms which demonstrated the potential to enter export markets quickly. Three years after start-up, 72.5 per cent of new firms created with selective financial assistance (now the Home Start and Export Start schemes) were still trading while 68 per cent of new firms started up with assistance under the enterprise programme (EG and BSP) were still in existence. All of this difference is accounted for in the first year and the difference is surprisingly low given the contrasting nature of the two groups of businesses. By comparison, academic studies in the UK suggest that 64 per cent of all new firms and around half of Enterprise Allowance scheme start-ups will survive the first three years (Storey 1994).

---

1   In our previous evaluation covering the period 1986–90 the growth of non-assisted small firms in Northern Ireland was similar to that of small firms in Leicestershire. This provided some confidence that non-assisted small firms in Northern Ireland do indeed provide a meaningful control group with which to compare assisted firms.

Of the 9060 jobs in surviving new firms in 1994, 3525 were in firms set up with LEDU Selective Financial Assistance (SFA) and 5535 in Enterprise Programme start-ups. However, 3261 (or 55 per cent) of the latter were in the services sector and the majority would not be eligible for further assistance due to the high levels of displacement.

Table 18.1 Employment change among LEDU assisted clients, 1989–94

Industrial sector	Manuf. sector		Service sector		All assisted	
	Firms	Emp.	Firms	Emp.	Firms	Emp.
Firms in existence in 1989	1426	14,236	738	4674	2164	18,910
minus closures	(365)	(1916)	(187)	(559)	(543)	(2475)
plus job growth in survivors	1070	2627	551	1052	1621	3679
plus new openings	1346	3941	2326	5119	3672	9060
equals firms in existence in 1994	3477	18,888	2877	10,286	5293	29174
Net change	990	4652	2139	5612	3129	10,264

Source: NIERC LEDU client database.

Comparative employment change 1989–93

As stated above an important part of our approach to the evaluation of LEDU's impact on job creation involves the comparison of the performance of firms assisted by LEDU with a series of control groups. These control groups include both non-assisted small firms within Northern Ireland and all small firms in two areas outside Northern Ireland: Leicestershire and the Republic of Ireland. The use of these two areas as external comparisons continues a sequence of evaluations undertaken at NIERC covering periods back as far as 1973 which is close to the inception of LEDU in 1971. In each case the control group includes the entire population of small firms and no sampling is involved.[2] The data is drawn from databanks developed or held at NIERC. Since the availability for external control groups is restricted to

2   The size of each of the control groups was as follows (see Table 18.2): Northern Ireland: 2324 small firms; Leicestershire: 4564 small firms; Republic of Ireland: 6658 small firms. The size and sectoral distributions of these control groups were broadly similar to the LEDU-assisted firms.

manufacturing industry, this comparative evaluation excludes service sector companies assisted by LEDU. Furthermore, the period for comparison is restricted to the four years between 1989 and 1993 due to the absence of 1994 data for two of the control groups. A detailed discussion of the characteristics and economic trends found within each of the external comparator areas can be found in NIERC (1996).

The method of comparison using control groups has two aims. The first is to put the performance of LEDU-assisted companies into context. We wish to know how well small firms in Northern Ireland are performing relative to those in other areas, and in particular, how those companies assisted by LEDU fare in these comparisons. Second, the comparisons are used in the measurement of 'deadweight loss'. In this case we wish to know the extent to which the favourable performance of firms assisted by LEDU is due to the assistance itself and would not have occurred in the absence of assistance.

Employment growth in small indigenous firms

Employment growth in small indigenous firms is defined in the following way:

> Change in the number of jobs in locally owned firms which were in operation at the start of the period

> **plus**

> Jobs at the end of the period in all new locally owned firms started during the period.

Under this definition, jobs lost in closures are subtracted from the total. Also, firms which grow in excess of 50 employees during the period are still included within the definition of small firms. Such growing firms can be new companies formed during the period, as long as their initial employment was below 50.

Employment changes between 1989 and 1993 are shown in Table 18.2 for companies assisted by LEDU and for their direct comparator groups. LEDU-assisted companies are those receiving letters of offer between 1988 and 1992 inclusive. Growth is measured over the slightly later period of 1989–93 to allow a time-lag in which financial and other assistance begins to be taken up.

Companies assisted by LEDU increased their employment by 29 per cent during the four years. This was a remarkable rate of expansion over a period which included a major UK recession. Moreover, it was a much more favourable rate of expansion than that of non-assisted manufacturing companies in Northern Ireland. These barely raised their employment at all.

Table 18.2 also identifies an intermediate set of companies. These are firms which received letters of offers of LEDU assistance prior to 1988. Some of these companies may have continued to draw down assistance after 1988. These firms increased their employment by 6 per cent between 1989 and 1993.

Since most firms in Leicestershire received little or no government assistance, they can be directly compared with non-assisted companies in Northern Ireland. Between 1989 and 1993 employment in small indigenous companies in Leicestershire contracted by 6.3 per cent (Table 18.2). Non-assisted firms in Northern Ireland had a more favourable growth record at 0.5 per cent. The 6.8 percentage point gap between these groups of non-assisted companies is a measure of the impact of the different macro-economic conditions in the two areas. Firms in Leicestershire were more affected by the recession in both consumer and industrial demand in

Table 18.2 Employment change in small indigenous firms in Northern Ireland, 1989–93

	No. of firms	Employ. in 1989	Change 1989–1993	Percentage
Northern Ireland				
Currently-assisted LEDU[1]	(1371)	12,399	+3632	29.3
Previous-assisted LEDU[2]	(436)	3925	+238	6.1
Non-assisted small firms in NI	(2324)	15,987	+74	0.5
NI all small indigenous	(4094)	29,841	+3713	12.4
Republic of Ireland				
Assisted indigenous SMEs	(2094)	19,326	+6102	31.6
Non-assisted indig. SMEs	(4564)	35,566	-3699	-10.4
Leicestershire[3]				
All small indigenous firms	(4564)	30,671	-1944	-6.3

Sources: NIERC and IDA industrial databases.

Notes: 1. Firms assisted between 1988 and 1992 inclusive.
  2. Previously assisted firms still in operation in 1989.
  3. There is a likelihood of under-counting of the number of very small new businesses formed in Leicestershire. Our estimate is that employment in small indigenous firms in Leicestershire in 1993 should be 1,000 greater than shown in these tables. This adjustment would reduce the decline for Leicestershire in the table above from -6.3% to -3.1%.

southern England. In Northern Ireland, where the recession was the mildest anywhere in the UK, local demand was more buoyant.

The gap in employment growth between LEDU-assisted firms and those in Leicestershire was a huge 35 percentage points. Our conclusion is that some 7 percentage points of this difference was due to the more favourable economic environment in Northern Ireland. Most of the difference (28 percentage points) is, therefore, likely to have been due to the direct effects of LEDU assistance. However, for the two reasons noted above one must exercise caution in accepting this difference as the 'LEDU effect'.

The second external comparison is with the Republic of Ireland. In the Republic, employment growth in small indigenous firms was 4.4 per cent. This level of growth was intermediate between Leicestershire and Northern Ireland. As in Northern Ireland, there was a large contrast in growth between assisted and non-assisted firms. Assisted firms in this case are those which were actively assisted during the 1989–93 period. The growth of the assisted group of companies in the Republic was similar to that of LEDU-assisted companies in Northern Ireland. Non-assisted firms in the Republic, however, fared worse than non-assisted firms in either Northern Ireland or Leicestershire. Since local macro-economic conditions were more favourable than in either Northern Ireland or Leicestershire, this suggests the possibility of a lack of competitiveness or enterprise among these firms. As in Northern Ireland, however, there may be a degree of self-selection. Those companies with growth potential may also have been those which applied for assistance.

The rapid 29 per cent expansion of LEDU-assisted companies generated 3632 extra jobs over the four-year period. Table 18.3 shows the different

Table 18.3 Employment change 1989–93 in LEDU assisted firms

	No. of firms	1989	1993	Change	Percentage
Employment in survivors	(931)	11,848	14,221	2373	20.0
Jobs lost in closures	(59)	551	–	-551	–
Firms open in 1989	(990)	12,399	14,221	+1822	14.7
New firms	(381)	–	1810	+1810	–
Total	(1371)	12,399	16,031	3632	29.3

Sources: IDA industrial databases.

routes by which this was achieved. A total of 1371 companies were assisted during the period, i.e. they received letters of offer between 1988 and 1992. Of these, close to three-quarters (990 firms) were in operation at the start of the 1989–93 period. The remainder (381 firms) were new firms which started up during the period.

Of the 990 companies already established in 1989, 59 companies (6 per cent) had closed by 1993, an aggregate loss of 551 jobs. The 931 surviving firms, however, expanded by 20 per cent, generating an additional 2373 jobs by 1993. These were further augmented by 1810 jobs in new assisted companies (Table 18.3). Hence, most additional jobs were generated by the expansion of firms which survived throughout the period. For a more detailed discussion of the mode of employment change in LEDU-assisted clients the reader is referred to the full evaluation report (NIERC 1996).

The additional employment created by LEDU

Summary: 1989–93

LEDU-assisted companies expanded rapidly between 1989 and 1993 despite the relatively unfavourable economic conditions. Employment in assisted firms rose from 12,399 to 16,031, an increase of 29 per cent. Non-assisted firms experienced little expansion, and hence the growth rate for assisted firms was 29 percentage points above that for non-assisted firms in Northern Ireland. It was also 35 percentage points above the growth of small indigenous firms in Leicestershire. Our conclusion is that Northern Ireland companies assisted by LEDU gained both from that assistance and from the fact that economic conditions were more favourable in Northern Ireland than Leicestershire during this period. The additional growth, however, came more predominantly from LEDU assistance than from locally favourable economic conditions. These figures give an overall deadweight estimate of 20 per cent, i.e. 7 percentage points of the 35 percentage point difference.

Net additional employment impact, 1989–94

In this section we present an overall estimate of the additional employment impact of LEDU over the full study period 1989–94. The data on comparative employment performance, which provide an estimate of 20 per cent deadweight, are now combined with an assessment of displacement to provide an estimate of net additional employment after allowing for deadweight and deducting any displacement in other Northern Ireland firms.[3]

Estimates of displacement were derived from data on sales and export growth and the location of competitors collected through the annual LEDU client survey. Putting the potential for displacement (as indicated by the proportion of any increase in turnover sold to the Northern Ireland market) together with the information on the degree to which firms selling in the local market were competing with other local firms, allows an estimate to be made of the actual level of displacement over the period.

Growth companies sold 43.6 per cent of increased turnover in the local market. However, 58.4 per cent of growth companies were competing solely or mainly with Northern Ireland competitors. This implies that around 25 per cent (i.e. 58.4 per cent of 43.6 per cent) of sales by growth companies may have displaced turnover and thus employment in other Northern Ireland firms.

For established companies the extent of potential displacement is estimated at 72.3 per cent. However, 77.7 per cent of these companies were competing solely or mainly with Northern Ireland firms. This results in an estimated level of displacement of 56 per cent (i.e. 77.7 per cent of 72.3 per cent). The weighted average estimate of displacement for all LEDU clients is 36 per cent reflecting the much higher weight for growth companies when measured in terms of sales rather than number of firms or employment. Those

Table 18.4 Components of employment change among assisted LEDU clients, 1989–1994

	Manuf.	Services	Total
Firms in existence in 1989	+711	+493	+1204
New SFA firms	+1667	+1858	+3525
New enterprise firms	+2274	+3261	+5535
All	+4652	+5612	+10,264

Source: NIERC industrial databases.

---

3   The comparative analysis provides one estimate of deadweights, but as mentioned earlier it is likely to underestimate the actual impact of LEDU assistance, and for this reason it should be seen as a lower bound to the degree of deadweight. However, it is interesting to note that the survey evidence on the level of deadweight for small manufacturing firms in Northern Ireland is only slightly higher at 25 per cent, therefore increasing the level of confidence in control groups.

LEDU clients which were assisted during the period 1989 to 1994 increased their employment by 10,264 or 54.3 per cent. The components of employment change are summarised in Table 18.4.

The results of the analysis presented in the previous section indicated that LEDU assistance (net of deadweight) led to the creation of around 3500 additional jobs in 'manufacturing' between 1989 and 1993. Employment in assisted manufacturing firms over this four-year period increased by 29 per cent. Over the longer period 1989–94 employment in existing and new manufacturing firms in receipt of selective financial assistance increased by 4652 or 32.6 per cent. Assuming the same differential survival and growth as for the shorter period this implies that LEDU assistance resulted in an additional 3722 manufacturing jobs (net of deadweight) by 1994. Displacement from other Northern Ireland firms by assisted manufacturing small firms was estimated at 33 per cent. This suggests that of the 3722 additional jobs (net of deadweight) created in manufacturing small firms around 1239 are displaced from other Northern Ireland firms. Thus, the additional net employment effect of LEDU assistance to small manufacturing firms is estimated as 2483 jobs.

No appropriate control group is available for assisted 'service' sector small firms in Northern Ireland. However, evidence on the possible degree of deadweight for this sector was obtained from specific questions on the 1995 LEDU client survey (see NIERC 1996 for fuller details). The net employment change among assisted small firms in the service sector was 5612 jobs between 1989 and 1994 (Table 18.4). There was very little change in employment among assisted firms which were open in 1989. The vast majority of employment created was in new firms (5119 jobs or 91 per cent of all jobs created).

The survey evidence suggests that the amount of pure deadweight associated with mainstream SFA to small service sector firms was 28.4 per cent.[4] This would imply that of the 2418 jobs created through SFA, 687 jobs would have been created in LEDU firms in the absence of assistance. The estimate of additional employment (net of deadweight) for this group is, therefore, 1731. Displacement among assisted service sector (growth and established) small firms is estimated at 40 per cent which means that the estimated number of jobs created (net of deadweight and displacement) among LEDU SFA-assisted service firms is 1039 jobs.

Survey evidence suggests that typical levels of deadweight for enterprise programme small firms is around 50 per cent. Furthermore, based on an

---

4 See Chapter 5 in NIERC (1996) for a full discussion of the survey evidence on deadweight.

analysis of returns to the 1994 LEDU client survey, around 78 per cent of sales from this group are to the Northern Ireland market. Of the 3261 jobs created in the assisted small firms service sector by the enterprise programme, it is estimated that 1630 represent deadweight and 1271 represent displacement. The employment impact of this group (net of deadweight and displacement) is estimated, therefore, as only 360 jobs or 11 per cent of the total jobs created.

Overall, it is estimated that LEDU assistance created an additional 3882 jobs over the 1989 to 1994 period, or 37.8 per cent of the total net employment change among assisted LEDU clients (10,264 jobs).

Cost effectiveness of LEDU assistance

For those firms which received a letter of offer between 1988 and 1993 total payments by LEDU to assisted firms totalled £85.7 million. Around three-quarters of grants (£62.9 million) went to small manufacturing firms and the remainder (£22.8 million) to small service-sector companies.

Growth clients, which accounted for 8.5 per cent of assisted firms (20 per cent excluding enterprise clients) and 35 per cent of employment (52 per cent excluding enterprise clients) at the end of the period, attracted just over half of the grants paid out. Established clients received around one-third of total LEDU assistance going directly to firms and enterprise programme clients around 13 per cent.

The average level of grant paid (against letters of offer accepted between 1988 and 1993) by 1994 ranged from just under £90,000 for Growth clients to just over £3000 for Enterprise clients. When standardised by the number of employees there was less variation between growth clients (£3876 per employee) and Established clients (£2588 per employee). However, payments to Growth clients were around twice the level of grants per employee paid to Enterprise clients (£1834 per employee).

In terms of the net gain in employment among assisted LEDU clients the cost per job created averaged £8345. This varied from £24,757 for Growth clients to £8948 for Established clients and £2181 for Enterprise clients. However, these estimates take no account of the degree of deadweight and displacement associated with the different client groups.

In the previous section it was estimated that net additional employment creation among assisted LEDU clients was around 3882 jobs at 1994. The implied cost per additional job created by LEDU assistance, among firms assisted during the period, is therefore £22,260. This compares with our previous estimate for the 1984/5 to 1988/89 cohort of assisted firms of up to £20,800 per job, at 1991 prices (Hart et al. 1993).

The estimates of cost per job are in respect of jobs in existence in 1994. To estimate the cost of each job year of additional employment generated requires some judgement as to the likely life of assisted jobs. Based on projecting forward the likely attrition rate of LEDU-assisted jobs, it is estimated that around 11 job years of employment will be achieved for each job created (Hart *et al.* 1994). On this assumption the projected cost per job year is around £2500 on an annuitised basis for firms assisted in the 1989 to 1994 period. Compared with other policies designed to create employment in Northern Ireland and the UK, it would appear that LEDU assistance is a cost-efficient method of creating employment in Northern Ireland.

At this stage of the analysis it would be normal to factor in a multiplier to take account of the indirect job creation that would occur as a result of LEDU assistance to small firms. However, the Department of Finance and Personnel (DFP) in Northern Ireland, along with the Northern Ireland Audit Office (NIAO), take the view when assessing the relative effectiveness of public expenditure under the various strands of the Industrial Development Programme (IDP) in Northern Ireland that a standard regional multiplier would be applied irrespective of the particular programme. For example, if the moneys allocated to LEDU to assist SMEs policy were switched to the Industrial Development Board (IDB) to encourage inward investment or to restructure a particular firm or industrial sector, according to the DFP, there would be a multiplier effect of roughly the same magnitude. Consequently, when undertaking the calculation of net additional job creation for LEDU, the multiplier component was excluded on the grounds that it is not appropriate for comparative purposes across the Northern Ireland IDP.

Conclusion

In terms of the relative performance of the Northern Ireland small firms sector, it is possible to conclude that in general LEDU appear to have achieved remarkably good results in the first half of the 1990s. Increasingly it seems that LEDU is having an influence on the fact that the small firm sector in Northern Ireland is outperforming the small firm sector in other parts of the UK and Ireland.

Furthermore, the level of net additional employment generated by LEDU assistance (776 jobs per year) between 1989 and 1994, and during a more difficult trading environment, is only slightly lower than the 1000 jobs per year estimated for the earlier 1984 to 1989 period. The evidence from this second major evaluation of LEDU assistance once again suggests that a regime of intensive grant assistance to small firms results in higher employment growth even with relatively high levels of deadweight and displacement.

Without doubt Northern Ireland has been transformed into an economy with an above-average dependence on small firms. The benefits that this affords to the local economy are varied. A greater degree of diversification in the industrial structure, controlled by owner-managers with a commitment to the local economy offers a cushion against the impact of the closure and contraction of multinational investment. Nevertheless, the reliance upon indigenous growth strategies to regenerate local and regional lagging economies is fraught with difficulties. Four issues merit comment.

First, as clearly indicated in the employment analysis, the majority of net employment creation was by very small new firms supported under the enterprise schemes during the period. This is a characteristic of LEDU assistance in the 1990s which requires careful monitoring as these enterprises are typically the most vulnerable and are associated with high levels of displacement.

Second, can the indigenous sector in Northern Ireland, and local small firms in particular, continue to create employment at the rate they have during this period? Essentially, is this growth the result of increasing entrepreneurship and self-sustaining growth through increasing sales to export markets, or is it simply a reflection of the high levels of government expenditure, supported by the £3 billion subvention from the UK exchequer, and the public service sector income that this generates. Although it is unlikely, regardless of the outcome of the current 'peace process', that the subvention from the UK exchequer will disappear overnight, it is very possible that it will gradually wither away. If this is the case then the question is to what extent is the indigenous manufacturing sector supported or hindered by the high levels of government expenditure, and public sector employment, in the province?

Some recent evidence (Hanvey, Scott and Hart 1995) indicates that the proportion of output exported by Northern Ireland small firms, assisted by LEDU, has been growing. The impact of LEDU assistance estimated in this paper, allowing for both deadweight and displacement effects, would suggest that not all of the growth in small firm employment is based on increased domestic market demand, fuelled by government expenditure, although clearly government assistance to the small firm sector is a component of this.

Third, the quality of the jobs created in small firms may be markedly different from those created elsewhere in the economy. They may, for example, be less well paid, less stable and offer considerably less protection for basic workers' rights than larger firms. Too often the debate on the economic impact of small firms concentrates on the quantity of jobs at the expense of a consideration of the types of jobs being created. Business development agencies, such as LEDU, must be sensitive to this issue and seek to investigate the precise nature of their impact on the labour market (e.g. wage rates, skill levels, labour turnover etc.).

Fourth, it must be acknowledged that small firms are not as independent as many observers would have us believe. They operate within broader economic frameworks that involve consideration by researchers and policy makers of the roles and strategies of large firms (indigenous and foreign). An understanding of the relationships and networks that exist between large and small firms is essential in order to comment accurately on the growth potential of small firms. Therefore, in our view small firm policy is only *one*, albeit important, dimension of an overall industrial development strategy for regional economic development. Accordingly, in practical policy terms one must question the wisdom of having two separate business development agencies in Northern Ireland which are demarcated solely on the basis of firm size.

In conclusion, therefore, assessing the impact of RDAs, or business development agencies with a clear regional remit, is an essential element of any discussion of their role in regional economic development. The analysis reported in this chapter has presented one methodology for measuring their effectiveness and the results demonstrate that it is possible to provide some quantification to a sometimes highly charged political debate. However, a key factor in the evaluation process has been the cooperation of LEDU itself. Without access to the internal records of LEDU the analysis presented above would not be possible. They have recognised the value in working with an independent research team in order to provide a clear understanding of the scale and nature of the impact that their financial assistance has had on the small firm sector in Northern Ireland. However, one suspects that their motivation for doing so rests more with the pressure placed upon them by the Northern Ireland Audit Office and the Northern Ireland Select Committee at Westminster to be accountable for their budget than a genuine desire to engage in a debate on the most effective ways to assist the development of small firms in a regional economy. Nevertheless, they have taken their responsibility seriously and are not afraid to publish on an annual basis the performance record of their client firms.

References

DED (1990) *Northern Ireland – Competing in the 1990s: The Key to Growth.* Belfast: HMSO.

Hanvey, E., Scott, R. and Hart, M. (1995) *The Performance of Northern Ireland Assisted Firms.* NIERC Working Paper, Belfast: NIERC.

Hart, M., Scott, R., Gudgin, G. and Keegan, R. (1993) *Job Creation in Small Firms.* Belfast: NIERC.

Hart, M. and Scott, R. (1994) 'Measuring the effectiveness of small firm policy: some lessons from Northern Ireland.' *Regional Studies 28,* 8, 849–858.

LEDU (1991) *Forward Thinking, 1989–94.* Belfast: Local Enterprise Development Unit.

NIERC (1996) *An Evaluation of LEDU Assistance to Small Firms in Northern Ireland 1989 to 1994.* Belfast: NIERC.

Storey, D. (1994) *Understanding the Small Business Sector.* London: Routledge.

CHAPTER 19

Regional Development Agencies in the New Europe

Patterns, Issues and Prospects

Henrik Halkier, Mike Danson & Charlotte Damborg

In the introduction to this volume we stressed that diversity was one of the most salient features of the great expansion in economic development activities based at the regional level, and the preceding surveys and case studies have certainly confirmed this impression. At least on a superficial level, bottom-up policy would seem to reflect the specific circumstances of individual regions and bring something genuinely new to regional policy: instead of relying on the traditional standardised policy programmes of central government, regional policymakers should now be better equipped to promote development on the basis of their own priorities and the specific economic and social needs within their locality.

The chapters in this book do, however, add up to more than a solemn reiteration of the virtues of the bottom-up approach in general and the desirability of RDAs in particular. Starting from the concept of a 'model RDA' – a semi-autonomous organisation supporting mainly indigenous firms by means of 'soft' policy instruments and being able to draw upon a broad range of policy instruments in an integrated manner – a number of conclusions have been suggested:

- Despite the diversity amongst regionally based development bodies, it is possible to develop a *typology* distinguishing between different combinations of organisational features and strategic orientations.

- *National patterns* with regard to bottom-up regional policy would seem to emerge, both with regard to individual development bodies and the way they are inscribed into broader patterns of regional governance.

- Cutting across national and regional differences are a number of *key issues* – accountability, public-private partnership, evaluation, and governance – that need to be addressed both by policy makers and academics.

This concluding chapter begins by charting the findings with regard to types of development bodies and national patterns, and then considers four key issues with regard to bottom-up policies. Finally, some pointers about the future role of RDAs in an increasingly diverse environment are put forward, along with an agenda for future research that would help illuminate the transformation of regional policy in the new Europe as it unfolds.

From typologies to national patterns – order out of chaos?

The survey of regionally based development bodies in Western Europe (Halkier and Danson, Chapter 2) demonstrated that, despite innumerable permutations, organisations active in bottom-up regional policy can be grouped according to the extent to which they comply with the criteria entailed in the description of the ideal-type 'model RDA'. As will be remembered, these criteria cover 1) the nature of the relationship between the development body and its political sponsors, 2) the overall strategic thrust entailed in its policies, and 3) the capacity to operate in an integrated manner by drawing on a variety of policy instruments. This results in a multi-dimensional picture that captures key characteristics of bottom-up organisations: Are strategic decisions taken by politicians or development professionals? Is the resulting growth strategy oriented towards indigenous or incoming firms? Can policies be delivered in an integrated manner in order to ensure efficiency and transparency in policy implementation?

On the basis of this, the organisations covered by the survey were distributed into three categories:

- *model RDAs*, either specialising in new policy areas or combining traditional and new activities

- *potential RDAs*, primarily organisations involved in relatively few policy areas

- *non-RDAs*, mostly organisations under close political control or specialising in traditional policy areas.

The ensuing case studies and surveys in this volume would seem to confirm the relevance of these distinctions. The vast majority of the development organisations appear to comply with the requirement to operate outside the apparatus of mainstream government, and although this undoubtedly is partly due to the selection of particular cases for study, it does confirm that arm's-length regional policy is a phenomenon that can be found across Europe. The picture is much more multifarious when it comes to strategic priorities and the capacity for integrated policy implementation. In the Western European survey, for example, we encounter organisations involved in a wide range of policy areas – Scottish Enterprise, Kärntner Wirtschaftsförderungsfond in Austria, SPRI in Spain – and organisations with a much more focused remit – such as the Dutch NOMs, Sønderjyllands Udviklingsselskab in Denmark and CITER in Italy – most of them specialising in areas relevant to the promotion of indigenous firms within the region.[1] The different types of development bodies originally identified in the survey in other words do recur in other studies of the bottom-up scene in Western Europe.

Given the short period in which RDA-like bodies have been in existence in Central and Eastern Europe and the rapidly changing economic environment in which they operate, it is not surprising that these organisations have been preoccupied primarily with finding a role at the regional level and seeking funds for development projects. At the present stage it is still difficult to distinguish patterns with regard to policy priorities and modes of implementation, but as can be seen from the three chapters on Poland, Hungary and the Czech Republic, diversity with regard to both size and activities is already in evidence.

In addition to identifying different types of development bodies, a recurring theme in this volume has been the origins of the pattern observed. Three major influences on the make-up of individual organisations were identified, namely the economic environment, the political-institutional environment and the regional policy paradigm dominant when the organisation was established. The thinking behind the bottom-up approach

1   Examples of organisations specialising in traditional policies such as the attraction of inward investment include Copenhagen Capacity (Damborg & Halkier, Chapter 5) and Instituto Aragonés de Fomento in Spain (Halkier & Danson, Chapter 2).

of course would like to see economic differences account for the variation because RDA policies are expected to reflect the specific problems of the individual region, but in practice the impact of economic factors appears to have been overshadowed by the influence of the institutional environment and shifting paradigms in regional policy. This opens up an interesting line of inquiry because the importance of institutional and historical factors points towards the possible existence of national patterns in bottom-up regional policy.

From the perspective of political institutions, the distribution of tasks between the different tiers of government are regulated at the national level, although the rights enjoyed by individual regions within the same country may not be identical. From an historical perspective regional policy was originally the responsibility of central government, and hence bottom-up initiatives were launched into an environment defined by the policy paradigm prevailing at the national level, and therefore even if RDAs have in fact developed policies addressing particular regional needs, the organisations will also have had to adapt to their specific political and institutional environment in order to be able to pursue their economic objectives effectively. The regional policies of central government, the capacity of sub-national government to pursue its own priorities, and the presence of other regionally based development bodies are in other words examples of institutional and historical factors that can have an important bearing on regionally based development initiatives, no matter how needs-driven they purport to be.

In the following the existence of national patterns in bottom-up regional policy will be discussed by drawing on the findings of the surveys and case studies presented in this volume. First, the existence of national patterns in key features of RDAs is explored, and then an attempt is made to identify possible origins of any such national characteristics.

In terms of size regional development bodies vary greatly. In Western Europe small agencies predominate in the relatively prosperous north-western parts, especially in smaller countries,[2] while larger organisations are more typical of the larger or less well off members of the EU.[3] In Eastern Europe a key factor setting the relatively large Hungarian agencies described by Lorentzen apart from the much smaller RDAs found in

2   This is typical for the situation in Belgium, Denmark, the Netherlands and France. Portugal may be the exception to the rule that small agencies are northerly and/or operate in a relatively prosperous national setting.
3   Spain, Britain, and Ireland comply with the economic requirements, Germany and possibly Italy with the geographical.

Poland and the Czech Republic would seem to be the scale of external financial support available. Size can give a first indication of the potential impact of individual agencies on the regional economy, but without a systematic comparison that takes the size of the regions, their 'institutional thickness', and the nature of their economic problems into account, the significance of the differences recorded is difficult to interpret.

With regard to policy profiles a difference can be observed between countries in which the individual organisations appear to be largely similar and other countries which display a much greater degree of variation. The studies in this volume appear to suggest that homogeneity is a characteristic of bottom-up organisations in the small and relatively prosperous Western European countries,[4] while the large or less prosperous EU member states generally display a much greater variation, both with regard to the overall strategic orientation and the degree to which the organisations specialise in policies of a similar nature.[5] Although perhaps less clear-cut due to the rather different circumstances in the transitionary economies of Central and Eastern Europe, RDA-type organisations in both Poland and Hungary appear to display a high degree of homogeneity, combining traditional and new policy instruments to promote regional development.

The pattern concerning the potential for integrated policy implementation is also reasonably distinct. Within the individual region, policy integration can be achieved either by concentrating most policies within one agency – a multi-function approach – or through a network of separate agencies each pursuing a more limited remit – what could be termed a single-function approach.[6] Here we find that while some small countries appear to favour single-function agencies,[7] organisations integrating a wide range of policy areas are prominent in most of the EU member states studied regardless of size.[8] Or to put it another way: large Western European countries are generally characterised by multi-function agencies while examples of both models can be found in smaller countries. Again the

---

4   Using the terminology developed in the Western European survey (Halkier & Danson, Chapter 2), Dutch and Danish RDAs specialise in new policy areas while their Austrian counterparts generally have mixed-new policy profiles.

5   This would seem to be the case in France, Germany, Spain, Ireland, the UK and Belgium (the latter being the only country being neither large nor relatively poor with these characteristics).

6   This dichotomy is inspired by the work of by Steiner and Jud (Chapter 3) who distinguish between single-institution and multi-institution approaches, but as most of the studies reported in this volume focus on individual organisations rather than geographical areas, using terms that characterise agencies rather than regions would seem to be preferable.

7   The Netherlands and Denmark in particular, the situation in Austria appears to vary between the regions (Steiner and Jud, Chapter 3).

8   Examples of this are Spain, France, Belgium, Germany, Ireland and the UK.

Table 19.1 National policy patterns: policy profiles and policy integration

		Strategic diversity	
		Homogenous	*Heterogenous*
Method of policy integration	Single-function agencies	Denmark The Netherlands Austria	
	Multi-function agencies	Poland Hungary	Spain Germany France Belgium Ireland UK

Note: The data situation does not allow inclusion of Portugal, Italy and the Czech Republic in the table.

situation in Central and Eastern Europe is less clear at this early stage, although at least in Poland and Hungary it appears that each region is being served by more than one multi-function agency RDA.

As a position at arm's length *vis-à-vis* their political sponsors would seem to be a general feature of regionally based development organisations, any systematic differences between the dominant patterns in individual countries will consist of specific combinations of strategic orientation and the way policy delivery is organised at the regional level. In order to get a first impression of the bottom-up scene in Europe, Table 19.1 uses as measures of strategic and organisational characteristics 1) strategic diversity (the extent to which RDAs in a given nation have similar policy profiles) and 2) methods of policy integration. Although the empirical foundation for identifying national patterns could certainly be improved upon – suggestions for further research can be found towards the end of this conclusion – this attempt to identify different national approaches to bottom-up regional policy would seem to suggest the existence in Europe of three basic models:

- *The homogenous single-function approach*, involving primarily indigenous oriented strategies and relatively small organisations. Examples are small and relatively wealthy EU members.

- *The homogenous multi-function approach*, involving broad policy profiles and relatively young organisations in East and Central European countries.

- *The heterogenous multi-function approach*, involving a variety of policy profiles and relatively large organisations. With Belgium as an exception, the recorded examples are large or relatively poor Western European countries.

While the Eastern and Central European situation is clearly still developing and the picture presented above therefore very much a snapshot of the mid-1990s, the pattern in Western Europe warrants further comment. It would appear that two distinct models of bottom-up regional policy are in evidence: some countries have regions with a large number of highly specialised development bodies pursuing strategies of a similar (indigenous-oriented) nature, while the regions in other countries are served by multi-function agencies with a broad mixture of strategic orientations. On the basis of the studies presented in this volume a systematic analysis of the origins of these difference cannot be undertaken, but still some preliminary suggestions can be put forward.

First, it must be underlined that although it is tempting to focus on the similarity between the homogenous single-function countries – small and relatively well off – the presence of Belgium and Germany in the heterogenous multi-function group shows that other influences than size of the country or level of economic development must be at work too.

National patterns could, for instance, reflect the historical origins of regionally based development bodies in the various countries. Some strategic and organisational choices might have been more relevant (or fashionable) at certain points in time, and one could hypothesise that multi-function agencies were attractive in the early years of bottom-up initiative where a powerful regional body would be needed to counter the dominance of central government policies, while at a later stage, when regionally based development activities had become more generally accepted, a host of smaller single-function agencies could be created to address particular problems. As can be seen from Table 19.2, the picture is less clear than one could have hoped for. Although development bodies in the homogenous single-function countries are generally relatively young,[9] the heterogenous multi-function approach has also been used in a nation relatively new to bottom-up regional policy, namely Spain.[10] The variations observed would

9   The Dutch organisations analysed by Sleegers (Chapter 4) were set up in the late 1970s.
10 The apparent youth of RDAs in the UK reflects the co-existence of some fairly old organisations and some very young ones, notably the Training and Enterprise Councils established in the early 1990s.

seem to reflect more than just different stages in the gradual transition from traditional to new-model regional policy in Western Europe.

Perhaps the most obvious explanation for differences between regions within nation states would be the degree of centralisation within the political system: the more powers enjoyed by the regions, the greater the freedom for regional government to set up new organisations and engage in new policy initiatives. According to this line of reasoning the ultimate outcome of decentralisation would be a heterogenous pattern where regions pursue their own priorities as best they see fit, and therefore Table 19.3 cross-tabulates the national patterns with an assessment of the overall degree of centralisation

Table 19.2 National patterns and the historical origins of RDAs

| | | National policy pattern | |
		Homogenous single-function	Heterogenous multi-function
Average year of origin	1982–	Denmark Austria	Spain UK
	1968–78	The Netherlands	Germany France Belgium
	– 1963		Ireland

Table 19.3 National patterns and degrees of political centralisation

| | | National policy pattern | |
		Homogenous single-function	Heterogenous multi-function
Powers of regions within national political system	Wide-ranging		Germany
	Advanced	Austria	Spain Belgium
	Limited	Denmark The Netherlands	France UK
	Few/no		Ireland

within the respective political systems.[11] Although the homogenous single-function countries tend to be fairly centralised, the exception of Austria and the heterogenous multi-function status of equally centralised countries like France, Ireland and the UK underline that there is no direct relationship between the political power of regions and their strategic and organisational approach to economic development.

All in all this would seem to suggest that although national patterns would appear to exist in bottom-up regional policy, this is not the product of one particular factor but should probably be traced back to a number of cross-cutting influences such as the nature of the economic problems, the broader political environment at the regional and national level with regard to policies and institutions, and the changing paradigms within regional policy at large. In other words, a series of more systematic comparative studies of RDAs across Europe would certainly be able to deepen our understanding of how and why policies and organisations are brought about.

Issues beyond the 1990s

Despite all the attempts to develop typologies and identify differences, it is also evident that some issues of common concern have emerged, transgressing individual case studies and national borders and constituting some of the key issues in bottom-up regional policy in Europe today. These issues touch upon all aspects of the policy process, and the following is therefore structured according to the traditional distinction between policy making, implementation and evaluation. Finally some more general questions with regard to the role of RDAs in regional governance will be addressed.

With regard to policy making the question of the *accountability* of individual RDAs is as sensitive as it is fundamental. While in formal terms the relationship of a very large number of organisations to their political sponsors can be described as arm's-length, what precisely this means in practice would be good to know. Most sponsors have a choice of strings to pull in order to ensure that an agency pays sufficient heed to their political priorities – financial, formal guidelines, informal advice and the ultimate risk of agency termination – but at the same time the economic expertise and the policy know-how embodied in the RDA coupled with public appreciation of the development work undertaken may be political resources that can be employed by the agencies to enhance their strategic and operational freedom.

11 The powers enjoyed by the regions in the nine Western European countries have been classified on the basis of the simplified categories developed by Wiehler and Stumm (1995).

The link between an RDA and its political sponsors therefore can be seen as a delicate balance of power, the exact nature of which will have to be investigated on an individual basis. It is, then, hardly surprising that the preceding chapters have documented both the differences between regions and agencies across Europe and the way in which the position of individual agencies may change according to the political circumstances.

The thinking behind the RDA approach originally assumed that political 'interference' in development activities was something that should be kept to a minimum, leaving the professionals 'to get on with the job', and thus implied a trade-off between political legitimacy and economic efficiency. Although this is certainly in many cases a very real problem – short-term party-political interests may not always coincide with the long-term needs of the regional economy – several contributions in this volume stress political legitimacy as an important resource in its own right for development organisations, at least with a view to building trust and cooperation between regional actors. While the trade-off between legitimacy and functional efficiency in the short run could be seen as favouring a technocratic approach, a greater degree of democratic involvement may well be desirable as a means of ensuring consensus and continuity in development activities from a long-term perspective.

Straddling the borders between policy making and implementation is the second issue, namely that of *public-private partnership*. The last two decades have seen a significant increase in the involvement of private sector organisations and executives in bottom-up policy, and this development would seem to have been propelled by a number of considerations. On the one hand an increased private sector involvement in the policy process could be a means of securing additional funds for development during a period of fiscal restraint. On the other hand both the liberal ideological climate of the 1980s and the more pragmatic attempts to build consensus and ensure efficient implementation would seem to prompt closer and more permanent links between RDAs and the key economic players in the regional economy, both on a general level and with respect to particular development initiatives. The exact motives in individual cases are difficult to establish because some reasons can be viewed as more palatable than others, and seen in the light of the European experience reported in this volume the consequences of giving private sector actors an increased role in regional policy would seem to be ambiguous. Although individual top managers may have a strong kind of 'place attachment' and therefore be willing to take a long-term view of development opportunities, the risks are also obvious: short-termism may guide the selection of individual development projects if financial returns are expected to match those of the private sector, institutionalised links may make private sector organisations more oriented towards public sector initiatives than market developments, and policy initiatives may ultimately be confined to areas of direct relevance to private sector economic activity. A radical version of this is the requirement of RDAs to earn sizeable parts of their income by means of market operations, a pattern seen both in Western and East-Central European countries.[12]

The third recurring issue is that of *policy evaluation*. Although regional policy has a strong political dimension – being seen to be doing something may in the short run be more important than the economic relevance of the policies – the results are of course not unimportant in a long-term perspective. Over the years attempts to evaluate the traditional regional policies of central government have demonstrated the difficulties involved in estimating their effects and efficiency,[13] but the contributions in this volume suggest that in some respects evaluating RDAs and their policies may be even more problematic. Evaluation of bottom-up initiatives may focus on different aspects of the policy process:

- The *strategies* pursued and their relevance given the structure of the regional economy. The temptation to go for quick-fix high-visibility strategies with good photo opportunities for political sponsors are of course ever-present, and hence the long-term viability of the strategic choices must also be subject to review, although this for obvious reasons is not always the most pressing issue from the perspective of the RDAs or their political sponsors.[14]

- The adequacy of the *resources available* is another issue that is highly relevant, especially in peripheral regions where development efforts have a weak local resource base or depend on external funding from central government or the EU.[15] Also this issue is highly charged, not only because adequacy in itself is difficult to specify but also because it is a potent reminder of the importance of territorial politics: at the end of the day regional policy is about strengthening particular regions at the possible expense of others and this may require the transfer of additional resources into the weaker regions. Such transfers are not only politically sensitive in

12 Examples include Poland (Gorzelak, Kozak and Roszkowski, Chapter 6) and the UK (Morgan, Chapter 13; Danson, Lloyd and Newlands (1993)).
13 See e.g. Ashcroft (1980), Diamond and Spence (1983), Stöhr and Tödtling (1984), and Holden and Swales (1995).
14 An example of this approach to evaluation is provided by Guzmán-Cuevas, Santos-Complido and Cáceres-Carraso (Chapter 16).
15 This issue is clearly present in the Hungarian case (Lorentzen, Chapter 8).

the stronger regions that pay the price, but may also limit the strategic freedom of manoeuvre of the weaker regions.

- *Output* such as grants given, factories built or firms advised are probably the most common way of measuring the activities of a development body in order to monitor its performance. While there is little doubt that keeping track of various forms of output is a prerequisite for other forms of evaluation and can be a useful way of seeing to what extent policy implementation complies with overall strategic goals,[16] the temptation to concentrate on the tangible – what is being done by the organisation – rather than the more elusive effects of the policies on the activities of private firms is a very real one indeed, and for obvious reasons.

- *Outcomes*, i.e. the resulting improvement of the regional economy, is from a functional perspective the acid test of success for any regional policy, but the small size of most programmes in combination with the high degree of variation in policy design between regions often complicates matters with regard to indicators, displacement effects and deadweight. While some types of programmes can be analysed fruitfully using methods similar to those employed when evaluating the generally larger and more standardised programmes of central government (cf. e.g. Hart, Scott, Gudgin and Hanvey, Chapter 18) assessing the impact of e.g. advisory services or sectoral schemes will often have to rely on more qualitative methods of evaluation (cf. Bellini and Pasquini, Chapter 14).

- In real life the *political evaluation* of a particular organisation or programme can, however, be much more important than functional considerations about the economic effects. An RDA can be a powerful symbol of commitment to the economic and social advancement of a region, and in several of the case studies the perceived success of an agency has been instrumental in bringing about political reviews and ultimately organisational change, albeit in very different ways. While the increasing difficulties of ERVET in Italy brought about a thorough political review, the very public profile of the Scottish Development Agency would appear to have prompted the political review that through mergers and

---

16 Examples of this approach to evaluation can be found in the work of Finnegan (Chapter 17) and Halkier (1992a, 1992b).

decentralisation created the structure now known as Scottish Enterprise.[17]

In short, evaluation of RDAs and their activities is a necessary but immensely complicated task that will require the introduction of new methods and the refinement of existing ones in order to keep track of the rapid development in policies.

The fourth major issue that runs through the studies in this volume is the way in which individual RDAs are inserted into the broader pattern of *regional governance*. Although the increased political importance in Europe of the regional level is disputed,[18] it is generally recognised that public authority is no longer the preserve of elected government and its administrative organisation[19] but can also be enjoyed by an array of institutions outside direct democratic control such as semi-autonomous development bodies.

On a general level it goes without saying that the increased importance of bottom-up initiatives has vastly increased the number of actors in regional policy in any given region. While most central government policies traditionally had been implemented by one organisation, we now see a host of regional bodies operating alongside central and local agencies, often with support from the European level. Although a certain level of institutional thickness is undoubtedly necessary to ensure maximum involvement of private firms in public development initiatives – duplication in other words is not necessarily a problem – a plethora of institutions may also result in competition for scarce resources and a limited number of potential clients. The presence of many actors and organisations does not guarantee efficient collaboration between them.

On the basis of the contributions to this volume at least three different institutional patterns can be identified at the regional level:

- *the functional network approach* in which a number of fairly specialised agencies are responsible for development policies on behalf of regional and/or central government

- *the complementary approach* where major multi-function organisations operate alongside powerful regional governments, providing

17 On ERVET, see Bellini and Pasquini (Chapter 14); on the transition from the SDA to Scottish Enterprise, see Fairley and Lloyd (Chapter 11), Danson, Lloyd and Newlands (1989), and Halkier (1992a).

18 While Marks, Houghe and Blank (1996) stress the role of the regions in an emerging system of multi-level governance, the general tenor of the volume edited by Jeffery (1996) is more sceptical.

19 See e.g. Kooiman (1993).

professional clout and operational flexibility in development activities through their arm's-length position

- *the compensatory approach* where major multi-function organisations operate alongside relatively weak (or absent) regional governments, not only promoting economic development but also providing political leadership and/or territorial cohesion.

The first two patterns involve transferring responsibility for regional policies, at least implementation, but sometimes also strategy development, to technocratic organisations while democratic legitimacy is still primarily provided by elected government through its sponsorship of the various agencies. Contrary to this, the weakness of elected government in the third pattern effectively means that the RDA can assume a leading role in the development of economic promotion and act as an informal broker of consensus at the regional level, although its legitimacy does not stem from votes but from being perceived as a successful promoter of regional development. Just like it was possible to measure the characteristics of individual development bodies by comparing them with an ideal-type 'model RDA', the identification of these patterns strongly suggests that it will also be possible to establish ideal types focusing on the way in which an RDA is inserted into the broader system of governance at the regional level.

RDAs and bottom-up policies – an agenda for future research

If we are correct in maintaining that 1) RDAs will play an important role in regional policy in the beginning of the next millennium also, 2) they will continue to operate in a fast-changing global economic environment, and 3) the way they relate to their institutional environment will become increasingly complex, then what are the key issues that further research will have to address?

First, more knowledge about individual organisations is clearly still needed. A systematic comparative study of European development bodies, their organisation, accountability, strategies, policies and evaluation procedures is required in order to be able to draw more wide-ranging conclusions about the current state of affairs amongst regionally based development bodies. Second, the increased importance of inter-organisational relations suggests that much more attention should be given to the way in which individual RDAs are embedded in larger policy networks: horizontally with other public and private institutions within the region, and vertically in relation to local efforts below and central and European institutions above.

All in all it would appear that future research would have to draw upon a combination of quantitative and qualitative methods, but that the balance would begin to tilt towards the latter, given the importance of institutional issues for the development of both individual organisations and the regional system of governance as such. It may well be that the second or third generation of development agencies that will operate into the next century can best be described as 'networked RDAs', and given the stupendous number of actors involved, undertaking comparative studies may seem to be a daunting task. The current economic and social importance of bottom-up regional policy, however, does suggest strongly that it is also a task that hardly can be ignored.

References

Ashcroft, B. (1980) 'The evaluation of regional policy in Europe – a survey and critique.' *Studies in Public Policy 68.*

Danson, M., Lloyd, G. and Newlands, D. (1989) '"Scottish Enterprise" – towards a model agency or a flawed initiative?' *Regional Studies 23,* 557–63.

Danson, M., Lloyd, G. and Newlands, D. (1993) 'The role of development agencies in regional economic regeneration – A Scottish case study.' In R.T. Harrison and M. Hart (eds) *Spatial Policy in a Divided Nation.* London: Jessica Kingsley Publishers.

Diamond, D.R. and Spence, N.A. (1983) *Regional Policy Evaluation: A Methodological Review and the Scottish Example.* London: Gower.

Halkier, H. (1992a) 'New lamps for old? The industrial strategies of Scottish Enterprise.' *Quarterly Economic Commentary 17,* 4, 56–65.

Halkier, H. (1992b) 'Development agencies and regional policy: the case of the Scottish Development Agency.' *Regional Politics & Policy 2,* 3, 1–26.

Holden, D.R. and Swales, J.K. (1995) 'The additionality, displacement and substitution effects of factor subsidies.' *Scottish Journal of Political Economy 42,* 2, 113–26.

Jeffery, C. (ed) (1996) *The Regional Dimension of the EU. Toward a 'Third Level' in Europe?* London: Cass.

Kooiman, J. (ed) (1993) *Modern Governance. New Government-Society Interactions.* London: Sage.

Marks, G., Hooghe, L. and Blank, K. (1996) 'European integration from the 1980s: state-centric versus multi-level governance.' *Journal of Common Market Studies 34,* 3, 341–78.

Stöhr, W. and Tödtling, F. (1984) 'Quantitative, qualitative, and structural variables in the evaluation of regional development policies in Western Europe.' In G. Demko (ed) *Regional Development Problems and Policies in Eastern and Western Europe.* London: Croom Helm.

Wiehler, F. and Stumm, T. (1995) 'The powers of regional and local authorities and their role in the EU.' *European Planning Studies 3,* 2, 227–50.

The contributors

Henrik Halkier is Associate Professor of International Studies, Aalborg University, Denmark.

Mike Danson is Professor of Economics, University of Paisley, Scotland.

Charlotte Damborg is Assistant Researcher, European Research Unit, Aalborg University, Denmark.

Nicola Bellini is Research Fellow, Department of Social Sciences, Scoula Superiore Sant'Anna, Pisa, Italy.

F. Rafael Cáceres-Carrasco is Lecturer of Applied Economics, University of Seville, Spain.

John Fairley is Professor of Public Policy, The Robert Gordon University, Aberdeen, Scotland.

Marie Finnegan is Economist, Northern Ireland Economic Council, Belfast, Northern Ireland.

Grzegorz Gorzelak is Professor and Director, European Institute of Regional and Local Development, University of Warsaw, Poland.

Graham Gudgin is Director, Northern Ireland Economic Research Centre, Belfast, Northern Ireland.

Joaquín Guzmán-Cuevas is Professor of Applied Economics, University of Seville, Spain.

Eric Hanvey is Researcher, Northern Ireland Economic Research Centre, Belfast, Northern Ireland.

Mark Hart is Reader in Industrial and Regional Policy, University of Ulster at Jordanstown, Northern Ireland.

Rik Houthaeve is Assistant Researcher, Department of Planning, University of Ghent, Belgium.

Jim Hughes is Director, Wales European Centre, Brussels, Belgium.

Thomas Jud is Senior Research Fellow, Institute of Technology and Regional Policy, Joanneum Research, Vienna, Austria.

Daphne H. Kooistra is Junior Researcher, Department of Human Geography, Faculty of Policy Sciences, University of Nijmegen, The Netherlands.

Marek Kozak is Director General, Polish Agency for Regional Development, Warsaw, Poland.

Greg Lloyd is Professor of Planning Research, University of Dundee, Scotland.

Anne Lorentzen is Associate Professor, Department of Development and Planning, University of Aalborg, Denmark.

Kevin Morgan is Professor of European Regional Planning, Department of City and Regional Planning, University of Wales, Cardiff.

Jan Olsson is Director of Novemus, University of Örebro, Sweden.

Francesca Pasquini is Partner, Laboratoria di Politica Economica Regionale s.r.l., Bologna, Italy.

Wojciech Roszkowski is Research Assistant, European Institute of Regional and Local Development, University of Warsaw, Poland.

F. Javier Santos-Cumplido is Lecturer of Applied Economics, University of Seville, Spain.

Ronnie Scott was, before his untimely death in April 1997, Senior Researcher, Northern Ireland Economic Research Centre, Belfast, Northern Ireland.

Wilfred Sleegers is Professor in the Department of Applied Economics, Erasmus University, Rotterdam, the Netherlands.

Michael Steiner is Professor of Economics, University of Graz, and Head of the Institute of Technology and Regional Policy, Joanneum Research, Graz, Austria.

Jan Vozáb is Project Manager with Most Regional Development Agency and Assistant Professor, Department of Regional and Local Development, University of J. E. Purkyne, Usti nad Labem, Czech Republic.

Subject Index

Aachener Gesellschaft für
    Innovation und
    Technologietransfer
    (AGIT) 28, 37
Aalborg 49, 142, 220
ACE (Institutional Background
    for Regional
    Development) Project
    107
accountability of RDAs
    351–352
Act on Foundations, 1994
    (Poland) 106
advisory councils in Denmark
    87
advisory service activities 33
agency as animateur, renewal
    and the WDA
    aid budget reduction
        229–230
    contradictory perspectives
        247–248
    divergent development 248
    economic strategy
        235–242
    expertise centres 240–242
    external perceptions 247
    institutional character
        232–235
    internal perceptions 248
    introduction 229–231
    inward investment
        235–239
    networking capacity 231
    political control 250
    public accountability
        249–250
    regulating the agency
        242–247
    self-regulation 244–245
    significance of social capital
        248
    support services 239–242
    technology audits and clubs
        240–242
    Welsh Office role 245–247
Agenzia Polo Ceramica,
    Ravenna 262
aggregated economic
    instruments 48
Alpes-Maritimes, Côte d'Azur
    Développement 28, 37
Alto Tamega, Associação de
    Desenvolvimento da

Região do (ADRAT) 29,
    37
American Political Science
    Association 275
Amt der Steiermärkischen
    Landesregierung 55, 62
analytical framework see
    framework for analysis
Andalusia 292–299
Andalusia, Instituto de
    Fomento de Andalucia
    29, 37
Andalusian Autonomous
    Community 299
Andalusian Council for
    Industry, Commerce and
    Tourism 299
Andalusian Society for the
    Development of
    Computing and
    Electronics (SADIEL)
    300
anti-cyclical patterns in
    Holland 68
Aragon 38
Aragon, Instituto Argenoés de
    Fomento 29, 345
Århus 85, 88, 90, 91
Association of County
    Councils (Denmark) 82
ASTER, Bologna 260, 261
Australia 307
Austria
    see also trends in
        organisation and
        activities in Austria
    functional variation between
        regions 347
    multi-institutional approach
        54, 55
    national policy patterns
        348, 350, 351
    proximity to West Hungary
        143
Austrian regional policy
    48–64
autonomy of RDAs 30–32

Baranya 143
barriers to progress in Poland
    120–122
Barsod-Abaúj-Zemplén (BAZ)
    County 102, 141–160
Basque Country (Spanish)
    292–299, 301
Belgian Chamber of
    Commerce and Industry
    176

Belgian Christian Democratic
    Party 177
Belgian Framework Law 171
Belgian General and Specific
    Expansion Legislation,
    1959 168, 174
Belgian Leiedal 166, 172,
    176
Belgian Planning Act(1962)
    168, 169, 176, 178
Belgian Planning Act(1996)
    176
Belgium
    see also changing role of
        RDAs in Flanders
    bottom-up experience 163,
        164
    changing role of RDAs in
        Flanders 166–178
    Flemish 'model' RDAs 39
    national policy patterns
        349–350
    policy variation 347
    similarities with Spanish
        experience 46
    small agency predomination
        346
Bellini, Nicola 227
Bergslagen 215, 221, 222
Berlin, Wirtschaftsförderung
    28, 37
Bielsko-Biala 109
Blekinge 215, 221
block grant allocations in
    Denmark 90
Bohemia, North RDA
    activities focus 136
    diverse financial resources
        137
    diverse ownership structure
        134
    establishment of RDA 131
    serving small cities and
        towns 133
    transitional features 130
Bornholm 84
Bornholms Erhvervfond 83
Bornholms Erhvervsråd 83
bottom-up initiatives
    advantages of 18
    comparison with top-down
        19
    future analyses 43
    growth 14, 26–27
bottom-up regional policy in
    Denmark
    bureaucratic autonomy
        87–89
    current situation 95–97

Author Index